THE IMMORTALS

Topics in Contemporary Buddhism
GEORGE J. TANABE JR., EDITOR

Establishing a Pure Land on Earth: The Foguang Buddhist Perspective on Modernization and Globalization
STUART CHANDLER

Buddhist Missionaries in the Era of Globalization
LINDA LEARMAN, EDITOR

Being Benevolence: The Social Ethics of Engaged Buddhism
SALLIE B. KING

Japanese Temple Buddhism: Worldliness in a Religion of Renunciation
STEPHEN G. COVELL

Zen in Brazil: The Quest for Cosmopolitan Modernity
CRISTINA ROCHA

Land of Beautiful Vision: Making a Buddhist Sacred Place in New Zealand
SALLY MCARA

Attracting the Heart: Social Relations and the Aesthetics of Emotion in Sri Lankan Monastic Culture
JEFFREY SAMUELS

The Buddha Side: Gender, Power, and Buddhist Practice in Vietnam
ALEXANDER SOUCY

Passing the Light: The Incense Light Community and Buddhist Nuns in Contemporary Taiwan
CHÜN-FANG YÜ

Experimental Buddhism in Contemporary Japan: Innovation and Activism for the Twenty-first Century
JOHN K. NELSON

From Comrades to Bodhisattvas: Moral Dimensions of Lay Buddhist Practice in Contemporary China
GARETH FISHER

The Immortals: Faces of the Incredible in Buddhist Burma
GUILLAUME ROZENBERG; TRANSLATED BY WARD KEELER

TOPICS IN
CONTEMPORARY
BUDDHISM

THE IMMORTALS

Faces of the Incredible in Buddhist Burma

GUILLAUME ROZENBERG
TRANSLATED BY WARD KEELER

University of Hawai'i Press
Honolulu

© 2015 University of Hawai'i Press
All rights reserved
Printed in the United States of America

20   19   18   17   16   15   6   5   4   3   2   1

Library of Congress Cataloging-in-Publication Data

Rozenberg, Guillaume, author.
   [Immortels. English]
   The immortals : faces of the incredible in Buddhist Burma / Guillaume Rozenberg ;
translated by Ward Keeler.
     pages   cm—(Topics in contemporary Buddhism)
   Includes bibliographical references and index.
   ISBN 978-0-8248-4095-2 (hardcover : alk. paper)—ISBN 978-0-8248-4096-9 (pbk. :
alk. paper)
   1. Weikza.   2. Buddhist cults—Burma.   3. Anthropology of religion—Burma.
I. Keeler, Ward, translator.   II. Title.   III. Series: Topics in contemporary Buddhism.
BQ418.R6813   2015
294.309591—dc23   2014028868

University of Hawai'i Press books are printed on acid-free
paper and meet the guidelines for permanence and
durability of the Council on Library Resources.

Printed by Sheridan Books, Inc.

For Major Zaw Win, an immortal if ever there was one

Contents

Series Editor's Preface

It is difficult to characterize this fascinating book, not just because it concerns thousand-year-old Burmese Buddhists who fly but also because its author has chosen, almost by necessity, unusual procedures for studying and writing about this strange topic. Readers will be charmed and/or vexed by this monograph that defies monographic conventions, this nonfiction account that often reads like fiction, this ethnographic study written in the first person by a participant who observes himself along with his subjects. As a social scientist, writer, and researcher of Buddhism, Guillaume Rozenberg breaks a lot of the usual rules to capture and represent as accurately as he can the curious makings of belief in a Burmese Buddhist community.

George J. Tanabe Jr.
SERIES EDITOR

Translator's Preface

In this book full of marvels, there comes a particularly startling moment when Guillaume Rozenberg ruminates on a thorny dilemma: whether to follow the express wishes of one of his principal informants and suppress much of the material the man has given the ethnographer—material that the latter wants to use as an important element in portraying the life of a Burmese Buddhist religious cult and the lives of its adherents—or instead, contrary to the man's wishes, to remain true to the anthropological project on which he, Rozenberg, is embarked—betraying perforce his Burmese friend. By presenting the choice so starkly, Rozenberg makes it clear that he is very much attuned to the rhetorical and, especially, the ethical concerns that have become prominent in anthropology over the past thirty or so years (particularly since the publication of such books as Edward Said's *Orientalism,* James Clifford's *Writing Culture,* and Marcus and Fischer's *Anthropology as Cultural Critique*). Yet he makes the decision to take his responsibilities as an ethnographer as primary; that is, to reveal what his friend would have had him hide. Putting the matter in such clear relief, and braving charges of political incorrectness by highlighting rather than obscuring the nature of the project he has undertaken and the means he has used in doing so, places Rozenberg on very controversial ground. One reason I took on the task of translating the book was because I admire Rozenberg's honesty, an honesty that makes many other anthropologists look pious but conventional by comparison.

Another dilemma confronts Rozenberg when, in Chapter 4, he has set out information about a group of martial arts practitioners endowed with invulnerability. Whereas in the instance just cited Rozenberg had to choose between his loyalty and gratitude toward a good friend, on the one hand, and his dedication to critical analysis, on the other, in this later case, when it comes to musing on the resonance between martial arts and the conditions of generalized tyranny that have characterized Burmese society—most egregiously for the past sixty years, but fairly consistently for the past several centuries—he must tread very carefully if he is to avoid accusations of blaming the victims. Yet he forges ahead, using Burmese material to address a centuries-old question: how do those subject to oppression participate in their own subjugation? Rozenberg's response is nuanced and undogmatically stated. Yet he will certainly not escape accusations of insensitivity, made by those who object to all generalizations about people suffering subjugation, unless those generalizations are highly idealizing (and so at best partially accurate and at worst distorting).

Actually, Rozenberg's determination to part ways with most contemporary anthropological writing shows most obviously not at these moments of high ethical and/or analytic drama, but rather in the overall format of the book, which is nothing if not surprising. James Clifford has made all anthropologists (and their readers) wary of the trope whereby the anthropologist enters the scene as an uncomprehending newbie but slowly becomes wise enough—we are to infer—to serve as a cultural intermediary, able to explain "them" to "us." Usually serving as an introductory rhetorical device, the trope frames the resultant text as the product of ripe reflection on a wealth of lived experience—most of which remains unrecounted, except for the occasional quote from the ethnographer's field notes. (This is yet another rhetorical ploy that readers should treat with suspicion, because it plays on the same "you are there" deception as photography.) Rozenberg chooses instead to make the process of gathering information about a Burmese Buddhist cult the connecting thread through all the topics he addresses. Only as information piles up, much of it hard to make sense of, does Rozenberg start to suggest how we might understand it. So the process of thinking through the data comes up from time to time, but always integrated with the process of data collection. This is much truer to the process of fieldwork—wherein someone is engaged constantly in observing, recording, and pondering people's actions and statements all at the same time—than any more tightly presented set of analytic remarks.

Rozenberg does, certainly, organize his material into relevant categories, and these categories give their names to the five chapters. But within each chapter, his aim is to keep us constantly aware of the way in which he obtained the information he is working with—or, for that matter, failed to obtain information, as in the story of an important figure's biography he was prevented from getting his hands on. He also wants to make us see how he has reflected on his material, shaping it in alternative ways as he considers it from one angle and then from another. We are to see not only the process by which he, as an ethnographer, gathered information but also the process by which he, as an analyst (aka an anthropologist), drew on his previous reading and his own intellectual inclinations to come up with a variety of possible ways to understand the ideas and practices he has learned about.

The advantages of this method are two. First, Rozenberg renounces all claims to the status of omniscient observer. He uses a first-person narration throughout the text to highlight the fact that he is yet another participant in the fashioning of the cult of four superhuman beings, with his own set of desires and preoccupations but no special, privileged access to any objective truth. Indeed, a reader eventually realizes that at no point does Rozenberg attempt to "get to the bottom" of the amazing goings-on he is constantly being told about and even on occasion observing. A social scientist's "objectivity" in this case takes the form of a studied refusal to be drawn into arguments about whether a specific medium's claims are to be believed. Because the drama of "believing" matters so much to the people Rozenberg tells us about, to try to get beyond people's experience to solve the problem of how a medium does what he does (or what four superhuman beings do through him) would be to leave aside the very people and their ideas that Rozenberg, as an anthropologist, wishes to learn about.

Yet Rozenberg does not renounce the right to apply his own analytic tools to what people tell him. He is not afraid to speak in his own voice about what he infers from what he sees and hears, inferences quite foreign to the thinking of the people he is working with. Indeed, he is an avowed and unabashed (although not a naive) subscriber to Durkheimian understandings of human societies. He believes that individuals' engagements with their communities are fundamentally important to any understandings of their actions. So he responds to matters that the crisis of representation has brought to our attention, questions concerning why we should set any store by an anthropologist's claims to knowledge and, especially, any claims to the right to tell us about (to represent) any "others." He does so by representing as faithfully as possible the process of doing fieldwork and then representing as faithfully as possible the process of drawing conclusions—tentative, intriguing, suggestive ones—about people on the basis of that fieldwork.

The second advantage of Rozenberg's method is the room for storytelling it allows him. For most of the period when I was translating this book, I was balancing my responsibilities as a translator with the demands of my own anthropological research in Mandalay. Yet I found myself looking forward every day to what amazing stories I would come upon as I turned the pages of this book: there was absolutely no telling what might happen next. And unlike some anthropologists whose storytelling seems to substitute for analysis, in Rozenberg's case, the storytelling lays the groundwork for deeply considered meditations on religious belief and skepticism, orthodoxy and its putative others, individuals' talents and communities' felt needs—in sum, for a whole series of topics that anthropologists have long engaged with but rarely on the basis of such vivid narratives. To my mind, therefore, Rozenberg's unorthodox gamble—to give up the standard anthropological format in favor of something less obviously academic and therefore more readable—has paid off impressively. His book teaches us about specific Burmese individuals with both sympathy and skill, while enabling us to better understand what a range of ideas and practices Burmese Buddhism can, in the view of some people at least, accommodate. Rozenberg has crafted a book about the extraordinary that is in itself an extraordinarily good and stimulating read.

Ward Keeler

Acknowledgments

The research for *The Immortals* was done in part when I was a postdoctoral fellow at the Asia Research Institute at the University of Singapore (from September 2003 to September 2004). I was able to develop it further when I became a member of France's National Center for Scientific Research (CNRS) in 2004. The fact that I was able to bring this book to fruition owes much to the freedom to work and think that these two institutions afforded me, as well as to the encounters with people holding other points of view that those institutions encourage.

I want to express my gratitude to all those who have contributed to this book's development. In addition to the people cited by name in the following pages, I thank very warmly Nicolas Adell, Jean-Pierre Albert, Marlène Albert-Llorca, Vanina Bouté, Bénédicte Brac de la Perrière, Céline Coderey, and especially Grégoire Schlemmer, who brought me back to my senses on a number of occasions. Granted, *The Immortals* is not such as they would have wished it to be. But their careful and critical readings and their intellectual generosity have enabled me to ameliorate a certain number of its defects and to catch a certain number of my errors. Others—Jason A. Carbine, John Clifford Holt, F. K. Lehman, Patrick Pranke—took up the burden long ago of reading an initial English-language version of Chapter 1. San San Hnin Tun kindly checked the translation of the bibliographical references' titles in Burmese. The anonymous readers of the English-language manuscript provided helpful remarks to improve the work. Patricia Crosby of the University of Hawai'i Press offered fruitful editorial advice throughout the publication process. The care she takes with manuscripts is exemplary.

I am greatly indebted to Ward Keeler, an anthropologist at the University of Texas, who took on the task of translating the book from French to English. It was an enriching experience to have the privilege of working with him. I do not think that the result will in any way diminish impressions of his talents as a wordsmith.

Note on the English Edition

The original manuscript of *The Immortals* was written between 2003 and 2009 and appeared in French in 2010. This English edition differs in several respects from the French one.

First, I revised and expanded the foreword, "A Word to the Reader," to convey more precisely the nature of the project. Second, throughout the book, the first person has been substituted for the third person ("Guillaume"). Some readers found the device of using the third person when I appeared in the guise of an ethnographer to be a distraction. Because it was not essential to the work's tone, I decided to dispense with it. (However, when relevant, I retained the third person "the anthropologist" when referring to myself.) Third, within each of the five chapters, the numerals that had served to separate and distinguish between the successive sections have been replaced by subheadings so as to help orient the reader along the way. Fourth, I added notes and a bibliography. These consist for the most part of materials I had included in early versions of the manuscript, before deciding to forego any critical apparatus in the published French edition. Finally, I expanded one of the sections in Chapter 1, titled "In Retrospect: What the Buddha Did," to respond to specialists in Buddhist studies who expressed a desire to see the argument placed in conversation with the most recent publications in the field.

Overall, this English edition remains completely true to the spirit of the original version while offering the reader, I hope, a more accessible and more engaging experience.

TRANSCRIPTION OF BURMESE WORDS

In this book, the transcription of Burmese terms follows the "standard conventional transcription" recommended by John Okell (1971: 66–67, with modifications in 2000). Tones are not indicated. Plurals are not marked.

A Word to the Reader

July 1952. A virtually illiterate twenty-six-year-old peasant, living in Mebaygon village (Central Burma), where he has a well-earned reputation as a rowdy, is suddenly possessed by *weikza*. Key figures in Burmese Buddhism, *weikza* are humans who have acquired extraordinary powers, including that of being able to prolong their lives. An individual who achieves the status of a *weikza* does not die, but rather "exits" this world and goes to live in an invisible place reserved for beings of his stature. From there, he can enter into relation with the world, notably through possession, in order to carry out salvational projects. *Weikza* care for people's temporal and spiritual needs while protecting and propagating the Buddhist religion. A unique feature of the cult that quickly forms around our young peasant is that the four invisible *weikza,* ranging in age from 150 to 1,000 years, whose medium he becomes, regularly appear in the flesh themselves as well. These apparitions soon attract devotees from all over the country.

This book focuses on this cult, which has existed for more than fifty years and constitutes one of the most remarkable religious phenomena in contemporary Burma. It is the second volume of a projected four-volume "cycle of the extraordinary," dedicated to figures of Buddhist virtuosity and related cults in contemporary Burmese society. Initiated with *Renunciation and Power: The Quest for Sainthood in Contemporary Burma* (2010), this anthropological cycle aims both to reveal and to invite reflection on some of the most striking forms that Buddhism takes in Burma—whether these forms pertain, for Burmese as much as for the anthropologist, to the phenomenal, the supernatural, the incredible, or the strange, or, indeed, all of the above. An individual's attainment of a condition like sainthood, the appearance in the flesh of invisible beings, becoming possessed by an entity or becoming its human intermediary: these represent so many instances, along with others, of the extraordinary. The task at hand is to take these manifestations as the starting point for reflecting both on what produces and defines the domain and experience of the religious and on what the religious domain and experience define and produce.

Each volume of this "cycle of the extraordinary" stands on its own and can be read without reference to the others. Each is written in a specific mode. *Renunciation and Power* is intended to answer a single question (how does one become a saint?) through the demonstration of a single claim—the correlation, in the making of sainthood, between detachment from and involvement in the world, between renunciation and power. *The Immortals* is conceived, in its form, as an exercise in reflexivity (see the later discussion). Yet to appear are a comparative study of cults found throughout Buddhist Southeast Asia and an ethnographic account of Burmese exorcism. Although self-contained, each volume should nevertheless take on an additional dimension when read as one element in an ensemble whose constituent parts resonate, complement, respond to, or critique one another. The cycle, taken overall, will recount a researcher's progress, including the times he got lost and had to correct his course.

The present volume developed out of fieldwork I conducted on Burmese Buddhism starting in 1997. At the end of the 1990s a photograph of a visibly old monk, with an emaciated face and his head covered with a piece of ochre monastic cloth, could be seen all over Burma. People stated he was a *weikza* aged more than one thousand years who shortly before had successfully undergone a spectacular life-prolonging ceremony to extend his life span. This *weikza* was U Kawwida, the eldest of the four *weikza* appearing in the flesh since the 1950s in Mebaygon village.

My first introduction to the cult of this *weikza* and his three counterparts took place in July 2000 when, through the intermediary of a mutual acquaintance, I met Major Zaw Win in Yangon. He had been a disciple of the cult since 1967. During this first meeting, the Major told me at length about the cult of the four *weikza* and showed me a clip from a video shot during U Kawwida's life-prolonging ceremony (which had been performed in December 1994). I was then committed to another project and could not follow up this topic. But the following year, in October 2001, I seized the opportunity of another research stay in Burma to investigate further this puzzling cult. I interviewed the Major about the cult several times in Yangon. I also spoke about the cult with a few other Burmese, including some who judged the whole thing to be pure and simple trickery. Most important of all, I went on a three-day trip with the Major to make inquiries at the place where the four *weikza* appeared, the cult's headquarters: a monastery established in Mebaygon village in 1973 by the four *weikza's* medium when he was ordained as a monk. These first glimpses convinced me that an in-depth study of the cult in all its many facets would prove worthwhile.

My next three research stays, each lasting about two months (August 17–October 14, 2003; January 16–March 4, 2004; and December 12, 2005–February 20, 2006), were for the most part devoted to the study of this cult of the four *weikza*, with the assistance of a Burmese research assistant named Victorious. Victorious and I stayed at the *weikza's* Mebaygon monastery four times, for a total of almost three months (September 7–September 30, 2003; October 7–October 11, 2003; January 26–February 13, 2004; and January 10–February 18, 2006). During these stays, we accommodated ourselves to the activities relating to the monastery and the cult. We had occasion to attend numerous séances in which the four *weikza* appeared in the flesh, forty-four séances in all, whose contents we often tape recorded. We spent time with the four *weikza*'s medium and with disciples of the cult who were living in the monastery or were visiting it for a short or an extended time. We conducted one or several interviews with many of these people: altogether we interviewed about eighty individuals. We also had discussions with monks and laypeople from the village and its surroundings, another dozen individuals. We studied the practice of alchemy—I was not gifted at this technique, but our companions and masters proved to be patient. We participated twice in the annual cult festival, which extends over several days (February 5–10, 2004, and February 12–17, 2006).

A second dimension of the field research consisted in visiting about twenty of the cult's most active disciples in their homes in Yangon or Mandalay to interview them, once or several times according to circumstances. We also took a close interest in a group that developed out of the cult of the four *weikza,* a group that purveys "knowledge" for making oneself invulnerable. We attended invulnerability demonstrations performed by members of this group in several parts of the country, and we made two brief stays (March 9–11, 2004, and December 23–25, 2005), at the group founder's home, in Kyungyi village (Irrawaddy Division, Lower Burma). Finally, we collected and translated writings in Burmese relating to the cult of the four *weikza.* These provided an essential complement to the data we derived from fieldwork.

This work is based on all these elements, as well as, more generally, on the knowledge I have acquired about Burmese Buddhism through my research experience since 1997. The cult of the four *weikza* raises a number of classic anthropological issues, particularly those of the anthropology of religion: the nature of the supernatural and of belief; the relations among religion, magic, and science; the experience of possession; the various constructions of personhood; the social mechanisms of subjection; and, ranging farther afield, alchemy and invulnerability. An effort has been made to link all these themes closely together because the cult of the four *weikza* presents them as forming a whole, as constituent parts of a single totality. At the same time, the cult of the four *weikza* provides a window on contemporary Burmese society, and this book is meant, by means of a study of this specific cult, to portray, even if only partially, Burmese society in its entirety.

To pursue these two ends—to grasp the cult of the four *weikza* as a phenomenon implicating a number of anthropological concerns and to allow a reader the opportunity to delve into the thick of Burmese society—*The Immortals* adopts an unconventional approach. Indeed, the approach itself reflects yet a third and final intention: to reflect on the matter of representation in anthropology or, more precisely, on the means with which anthropology uses description and the interpretations that description occasions to make sense of what it studies (e.g., a religious cult, village politics, economic globalization, a male initiation ceremony, etc.). A question much on my mind at the time when I began writing *The Immortals* was whether it was possible to develop a mode of representation in anthropology combining a narrative style and theoretical reflection.[1] Or, more precisely, could anthropology get turned into a story?

My intention was not to recount the fieldwork experience, its ups and downs, and the encounters, discussions, and adventures to which it gives rise. Anthropology is not reducible to fieldwork. By the time I was conducting research for this work, I had lost, for that matter, all illusions about fieldwork, at least about the possibility that it might constitute not only a necessary but also a sufficient condition for the creation of an anthropological work. Fieldwork, although indispensable, did not in itself move me. On the contrary, it eradicated my initial enthusiasm. "For someone who has never seen the Orient, a lotus is still a lotus," Gérard de Nerval once said to Théophile Gautier. "For me, it's just a kind of onion."[2] My research trips to Burma for this book rarely provided great excitement. In the field, an invisible wall separated me from my interlocutors. To fill the gap, I had to distance myself from them: only after I had left the field and returned to my desk, as I worked to reconstruct reality on the basis of the inert fragments conserved in my notes, did I experience an intimacy with Burmese that had been lacking when I was there. Thus for me writing anthropologically was a way to turn the onion back into a lotus. It seemed to me that a work of anthropology should not only entice the intellect but also arouse the imagination, that it should re-enchant reality, in one way or another. On such a condition anthropology would be true to reality and its vertiginous depth.

I wanted therefore to take account of the reality under study, but at the same time to take account of the anthropological endeavor itself; that is, to demonstrate how one comes gradually to an understanding of what one observes and to display the various benchmarks along the way: both the inner dynamic and the progressive elaboration of an anthropological interpretation.

It is now standard practice to provide in a book such as this one a general introduction setting out the state of the field for the subject under consideration, a summary of the work's major arguments, and a précis of the chapters to follow. In other words, it is customary to show at the outset what the author arrived at only after years of research, reflection, and writing. The procedure has more than proved its worth. In addition to its didactic intent, it arouses a reader's curiosity; it generates suspense and a felt need to see the details of the argument. Readers then know why they must read this book and what the book contributes to the field of research to which it pertains. But even aside from having become a bit tiresome by dint of overuse, this rhetorical strategy fails to reflect the process of anthropological analysis. It does not show how, on the basis of disjointed elements—not only lived experience, events, encounters, and discussions but also the reading of scientific works and personal reflections, which he or she must, through trail and error, fit together in a concise and illuminating way—an anthropologist finally formulates an interpretive scheme. Yet it is precisely this process, this *doing* of anthropology, that I wished to foreground. I do not mean to claim that anthropology should refer only to itself. I mean only to suggest that, between the smooth surface of a fully developed anthropological work, on the one hand, and on the other, the successive and fragmentary attempts and occasional disorder built into the process of anthropological analysis, there exists a balance point wherein the writing can make clear to a reader both the indigenous take on reality and the work of anthropological understanding as it is being elaborated, along with the ties that connect the latter to the former. It is at this medial point that *The Immortals* is set, because it seems to me an effective way for a reader to accompany the anthropologist and in that way to grasp—to take up and make one's own—the anthropologist's interpretations and the realities to which they pertain.

Yet even more challenging than describing what I intended is to characterize the end result. The work does indeed take on an unusual form, difficult to define, and therefore disconcerting. It is telling in this regard that its readers, whether anonymous reviewers of this English edition or people who published reviews of the French edition, all of whom were scholars trained in either Buddhist studies or anthropology, have formulated divergent, if not opposite, assessments of it, even though they agree that the scholarship is fundamentally sound. Thus, while Reviewer A judges that "the book is remarkably free from anthropological theorizing" and characterized by "an anti-theoretical bias," Delphine Ortis (whom I have never met), in a review published in *L'Homme: Revue française d'anthropologie,* sees it on the contrary as "a gripping book, full of wit, and legitimizing the original and essential contribution of anthropology to the study of religion." Reviewer B, for his part, thinks that "the informal style of the book is such that I could leisurely read it by picking it up whenever I felt like it without having to worry about following a sophisticated academic argument," and that "instead of a serious anthropological study of religion, it reads very much like a travelogue or a '(The Author's) Adventures in the Land of Burmese Wizards' kind of non-fiction, adventure book." Yet, from Bénédicte Brac de la Perrière's point of view, expressed in a review published in *Archives de sciences sociales des religions,* the work, although it is indeed elaborated on the "[narrative] standpoint of travelogue" and "does not look like" an academic monograph, nevertheless remains "first of all a monograph of a cult" and "a brilliant analysis of the cultural inner workings of *weikza* cults."

Even more disturbingly, each reader's views seem internally inconsistent or indecisive. Reviewer A underlines "the highly digressive nature of [the book's] writing" and explains that "the leitmotif of the text as a whole and, indeed, of the cult itself is of endless deferment." "In a sense," this reviewer writes, "we are led to the essence of religiosity itself, but on a more prosaic level the reader can not quite escape the unsettling feeling that this is really a film scenario—a sort of Burmese *Waiting for Godot* rewritten in the style of Carlos Castaneda—masquerading as a work of anthropology." This reviewer nonetheless considers the book "an extraordinary achievement representing a distinctive exploration of a little known form of religiosity in a methodologically unique manner." For Reviewer C, "in many ways, *The Immortals* reads more like a relaxed research journal than a standard academic text." It "is essentially a saga of how four specific *weikza* are venerated by devotees," a saga whose subject "often appears as complex as a Russian novel." And yet, this reviewer also asserts that "the book is important largely because of the detailed anthropological analysis it brings to the *weikza* cult in Burma over the last half-century or so." Reviewer B finds that, rather than resembling a "relaxed research journal," "the book reads like a piece of fiction or a collection of short stories." But this reviewer also speaks, as we have seen, of a "kind of non-fiction, adventure book" and simultaneously describes it as a "great book" and a "valuable addition to the field of Buddhist/sorcery/anthropology/history studies of Burma and Southeast Asia."

The multiplicity of images and analogies to which the quoted commentators resort, as well as the internal contradictions in their words, show that each and every one of them has wondered about what kind of book they had in their hands and has strived to define its genre without succeeding in formulating a fully consistent and satisfactory characterization. To the question, "what is this book, exactly?," these readers offer strikingly different and complex answers. As a matter of fact, inextricably narrative and scholarly, neither clearly academic nor nonacademic, the work blurs genres, and so much so that any univocal characterization turns out to be inadequate. Usually, works about Buddhism in past or present-day South and Southeast Asian societies written by anthropologists or by Buddhist Studies scholars tell the reader *what* Buddhists believe and practice, and *why* (e.g., the genealogy and history of Buddhist beliefs, institutions, and practices; their social, economic, and psychological functions; their symbolism; the principles of their effectiveness; and their interrelations). This book tells *how:* it speaks, "in a methodologically unique manner," about the experience(s) of believing and practicing—experience being understood here not in the sense of an ungraspable inner state of mind but in the sense of culturally and socially configured situations of interaction, points of view, and affects. To convey the experience(s) of Burmese Buddhists in relation to the cult under study, but also to make of anthropology itself a perceptible experience, I renounced, it is true, bread-and-butter academic routines. This does not mean, however, that the book is a mere description of the cult, a "journal" or a "travelogue." It suffices to look at the form and content of the book to realize that it actually resembles no journal or travelogue yet known. Nor does the book's unusual format mean that it displays an "anti-theoretical bias." I do "theorize" or at least "interpret" various aspects of the cult, including the incredible. My concern for the incredible is not a way to escape interpretation, thus to remain in the position of fascinated outsider. Instead it reflects the focus of Burmese discourses and practices in this context, a focus that the work tries to conceptualize and understand.

In sum, *The Immortals*—a title referring both to the four *weikza* and to all the men and women who participate in the fashioning of the cult and fill the book's pages—provides the reader, if he or she is ready to comply with the rules of the game (as some readers obviously will not), with a way of delving into a Burmese Buddhist cult and its inner workings, a way that more orthodox, static, and distancing anthropological rhetorical strategies, whatever their indisputable merits, do not provide.

Nevertheless, the book undeniably fails to offer to scholars of Buddhism and Buddhist societies two important things. The first is a general conceptualization of Burmese *weikza* cults, inspired by the study of this particular cult, that would take up and counter previous scholars' interpretations of such cults. The second is a comparative perspective that would situate Burmese *weikza* cults within the larger world of Buddhist cults in Asia. Neither of these projects fit within the scope of a monograph of the cult of this sort. I must also confess that, at the time of writing (2003–2009), I had no well-articulated argument to make with respect to either of these two topics. They will, however, be addressed in a long essay to appear in the next volume of the "cycle of the extraordinary." Written in a conventional scholarly style, that essay formulates an approach to and a characterization of the highly diverse Burmese *weikza* cults. It diverges from previous scholarship to the extent that it does not force the phenomenon into one of the accepted categories ("esotericism," "millennialism," "mysticism") with which scholars in religious studies and anthropology usually label it. Instead, the essay seeks to design a specific frame of analysis based on the elaboration of a distinctive terminology with which to apprehend, render, and organize ethnographic realities. Furthermore, it endeavors to go beyond the apparent singularity of *weikza* cults and to inscribe them in a comparative perspective that makes these cults more intelligible. The research undertaken for *The Immortals* was critical for the subsequent elaboration of this essay.

I think readers are now sufficiently warned about what awaits them in the following pages: what they can and cannot expect from this book. There remains for them to form their own opinion of the work much as Burmese, after having heard reports about a certain *weikza* cult, must form, through firsthand experience, their own opinion about the cult.

Dramatis Personae

The following is a list of people who appear in this book with information, when known, as to their place of residence and their age in 2003–2004 or at the time of their death, indicated by the symbol † (in parentheses). Some Burmese proper names lend themselves to literal translation, but only one of them has been translated in this book, that of my fellow researcher, Victorious.

The prefix U used before the name of a monk or an ascetic can be rendered as "Venerable."

Bo and Bodaw, titles used before the name of a lay *weikza,* mean "Grandfather" and "Noble Grandfather."

The four *weikza*

U Kawwida (Dragoness Mountain, 1,035)
U Pandita (Dragoness Mountain, 748)
U Oktamagyaw (Dragoness Mountain, 550)
Bodaw Bo Htun Aung (Dragoness Mountain, 192)

The four *weikza*'s medium

Htun Yin, *alias* Saturday's Son (in Burmese, Sanay-tha), *alias* U Tilawkeinda (Energy Monastery, Mebaygon, 77)

Disciples of the four *weikza*'s cult

Monastic disciples

U Sanda Thuriya (Energy Monastery, Mebaygon, 90)
U Sandima (Energy Monastery, Mebaygon, 57)
U Thakkara, *alias* Monk Taungtha (Energy Monastery, Mebaygon, 41)
U Thilasara (Aunglan, 44)

Lay disciples

Aung Khaing (Yangon, ?)
Aung Khaing (Loikaw, 57)
Aung Thaung (Kyungyi, 66)
Ba Htay (?, †)
Ba Yi (Mandalay, 73, † 1999)

Chit Kyaw (Mandalay, †)
Hpay Myint (Pyay, approximately 81, † ca. 1993)
Hsami (Mandalay, 47)
Htu Aung (Mandalay, 50)
Kyaw Khaing (Minbu, †)
Kyi Shwe (Yangon, †)
Kyin Myaing (Yangon, 83, † 2003)
Maung Maung (Minbu, 95)
May Aung (Magway, approximately 50)
Mingyi Sein Hlaing (Yangon, 66, † 1977)
Mya Maung (Yangon, † ca. 1974)
Mya Nan Nwe (Energy Monastery, Mebaygon, † 2002)
Mya Than (Mandalay, 66)
Myint Hsway (Aunglan area, 38)
Myo Lwin (Yangon, 68)
Ohn (Yangon, †)
Pan (Minbu, †)
Pyizon (Mandalay, 58)
Sein Yi (Yangon, 72)
Shwe Pyi (Ledaing village, ?)
Tayza Htun (Yangon, 49)
Thein Han (Yangon, 89)
Yan Shin (Mandalay, 52)
Zaw Win (Mandalay, 50)
Zaw Win (Yangon, 77)

Others
Weikza
U Nareinda (Brown Mountain, ca. 500–600)
Bo Paukhsein ("exited" in 1965)

Monks
U Pyinnya (Mebaygon, † 1992)
U Thitala (Yangon, 33)
U Thondara (Dammarattita Monastery, Mebaygon, 49)
U Zawana (Ywa-Le Monastery, Mebaygon, 69)

Laypeople
    Gyan, *alias* Weikza Gyan (Letkhotpin, 73, † 2005)
    Tin Ko Ko (Singapore, 37)
    Victorious (Yangon, 33)

1　From Belief to Believing

ENCOUNTERING THE INCREDIBLE

Tuesday, September 30, 2003, 7:00 p.m. The apartment, which is located on an avenue running along the moat of Mandalay's palace, is suddenly plunged into darkness. The power's out. Yan Shin, interrupting his story, asks his wife to light some candles. He resumes:

> "It was in 1998, at the time of the ceremony to put the finial on the Pagoda of Sighs [Lwan Zaydi, a religious construction put up in memory of someone who has died]. It was my job to get the finial there. We left Mandalay in two small vehicles. I was driving the one in front. My wife and son were sitting in the cab, next to me. A group of people and the finial were in the open back part of the truck. Suddenly [the *weikza*] Bodaw Bo Htun Aung appeared [flying] in the sky. My son saw him first. Bodaw Bo Htun Aung followed our truck for a moment. I stopped the truck and got out to look at him. He turned halfway round and disappeared. The others didn't see him. Just my wife, my son, and me. He had come to greet the finial."

Zaw Win,[1] looking satisfied, takes pleasure in this story, which he already knows well. It is he who has brought my friend and research assistant, Victorious, and me to meet this rich contractor. Victorious and I sit facing the two men, all of us seated on plastic chairs placed in the room reserved for the Buddha altar. Victorious does not have to do much: our host is talkative and keeps his remarks coming. Yan Shin has for that matter said repeatedly, "You could talk about this stuff endlessly; you could fill books with it." I take notes, stopping him from time to time when a phrase or a situation puzzles me. Yan Shin's wife, a small, slightly chubby woman, remains standing at a respectful distance, her eyes shining with excitement.

"There's another [extraordinary thing]. It was five years ago. My older sister had lung cancer. The doctor said she would die within six months . . ."

I am feeling a bit fed up. How many of these stories, each one more incredible than the last, have I recorded in the past month and a half? Weariness overtakes me. And on top of weariness, helplessness. Coming upon what I had set out to find—the extraordinary, which people provide me without letup—I am confounded. What to do with men who fly?

FIFTY YEARS EARLIER

September 1957.[2] Hpay Myint takes up residence in Minbu (Central Burma). He has been named to the recently established post of District Officer of Religious Affairs, headquartered in that town. It falls to him to oversee the proper functioning of the local Buddhist institutions.

On taking up his post, Hpay Myint enters into discussion with notables Maung Maung, civil affairs officer for the district, and Pan, representative of a national organization for the promotion of Buddhism, the Buddha Sasana Council. These two men describe the local situation: the number of members of the monastic community, the activities of the religious organizations, teaching and meditation sites, and so on. They also refer to two *weikza* cults. In the Paygon village monastery, near the town of Sagu, U Nareinda, a *weikza* monk who, since "exiting" the human world, has lived in an invisible place called the Brown Mountain (Taung Nyo), regularly possesses (*dat si-*) a twenty-five-year-old woman, Gyan. Through her, he teaches the faithful the practice of meditation. In the village of Mebaygon, about ten kilometers from Minbu, two "exited" *weikza* residing at the Dragoness Mountain (Nagama Taung), the monk U Pandita and the layperson Bodaw Bo Htun Aung, possess Htun Yin, better known by his nickname Saturday's Son (Sanay-tha). Using him as an intermediary, they deliver sermons and demonstrate their supernatural potency (*dago*). Remarkably, these two *weikza* appear just as frequently in the flesh. Maung Maung and Pan, both disciples of the Mebaygon cult, report many extraordinary incidents, which in Hpay Myint's opinion can only be figments of their imagination.

Hpay Myint was born and raised in Minbu. In his youth, he often heard about *weikza* and *weikza* cults, about the Prince of the Universe (Setkya Min), about the Nine Powers of Noble Success (*aungdawhmu zay ko-lon*), and many other amazing matters. But all that remains so much hearsay. Not that he doubts the existence of *weikza*—it is just that he has never met any genuine *weikza*. People who claim to have had dealings with real *weikza* never provide definitive proof of their claims. Although he listens respectfully to his interlocutors' words, still the religious affairs officer remains unconvinced, looking at the speakers with some condescension. He himself feels in no way inclined to believe (*yonkyi-*) in these so-called *weikza*.

Hpay Myint's duties entail consulting with the most prominent monks in the district and visiting the most famous monasteries. In the course of the second week of November, he goes with Pan to the village of Paygon, where the Yadana-bonpyan monastery is located. The monastery is commonly called "Gyan's meditation center," alluding to the young woman who officiates there.[3] Gyan is the daughter of poor farmers from the village. When she was a child, the family moved to Letkhotpin, closer to Sagu. Gyan attended school until the fourth grade, the last year of primary school. She then started selling fried squash and onions. Until the *weikza* U Nareinda showed up in her life, she knew nothing of *weikza*. She was happy simply to venerate the Three Jewels: the Buddha, his Teachings, and the Community of Monks. Everything got started when, twenty years old and still not yet married, she suddenly experienced worrisome menstrual difficulties. Her periods grew irregular, then soon ceased. Thinking an evil spell must be the cause of her problems, her family sought the help of a monk who was visiting the village. He was known to be a member of the Left Hand Congregation (Letwe Gaing), a group of practitioners of the *weikza* path specializing in exorcism. (The right-hand path is focused on the quest for nirvana.) The monk told her that, if she wanted to be relieved of her affliction, she must become a member of the congregation. The young woman, after committing herself to reciting her prayer beads daily using the formula of the Nine Supreme Qualities of the Buddha, ingested the medicine (*hsay*) with which the congregation initiates its members.

One day, while tending to the Buddha altar in her home, Gyan suddenly sensed herself inhabited by an external force. U Nareinda, one of the Left Hand Congregation's four *weikza* masters, had possessed her. He signaled that energy ashes, powder produced from his own alchemy ball, were to be found in the plate reserved for food offerings to the Buddha. Gyan gathered these ashes and swallowed them with water. It was Friday, January 4, 1952 (eighth day of the waxing moon of the month of Pyatho, in the year 1313 of the Burmese calendar). Not only did the young woman's menstrual problems then cease but she also acquired the ability to lift spells, a skill that the *weikza* urged her to exercise for the benefit of all. By giving a glass of water to the victim of sorcery, Gyan lifts the evil spell, and by placing her hands on a snake's bite, she neutralizes the venom.

Early on, U Nareinda, although he possessed the young woman to deliver Buddhist sermons, had not furnished proof of his identity. People wondered whether a witch or some invisible entity with malicious intentions might not be pretending to be a *weikza*. To decide the matter, a group of experts, four monks and four laypeople, was assembled to put Gyan's discourses or, rather, those of the *weikza* U Nareinda to a careful test. The experts were obliged to acknowledge the orthodoxy and worth of the teachings. On this occasion, U Nareinda, possessing Gyan, explained who he was. He stated that he had "exited" (*htwet-*) five or six hundred years ago, after having "succeeded" (*aung-*) in his practice of alchemy, using a ball of mercury.

The *weikza*'s sermons enjoyed an immediate success. The young woman, known from then on as "Weikza Gyan," was invited to Minbu. She lived for several months at a layperson's home, where people gathered to listen to the *weikza*'s sermons. It was there, in August 1952, that U Nareinda started, through Gyan, to show the faithful the practice of meditation. As a result of these developments, the head monk of the Yadanabonpyan monastery requested that Gyan teach at his monastery, and the young woman took up residence there.

When Hpay Myint visits the center, it has already been five years that Gyan, facing her audience, has been possessed by U Nareinda from four or five in the afternoon until midnight every day. Some people come after work; others take up temporary residence at the monastery. At times of high attendance, during the three months of the annual monastic retreat, séances take place during the day. Simply prostrating herself before the Buddha altar suffices for the young woman to make the *weikza* "come" (*kywa-*). Gyan, imperceptibly possessed, then turns back to face her listeners, sitting as for meditation (her legs crossed and her hands stacked at the level of her thighs, palms up), and starts to preach. Even her intonation shows no change. The fact that the *weikza* is done and has withdrawn his presence becomes clear when his medium, changing position, puts her legs to the rear. Never does Gyan recall the sermon that U Nareinda has delivered through her. When not attending these séances, people engage in solitary meditation in small outbuildings constructed for that purpose. Every time the *weikza* comes, disciples have a chance to inform him of their spiritual experiences and to ask him for his guidance. The center's success is obvious. It enjoys official recognition and, on that basis, financial support from the national organization for the promotion of Buddhism of which Pan is the local representative. Monks in the area support the center's work. Two affiliated centers opened in the district.

This visit makes clear to Hpay Myint what possession by a *weikza* implies and what opportunities it might offer for religious development. Putting aside questions of believing, his interest is aroused. He decides to visit the village of Mebaygon to learn a bit more about the other *weikza* cult that Maung Maung and Pan have told him about. The prospect of his making this excursion evokes strong reactions from his acquaintances in Minbu, many of them dismissing the cult as trickery pure and simple. Such condemnations, far from persuading Hpay Myint to give up the plan, only egg him on. He is not in the habit of letting others tell him what to think. He would never accept or reject a point without having looked into it himself: he would form an opinion based on his own investigation. Granted, the district head has urged him to be vigilant. It is a fertile time for charlatans. The district head cited the example of a man in a village near the capital, Yangon, who had claimed to be able to summon *weikza,* spirits, ogres, and so on, and make them visible. Respected figures and political leaders were counted among his generous devotees. Great was their shame, as well as that of the enchanter himself (whose accomplices disguised themselves as *weikza,* spirits, etc.), once the trickery was revealed. One must not put faith in any of these things, Hpay Myint thought to himself while listening to this story, unless one can do so with complete certainty.

Maung Maung and Pan are more than happy to accompany their colleague on the trip. They take care of renting a jeep. One Saturday at about 6:30 p.m., the three men and their driver leave Minbu, setting off on the main road to the city of Sagu. Pan and Hpay Myint sit in the front seat, Maung Maung in the rear. When they have gone about five kilometers, the driver turns off to the right, following a cattle track. He reduces his speed to fifteen kilometers an hour at most. The path is bad and the vehicle in sorry shape. The crossbars of the roof, which threatens to collapse at any moment, are fastened with wire. Pan touches the roof.

"I was checking to see if the *weikza* had arrived," he explains to his astonished companion.

"Impossible!" exclaims Hpay Myint with a skeptical smile.

About five or six hundred meters farther on, as Pan checks the roof once again, a voice can be heard: "Hey, who's feeling my ass?" The question is put brusquely.

"It's me, your disciple Pan, Venerable. I wanted to know whether the *weikza* were following us."

The voice addresses the driver: "Hey, speed up! Are you afraid a *weikza*'s going to fall down? Come on, speed up!"

Disconcerted, Hpay Myint thinks a moment. If it were an ordinary person sitting on the roof, the jeep's roof would have collapsed or at least sagged deeply.

Yet it hasn't even moved. While the puzzled official wonders—what is this, a pagoda's guardian spirit (*okzazaung*), a ghost (*thaye*), or really a *weikza?*—Bodaw Bo Htun Aung himself, dressed in his white outfit and with a staff in his hand, appears on the hood of the moving vehicle. The *weikza* moves two steps forward and two steps backward, balancing himself without any trouble, and then sits down cross-legged. Eight hundred meters farther on, he makes the jeep stop and the passengers get out. Standing on the hood, he speaks to them:

> "Disciples, when you come to our energy center (*dat zakhan*), be of calm mind. Venerate the Three Jewels. Recite your beads! Don't think about *weikza!* Don't put them before the Buddha! *Weikza* can't save (*ke-*) you; only the Three Jewels can save you. But we don't want those who come to our energy center to encounter any difficulty, or any danger. The *weikza* have to honor their reputation . . ."

Bodaw Bo Htun Aung speaks another moment and then tells the passengers to get back into the car, which sets off once again. Now he is walking ahead of the jeep, which is moving at fifteen kilometers per hour. The *weikza* and the jeep proceed in concert for a little less than a kilometer before Bodaw Bo Htun Aung, speeding up and putting a distance of more than thirty meters between himself and the jeep to his rear, suddenly disappears. Hpay Myint is taken aback.

The jeep enters the village of Mebaygon. The Energy Center, the place where the *weikza* appear, is a big wooden house. It belongs to the parents-in-law of Saturday's Son, the medium. This couple, their daughter, and her husband live on the ground floor. The room upstairs, with the Buddha altar, is dedicated to the *weikza* cult. Guests go up the stairs. The altar to the Buddha, placed on the east side of the room, is magnificently decorated with paintings and further adorned with flower pots. There is a statue of a standing Buddha, two of seated Buddhas, as well as two photographs of *weikza,* one of U Pandita and the other of Bodaw Bo Htun Aung. Hpay Myint is impressed by the splendor of it all.

Once he has paid homage to the Buddha, the official goes back downstairs to have a look around. He tries to see if there is a secret entryway, some opening that would allow the so-called *weikza* to get access to the upstairs without being seen. He also checks out the area nearby. When he goes back upstairs, Saturday's Son is talking with Maung Maung and Pan. The three men are drinking green tea. Hpay Myint joins the conversation. Soon Maung Maung asks Saturday's Son to invite the *weikza.* The young man—he is thirty-one—sits in front of the altar to the Buddha and starts to recite a respectful formula. He fails to reach the end before Bodaw Bo Htung Aung takes possession of him. The *weikza* addresses the visitors through the offices of his medium, whose voice now takes on a noticeably pleasanter timbre. Much as he has done on the road to Mebaygon, Bodaw Bo Htun Aung exhorts his listeners to revere the Three Jewels, to recite their beads, and so on. He addresses Hpay Myint directly:

"Great Disciple Hpay Myint, you are in charge of religious affairs and you must conduct investigations. So investigate! There have been photographs taken of us. If you find someone around here who looks like the figures in these photos, you can take action. No ordinary person would dare pretend to be U Pandita or Bodaw Bo Htun Aung and get photographed as such. We possess Saturday's Son, who isn't worth two pence, and we're supporting the religion. Don't make us gifts of nine yards of cloth or nine twenty-five-cent coins, or trays of offerings. Those things are for people who lie and cheat. There's no point making gifts to *weikza*. *Weikza* don't need to eat bananas from trays of offerings the faithful make up for them. If we can watch over you, we will do so. Be calm and happy! We'll keep problems at bay for you. Rest assured! Furthermore, Great Disciple Hpay Myint, take a lamp and check this house out carefully. See if there are any secret doors or anything like that so as not to have any more suspicions. You never know where U Pandita shows up from. He may come from over by the altar or from someplace else. Look everywhere so as to get over all your suspicions."

Hearing these words, Hpay Myint realizes that the *weikza* knows all about how he was checking out the house.

"Come closer, Great Disciple Hpay Myint! Do you know the song of Bobo Aung [Grandfather Success, a famous *weikza*]?[4] If you erase one *wa* [the letter o], two *wa* appear. If you erase two *wa,* four appear. And so on. Do you know this song?"

"Yes, I know it, Venerable."

"Have you seen a *wa* that couldn't be erased, that even makes two *wa,* four *wa,* and so on?"

"I've never seen such a thing, Venerable."

"Would you like to?"

"Yes, I would, Venerable."

"Give me your hand!"

Saturday's Son takes Hpay Myint's left hand and covers it with a handkerchief. Grabbing a pen from the visitor's shirt pocket, he draws three circles in the air without touching the handkerchief, each time intoning, "It's written! One *wa!*" He removes the handkerchief. Three circles have appeared on Hpay Myint's hand, as clear as if they had been drawn with red paint.

"Go ahead, erase them!"

Hpay Myint, using his right hand, tries in vain to make the little circles disappear.

"Are they getting erased?"

"No, they're not getting erased, Venerable."

"Then try erasing them with water!"

Hpay Myint takes a little water from a nearby pot and starts in. Not only do the circles not disappear but the more he rubs, the more they proliferate. Soon his hand is covered with them. The *weikza* asks him to put the handkerchief back on his hand and then declares, "There are none left!" He takes the handkerchief away. The circles are no longer there.

Bodaw Bo Htun Aung talks for a moment with Maung Maung and Pan before ending the conversation:

"Great Disciples, recite your beads and then sleep! Don't wait for the *weikza*. Focus your mind solely on the Three Jewels. I'm leaving."

Bodaw Bo Htun Aung "separates his *weikza* essence" (*weikza dat kwa-*) from Saturday's Son, who regains consciousness. Hpay Myint doesn't know what to think. Saturday's Son is ordinarily a simple, countrified sort of man; there is no way he could express himself in the remarkable way he has just done. His gestures and his conduct when he is possessed differ from his usual demeanor. It couldn't be a hoax intended to fool the naïve and extort gifts from them. Hasn't Bodaw Bo Htun Aung insisted that making offerings to *weikza* is useless? Hpay Myint, plunged in thought, has no intention of sleeping. But Saturday's Son, taking leave of the visitors, invites them to rest. When he goes downstairs, he turns off the main light, leaving only a night light on.

Hpay Myint wants to take a moment to meditate in front of the Buddha altar before sleeping. When he has been saying his beads for about fifteen minutes, something strange happens. The flowers set on the altar shake slightly. From that very place emerges U Pandita, in the flesh, his monastic robe covering his head. The *weikza* comes toward Hpay Myint in measured steps and speaks to him. Reiterating Bodaw Bo Htun Aung's exhortations, he urges him to venerate the Three Jewels, to say his beads, not to concern himself with the *weikza,* not to give them gifts, and so on. He then pronounces a wish on his behalf: "May you be successful, may you be successful! May you be satisfied, may you be satisfied!" Whereupon he withdraws, going down the stairs. Hpay Mint follows him. But when the *weikza* reaches the bottom step, he disappears into thin air. Hpay Myint looks everywhere underneath the house, to no avail. He then goes upstairs, joining his companions, but having witnessed something so extraordinary makes him too excited to sleep.

Bodaw Bo Htun Aung soon appears. He pops in through a door from a side room. "How did he do that?" Hpay Myint asks himself. The room is much too high for him to have climbed up outside. Bodaw Bo Htun Aung quizzes Hpay Myint while tapping him on the head.

"Great Disciple Hpay Myint, are you content, are you satisfied? What did the *weikza* U Pandita tell you?"

He offers his companions and him bananas, even though the *weikza* had brought nothing with him. Hpay Myint, in any case, has seen nothing, despite the fact that the moonlight is bright that night and you can see the shapes of things clearly.

Ten minutes or so later, Bodaw Bo Htun Aung, about to leave, questions Hpay Myint one last time:

"Now do you understand?"

Bodaw Bo Htun Aung goes down the stairs. Hpay Myint follows him with his eyes. This time, the *weikza* doesn't disappear as soon as he reaches the bottom. Walking back and forth in front of the house, he discusses matters with the visitors standing at the windows.

"Great Disciples, be reassured, sleep well!" he tells them finally, before suddenly disappearing.

As he lies down, Hpay Myint delightedly recalls all the different ways the *weikza* have demonstrated their supernatural potency in the course of the evening.

The next morning at 5:00 a.m., the three men and their driver leave Mebaygon to return to Minbu. Along the way, Hpay Myint turns over in his mind everything that he has seen. How grateful he is to Maung Maung and Pan for having allowed him to meet the *weikza*.

So ends the story of Hpay Myint's first visit to the Mebaygon Energy Center at the end of 1957. Its protagonist related this story as the opening of a book he dedicated to the cult of the four *weikza*, which was published fifteen years later, in 1972. (In addition to the two, Bodaw Bo Htun Aung and U Pandita, mentioned so far, the *weikza* include the monks U Kawwida and U Oktamagyaw.) Hpay Myint had left Minbu long before. In November 1959, he had been transferred to Pyapon District, in Irrawaddy Division. But in the course of his two years in Minbu, as had Maung Maung and Pan, he had become a fervent disciple of the Mebaygon *weikza*. Nonetheless it had taken this religious affairs officer two more visits, which he describes in just as much detail, for him to become convinced. The opening chapter of his work, which gives an account of this personal experience, is made up of the many prodigious feats accomplished by the *weikza*, feats that the skeptical visitor considers carefully. The chapter consists of thirty-six pages filled with facts each more extraordinary and incredible than the last, supplemented with the author's ruminations, to which the hundred pages of the fourth and final chapter add material in the form of transcriptions of testimonials gathered by Hpay Myint from nine eminent disciples of the *weikza,* including three medical doctors. Thus fully half of the original edition of the work is given over to such stories. Hpay Myint makes it clear what is at stake when he poses this question, formulated as the title of the account of his own experience: "Should one believe in *weikza?*" (*weikza hsoda yonkyi ya hma la*).

A FUNCTIONALIST EXPLANATION FOR FLYING MEN

Early 1961. The American anthropologist Melford E. Spiro arrives in Burma. Forty-one years old, he is a seasoned ethnographer and an inspired theoretician. His approach straddles both functionalist conceptions, after the fashion of Bronislaw Malinowski, and those of the "Culture and Personality" school, placing him in an iconoclastic position—one he assumes with gusto, at a time when both of these theoretical streams are being subjected to vigorous criticism within the discipline. Spiro pointedly distances himself from Claude Lévi-Strauss's structuralism, at the time reaching its fullest flowering. He does not see in myth and ritual the result of a symbolic logic, the infinite capacity of the human mind to combine elements in order to confer on the world order and meaning. For him, myths, rites, and all other cultural manifestations have first and foremost an objective, or several objectives, both conscious and unconscious. It is these objectives, what R. K. Merton calls "manifest and latent functions," that must be uncovered. The questions that Spiro poses begin with "Why?," not "How?," and the responses he formulates consist of causal explanations of a psychological nature.[5]

In the 1950s, Spiro conducted research on the institution of the kibbutz in Israel. He was struck by the supramundane elements—touching on matters of salvation—of the ostensibly secular and socialist ideology of the kibbutz. He then wished to study this collective tendency to formulate a supramundane horizon in a society in which such a tendency derived directly from a religious ideology. Thus his choice of Burma, a country in which Buddhism constitutes the base of its culture and social organization.[6]

After spending four weeks in Yangon, Spiro heads upcountry. A village in the area of Mandalay catches his fancy. His family sets up house in the former royal capital, the country's second largest city. Thus Spiro, while living in the village, travels regularly to town, taking the opportunity to study the features of "urban Buddhism."[7]

Spiro will not travel to Minbu, let alone to Mebaygon. He will not meet Hpay Myint, now posted to Pyapon, in the southwest of the country. Nevertheless he cannot help but stumble on the phenomenon of *weikza*. These cults proliferate wildly. Ideas linked to the *weikza* path (*weikza lan,* the path for becoming a *weikza*) are widespread among all layers of Burmese society. Alchemy is practically a national pastime. Many are those who, using fire to purify and fortify a little ball of metal to endow it with extraordinary powers, hope to attain the status of a *weikza*.

In a chapter of the work he publishes ten years later, appearing at almost the same time as Hpay Myint's book, Spiro, then chair of the Department of Anthropology at the University of California at San Diego, labels the *weikza* phenomenon "esoteric Buddhism" and analyzes it at length.[8] The Burmese "beliefs and practices" related to *weikza,* he asserts, derive their fundamental raison d'être from universal human aspirations, such as the desire for immortality and the quest for supernatural powers. Nevertheless, the fascination they exert on the Burmese social and intellectual elite requires a more specific explanation. Spiro has observed a passionate engagement with the practice of alchemy on the part not only of villagers but also of people from "educated" and "Westernized" urban milieus: civil servants (such as Hpay Myint), university professors, writers, legal specialists. Spiro suggests that belief in *weikza* works as a compensatory mechanism for Burmese in general and for the elite in particular, who still suffer from a double trauma: the trauma of British conquest and colonization in the nineteenth century, which revealed Burma's technological backwardness, and the trauma of the country's economic collapse after independence (1948) and its consequent incapacity to institute a system of industrial production capable of responding to the popular desire for modern goods.

> It is out of desperation, therefore, a desperation stemming from the discrepancy between what they have and what the West has been able to create, that, in my opinion, these upper-class Burmese turn to alchemy and the belief in weikzahood. They may not be able (as their erstwhile Western

masters are) to manufacture autos, but as *weikza* they are able to travel even faster than the speed of autos; they may not be able to manufacture planes, but as *weikza* they are able to fly through the air without them; they may not be able to manufacture bullets, but as *weikza* they are able to become invulnerable to them; they may not be able to manufacture radios, but as *weikza* they are able to communicate over long distances without them.[9]

More than forty years later, at a time when Burma ranks among the world's least developed countries, Spiro's analysis still seems applicable to the Burmese state of mind. Burmese discourse remains imbued with a hierarchical distinction between "*weikza* knowledge" (*weikza pyinnya*) and "scientific knowledge" (*theik-pan pyinnya*), the word *pyinnya* naming in the case of *weikza* both a type of knowledge or skill and its attendant power. To cite just one example, here is what a monk told me one day; that is, what the monk said to a foreigner presumed not to believe in *weikza,* not to be Buddhist, and to incarnate in the eyes of his interlocutor Western civilization:

"Granted, Burma is a poor and under-developed country. But even if it is lacking in material things (*yok-wada*), it does not lack for spiritual ones (*seik-wada*).[10] In this domain, Burma ranks in the forefront of nations. Where in the world can you find *weikza* other than in Burma and Tibet? If you want to go on a trip, you have to buy a plane ticket, get a passport and a visa, go to the airport, fly for several hours and maybe die in an accident. But a *weikza,* he gets wherever he wants to go in the blink of an eye."

Yet it is worth asking whether the opposition between *weikza* knowledge and scientific knowledge stems from Burma's brutal confrontation with the West and modernity or whether it represents a reformulation, brought about by historical circumstances, of an older concept antedating that confrontation. What is at issue is an estimation of the impact the encounter with the West had on the Burmese system of representations. To what extent did Western civilization determine and does it continue to determine Burmese cultural developments?[11] Taken to its logical limit, Spiro's argument would lead to the following conclusion: "magical beliefs" of whatever sort (whether pertaining to *weikza* or other matters) will disappear from Burmese society once the country fully enters the era of scientific and economic development, once its population enjoys the same material privileges as Western populations. Yet, as suggested by the case of neighboring Thailand, which experienced a spectacular economic boom and at the same time an intensification of "magical" practices in the 1990s, the two phenomena turning out to be completely compatible, couldn't exactly the opposite take place instead?[12]

Spiro, in a footnote, cites two authors, Howard Malcolm and John Crawfurd, who, writing in the 1830s, underline in similar fashion the remarkable interest in alchemy shown by both Burmese scholars and officials, including the king.[13] He could by the same token have referred to the testimony of Father Sangermano, who lived in Burma from 1783 to 1808, well before the First Anglo-Burmese war (1824–1826) and the catastrophe it brought down on the kingdom.[14] In other words, the Burmese elite devoted itself to practices similar to the *weikza* path prior to the traumas of colonization and modernization. The elite did not need to experience these traumas to become enthralled with these practices. Such an inclination demands a different explanation or, perhaps better, an interpretation, should one feel the need for one—such as Spiro encourages us to seek—that gets beyond seeing in the *weikza* phenomenon the expression of universal human aspirations. What could it have meant to Burmese, two hundred years ago, to practice alchemy and acquire supernatural faculties (immortality, the ability to transform metals into gold) or to venerate a deceased person who was a master of alchemical work and so endowed with supernatural abilities? Accounts of observers at the time do not enable us to provide a conclusive response. Spiro, for his part, looks at the practice of alchemy as belonging to an age of magic, an age before Westernization, destined in theory to decline with the expansion of scientific reasoning. He therefore finds it paradoxical that the Burmese elite, educated in the European tradition—that is, enlightened by the scientific view of the world—should continue to be fascinated by alchemy.

But do understandings of the *weikza* phenomenon need to be broken down in tandem with class, status, and other social divisions? Can we differentiate a Buddhism of the elite from a popular Buddhism, or an urban Buddhism from a rural one? Such an approach gives us the image of a religion in layers. Yet in observing contemporary Burmese society, we are obliged to note that "magical beliefs" are spread among all social strata, as are "rationalist" interpretations of Buddhism. Further complicating matters is the fact that the same person will, according to the context or interlocutor, speak or act alternatively in "magical" or "rational" terms. At this point, the work of understanding depends on considering the facts with respect to their cultural pertinence rather than with reference to sociological categories. A phenomenon running through the entirety of a society, as is true of the *weikza* phenomenon, owes its existence and meaning to its relation to the totality in which it takes part, a totality with its own language and logic.

From this perspective, and in spite of the fact that some elements do support Spiro's analysis, it turns out that his way of making sense of the *weikza* phenomenon differs from that of the Burmese. Spiro claims to clarify the "motives" and "functions" of "beliefs" pertaining to *weikza* in the context of a comparative anthropology. He approaches and explains this phenomenon both as the manifestation of universal human desires and as a reaction specific to Burmese society in the face of a historical conjuncture that is shared by many contemporary nations. In doing so, he uses the term "belief" in its conventional anthropological sense. A belief is what members of a society consider collectively—which is to say, culturally—real or possible. Thus the Burmese "believe that" individuals, having acquired the status of a *weikza,* can fly and prolong their life, or they "believe in" *weikza*—that is, in the existence and the powers of *weikza*— "beliefs" that can be explained in a number of ways. Yet one of Spiro's interlocutors told him, "If important people like U Nu [then prime minister] and U Kya [*sic*] Nyein [leader of the opposition party] and other officials and important businessmen believe in him [the alleged *weikza*], then I'm prepared to believe, too."[15] To speak in this way shows that believing—that is, "believing in" one or several *weikza*—was not self-evident. Indeed, didn't Hpay Myint's entire story, so carefully elaborated, turn on that very point? But Spiro, in his reflections, ignores the point of view implicit in his interlocutor's statement. He thereby ignores what is at the heart of the Burmese discourse on the subject: a questioning not of the basis for belief in *weikza* in general, but rather of the basis for belief in one or several specific *weikza* in particular. Where Spiro is surprised at the Burmese belief in *weikza* and tries to justify it, the Burmese are surprised by their belief in one or several *weikza* and try to justify that. Shouldn't we be surprised by their surprise?

RETURNING TO BASICS: BURMESE WORDS FOR "BELIEF" AND "BELIEVING"

Monday, November 10, 2003, 8:00 a.m. Sitting at my desk at the University of Singapore, I write the first pages of what will become *The Immortals.* Yan Shin's noticing the *weikza* Bodaw Bo Htun Aung flying through the air is already included in the manuscript, along with Spiro and his explanation of the *weikza* phenomenon, although these descriptions remain in the form of sketches. Hpay Myint's narrative of his visit to the Mebaygon Center of Energy in late 1957 will be brought in later; it will replace an introductory account of the figure of the *weikza* that I later dispense with. The problem—"Where is the problem?" asked Bronislaw Malinowski tirelessly, in the manner of Socrates[16]—that runs throughout these pages presented itself to me within the first two months of my fieldwork, between mid-August and mid-October 2003. But I still need to articulate it clearly.

There are at least two verbs in Burmese corresponding to the English verb "to believe." These two terms do not denote the same type of engagement, because one might say—twisting a grammatical metaphor—that the social conjugation of the verb "to believe" permits both an active and a passive voice. Granted, the difference is not always apparent in daily usage: not as clear, at least, as the anthropologist might wish. Nonetheless, an essential nuance distinguishes *yuhsa-* from *yonkyi-* (or simply *yon-*). The former means "to believe that," "to consider that," or to "suppose that;" the latter "to believe in," "to be confident that," "to count on," "to depend on." The two verbs are like the two faces of the English "to believe," the sense of which inclines, according to the situation, either toward "to believe that" or toward "to believe in." Each Burmese verb generates a substantive form, *ayuahsa* and *yonkyihmu*. But in English there is only one nominalized form available, that of "belief," which refers, in specific cases, to one or the other of the semantic registers of the verb "to believe." How to escape the terminological ambiguity without shirking the responsibility to make a translation?

Ayuahsa refers to a statement that requires no argumentation or proof. It is the expression of an opinion as to the truth of a phenomenon not amenable to practical demonstration: it is both an individual (idiosyncratic) opinion and, more important, an opinion held in common; that is, a collective representation. "We believe that there are tree spirits"; "When you give money to monks, you acquire merit; that's a Burmese belief (*ayuahsa*)." This type of formulation is addressed to a foreigner in order to lay out the content and principles of Burmese culture, "Burmese beliefs" (*bama ayuahsa*). Thus *ayuahsa* designates beliefs as customary understandings, particularly with reference to religion, magic, and ritual, characteristic of a specific culture just as classical ethnographic description conceives of them. The Burmese substantive noun has no direct opposite, and the verb is usually used in the positive, just as, for the anthropologist, there is no domain or word pitting against "beliefs." The category of "unbeliefs" is meaningless in anthropology. Beliefs simply vary from one culture to another. That's all there is to it.

The second term, *yonkyihmu,* contrasts with the first inasmuch as it implies on the part of the speaker some psychological or social involvement that is absent or only latent in the statement of a conventional belief. A Burmese person who, as occurs frequently in the religious domain, states with reference to a being or a category of beings, "I believe" (*yonkyi-*), articulates two things simultaneously. On the one hand, this person takes a position on a terrain in which not to believe (*ma yonkyi bu*) is perfectly possible and admissible—so much so that "to believe" differs from "to know" (*thi-*) precisely because the former implies the possibility of doubt. On the other hand, that individual acknowledges the power of the beings in question and the influence they may exercise over his or her person and life course. "To believe" in this sense means not just to consider something to be the case but also to revere and, to a certain degree, to fear. To affirm, for example, about tree spirits that "I believe" (*yonkyi-*) amounts not only to assuming their existence but even more to asserting that these beings can be harmful or beneficent and that it is imperative to conduct oneself accordingly. To state, in contrast, "I don't believe (in tree spirits)," does not deny the existence of such spirits, but rather indicates that you are unconcerned about their existence. *Yonkyihmu* thus labels, in the realm of religious matters, belief understood as adherence to the cult of one or several figures and someone's involvement in practices relating to them—an individual choice that may cause tension or even rifts among parents and children, brothers and sisters, teachers and students. To avoid all ambiguity, in place of "belief," I use the word "believing." The word "faith" would have passed muster were it not colored with a heavy suggestion of belief in a religion, not in one being or a category of beings. Faith, furthermore, is a feeling of blind and absolute confidence, whereas believing (*yonkyihmu*) combines a greater range of affects, among them fear.

A collective belief or representation (*ayuahsa*) does not necessarily bring about individual believing (*yonkyihmu*). There exists no mechanical relation of cause and effect between customary belief in the existence of *weikza* and believing in one or several specific *weikza*. The Burmese, for the most part, accept as real the existence of *weikza*. Nevertheless, a certain number of Burmese are adepts of no cult and, by this very fact, say that they do not believe in *weikza* (*ma yonkyi bu*); that is, they worship no *weikza*. Thus we must distinguish two different levels: belief at the first level, which applies to the full extent of the society in question, and within this community of believers, the second level of believing, marked by individual variability.[17] So not to believe in *weikza* (*ma yonkyi bu*) must not be equated with unbelief properly speaking, which is practically impossible in Burmese society. Given that belonging to this society, being culturally Burmese, implies believing that *weikza* exist, unbelief would require that an individual give up some portion of his or her Burmeseness, not an easy thing to do.

In in the late 1970s, a communist living in the city of Monywa came to the Energy Monastery, founded in Mebaygon village by Saturday's Son, who had then become a monk. The man had been led there by a friend, a member of the cult. In the eyes of some Burmese communists prominent in the 1950s and 1960s, organized in independent communities in rebel-held areas, religion was the opiate of the people, the cause of stupidity and subjugation. These communists rejected the ideas—central to Buddhist dogma—of karma and of rebirth, which they considered mystifications. Every individual should be considered immediately responsible for his or her actions and fortunes. Only on this condition would people fight for their liberty and their progress, instead of resigning themselves to their condition, attributing it to the inevitable effect of actions committed in earlier lives.[18] In the evening, on the appearance in the flesh of the first *weikza,* the visitor therefore took on a defiant tone and acted in an insolent manner. Instead of paying homage to Bodaw Bo Htun Aung and requesting his benediction, the communist challenged him:

> "Aren't pagodas [buildings sheltering Buddha relics or those of saintly individuals, the main sanctuaries for Burmese] made of brick? Stairs, houses, and bathrooms are also made of bricks. So why should I pay homage to a pagoda? Why should I pay homage to bricks? I'm going to go urinate on the pagoda!"

The man was referring to one of the three pagodas standing on the monastery grounds. The *weikza* thought for a moment in silence, then questioned the impious man:

"Do you have a mother?"

"Yes," answered the communist.

"Do you have brothers and sisters?"

"Yes, we are two brothers and three sisters."

"Are you married?"

"Yes."

"Your mother, your sisters, and your wife are all women, isn't that right? So you could sleep with all of them!"

The *weikza,* in assimilating, for the purposes of his apologue the incest taboo and the Buddhist faith, treated the two axioms as equally essential for the collectivity, for its social and cultural life. The elementary notions undergirding Burmese Buddhist conceptions, such as the notion of karma and of rebirth, as well as the idea that suffering is inherent in any existence and that it is possible to put an end to it by obtaining nirvana, cannot be put into question. This Buddhist way of being precedes believing; it constitutes a primary identity, one that is not the fruit of individual decision making or will. Buddhism makes the Burmese. It is not without reason that for a hundred years foreign observers have continued to repeat the same formulaic remark, "To be Burmese is to be Buddhist," often taking it—erroneously but tellingly—to be a Burmese saying.[19] When identity and religion are confounded to this degree, a person without religion is a person without identity, a disconnected and errant individual, marked by a fundamental deficiency: a "communist," a strange being living on the margins of society. A Burmese does not ask a foreigner, "Do you have a religion?" but rather "What is your religion?" (*ba batha kokwe tha le*), as if the fact that one has a religion were self-evident.[20]

The brash communist, the rest of the story goes, thought over Bodaw Bo Htun Aung's response the entire night. In the morning he was converted. He donned the monk's robe temporarily at the *weikza* monastery and returned regularly thereafter. A surprising reversal—one among many—only if one forgets that before being a communist the man was a Burmese; in other words, that despite his proclaimed unbelief, he was basically Buddhist and believed in *weikza*. In the end, to speak of "unbelief" is acceptable only if individuals declare that they can say neither "I believe" (in the *weikza* of Mebaygon, for example) nor "I do not believe;" that is, only if they declare themselves both beyond the reach of and indifferent to the cultural basis of the discussion. Rather than unbelief, the Burmese attitude that contrasts with believing is incredulity, whether an expression of skepticism or doubt in the face of a particular individual's claims to the status of a *weikza,* or in the face of a particular cult, or even in the face of certain commonly accepted verities. Yet such skepticism and such doubt remain informed by the conceptual frame of Burmese Buddhist thought.

There is, in sum, a disparity between a belief's "passive" mode and its "active" one, between a belief that remains in the latent state on the part of an individual who shares it with the other members of society and such a belief's activation when that same individual experiences its truthfulness and content, when the belief turns into believing. What we might be inclined to call the "drama of believing," in light of the element of conversion evident in the striking stories told by interested parties (Hpay Myint and many others), stems from this disparity. The plot develops in such a way as to make meaningful and legitimate the conversion that takes place, a conversion based on an experience of the extraordinary. It is precisely this drama that Spiro overlooks, and in so doing, he prevents himself from grasping fully the nature of the *weikza* phenomenon—

because it is through the drama of believing that Burmese conceptions of *weikza* express themselves.

Spiro is aware of what he is doing. He finds it more appropriate and more conclusive to establish what people believe and to explain why they believe it—the content, motives, and functions of their beliefs—than to examine how they come to believe and to interpret how they make sense of this experience. In other words, he overlooks the process by which believing and indigenous discourse on this subject are generated. In an earlier work focusing on "supernaturalism" (that is, Burmese belief in the existence of such beings as ghosts, demons, witches, and spirits, with their associated ritual complex), which treated it as a religious system distinct from Buddhism, Spiro had devoted more attention to the modalities of believing.[21] His approach to Buddhism and *weikza* turns resolutely aside from this matter. Although an explanation in functionalist and psychological terms is not without merit, an effort to understand the principles generating and sustaining a cultural production would benefit from a more attentive analysis of what people say and how they say it. It is significant that Hpay Myint introduces the narration of his experience by the following question—"Should one believe in (*yonkyi-*) *weikza?*"—one that runs throughout the whole of his work. It is also significant that he responds not with an argument about the phenomenon of *weikza* in general—he admits their existence a priori in stating that he had never yet seen a "real" *weikza*—but by recounting individual experiences, his among them, of confrontations with the four *weikza* of Mebaygon village and their medium. Either Hpay Myint and the rest of the Burmese with him speak in order to express nothing other than their aspirations as human beings and their frustrations as budding modern individuals, in which case, indeed, why bother to listen to them? Or they have a story to tell, a meaningful story, in which case we must listen to them, no matter how unbelievable it appears. The problem for anyone who wishes to understand what a *weikza* is consists of penetrating the drama of believing: its conditions, its development, its characteristics, its language. And a drama does not lend itself to quick summary without the loss of its intensity and its complexity. On the contrary, it is better to let it play out in all its richness.

SKEPTICISM AS THE FOUNDATION FOR BELIEVING

Wednesday, August 27, 2003, early afternoon. Two days having passed since my arrival in Mandalay, I go to the Yasagyo Monastery, where Saturday's Son, the four *weikza*'s medium, is spending the annual three-month monastic retreat. When I appear, the distinguished man is taking his siesta. He comes out twenty minutes later and seats himself on a chaise lounge in the middle of the room, facing a small television set, and starts watching a videocassette.

I strike up a conversation with a cult disciple who provides Saturday's Son his midday meal every day. Zaw Win is about fifty years of age, but looks younger. This, he says, is because he eats youth-maintaining fruit that the *weikza* provide. These fruit are gathered at Dragoness Mountain, Nagama Taung.[22] Located in the heart of a forest in Central Burma, in the region of the Shwesetdaw Pagoda (a national pilgrimage site whose founding is attributed to the Buddha himself), the place is invisible and inaccessible to ordinary people. The four *weikza* who appear in the flesh at Mebaygon live, along with numerous other masculine and feminine representatives of their kind, inside the mountain, in a vast cavern of more than three square kilometers, whose inner walls are of alabaster and quartz and whose floor is covered with precious stones. At its center stands a pagoda made entirely of gold, thirty-two cubits high (about fifteen meters), named "Great Pagoda of the Cessation of Hostility and Evil Sentiments" (Yan-pyay Man-pyay Zaydidawgyi); it is encrusted with nine kinds of precious stones. The cavern contains many grottoes, divided up into several halls. There the *weikza* practice meditation, alchemy, and other arts appropriate to their condition. One of the grottoes is reserved for women; in it liquid gold flows drop by drop. In the highest hall lives U Kawwida, the "great monk commander of the *weikza*" (*weikzado gainggyok hsayadawgyi*), more than a thousand years old. On the exterior of the mountain, a magnificent waterfall flows down from its summit. Rocky platforms, suitable spots for prayer-bead recitation, are spread about the gem-encrusted slopes. At the foot of the mountain and in surrounding areas are to be found many tree-filled parks, rich in aromatic plants and fragrant flowers; water tanks decorated with lotuses; and forests with immense trees (mango trees, jackfruit trees, banana trees) that bear fruit all year long. When the four *weikza* come to preach at the Energy Monastery in Mebaygon, they often bring along some of these fruit to distribute. Although the fruit may appear quite ordinary, the disciples say that their taste and fragrance always turn out to be extraordinary. Zaw Win often receives a mango.

Zaw Win's mother, who died the year before, was a fervent disciple of the four *weikza,* who declared that she had been the mother of one of them—U Pandita—in a previous existence. But her intense devotion did not please her family, least of all her eldest daughter. At the end of the 1970s, the daughter decided to send her brother, Zaw Win, on a mission to Mebaygon, in the hopes that he would unmask the four supposed *weikza*'s tricks and make the truth burst on their deluded mother.

"My older sister, who has a bachelor's degree in the sciences, told me:
'Our mother is being deceived by fake *weikza* (*weikza tu weikza yaung*). She's rich and they're going to defraud her. Go there and see what's going on.'
'What will you give me if I go there?'
'What do you want?'
'Give me a flashlight, the kind that takes three batteries.'

She agreed. She also promised to reward me with 300 *kyat*. That was quite a lot of money. In those days, you rarely saw a 20-*kyat* bill. A banana only cost fifteen hundredths of a *kyat*. I had never held 300 *kyat* in my hands. Had you opened my money box, you would have found 50 *kyat* at the very most. I decided to go. I was curious, for that matter, to see some *weikza*.

I set out with Shwe and San San Aye, who lived on 27th St., between 79th and 80th Streets [in Mandalay]. They were going to have their son become a novice in Mebaygon. The ceremony took place the day we arrived. A sermon by the *weikza* was planned for the evening. I wanted to spy on things on the outside. I thought the *weikza* got up [to the window of the hall where they appeared] with the help of a ladder or of some other people. I was trying to get to the bottom of their tricks. At the moment that the *weikza* came to preach, I looked down at the foot of the Monastery of the Noble Success [the building where the *weikza* appear in the middle of the Energy Monastery]. There was no one there. I went down. I was a bit frightened. I circled around the building. Saturday's Son was seated on the bench around the base of the big tree along with two other individuals. Up above, the monks started their recitation [the signal of the *weikza*'s imminent arrival]. I went to sit on the steps of the Monastery of the Peace of the Noble Country. There was a little bit of light because of a bulb hanging nearby. I could see my shadow in front of me. I looked at the Monastery of the Noble Success. The recitation stopped. I kept watching. Suddenly, the light went out: the power was out. It was dark. I began to feel afraid. I was alone. What to do? Where to go? Should I rejoin the others? No, I had to stay there. I went on sitting there watching. A moment later, the light came back on. I heard the voices of the *weikza*. They were preaching in the Monastery of the Noble Success. Ha?!

How had they gotten up there? Despite the darkness, I could see fine and I had observed no one. No doubt they had climbed up the other side. I started to sweat. I didn't know what was going on. My whole body was

sweating, I was so hot. My stomach was in knots. I felt like crying.
Nothing like that had ever happened to me before. I saw my shadow
on the ground. Ha! I was no longer alone. Bodaw Bo Htun Aung was
standing in the air above my head, a stick in his hand. Impossible! I was
terrified! I jumped down to the foot of the stairs and tried to get away.
Bodaw Bo Htun Aung calmly followed me. He was laughing. Up above,
the preaching had stopped and people were laughing. The two people
on the bench were laughing, too. I felt terrible shame. My heart was
beating wildly. It was impossible for someone to stand in the air like
that! But Bodaw Bo Htun Aung was demonstrating his supernatural
potency (*dago pya-*). I didn't know what to do. Bodaw Bo Htun Aung
questioned me:

'What are you doing here?'

'My sister sent me here,' I replied, shaking. 'She promised me three
hundred *kyat*. She gave me a flashlight, too. She sent me here because she
thinks some fake *weikza* are fooling our mother. I didn't want to come
here. It's because my sister told me to do it.'

'All right. What is it you need [such as protection from misfortune,
success in business]?'

'I don't need anything.'

'Then go back up there.'

'Yes, Venerable.'

I was so terrified that I ran. When I got to the foot of the double
staircase of the Monastery of the Noble Success, a *weikza* was coming up
from the other side. He was holding a stick, and he had a section of his
monastic robes covering his head. It was U Pandita. I went racing up the
steps. U Pandita ascended calmly, one step at a time. When I got to the top,
he was facing me. Impossible! And yet, I was seeing him with my very own
eyes. I went to sit down in the hall in the middle of the crowd. U Pandita
came into the hall. He came toward me. He hit me with his knee and said,
'I know what you're up to.' He then proceeded to the front and started to
preach: 'Some people who do not believe have come into our monastery,
acting as if they were believers. And they're looking around on the sly. I'll
show you how to distinguish between *weikza* and science (*theikpan*).' U
Pandita preached for a long time. I was incapable of listening. I was still
shaking, thinking about Bodaw Bo Htun Aung appearing above me. That
night I couldn't sleep. I kept repeating to myself, 'I was wrong, I was
wrong. These are real *weikza* (*weikza asit*)!'"

"One real, a thousand fakes, and a hundred thousand imposters" (*asit tit-khu, atu tit-htaung, ayaung tit-thein*) goes a common Burmese saying. Burmese think that the world of *weikza* abounds in charlatans, individuals who exploit the credulity of the faithful by claiming to have supernatural powers or to be the mediums of *weikza* who have already "exited." Still, as U Zawana, head of a monastery at the edge of Mebaygon village, put it in a Wittgensteinian manner to Victorious and me one day, "How can you say 'He's a fake *weikza*,' when no one has ever seen a real *weikza*?" At the time, the significance of this sibylline statement escaped my attention. I did not realize its potential import until long afterward. There is in fact no absolute and definitive criterion with which to establish whether an individual is a real (*asit*) or fake (*atu*) *weikza*. The question of what a "real" *weikza* is and, consequently, what a *weikza* is, is never posed a priori. No identifying principle is ever formulated. If someone is not a fake, then he must be real. The conception someone has of a *weikza* develops on the basis of his or her experience of the phenomenon: the one or several *weikza* in whom someone comes to believe are taken as the generic model for *weikza*. For this reason, at the end of the story, someone like Zaw Win, who on the eve of his first visit was just curious to "see" some *weikza,* can cry out, "I was wrong, I was wrong. These are real *weikza!*" There are no "fake" *weikza* because every *weikza* is real for those who believe in him. There are no "real" *weikza* because every *weikza* is a fiction whose only reality stems from some people's believing. The question of the real and the fake is a false problem. So suggests a Burmese village monk in an aphorism of his own coinage (if I understood him correctly), and so posits classical anthropological theory.

Nevertheless, Burmese, including U Zawana himself, who in other circumstances expressed himself differently—speaking with conviction of certain (real) *weikza*—rarely content themselves with such imperturbable relativism. In their eyes, there are indeed both real and fake *weikza*. Making this distinction turns out to be at the heart of discussions about *weikza*. These passionate discussions, which make up, along with other matters pertaining to the strange and the extraordinary,[23] a considerable part of people's conversations about religion, do not concern the objective content of belief, such as the existence and extraordinary powers of *weikza*. They hinge on the credibility of such and such a claimant to the title of *weikza,* on the reasons why it appears justified or not to believe in him. Given the fact that no one knows how to distinguish between real ones and fake ones, it is impossible to arrive at a consensus. Some people, if they are not personally connected to the *weikza* under discussion, will dodge the dispute, concluding that after all, it's just a matter of believing, a subjective question, a personal judgment. But believers accept such a conclusion with difficulty. Their discourse is shot through with a tension inherent to the nature of believing. What they believe in—one or several *weikza* and their powers—stands, they say, beyond ordinary human understanding. The phenomenon relates to an alternative mode of reality, a reality ruled by a logic that the common run of mortals are incapable of grasping or explaining. If this were not the case, then they would not believe. Only the extraordinary generates believing. At the same time, believers prove themselves to be in a position to observe the manifestations of this supranormal reality due to the feats or miracles accomplished—either directly or through a medium—by the worthy individual(s) in whom they believe. And for these believers, such manifestations represent an objective and indubitable proof of the authenticity of the individuals in question and of their powers. In other words, believers know that what they believe in cannot and must not be amenable to refutation, yet they still claim that it is verifiable and seek desperately to make it so. Believing, even though it is necessarily built on an inscrutable foundation, must be motivated: it originates in the observably inexplicable. Hence the typical exclamation of believers in the making, "Impossible!," while some prodigious feat takes place before their eyes.

Thus skepticism, as opposed to unbelief (which is absent), is endemic in Burmese society. Rather than eating away at believing, skepticism is a constituent part of it, precisely because believing would have no place were a phenomenon not unbelievable, were it not taken at first to be so and thus in need of no proof. Believers' frequent insistence on their initial skepticism substantiates the unbelievable; it helps represent the phenomenon depicted as extraordinary. They present themselves as self-described skeptics. They have forged their own judgment, they assure us, on the basis of "firsthand experience" (*lettway*) and not on the basis of hearsay. They were doubtful and have looked into things in "doubt" (*thanthaya*); their two watchwords are "studying" (*layla-*) and "putting things to the test" (*san-*). The credulous (*yonkyi lwe-*, "those who believe easily"), that describes other people: those who "are without education" (*pyinnya ma shi-*), those who "are backward" (*khit ma mi-*), those in whom "the critical mindset is lacking" (*athi nyan ma shi-*), or who are inclined toward believing for illegitimate reasons, most notably the hope for material gain ("greedy people," *lawbathama*). These believers, for their part, did not believe (*ma yon bu*) at first. They consented to "believing" (*yon-*), they "have accepted" (*letkhan-*) the phenomenon, they "credited" it (*athi ahmat pyu-*, the phrase denotes a legal acknowledgment) only once there was, in their eyes, no longer the shadow of a doubt.

What is peculiar to believing, in the end, lies not in a state of mind that the psychoanalyst, Octave Mannoni, summed up in a phrase that has become famous, as "I very well know, but still . . . ,"[24] but rather in the possibility, if not the necessity, of a reversal summed up rather differently: "I didn't believe it but there you have it . . ." Mannoni, looking into the Hopi Indians' belief in masks as an example, put forward the idea that an individual's perception shifted at the time of initiation ceremonies, in the course of which a Hopi boy discovered that it was adults who, hidden behind the "Kachina" masks, played the role of spirits. From a literal belief—that the masks are the spirits—the boy on the path to attaining manhood evolved toward a revised belief based on this point of view, as described by Mannoni: "*I very well know* that the Kachina are not spirits, they are my fathers and uncles, *but still* the Kachina are there when my fathers and uncles dance with the masks on."[25]

Now the evolution undergone by the Burmese Buddhist when he or she flips over to believing is different, practically the opposite. From a situation in which the *weikza* were a fuzzy phenomenon, almost unreal, when he or she might even have spoken of some *weikza* cult as a scam, a comedy, an old wives' tale, the individual moves to total participation in and adherence to the phenomenon. "I didn't believe in *weikza*," that person might assert, stating in effect that he or she made obeisance to no *weikza*, "but here's what happened, here's what I experienced myself, personally, the person who's speaking to you right now." The *weikza* impose themselves as reality, and this personal revolution in someone's point of view is said to be based on an experience of the extraordinary. If believing is not knowing, it is at least experiencing personally. But experiencing what? To what reality does believing and the experience on which it is based give access?

PERFORMING THE EXTRAORDINARY, EMBODYING THE BUDDHA

Sunday, August 8, 2004, 10:00 a.m. Seated in a large seminar room at the University of Singapore, Tin Ko Ko and I are working on a translation of one of the four *weikza*'s sermons that I recorded during my last stay in Burma, from mid-January to mid-March. Tin Ko Ko, a telecommunications engineer, has been living in Singapore for ten years. He has never been to Mebaygon but he is interested in the *weikza* path, which he thinks of as a (distant) alternative to his current existence. Forcing himself to find his way through the meandering discourse of Bodaw Bo Htun Aung, he paraphrases and comments on the sermon in a Burmese mixed with English. On the slightest pretext, he jumps up to illustrate his explanations with some drawing on the board. Every statement, every action and gesture of the *weikza* not only gets interpreted but is also weighed and evaluated against his claims. Still, Tin Ko Ko refuses to commit himself. He wishes to see the evidence.

I want to have the content of these sermons—which I attended but of which at first I hardly understood anything—clarified. The morning after each appearance in the flesh of the *weikza,* I went over the course of the session from the night before with Victorious. Victorious set to work transcribing the sermons in their entirety. In the course of a year, 2004–2005, staying in France, the Burmese man will spend many hours in my Paris apartment sorting out these texts, along with other documents concerning the cult.

The *weikza*'s sermons take place in the evening, after darkness has fallen. People present at the monastery are expected to attend the sessions, which begin at about 7:30 p.m. No one is permitted to remain downstairs. Here is Bodaw Bo Htun Aung, dressed all in white, a turban covering his head, making his entrance into the hall on the upper floor of the Monastery of Noble Success. He pops up outside the window frame in the front left corner of the hall, three or four meters above the ground: doing so, the *weikza* demonstrates his ability to fly. He has come from his invisible realm, Dragoness Mountain. Contrary to what I long imagined, a *weikza* does not glide through the air like a bird or a plane—a loony idea for Burmese. He moves in a vertical position, remaining dignifiedly erect, in imitation of the Buddha and his five hundred saint-disciples traveling through the air, a scene that is often depicted in pagoda and monastery paintings. In this case, Bodaw Bo Htun Aung's hands can be seen gripping the base of the window (there is no glass, just wooden shutters, one of which is open); then his head can be seen in the window frame, before the *weikza* jumps quickly inside. Disciples never fail to point out that because Bodaw Bo Htun Aung is a layperson, he is not constrained by the rule that forbids monks from showing off their supernatural powers in front of the faithful. The three other *weikza,* as monks, must in principle—and in the case of the most energetic among them, U Pandita, it is only in principle—act with greater restraint. When they appear, later in the evening, they make their entrance walking, coming from a little room located in the right front corner of the hall, which serves as a passageway between Dragoness Mountain and the human world.

Shortly after the eagerly anticipated arrival of Bodaw Bo Htun Aung, some coconuts and candles fall among the audience members, as though tossed supernaturally by the *weikza*. People seize them feverishly. They are filled with energy of success (*aung dat*). Bodaw Bo Htun Aung, meanwhile, has begun to deliver a kind of sermon that he punctuates with several amazing feats to display his supernatural potency (*dago pya-*). The *weikza* chooses several among those people who are visiting the monastery for the first time and invites them to check out the window through which he has just come. They are asked to lean outside. They note that the height above the ground is such that no ordinary man would be able to jump all the way down; there is no ladder to help the *weikza*. After he has sent them back to their places, Bodaw Bo Htun Aung jumps or rather flies through the opening in the window, disappearing from the audience's sight. He reappears a few seconds later through the door of the little room in the front right corner of the hall. This performance will be repeated a second time in the course of the evening, the exit and reappearance taking place in other locations.

The other feat performed by the *weikza* is to transmit an energy ball (*datlon*)—derived from the practice of alchemy—between two people standing a good distance from each other. Bodaw Bo Htun Aung asks a member of the audience for a piece of cloth, a handkerchief or a scarf. He wraps the energy ball in it and rubs it three times between his hands before giving it to the person who gave it to him, who then moves to a specified place in the hall. A second member of the audience in turn gives Bodaw Bo Htun Aung a piece of cloth, which he takes for a moment in his hands, makes into a ball, and then gives back to that person. Everything is ready, and the *weikza* instructs the first person to pronounce the following vow: "May the energy ball I have reach the other cloth!" This person then unfolds his cloth, and the ball is no longer there. The *weikza* tells the other person to check his piece of cloth: the ball is there.

The flying entrances and exits and the falling candles and coconuts, like the invisible transmission of an object from one person to another, constitute the standard feats accomplished by Bodaw Bo Htun Aung at each of his appearances to prove his supernatural potency, the guarantee of his identity as a "real" *weikza*.[26] Sometimes, however, the four *weikza* must deal with visitors whose radical skepticism requires recourse to the heavy artillery of the extraordinary. I belong in their eyes to this category of ultra-skeptics. Victorious and I have already been reprimanded several times in the course of sermons by Bodaw Bo Htun Aung or U Pandita for our inquisitorial behavior. We have been reproached for going into the village (we have gone to see U Zawana, among others), when it is well known that the people of Mebaygon and its surroundings are doubtful as to the existence of the four *weikza* and the validity of the homage they attract. "Does our monastery not feed you?" U Pandita asked us in the course of an appearance. He meant that the *weikza* supply you with room and board and everything you need. As a result, you have no reason to wander about elsewhere; you don't bite the hand that feeds you. As for your questions, he added, there are many people right here at the monastery who are ready to answer them. Believers or not, Victorious and I, who had been staying here for a while already, found ourselves feeling ill at ease. Victorious, especially, found this public censure hard to bear. By what right could we allow ourselves to torment the *weikza* and their disciples? Should such a thing happen again, he has warned, he will hand in his resignation. The threat carries considerable weight: the reassuring presence of this Burmese man has been more than a little help in ensuring the anthropologist's acceptance at the monastery, not to mention the precious linguistic help he has provided and the sage wisdom with which he has tempered my impatience.

But in a certain way, the *weikza* need the anthropologist just as much as he needs them. My barely intelligible attitude certainly causes them some puzzlement, and that in two ways. Perhaps I have decided on the basis of my detailed investigations that they are not real *weikza*. But in that case, why would I remain here? Perhaps I am now convinced of the legitimacy of their claims. But then why do I insist on meeting with and questioning unbelievers? And why do I not show the outward signs of believing? This situation, although disconcerting, nonetheless offers the *weikza* a chance to confront and confound one exemplar—a foreigner to boot—of that group of individuals highly resistant to believing. The *weikza* have done this in the past in memorable fights that have become oft-cited incidents within the circle of the cult's disciples.

It is on the eve of the Festival of Success (Aung Bwe), the cult's annual festival, that the *weikza* decide that it is time to be done with what they take to be my persistent doubts. The circumstances lend themselves to this decision. The crowds are at their peak, and they expect the *weikza* to live up to their reputation. On Tuesday, February 3, 2004, people have begun to arrive as early as 5:30 p.m. to make sure they find places at the evening session in which the *weikza* will appear. When we arrive at about 6:15 p.m., the hall is already full. How many people are there? Eight hundred, a thousand, maybe more. Night has fallen; the scattered light bulbs hanging from the ceiling provide only dim light. Victorious goes to sit a bit toward the front on the left, near the lay disciple charged with running the sound system (microphones are set up in front of the sermonizers' chairs to enable the *weikza* to be heard by their listeners and he operates a cassette player). The disciple is using a small electric lamp to see what he's doing, and its light enables Victorious to take notes without difficulty. With the tape recorder protected from the crowd's sudden movements, Victorious can record the session without worry. I sit at the rear of the hall, next to a group of older women, my notebook, pen, flashlight, and watch all within reach.

While waiting for the session to start, the disciple puts on a cassette, the recording of a sermon by the oldest and the head of the four *weikza,* the monk U Kawwida. Just after 7:00 p.m., Bodaw Bo Htun Aung appears. At festival events, the *weikza* comes early, responding to the crowd's impatience. He arrives, as is customary, through the window located in the front left corner. His spectacular entrance immediately captures everyone's attention; the noise of conversation ceases instantly. Bodaw Bo Htun Aung walks up to the main sermonizer's seat and takes his seat. The disciple turns off the cassette and strikes a gong once. The *weikza* addresses the crowd. He speaks at a rapid pace, moving from one subject to another in a sometimes incoherent manner. His speech is punctuated with interpellations to his listeners—"You understand?" "Is that right?"—to which the audience members respond in unison: "We understand, Venerable," "It's true, Venerable." Although Bodaw Bo Htun Aung is not a monk, people address him as they would a monk, in light of the reverence due a *weikza.*

After recounting a short story, a lesson about the necessity of attending not to the *weikza*'s appearances but rather to the teaching they impart (teaching that bolsters their status as spiritual figures), Bodaw Bo Htun Aung invokes the Buddha's funeral:

> "When the Buddha entered final nirvana [i.e., died], his extraordinary
> relics (*datdaw*) emitted light, manifesting their supernatural potency.
> However, in our day, some people have never seen the Buddha's supernatural
> potency. Everything I tell you is so that you'll understand. For the
> moment, I'm just explaining in speech, I haven't really started to preach.
> Once we [the four *weikza*] have preached all the teachings (*tayadway*), you
> will understand everything! Some people listen to our teaching because
> they are knowledgeable. Others are not familiar with our teaching. And
> some people come to study what sort of beings we are. Yes, there are such
> observers. I know that; we know that. We are going to do something so
> that these people will understand. We want everyone to become aware of
> the Buddha's teaching."

While the *weikza* goes on preaching, a man of about forty years of age works to get close to me. I have never seen him before at the monastery. He is holding in his hands two perfume bottles, both wrapped. He tells me to take them and to ask Bodaw Bo Htun Aung to "invite the relics" (*datdaw pin-*). I hesitate a moment. I have heard about this ultimate feat of the four *weikza.* But what would be the point of asking me to solicit its enactment? No matter what the answer might be, I do not wish to be the center of such a large crowd's attention. "I am not a Buddhist," I reply in order to decline politely. The stranger insists, bothered by my refusal.

"Hey, what's going on down there?" asks Bodaw Bo Htun Aung from the other end of the hall.

Plowing through the packed crowd seated on the floor, the *weikza* moves to the rear. The stranger quickly hands one of the perfume containers to me, then responds to the *weikza*'s call:

"He wants to invite the relics, Venerable!"

"So be it," says Bodaw Bo Htun Aung, "I will invite the relics for this foreigner. Come here, come!"

There's no getting out of it. I move to the front of the hall in the company of the stranger. Each of us holds a container in our hands. It isn't easy to move through the audience. Once we reach the front of the hall, Bodaw Bo Htun Aung runs through a checklist.

"Are the containers wrapped in plastic?" he asks me.

"Yes, Venerable!"

The stranger and I rip the plastic, open the containers, and take out the bottles.

"Are the bottles full?"

"They are full, Venerable!" I assure him.

The bottles are passed along among people sitting in the front rows so that audience members can see, using their flashlights, that they contain perfume and nothing else. They are then returned to the stranger and me, who remain standing before Bodaw Bo Htun Aung. The latter addresses the chorus of young women who take part in every sermon and recite various texts according to the instructions of the *weikza*. "Concentrate on the Buddha and his doctrine, and invite the Buddha (*hpaya pin-*)," he tells them.

The chorus chants:

"O Buddha, you who are a true descendant of the solar race of the Sākya, who possess the thirty-two principal marks and the diverse secondary marks of the nobleman, who are like the great solar star, who have eliminated all the impurities and obscurities of existence, such as delusion, make relics come into these bottles, so that virtuous people may venerate them!"

"Have the relics of our noble Buddha Gotama appeared [*kywa-,* literally "come"], as they did in such an extraordinary way after his cremation?" asks Bodaw Bo Htun Aung once the recitation is done. The stranger and I use a flashlight to look inside the bottles. The relics are there, about a dozen small white bits, looking like smooth tiny pebbles, at the bottom of each bottle.

"They have appeared, Venerable!"

"It is the Buddha, not an ordinary person (*lu*)," Bodaw Bo Htun Aung explains to his listeners. "The Buddha himself must do something since some people are not respectful. Certain people come here to study [investigate]. I have to explain things to them because they might fall into error. Today, it was a kind [of demonstration]. Tomorrow we'll do something else. Tomorrow we'll disappear. Do you want to see a *weikza* in the middle of a crowd suddenly disappear?"

"Yes, we do want to see that, Venerable!" those present shout excitedly.

Bodaw Bo Htun Aung sends me back to my place. I take the two precious bottles with me. It is hard to get across the hall. The atmosphere is feverish. Everyone wants the bottles. They get passed from hand to hand. People point their flashlights up to see the relics. Some people hold them up to their foreheads in a brief gesture of veneration. At the same time, the *weikza* U Kawwida enters the hall. He sits down on the largest of the sermonizers' chairs. At his command, the crowd requests permission to pay him homage, as well as, more generally, to pay homage to the Three Jewels. The recitation enables laypeople to purify themselves by erasing faults they have committed—whether intentionally or not, physically, verbally, or mentally—before reiterating their devotion to the Five Precepts, the minimal ethical code for Buddhist laypeople. After having them recite the Five Precepts, U Kawwida questions the audience members:

"Are you happy?"

"We are happy, Venerable!"

"Doctor Sein Yi, since you are one of the oldest and most prominent of our disciples, haven't we shown our supernatural potency in many ways?"

"Yes, indeed, Venerable," responds the doctor, sitting in one of the front rows.

"Great disciple Aung Khaing!"

"Venerable!"

"Haven't you brought these foreigners [Victorious and me, the former now grouped with me] to Magway, and haven't you shown them all sorts of extraordinary powers?"[27]

"I have done so, Venerable!"

"There's no use showing them, it doesn't work [they do not believe]. We do the same things as were done in the time of the noble Buddha, your master. The Buddha had to show his extraordinary powers to those who were capable of being liberated [to attain spiritual perfection and so nirvana]. Thus at the time of the Buddha, there lived a very learned Brahman. He could say who was a real Buddha, because he knew the thirty-two principal marks and the eighty secondary marks characteristic of buddhas. From time to time, individuals who claimed to be buddhas, such as Kawthala or other leaders of heretical groups, came to see this Brahman. But they were not in a position to show him the characteristic marks, and he, as a learned man, flatly rejected their claims. One day, this Brahman heard a rumor about the Awakening of Buddha Gotama. He sent one of his young disciples, Ottaya, to determine whether or not this Gotama had the marks of a buddha. When he got there, Ottaya looked carefully at the Buddha's marks. He found all but one of them. This was a mark involving the Buddha's penis, which was covered by his clothing. The investigator went back to his master to present his results. The Brahman decided to issue an invitation to the Buddha in order to conduct his own test. The Buddha came. Knowing the Brahman's thoughts, he made use of his supernatural potency to show his penis to the Brahman alone and no one else. The Brahman exclaimed, 'Forgive me, oh Master [for having doubted your word]!' And he prostrated himself in front of the Buddha, placing his forehead on the Master's feet."

The four *weikza* make frequent reference to the Buddha's supernatural potency (*dago*) or extraordinary powers (*theikdi*). More precisely, they explain how and why the Buddha was induced to make his potency manifest (*pya-*), in the sense of both showing and proving it. Having set about spreading his teaching, the Master, they say in substance, encountered both suspicious interlocutors and self-declared skeptics. He lived, furthermore, in an environment in which other individuals had ambitions similar to his. This made it absolutely imperative that he make an immediate assertion of his superiority. Making his supernatural potency manifest represented an essential tool for the Buddha in his campaign of persuasion; it was the means of demonstrating the legitimacy of his claims to the status of having been enlightened, and so of teaching the way to salvation. The Buddha, the *weikza* go on to say, strove to dispense his doctrine in accordance with the personality and expectations of his listeners. This implied manifesting his supernatural potency and his greatness in a way as to inspire believing. That indeed is why, the *weikza* conclude, he is called a buddha.

Now this account does not apply only to the Master: it applies to the *weikza* as well. In the same way as the Buddha, they say, they are obliged to provide proofs and edifying examples (*thadaka*) of their supernatural potency to show people that they are real *weikza*. The demonstration of their potency is, of course, not the end; it is only a means. The point, they emphasize, is to incite people to venerate the Three Jewels and to lead a virtuous existence. But such an objective can be realized only if the basis of believing is solidly established. The Burmese word meaning "to persuade," *khyaw-,* also means "to cajole." People, observe the *weikza,* are devoured by doubts about their authenticity or burn with the desire to see a manifestation of their supernatural potency, and it is necessary to rescue them from these fires that consume them before steering them along the right path. The *weikza* also declare themselves constrained, again in the Buddha's image, to preach at times in an arrogant manner and to berate their disciples, with a view to their spiritual liberation. And once again like the Buddha, who was confronted particularly by the actions of his diabolical cousin, Devadatta, they experience many difficulties and suffer many criticisms and false accusations.

Although the *weikza* may push, as far as they do, the analogy between the Buddha and their own persons, still they are careful, ostensibly at least, to claim no express equivalence. They never stop insisting on the distinction that exists between the Buddha and *weikza* and on their relative hierarchical positions: whereas the Buddha had no teacher and discovered the Four Noble Truths on his own, they themselves do have a teacher, none other than the Buddha himself, and as a result they cannot be compared to him. The Buddha and his saintly disciples (*yahanda*), they declare, are "supramundane *weikza*" (*lawkoktara weikza*), because they have attained full spiritual perfection. The *weikza* describe themselves, by contrast, as "mundane *weikza*" (*lawki weikza*). A mundane *weikza,* according to their definition, is an individual who has acquired supernatural abilities due to his success in a particular technique, such as alchemy or the cabalistic arts (the science of combining numbers, letters, or signs in esoteric diagrams that have special powers). That success was made possible by the *weikza*'s observance of the Buddhist precepts and his practice of meditation. Among a *weikza*'s abilities figure the capacity to prolong his existence beyond the normal course of a human life. This capacity grants him the hope, if not the assurance, of being present at the moment when the Gotama Buddha's relics are reassembled, expected at the end of the current religious era, in a little less than 2,500 years. The Master's final reappearance in the world will be the occasion of his final sermon, recapitulating his teaching. According to Burmese belief, those who have the privilege of seeing and hearing the Buddha at that time will reach full spiritual perfection or, for those less advanced, will enter definitively on the path leading to it. (Some *weikza* and those aspiring to that status, however, are betting on the longer term, namely, the advent of the fifth and last Buddha, Metteyya, of this world's cycle.) In other words, the mundane *weikza*'s longevity promises him future access to nirvana, in the place of a saint's (*yahanda's*) immediate accession thereto.[28]

Nevertheless, in spite of their vehement insistence on the preeminence of the Buddha, the *weikza* still appear to replace the Buddha. Rather than being disciples of the Master, they tend to be conflated with him; rather than imitate a model, they are assimilated to it. They do not content themselves with explaining who the Buddha was, what happened to him, what he did, and what he said. Instead, they enact the Master in their own fashion: they actualize him. Distributing relics is a typical gesture of the Buddha, who in his lifetime is supposed to have done just that in several places in what is today Burma after he had converted the population. The *weikza's* repeated protestations—"Don't think about *weikza,* don't place them before the Buddha, *weikza* cannot save you"—only heighten suspicions of a power move that takes place surreptitiously, the cardinal function of *weikza,* in everyone's eyes, being precisely to "save" (*ke-*) people. When Bodaw Bo Htun Aung asserts, "The Buddha himself must do something personally because certain people are not respectful," he is speaking of himself. In fact, it is he, the *weikza,* who has just brought about the miracle of the relics' appearance. Didn't he, for that matter, announce the miracle in the following terms: "We [*weikza*] are going to do something so that these [skeptics] may come to understand"? And didn't the *weikza* proclaim, following the extraordinary apparition, "Today's was one kind [of demonstration]. Tomorrow we'll do a different kind." Bodaw Bo Htun Aung's words, shifting imperceptibly between "I" or "we" and "the Buddha," scramble the difference between the *weikza* and the Master.

This scrambling is attested to further by the status accorded to the *weikza's* words. For the edification of their listeners, the *weikza* take up and adapt incidents found in the fundamental Buddhist texts, deemed to be faithful records of the Master's words and experience. The noticeable transformations that they introduce into these stories are not considered deviations. The cult's disciples go so far even as to confer a canonical pedigree on stories the *weikza* make up out of whole cloth. Evidently, they do not expect *weikza* to stick closely to the scriptural text. The cult's disciples feel no need to refer to the texts to verify the exactitude of the *weikza's* remarks, simply because the *weikza* substitute for the texts as a source of the truth. It is in these terms that we should understand the four *weikza's* recurrent assertion that they "make everything clear on the basis of the Buddha's own words" as a claim to being able to formulate the Master's own speech directly, beyond the texts supposed to account for it.

Should one be in doubt about such a scrambling, the course the possession séances take would remove all uncertainty. When the four *weikza* do not come—that is, appear in the flesh—then they come into their medium and express themselves through him. (In either case, Burmese say *kywa-*, "to come," a term whose usage is reserved for beings of an elevated condition: Buddhas, monks, *weikza*, kings, and so on.) This is what happens in the course of visits that Saturday's Son grants disciples at their homes. When circumstances permit, the medium is accompanied by some members of the chorus. These young women, in order to make one or another of the *weikza* come, start reciting an invitation to the Buddha (*hpaya pin-*). Such a type of recitation is common; it is done, for example, on the occasion of a collective ceremony at a pagoda or when paying homage to the Buddha in front of a household altar. Even if the content of the formula pronounced varies—a simple "O Buddha, come!" suffices in theory—the objective is identical: to cause the Buddha to come so one can make him an offering (of water, flowers, food, and so on). The Buddha never responds to the invitation, but one acts "as if" he had responded and was there. Now, in the special case of Saturday's Son's séances, the invitation is not a dead letter. The possession surpasses the register of "as if" to produce an actual presence and institute an effective relationship. It is more than a manner of "presentification" in the sense that the Hellenist Jean-Pierre Vernant coined and used the term, which is to say the establishment, by means of symbols and ritual, of communication with an entity deriving from a different level of reality.[29] Presentification, for Vernant, relates to a truncated communication in that it maintains the cosmological abyss between the entity to whom the ritual is addressed and the human world: within the frame of the relationship established, that entity remains invisible, intangible, inaudible, its presence presumed but not manifest. Possession, on the contrary, makes the presence of the entity available to the senses through the offices of the medium. Rather than presentification, it would be more appropriate to speak of "embodiment." But although it was the Buddha who was invited, one of the *weikza* appears: the *weikza* takes the place de facto of the Buddha. How better to suggest the *weikza*'s tendency to take on the Buddha's being? In other words, possession makes it possible to force the conjunction and coincidence of levels that should, in principle, remain apart. The persistence of the split is signaled by a basic impossibility: for the Buddha to possess an individual. But its diminution is signaled by the coming of a *weikza* who substitutes for the Master.

An appearance in the flesh and possession both tend in similar ways toward an actualization of Buddhahood, if to a different degree (the effect of embodiment being stronger in an appearance). The Buddha, although out of reach and imperceptible, becomes a living reality. He is there, even though it isn't he. This tendency to bring Buddhahood forth into reality, reaching its most extreme expression in the case of the four *weikza,* can be found in other actors on the Burmese stage. Observers, myself certainly among them, have not recognized it fully, probably because they have internalized one of the fundamental dogmas of Theravada Buddhism, a dogma known to every Burmese, according to which there can exist only one Buddha per religious era. After conducting fieldwork earlier on another topic, following others' example, I was happy to point out how the careers of contemporary Burmese forest monks, eminent spiritual figures, evoked many episodes from the Buddha's extensive biography, from his previous existences to his ultimate one, that of the Awakening.[30] But I failed to note sufficiently that these resonances represented more than a hagiographic convention, one consisting in taking up the elements of an archetype to glorify a person. A living person considered a saint or a *weikza*—he can be both at once—reimagines and personifies Buddhahood: he makes the Buddha visible and alive. "I don't have any chance of seeing the Buddha, but I can see *weikza,*" a disciple of the four *weikza* told me. Years earlier, an interlocutor had stated with reference to the most revered saint in Burma, the great monk of Thamanya (1912–2003), "To see the great monk is a singular stroke of luck; it's like seeing a Buddha." And didn't the great monk of The-in Gu (1913–1973), a virtuoso of meditation, go so far as to give himself the remarkable title of "little Buddha" (*hpaya-nge*)?[31]

Thus the question as to the status of the Buddha, to which observers of Theravadin societies (Burma, Cambodia, Laos, Sri Lanka, Thailand) keep returning, is one that Burmese Buddhists encourage us to reconsider in their own terms. Schematically, the problem has been to decide whether, in the eyes of Theravadin Buddhists, the Buddha is a man or a god, "absent" or "present." In fact, these Buddhists describe the Master as having entered into final nirvana at the time of his death and so as being inaccessible, even as they constantly invoke him as though he were living, available, and approachable, like a divinity. Questioned on this matter, Burmese provide apparently contradictory responses. Bodaw Bo Htun Aung's remarks combine both possibilities quite flagrantly. The *weikza* refers to the Buddha's accession to final nirvana even while proclaiming the Master's present intervention in an effort to convince unbelievers. Nothing could better illustrate the paradox of the Buddha's absence and presence. This logical paradox has caused the spilling of a lot of ink: various and sophisticated solutions have been advanced.[32] Yet from the point of view of Burmese Buddhists, the question is badly stated.[33] The problem is not knowing whether the Buddha is alive and present but whether Buddhism is alive and present. Burmese are not so much concerned about the postmortem condition of the Awakened One as with the current state of his legacy. Keeping Buddhism alive means living in the presence of the absent Buddha.

Some time before the expected death of the Master, his personal assistant Ananda asked him to speak to the members of the monastic community he had founded to instruct them in the measures they should take after his disappearance. The Buddha said the monks would have no need for a leader. They should simply live in conformity with the doctrine he had taught.[34] For Burmese, however, the Buddha did not only transmit a doctrine or teaching (*taya*). He left in place his faculty for accomplishing miracles and wonders, his *dago*. Relics' appearance in perfume bottles is one concrete illustration of this fact. This is not an isolated case: it exemplifies the Burmese belief in the permanence of the Buddha's supernatural potency—"supernatural" because uncommon, supranormal, extraordinary. *Dago* is a potency that surpasses all other powers. About a vigorous individual, one says in Burmese that "he [or she] has strength" (*a shi-*); about the Buddha, but also about a saint or a *weikza* that he "has great *dago*" (*dago gyi-*), an expression denoting potency of a completely different nature. The qualifier "supernatural" denotes this super-humanity and nothing else: it doesn't amount to attributing an extrahuman (particularly a divine) origin to the Buddha's potency, which it does not have, because the Buddha—like *weikza*—was a man and he achieved Awakening and its attendant faculties by means that were exclusively human. The supernatural potency of the Buddha is contained and localized in his representations (statues), as well as in his relics enclosed within various pagodas: material relics (objects that belonged to him) and especially corporeal relics (whole bones or elements resulting from the physical transformation of his being that took place at the moment of his cremation, such as the relics that appeared in the perfume bottles). These elements constitute objects of veneration because they perpetuate not the presence of the Buddha strictly speaking but rather his legacy, which must be supported and kept alive. Doctrine and supernatural potency are the double and indissociable legacy of the Buddha; they *are* Buddhism. If Buddhists live according to the Master's doctrine, they will benefit by his supernatural potency. Conversely, if that potency should show itself, such as when a pagoda in which his relics have been enclosed miraculously emits light, it is because the Master's doctrine is alive and that the ultimate end that it proposes, nirvana, remains attainable. A saint, he who has attained spiritual perfection, embodies without distinction the Buddha's doctrine and his supernatural potency: up to a certain point, he embodies the Buddha. Thus it would be an error to treat the cult offered to the Buddha in isolation, considering it independently from what it supports. Because what in the end Buddhists venerate is not the Buddha but Buddhism, the spirit of their collective existence.

When the *weikza* bring about their masterwork feat, the relics that appear in the bottles are often gathered up to be enshrined in a pagoda under construction. They return in this way to their natural habitat because, as was explained to the anthropologist (who has a knack for asking odd questions, no one ever concerning themselves with the relics' origins), they come from a pagoda—relics being able to multiply and displace themselves. Otherwise, the lucky beneficiaries of the feat take the bottle back home, where they keep it on the domestic altar, without subjecting it to any special treatment. Visitors who stop by the house will be shown the relics. The discussion will then concern not the authenticity or the origin of these precious objects, but rather the modalities of their appearing. As it happens, these modalities alone matter to believing: the *weikza*'s capacity to act—in the same manner as the relics—as depositaries and mediators of the Buddha's supernatural potency and, by extension, his doctrine. The *weikza* are at one and the same time themselves (beings endowed with extraordinary faculties, including an exceptional longevity that guarantees their access to salvation) and more than themselves, a living image of the Buddha, the vehicle of his word and of his power. Relics, statues, saints, *weikza*—all *are* the Buddha, all participate in his nature and his existence by embodying and by actualizing in various ways his legacy. The Master's presence comes via his manifestations' principle of plurality, through the action of what Burmese Buddhists call precisely his "substitutes" (*koza*). Substitution does not mean an absolute identity, rather a supplementarity, the ability to fulfill the functions of someone who is absent (with all that implies about the possible confusion among the two entities). The Buddha's transcendence and immanence—those of the Buddha and even those of his predecessors—are in this way combined. Is it really an accident that there are four *weikza* of Mebaygon, when the four Buddhas to have appeared in this world cycle (the last one being Gotama) turn out to be a constant reference point in Burmese Buddhism?

Considered from the point of view of the spectacular demonstration that the appearance of the Buddha's relics in some perfume bottles represents, the Burmese notion of supernatural potency (*dago*) is related to what Rudolph Otto called the "numinous" dimension of religion.[35] The category of the sacred, according to Otto, includes both rational and irrational dimensions. The nonrational aspect is what characterizes the domain of the numinous, the complex of sentiments that is at the foundation of every religion—rational elements emerging in a secondary manner out of this primitive base. The numinous is ineffable; it surpasses all understanding and conceptual formulation. Nevertheless, individuals go right on invoking the emotions characteristic of its experience, and its typical traits can be described as follows: incomprehension before the absolutely other, reverential fear, fascination, complete submission, and a sensation of energy. Otto condenses all of these affects into a single term, the "huge" (etymologically, "what escapes the rule"). The story Zaw Win tells of his first visit to Mebaygon, with all the feelings he relates, exemplifies this experience of the huge. The reader of this story will be quick to comment that, by the simple fact of telling this story, the individual lives it, creating the experience as much as believing in it: deluding him- or herself without realizing it. For it is simply "impossible" that Bodaw Bo Htun Aung could stand in the air above a person's head, but all the same, the *weikza* does indeed fly, as is demonstrated by his arrival through the monastery's window at every gathering. No doubt Bodaw Bo Htun Aung's entrances, his exits, and his reappearances are more evocative than altogether demonstrative. The *weikza* jumps across the windows or comes back running through the rear door, rather than actually flying. The monastery's walls conceal from those present the real nature of his movements, to the point that the members of the audience have to imagine and represent it to themselves in their own minds. Be that as it may, this mental representation is not the work of a storytelling believer wishing to exalt the *weikza*. Rather it forms part of a collective elaboration, drawing on a concrete representation provided by the *weikza*.[36] There is a feeling that an experience of the huge is necessary, that the Buddha's religion should be supported by an actualization of the supernatural potency that undergirds and animates it. And all of the participants, from the *weikza* to their disciples, cooperate to keep the numinous factory running. "Do you wish to see a *weikza* in the middle of the crowd suddenly disappear?" asks Bodaw Bo Htun Aung. "We do want to see that, Venerable!" responds the crowd feverishly.

IS IT MAGIC OR RELIGION?

Thursday, September 18, 2003, late afternoon. When Victorious and I come back from the Site of Success, an outstation of the Energy Monastery (the four *weikza*'s monastery) set up a distance from the village, a man of about fifty shows up, along with three adolescents. Clearly wishing to become acquainted, he approaches us. Tayza Htun is the son of Mingyi Sein Hlaing, a famous disciple of the cult who died in 1977. A lecturer in botany, Tayza Htun left the university about ten years earlier and gives private courses in Yangon to students preparing to take their final high school exams. The three adolescents are students originally from

Irrawaddy Division whose wealthy parents have sent them to secondary school in the capital. They live as boarders at Tayza Htun's house. Tayza Htun has taken on his father's role in the cult and comes regularly to Mebaygon.

That evening, two of the *weikza,* Bodaw Bo Htun Aung and U Pandita, appear in the flesh at the upper floor of the Monastery of Noble Success. The teacher invites Bodaw Bo Htun Aung to give a sermon to his students, who are taking a bad turn: they are smoking. The *weikza* enjoins the adolescents to respect the Five Objects of Veneration (the Buddha, the teaching, the monastic community, their parents, and their teachers), to avoid all immoral action, and to recite their beads regularly. He makes them take a vow, facing the Buddha altar: "If I smoke, may I vomit blood!" He then gives each of them a prayer bead. One boy in particular worries Tayza Htun. At sixteen, he is a difficult young man and a tormented one, whom his parents can no longer control. He daydreams constantly and is incapable of concentrating. His skin is ravaged by illness, some sort of acne that produces sores that an eminent dermatologist in Yangon has failed to heal. Tayza Htun is sure of it: a spell has been cast on the boy. That's the reason why Tayza Htun has brought him to the monastery. Bodaw Bo Htun Aung presents the young man with a small medicinal cone made by the *weikza.* The teacher, who is suffering from a terrible toothache, receives for his part an apple, which he bites into immediately. Although its flesh is fresh and juicy, the heart of the apple is brown and bitter, as though it was rotten. The *weikza* have probably injected it with some medicine, thinks Tayza Htun, who eats a part of the core and saves the rest in a handkerchief to eat later.

The next morning, at about 7:00 a.m., the teacher takes his students to the Site of Success. He wishes to consult with U Sanda Thuriya, a disciple of the *weikza* path whose specialty is to treat (*hsay ku-*)—in other words, to lift—spells. The man, whose face sports a long, fine white beard, says he is ninety years old. A retired army captain, he has been an ascetic (*yathay*) since the death of his wife about ten years ago. He is an ascetic rather than a monk, because, in his view, treating people could not be, at least not as obviously in any case, the principal activity of a monk: monastic discipline forbids it. Now having resided for six months at the Site of Success, he treats those who come seeking his assistance. The rest of the time he practices meditation to increase his power of mental concentration (*thamadi*).

U Sanda Thuriya confirms the teacher's suspicions by diagnosing that a spell has been cast on the troubled young man. The person responsible for it would have been an individual of Arakanese origin. (Arakan is the westernmost region of the country.) As a matter of fact, the boy's family has an Arakanese friend who is suspected of envying the family's wealth and the academic success of their children. With the help of a tattooing needle, the ascetic pricks the boy's shoulders and back in order to inject a powder mixed with a liquid. He does not compound the substances he uses; they are provided to him by his *weikza* masters, among them U Kawwida. A few hours later, he has his patient drink a powder mixed into coconut juice, a medicine whose power he has activated by murmuring a verse. Then he puts his hand on the boy's head and recites a long list of names, thirty-seven altogether (names of the five buddhas of this world cycle along with those of *weikza*), beings whose support he requests to break the spell of which the boy is a victim. He taps the boy's head three times before concluding by proclaiming: "Success!" (*aung byi*). The treatment is finished. The four *weikza*, Tayza Htun explains, are of much too high a station to cure people in this way. They delegate the job to others, the ascetic among them, while transmitting to them the energy (*dat*) necessary for the success of the operation.

The teacher devotes a good bit of the afternoon to Victorious and me. During the previous evening's sermon, the *weikza* had urged the teacher to share with us his experience and his knowledge of the cult. The interview takes place in the shade of the Site of Success's two intermeshed Bo trees. Even as he speaks, Tayza Htun continues to count off the prayer beads that he keeps in his hands the entire time he stays at the monastery. The conversation moves from one subject to another: his father, Mingyi Sein Hlaing's, story, the definition of *weikza*, the practice of alchemy, the meaning of the word *dat*, the wickedness of U Zawana (a monk in the village whom Tayza Htun deems an enemy of the *weikza* and compares to Man Nat, Māra in Pali, the god of evil and death and the Buddha's adversary), and the teacher's activities as the secretary of a religious association and coordinator of a missionary program in the outlying regions of the country. I take the opportunity of this relaxed exchange to bring up a judgment expressed by some of the cult's detractors and repeated by some disciples anxious to refute it, a judgment I continue to find puzzling: that the four *weikza*'s supernatural potency came from their having "succeeded in getting powers from a tree spirit" (*yokkhaso hmaw aung-*). If true, they would not therefore be real *weikza*. A tree spirit, the teacher comments, has attained this state thanks to the merit that it has accumulated in its previous lives. But its condition prevents it from accomplishing new acts of merit. Someone who can get merit for it will enjoy its favor. To do this, one has to meditate for a certain time, at least ten days, under the tree inhabited by the spirit and then share any merit acquired with it. In return, the spirit will support (*ma-*) you. He will protect you and endow you with supernatural abilities, including the capacity, similar to that of the four *weikza*, to appear and disappear at will (*ko hpyauk pyinnya,* the power of invisibility). "But just take a look around you," exclaims Tayza Htun, pointing out all the buildings that have sprung up at the Site of Success because of the cult's popularity. "How could a tree spirit make all this happen?"

Even when an individual's supernatural potency (*dago*) has been demonstrated incontrovertibly, such a person's claim to be a real *weikza,* although accepted by his disciples, will not necessarily be accepted by others. The source and significance of this supernatural potency remain subject to debate and to evaluation; the exact nature of the phenomenon is open to argument. Any discussion of believing and its legitimacy takes as its premise a discriminating conception that, schematically, attributes an individual's supernatural potency—provided it is not of a maleficent sort—to two types of bases, each one having a different value: an internal force and an external force. Does supernatural potency originate in the individual, or instead does it derive from an agent exterior to him? The two possibilities are not mutually exclusive. The development by an individual of his internal force encourages the assistance and efficacy of one or several external forces. The problem is to determine the primary source of this potency, a determination that will be decisive for the significance it will be granted.[37]

An individual's supernatural potency can be the result, on the one hand, of the practice of concentration meditation, a contemplative technique consisting of focusing the mind on an object, an idea, or a sensation. Such a technique engenders a temporary state of absolute quietude, of indifference to the movements of the external world; it confers, after a certain degree of mental concentration (*thamadi*) has been attained, supernatural abilities. The latter are called either *eikdi,* from the Pali *iddhi,* sometimes translated as "psychic powers," or *zan,* from the Pali *jhāna,* designating the different degrees of mental absorption brought about by concentration meditation. These powers include the capacity to fly, to make oneself invisible, to multiply oneself, and so on.

An individual's supernatural potency can, on the other hand, be the result of a relationship he or she has established with an invisible entity endowed with extraordinary powers (a *weikza,* a tree spirit, a kind of ghost, etc.) or of the help brought by someone whose status grants this individual special capacities (a monk). For example, a man sets out at night to take up a place in the forest where he will recite a secret verse continuously while holding in his mouth a piece of dried beef, in order to attract a ghost or spirit whose support he wishes to gain. Soon a snake arrives and crawls up his body, wraps itself around his neck, and then leaves. This is a sign that the man has succeeded. He is now possessed of several extraordinary powers, including invulnerability, powers called *theikdi*—

the word comes from the Pali *siddhi* (accomplishment, success) and designates a *weikza*'s supernatural abilities as well. He has, it is said, "gained the knowledge or the power of *hmaw*" (*hmaw pyinnya aung-*), *hmaw* constituting one kind of supernatural potency. People also say, "*Hmaw* has been breathed into him" (*hmaw thwin-*), an expression that shows well the external origin of the potency he now holds. The practice of meditation, when it makes up a part of the proceedings, acts like a means not for the growth of an interior force but for the domestication of an exterior one. Here is another example: a man swallows some lime (an ingredient that is usually mixed with pieces of areca nut when chewing betel leaves), which has been charged with power as a result of a mantra pronounced by a monk. That evening, in the course of a stage show given on the occasion of a monastic funeral, a fight breaks out between gangs from different villages. Ten or so policemen intervene to restore order. The young man, rendered invincible by incorporating the mantra, makes short work of them. Reinforcements arrive. He flees, hotly pursued. He faints after jumping on top of a fence. The next morning, the village chief has no trouble arresting the troublemaker. The mantra's effectiveness was limited to a few hours. The power conferred by *hmaw,* precisely because it is of external origin, can vanish into thin air, be withdrawn, or eliminated at any time.

Observers of Burmese society have largely ignored the notion of *hmaw.* The only study extant, which appeared in 1912 in the *Journal of the Burma Research Society,* although quite detailed, provides an inadequate translation—"hypnotism"—of the term and does not explain the relationships between it and other Burmese ideas about the supernatural (understood, once again, in the sense of the extraordinary, that which surpasses common experience).[38] *Hmaw* refers to a potency that can be either beneficial, protecting people from danger or making it possible to eliminate a spell, or harmful, giving people the means with which to attack others. It is in the latter sense, limited and negative, that many people understand it today: the idea of *hmaw* is often identified as the occult art of sorcery. By all accounts, the potency of the *hmaw hsaya,* the *hmaw* teacher, is, in contrast to that of the *weikza,* of a mundane character. The origin of this potency does not lie in spiritual accomplishments, and its acquisition is not linked ideologically with the obtaining of nirvana. Thus even if the *hmaw hsaya* and the *weikza* have similar powers—for example, the power of invisibility—the value of these powers differs. In the Burmese Buddhist perspective, to say of an individual laying claim to the status of a *weikza* that he possesses the science of *hmaw* comes down to saying that he is not a real *weikza.* The notion of *hmaw* is analogous to the Western notion of magic when it is distinguished from religion. The analogy hinges on the opposition between two spheres, that of magic and that of religion, and not on what each of these two spheres might contain. Indeed, what we would label spontaneously as religious, such as the cult of a tree spirit (which we would speak of as "animist religion"), Burmese would conceive of as magic or in any case outside the domain of the religious, strictly speaking. And what we would take to be magic, for example alchemy or the cabalistic arts, Burmese would tip toward the religious. Were any Burmese to read James Frazer, they would judge the eminent British anthropologist of little discernment, despite his impressive erudition. Frazer, translating into scientific terms a widespread Western concept, differentiated actions undertaken to influence the course of things on the basis solely of a ritual, without appeal to a divine force (magic), from a belief in nonhuman entities, superior to people, possessing a binding power over reality, of whom mere humans request help or indulgence by means of prayer or offerings (religion). For Frazer, magic functioned according to an (erroneous) understanding of the laws of nature, religion according to the putative laws of a supernature, understood to be a world of spirits or divinities.[39] But clearly, Burmese do not draw the border between the two on this spot. Still, like us, they do demarcate between what relates to religion and what does not, the latter to be sectioned off in a domain such as magic.

The question of the relations between religion and magic has figured prominently in anthropological reflections for a long time. It now appears obsolete, among other reasons because the categories of "religion" and "magic" have been put through the critical wringer, denounced for having been used abusively and being tainted with ethnocentrism. Burmese, nevertheless, still consider the question worthwhile. The terms they use to label a phenomenon do not, certainly, correspond to ours: opposed pairs such as *hmaw pyinna / weikza pyinnya,* or *lawki pyinnya / lawkoktara pyinnya* (mundane knowledge / supramundane knowledge), or *auk-lan pyinnya / ahtet-lan pyinnya* (knowledge of the lower path / knowledge of the upper path) are not literal equivalents of the pair magic / religion. But the opposition between magic and religion, however approximate it may be, enables us to take account of the spirit if not the letter of Burmese understandings. And we might say, without risk of betraying the indigenous point of view, that in his disciples' eyes, the supernatural potency of a *weikza* is of a religious, not a magical, order or, more exactly, of a mystical one, in the sense in which this potency is correlated with the *weikza*'s progression toward the supramundane goal of nirvana.[40] Far from extending over a single and homogeneous domain, what we have so far labeled "supernatural" in such expressions as "supernatural powers or abilities" is duplicated on two distinct levels: a magical sphere, which remains in the domain of the mundane and the immanent, and a mystical sphere, which touches on the supramundane and the transcendent. These two orders of potency, magical and mystical, must not be conflated.

Our choice of words, therefore, matters. To call the Buddha's supernatural abilities, for example, "magic powers" comes down to either denying their pertinence to both the quest for nirvana and the Master's way of transmitting his teachings, and thereby ignoring an inherent element—so the four *weikza* tell us—in the construction of the Buddhist religion since its very beginning, or—if the adjective "magic" is used in a neutral sense to characterize the human production of phenomena contrary to or escaping from natural laws—misunderstanding the Buddhist perspective in failing to distinguish between mystical potency and magical potency. And what applies to the Buddha applies to the *weikza*. So when Spiro chooses to assimilate *weikza* with magicians, he agrees with his theory, according to which the *weikza* phenomenon is "anti-Buddhist."[41] Burmese, in contrast to the American anthropologist, do not see the phenomenon as contrary to Buddhism, although they are ready, when the case arises, to discredit one or another of its manifestations by deeming it magic. The believing of such a cult's disciples is thereby delegitimated.

Under these conditions, the distinction between reason and believing, between the apprehension of a situation on the basis of intellectual and logical faculties and its apprehension on the basis of affects and an altered perception of phenomena, is revealed to be too simple, if not simplistic—because an individual can acknowledge the accomplishment of something unbelievable and nevertheless object to believing by terming it a magical feat.

BETWEEN A STRUCTURAL AND A DYNAMIC VIEW OF FLYING MEN

Wednesday, September 17, 2003, 9:30 a.m. Up since 5:00 a.m., I have finished organizing my notes from the day before: remarks, information, personal observations scribbled in a pupil's notebook in the course of meetings, conversations, and incidents. I decide out of curiosity to pay a visit to U Thondara, head monk of the Dammarattita monastery, which adjoins that of the four *weikza*. Lay people receive instruction there about the practice of insight meditation (*wipathana*), the path par excellence to spiritual perfection. The teaching follows the method of a famous Burmese teacher, the great monk of Mogok (1899–1962).

Victorious, as usual, begins by introducing me and my work on the cult of the four *weikza*. U Thondara responds hostilely. He knows nothing about the *weikza*'s path, he claims; he only knows about the word of the Buddha. The four *weikza,* whose principal activity is to display their supernatural potency, belong to the mundane path (*lawki laing*), whereas his monastery, dedicated to the practice of meditation, concerns the nirvanic path (*neikban laing*). Were he himself to find that he possessed extraordinary abilities, he would never make a show of them. That is contrary to monastic rule (*wini*). The three *weikza* monks, it's true, are not troubled by these considerations. They "have no *wini*" (*wini ma shi bu*)— that is, they do not observe the monastic rule: this is a way for U Thondara to downgrade them to the status of laypeople. They trick the faithful to get donations from them. Because what looks more attractive in the eyes of the devout, giving a gift to a normal monk or to individuals exhibiting supernatural potency? The faithful venerate the *weikza* because they are dominated by believing (*yonkyihmu*) and lack all critical acumen (*athi nyan*).

Even though he has just declared with some force that he knows nothing of the *weikza*'s path, U Thondara launches into a definition of the phenomenon while Victorious and I, disconcerted by his diatribe, dare not say a word. Real *weikza* do exist, the monk states. But they never manifest themselves physically to ordinary humans, because their body and spirit are separated and experience different fates. The four *weikza,* consequently, are not real *weikza.* They belong, says U Thondara, to the category of *dago-shin* (individuals endowed with supernatural potency) or *hpandi-shin* (individuals capable of making what they want happen), people who have obtained their powers by means of such practices as vegetarianism and concentration meditation (as distinct from insight meditation). Now none of that pertains to the quest for nirvana, asserts the monk. U Thondara likens the four *weikza* to those ascetics who, before the advent of Buddhism, devoted themselves to concentration meditation in the forest, eating only fruit, and thereby acquired a certain supernatural potency. These ascetics, he emphasizes, even though they attained a high degree of perfection, could only live 120 years. How could the four *weikza* claim to live several thousand years?

In other words, an individual's supernatural potency could have an internal source and still incline toward magic. The distinction between the spheres of magic and mysticism, which is connected to the meaning of supernatural potency, does not coincide with that concerning the source of this potency, internal or external. Everything hinges on what this potency reflects on the order of spiritual accomplishment. Such is what the anthropologist later gathers, long after the fact, from this morning's tempestuous interview; it will eventually cause him to refine his analytic schema. For the moment, this visit to one of their fiercest critics, their neighbor, will not escape the four *weikza*'s notice.

If opinions are divided about the source and significance, and so the value, of the four *weikza*'s supernatural potency, if no agreement can be reached on this topic, it is because a *weikza* is an essentially ambiguous figure, a paradoxical and troubling one. A *weikza* acquires his supernatural faculties (*theikdi*) thanks to his success in the practice of techniques apparently alien to the Buddha's teaching, such as alchemy and the cabalistic arts. Nevertheless, this success is the condition for his accession to nirvana: it enables him to prolong his life, guaranteeing his enjoying, in a distant future, the privilege of hearing a Buddha preach. A *weikza* puts endless emphasis on the supramundane goal of nirvana. Nevertheless, he provides first of all for the mundane expectations of his disciples, such as the desire for prosperity, success, and protection. A *weikza* lives outside the ordinary human world, in an inaccessible and invisible place where he is thought to practice meditation. Nevertheless, he intervenes repeatedly in the world. A *weikza* is not a divinity. Nevertheless, he has the capacity, like a divinity, to act at a distance on behalf of those who venerate him, even to make them the intermediaries for his potency, assimilating them then to masters of *hmaw* (whose power is of external origin and of a mundane nature). A *weikza* is deemed a virtuous being (*thudawgaung*) who has vanquished impermanence and death in order to attain nirvana. Nevertheless, he communicates by means of possession, the typical mode of manifestation of inferior invisible entities, ones liable to cause harm. A *weikza* can wear the robe. Nevertheless, when that is the case, he fails to observe one of the essential rules of the code of monastic discipline, which prohibits a monk from making any demonstration of his supernatural powers. In a word, a *weikza* is a double being who combines and joins the mundane and the supramundane, who converts magic into mysticism and thereby modifies its value. Significantly, the Pali term *vijjā,* from which the Burmese *weikza* derives, is used to label either a mundane form of knowledge, especially a magical knowledge such as the science of spells, or a supramundane one. Although the mundane is the sphere of the layperson and the supramundane that of the monk, the *weikza* brings about the synthesis of the two domains. For this reason he is beyond the lay/monk distinction. A *weikza* is completely of this world and completely outside this world.

This third state, while it raises numerous ambiguities in the *weikza*'s identity, nevertheless makes it possible to resolve the tensions between the mundane and supramundane aspirations that inhabit the Burmese Buddhist system of representations. The commonly accepted distinction between the two domains is based, on the one hand, on the idea of an ontological rupture between nirvana and all other possible states of existence and, on the other hand, on a hierarchy of values, some practices being conceived of as mundane (such as astrology) and others as supramundane (such as insight meditation). Still, a strictly binary approach, drawing on Buddhist ideology to oppose and hierarchize the mundane and the supramundane, cannot account for the existence of mediating phenomena or figures between the two domains. This is not the same as saying that the categories of the mundane and the supramundane are the two poles of a continuum. The disjunction between them remains, in spite of the fact that a mundane action may well express a supramundane reality and a supramundane accomplishment is made manifest through a mundane act.

In light of all this, we can better understand the difficulty for Burmese of defining a *weikza,* because they may look on him either from the angle of his mundane orientation or from that of his supramundane one. We can appreciate at the same time how difficult it is to characterize a practice a priori as magic or religious. For if the value assigned a practice depends on the meaning it is given and not on its content, it is possible—as is the case for the cult of the four *weikza*—for the same practice to be identified, in the midst of a society and a culture, by some as magic and by others as religion. Certainly, some phenomena can be classed, without any possible hesitation in the eyes of Burmese, either as magic (the practice of witchcraft, for example) or as religion (insight meditation). But others do not lend themselves to such absolute characterization. Their designation as magic or religious practices, as directed toward the mundane or the supramundane, is a matter of interpretation: it will vary according to the point of the view of the speaker. The boundary between magic and religion turns out to move about. A dualist approach to magic and religion—that is, an approach that insists on determining and distinguishing the characteristics of magic elements and religious elements in order to lead to a discrete classification of each phenomenon in one or the other category—hits up against reality.[42] The same happens to Burmese themselves, who in trying doggedly to classify activities according to the opposition between mundane and supramundane, hit up against the *weikza* phenomenon and find themselves incapable of agreeing on the nature of its protagonists. The anthropologist, to put an end to the indeterminacy, might well be tempted to speak of "magico-religious facts." Such a solution, however, would simply dodge the problem by masking the divergent interpretations to be found at the heart of the society under study.

When they leave their invisible realm to come preach in the village of Mebaygon, the four *weikza* cross the border between the mundane and the supramundane. Arriving from Dragoness Mountain (in some sense the threshold of nirvana) by flying through the monastery window, Bodaw Bo Htun Aung does not only show his supernatural potency. He sets up a bridge; linking the two domains, he indicates that he can respond to disciples' aspirations both mundane and supramundane. This point sheds new light on the impatience with which his dramatic entrance is awaited. The effectiveness of the performance lies in its power to represent the ambiguous nature of a *weikza* and the possibilities this ambiguity generates. The performance itself expresses the essence of a *weikza*.

We might congratulate ourselves at having arrived so quickly at such a characterization of the figure of the *weikza*—because the scientific objective at the outset of our inquiry was to try to get a hold of this elusive figure—were it not for the painful impression of having met with failure in the very process of getting here. However satisfying it might appear for one in search of a transparent representation of the facts and beings in question, this solution to the enigma of the *weikza*, with its whiff of structuralism (a fundamental opposition transcended by a mediating figure), accounts only imperfectly for the reality that we are determined to adhere to. To render in a schematic form the Burmese theory of supernatural potency that we have tried to trace, we might draw the following diagram, in which the vertical axis designates the source of supernatural potency (of external or internal origin) and the horizontal axis its signification (magic or mystical), while the left side corresponds to the domain of the mundane and the right side to the domain of the supramundane.

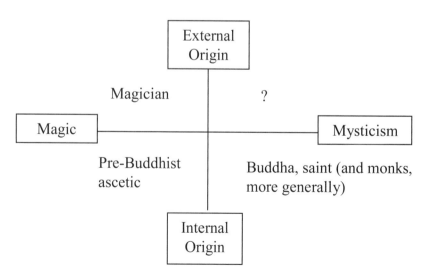

Figure 1   A schematic representation of the Burmese theory of supernatural potency

Putting aside for the moment the question mark, which alludes to a possibility not yet seriously addressed (that of the medium or person subject to possession), where and in what way should the four *weikza* of Mebaygon be placed? At the center of the diagram, in accordance with the general but static characterization of the figure of the *weikza* that we have just arrived at? Or instead nowhere, letting the four *weikza* move about among the different possibilities, thereby taking account of the variety of identities attributed to them (magician, ascetic, Buddha, or saint, ignoring the view that the cult is chicanery pure and simple)? Should the *weikza* be represented as single or multiple?

HOW THE INSTRUMENTAL (OR MUNDANE) MAKES THE SOTERIOLOGICAL (OR SUPRAMUNDANE)

Thursday, January 4, 2007, 11:00 a.m. Holed up in my office at the Center for Social Anthropology in Toulouse, I revise these pages for the *n*th time. For more than three years I have been working, intermittently, on the first chapter of the *Immortals.* By dint of circumstance and necessity, I have read and reread Spiro, Lévy-Bruhl, Weber, Malinowski, Hume, Evans-Pritchard, Needham, Lévi-Strauss, Mauss and Hubert, Pouillon, Horton, and Tambiah, among others.[43] The text has gone through multiple versions, among them an essay in English pompously titled "On Flying Men in the Land of Buddhism: Religion, Magic, and Science in Burma," for circulation among American readers. Doubts and detours. In the course of the successive reworkings, I have found myself increasingly inclined to substitute for a linear exposition, homogeneous and solid, which gives a work its scientific air, a project of breaking things down, one that unties what was at an earlier stage too willfully bound together, one that erases the usual procedures for formulating an argument, one that compromises the fluidity of the demonstration. How might it be possible to relate the different moments, the various sites at which thinking and writing occurred and the stages in the development of a research project? In what way might the figure of the *weikza* be allowed to sketch itself, by depicting the ways in which it is constituted, perceived, described, and solicited and by following the men who activate it, reactivate it, invest it with meaning—in brief, give it life?

Friday, January 30, 2004. At the monastery of the four *weikza,* where Victorious and I are staying for the third time, a thirty-three-year-old monk arrives who has the distinction of being of Russian or, actually, of Mongolian descent. After completing his military service, U Thitala became a novice in his natal city in Siberia, not out of spiritual commitment, truth be told, so much as out of a desire to be trained in herbal medicine, an art in which Siberian monks excel. Decades of communism, he relates, had deeply shaken the region's Buddhism, with its Mahayana commitments. Monks married, had children, and lived half the time at home. They only wore the robe when they were staying at the monastery. Once the communist regime was gone, some monks, having traveled to India, Nepal, or Tibet and having brought back a more rigorous conception of religious discipline, undertook to reform monastic morals. In 1991, during an international conference that brought together representatives of all the great religions in a Siberian city, U Thitala's master met a delegation of Burmese monks. They decided to set up an exchange program of Russian and Burmese novices. The following year, U Thitala, having been a novice for only three months, left for Burma, knowing not a word of either English or Burmese. He learned both languages, was ordained as a monk in the Theravadin tradition, and rose through several grades in the Burmese monastic curriculum before enrolling at the International Theravada Buddhist Missionary University, recently established in Yangon.

Sitting with the anthropologist at the teashop at the foot of the Monastery of the Noble Success, U Thitala speaks of his parents far away in Siberia. He describes them as full of a "blind faith" in Buddhism, considering anything that comes out of the monastery to be worthy of reverence. For his part, the monk describes himself as a "half-believer." He is not ready to take everything on in a single block; he takes up issues one by one to form an opinion. Thus reading a passage in the Buddhist canon asserting that ten thousand people attained nirvana after having listened to the Buddha's teaching left him feeling perplexed. Ten or fifteen would have seemed to him a plausible number, but not ten thousand. He spoke about this to one of his teachers, an erudite Burmese monk. The monk explained that the number should be taken in a metaphorical sense, that it was a way of emphasizing the Buddha's greatness.

This is U Thitala's second visit to the *weikza*'s monastery. He says in English that he is only at the stage of "studying" the phenomenon, that he is not yet a "true believer." He declares himself as much skeptical as disconcerted. He considers the *weikza*'s demonstration of their powers as excessive, a deviation from what he understands to be the ideal as put forth by Theravada Buddhist doctrine. Certain facts, however, remain inexplicable for him. Where could the coconuts and candles that fall among people during the séances be falling from? How is it physically possible for a man who appears to be older than eighty years of age— Bodaw Bo Htun Aung—to go in seventeen seconds (the monk has counted them) along the exterior of the monastery at several meters off the ground, from the front left window of the main hall all the way to the rear entrance, with coconuts in his arms? U Thitala has paid close attention to the *weikza*'s preaching. The content of that preaching strikes him as orthodox, because it addresses the quest for nirvana by means of the practice of moral virtue and meditation. Some people, he notes, deem the *weikza* path foreign to Theravada Buddhism. But one of the professors at his university, to whom he reported this view, countered that the *weikza*'s supernatural powers were acknowledged by Theravadin doctrine; the danger was becoming attached to them and making of them an end in themselves.

On a Sunday two days later, in the course of a discussion in the anthropologist's presence, U Thitala, who is not afraid of expressing his doubts, confronts Doctor Sein Yi, an elderly and respected disciple of the *weikza,* directly. "I came here a few months ago. At that time, I saw the faithful give big donations. Now that I'm back, I note that no improvements have been made to the monastery buildings. So where does the money given to the *weikza* go?"

The next day, U Thitala asks to meet Saturday's Son, the monk and *weikza*'s medium. The anthropologist does not attend the interview. The discussion is brief. U Thitala mentions the resemblance between the features and voice of Bodaw Bo Htun Aung, of U Pandita, and of Saturday's Son. "Everything depends on what you see," replies the medium. At a second interview the next day, Saturday's Son responds to the Russian's skepticism by reminding him that the four *weikza* have been confronted by equally tough skeptics in the past and that these people have ended up falling into the believing camp after they have put the *weikza* to the test. To support his remarks, he cites a famous feat in the history of the cult. Then he challenges U Thitala: if the Russian wants, Bodaw Bo Htun Aung will land on his shoulders that evening. After declaring that what each person sees depends on believing (*yonkyihmu*) and that some people are not yet ready to see the *weikza* for what they are, Saturday's Son puts an end to the interview, stating, "It doesn't much matter if you can spot the hands or feet of *weikza,* or anything else [that would reveal that they are not real *weikza*]. The only thing that matters is the effect the *weikza* have on their disciples, the way in which they foster their practice of Buddhism."

This assertion contrasts sharply with the customary rhetoric of the cult's disciples: it resembles the traditional anthropological view. It puts the question of the true and the false aside to draw attention to what gets implemented by means of believing, to what believing makes possible. This perspective is typical of those who, while still harboring doubts about the four *weikza,* judge the cult to be beneficial. Victorious and I have made a habit, during our stays at the monastery, of taking a brief walk around at nine or ten o'clock in the morning, once

I have finished putting my notes from the day before in order. We go out the monastery's main gate, walk through the village and beyond it, making a loop around the back and often stopping when we reach the edge of the Site of Success. It is in the course of these walks that Victorious confides in me his impressions of the cult. The Burmese man reveals himself to be undecided. He refuses to accept as established fact the stories we have heard about the four *weikza*. These endless stories of wonders, he comments, are born out of the disciples' imagination (*seikku yin-,* in the sense of indulging oneself in fantasy, to convince oneself by inventing stories). In his view, we lend our interlocutors too ready an ear; in so doing, we reinforce these people's tendency to ramble. Having said that, though, he has himself witnessed some strange, if not extraordinary, things. One event in particular has struck him. In the course of one of the *weikza*'s appearances, a coconut, following its startling fall, landed in the tiny space between him and the camera he had put on the floor. A few centimeters difference in one direction or the other and either he would have been hurt or the camera damaged. Unable to reach a definitive opinion and not wishing, given the circumstances, to criticize the *weikza,* Victorious adopts a position of neutrality. Whatever the real identity of the *weikza* might be, what he has witnessed at the monastery remains praiseworthy. People in disarray have found support; depraved people have repented of their ways. Rationalizing what the disciples say about the effects of their believing, he reveals to the anthropologist the psychological mechanism in which, he thinks, the effectiveness of the cult originates. Believers, because they feel themselves bolstered up and protected, are ready to confront with confidence and courage any uncertain and trying situation—illness, any personal matters of some delicacy, travel abroad—thereby faring better. Such is the miracle of believing.

Burmese generally maintain that there exists an inherent effectiveness in believing. A common remark is, "Without believing, nothing gets done" (*yonkyihmu ma shi bahma ma hpyit*). Its meaning is ambiguous, because the individual who states it, depending on his or her relationship to the person or cult under discussion, will attribute the effectiveness of believing either to a psychological mechanism or to a supernatural one. In any case, no one can expect to benefit from the four *weikza*'s potency in the absence of an absolute commitment. Believing is posited as a necessary condition for enjoying their support. It is tempting to say, in imitation of the famous formula that defines a Buddhist as someone who has taken refuge in the Three Jewels (the Buddha, his Teaching, and the Community of Monks), that one must "take refuge in the four *weikza.*"

Zaw Win, Victorious, and I got to Htu Aung's home about 10:00 a.m. on Sunday, October 5, 2003. The man lives in an outlying area of Mandalay, beyond the statue makers' neighborhood. Part of his house, made out of plaited bamboo, is rented out to wood carvers. He himself employs two or three people in the preparation of a Burmese medicine intended to rid children of coughing fits. Zaw Win places orders and sells the remedy at a counter installed in his family's house downtown. Zaw Win's father was a famous specialist in Burmese medicine. Now the business struggles along, maintained lackadaisically by his son.

Htu Aung has invited his guests to sit on bamboo chaise lounges outdoors in the shade. After responding to the anthropologist's eternal question—what is a *weikza?*—the disciple has insisted on this point: "To venerate the [four] *weikza* is to be protected against all dangers." And he recounted how his sister had been miraculously saved.

"It was in 1998. My older sister had malaria. She had fallen into a coma. We took her to the Taw Win Clinic [a famous private clinic in Mandalay]. The doctor examined her and said that it was hopeless, that there was nothing left to do. She was to be taken home the next day. People in her neighborhood started getting the house ready to receive the body and hold a wake. She was fifty-three years old. I said to myself, if the scientific method (*theikpan ni*) has failed, then only the *weikza* method (*weikza ni*) can succeed. I went to consult Khin Lay Lay. She has the power of clairvoyance. She told me, 'Htu Aung, only you can save her!' She explained to me how to change the course of fate (*yadaya khyay-*).[44]

The doctor had made his diagnosis in the late afternoon. It was nine in the evening by the time I got to the Pagoda of Noble Success (Aungdawhmu Hpaya), east of the Mandalay palace. My sister was born on a Wednesday morning and I went to the corresponding side [a spot on the south side of the pagoda].[45] I lit some candles and some incense sticks. I recited the Five Precepts,[46] then a verse in Pali composed by [the *weikza*] Bobo Aung, before pronouncing a declaration of truth (*thitsa hso-*)[47]:

'O Five Buddhas,[48] great monks U Kawwida, U Pandita, U Oktamagyaw, and Bodaw Bo Htun Aung, *weikza* specialists in medicine (*hsay weikza*), *weikza* specialists in mercury-based alchemy (*byada weikza*), *weikza* specialists in the cabalistic arts (*in weikza*), *weikza* specialists in iron-based alchemy (*than weikza*), *weikza* specialists in incantations (*mandan weikza*),[49] great monks [*weikza*] Baliba, Batamaw, Yakyaw, guardian divinities of the universe (*sakyawala saung nat mingyi*), guardian divinity of the earth (*wathondayay saung nat mingyi*), all of you together make it so that my older sister, born on a Wednesday morning, is cured as quickly as possible!

'I, your disciple, will recite my prayer beads twenty-seven times,[50] repeating the phrase, "loving-kindness of the perfect man deserving adoration and worship" (*arahan myitta*).[51]

'O Buddha, in light of this declaration of truth, make Wednesday's daughter be cured as quickly as possible.'

It was about ten at night. I went to the clinic and cut some strands of my sister's hair. I mixed them with one hundred and eight young bamboo leaves (*wa nyunt*).[52] Khin Lay Lay had told me to go to the Mahamuni Pagoda [a sanctuary in Mandalay, housing the most venerated Buddha image in the country] by seven or eight in the morning. There are always employees there watching the faithful who climb onto the statue of the Buddha. People are allowed to stick gold leaf on it, nothing else. It's quite extraordinary (*htuzan-*), but that morning no one prevented me from doing what I intended. I climbed onto the statue. I put the bottle containing my sister's hair and the bamboo leaves in the Buddha's hand. It was 7:15 a.m.; that was the time I had chosen. Once you undertake such a task, believing is essential. Without believing, nothing gets done. I stuck gold leaf on the statue. Then I climbed down and went through the same procedure as the night before. While I was concentrating, reciting my beads, I had a vision (*ayon*): a halo of white light was emanating from my sister's body. After that, I went back to the clinic. The street before I got there, [the chief of the four *weikza*] U Kawwida appeared to me. I was really relieved now that I knew that the four *weikza* were looking after my sister. At the clinic, the nurse told me that my sister had regained consciousness but had not yet opened her eyes. I mixed some medicine the *weikza* had handed out with some water and had her swallow it. I also ran a bamboo stick with a dragon's head that the *weikza* had given me above the length of her body. The doctor cautioned me: even if the sick woman woke up, her brain had been affected and she would be mentally handicapped.

She came to several hours later. She gesticulated like a madwoman. She had lost her memory; she recognized no one. I sprinkled the upper part of her body with water mixed with the *weikza*'s medicine. Six days passed. Then, during the night, close to three in the morning, she saw a monk approach her and then leave again, flying through the air. She described it to me later. It must have been U Kawwida. The following morning, she was in a position to leave the clinic and return home. She was doing well and had regained her memory. Imagine the looks on people's faces when she got to her neighborhood! Everybody thought she was dead!"

Most stories concerning extraordinary cures that occur thanks to the intervention of the four *weikza* hardly display such an elaborate plan as Htu Aung's narrative. The curative measures of the *weikza* consist as a general rule of the distribution of their medicine—in the form of a small, reddish-purple cone with a flat top—and above all in the pronouncing, sometimes in the absence of the patient, of a formula consisting of a single term, "Success!" (*aung byi, aung* meaning "to succeed, conquer, triumph, overcome" and *byi* being the grammatical marker for the past, for completed action). The formula refers to the Buddha's success in his quest for Awakening. Its complete version, which adorns the domestic altar of every disciple of the cult worthy of the name, is "The Buddha has succeeded!" (*Bokdaw aung byi*).[53] It admits of limitless extensions, with reference, for example, to the Three Jewels: "The Buddha has succeeded, the Teaching has succeeded, the Community of Monks has succeeded!" (*Bokdaw aung byi, Dammaw aung byi, Thangaw aung byi*). Both in its short form, without specification of the subject, and in its complete form, with mention of the Buddha, it serves as a motto for the four *weikza* and their disciples. Every endeavor, no matter what its nature or objective, is inaugurated and concluded by its pronouncement, which fosters and celebrates success in general. Said by one of the *weikza* for the benefit of someone who is ill, the formula suffices in itself: it is the means and the guarantee of a cure.

Clearly, the four *weikza*'s curative action, when they act without any intermediary, does not depend on the mechanism of symbolic effectiveness as Claude Lévi-Strauss characterized it.[54] Lévi-Strauss developed his analysis drawing on the example of a shaman's treatment of a difficult labor among the Cuna Indians of Panama. Whereas the shaman's intervention is implemented and is effective on the basis of identifying the force responsible for the disorder, a force then made the target of the operation, the *weikza*'s intervention does not take into account the origins of the sickness, attributed indifferently to bad luck or a physiological process diagnosed by medical science. Whereas the Cuna shaman's incantation, intended to sustain the painful work of childbirth, is the exuberant recitation of a symbolic (mythic) journey—yet an expressive and often even literal one—through the reproductive organs of the woman giving birth (a journey that Lévi-Strauss relates to the working process of a psychoanalytic cure, "inducing an experience" and "recreating a myth which the sick person must live or re-live"), the *weikza* pronounce this simple word, "Success!" Whereas the suffering and its reduction give rise to an explicit representation, through the shaman's discourse, of a system of meanings culturally intelligible to the patient,[55] the *weikza* neither furnish nor generate the formulation of any "language," of any symbolic idiom that would induce a cathartic effect in the patient. In short, whereas the Cuna shaman enters into a direct and intense relationship with his patient, the *weikza* remain at a distance, contenting themselves with allusive signs that make their protection clear. It falls to those who would wish for more expressivity in the curative process to fill the void by drawing on the shared symbolic repertoire, such as can be seen in the case of Htu Aung who, with the help of a clairvoyant, turned to a *yadaya,* an action reversing the course of fate.

The differing conditions of the shaman and the *weikza* form the basis for this divergence between their respective therapeutic methods. The shaman and his patient belong to the same order of reality, and the former, to accomplish his task, must count on the assistance of supernatural forces, tutelary spirits as it happens, who are external to him but influence the course of things from the in-side. In contrast, the *weikza* and their patient belong to different orders of reality, and the *weikza* count on their own power, drawing on their strength based on their spiritual accomplishments and their mastery of techniques such as alchemy or the cabalistic arts. Whereas the shaman operates to reestablish the normal order of things, the *weikza* operate by surpassing it. A shaman produces no mira-cles; the *weikza* do. A man is said to be condemned to die. The doctor has pronounced the verdict: he will die soon, he is already thought of as dead because his house has been readied for the bereavement. Nevertheless, he survives. He is living proof that fatality can be undone. His story, reported in wearying detail, invites believing—defying death and rebirth, escaping the normal order of things, in short, working for one's salvation. The miraculous story reminds the community of its supramundane ideal.

Thus it is hardly surprising, indeed it is practically inevitable, that the four *weikza*'s curative action should be so ritually impoverished. The more compli-cated and extravagant their performance became, the more the *weikza* would lay themselves open to suspicions of trickery or of having recourse to external forces that they would be obliged to mobilize in support of their action, which would amount to the exercise of a magic potency. The ritual spareness is a guarantee of their supernatural potency's source and of its effectiveness. When they use the power of language, the *weikza* pronounce only a single word, as though an utter-ance's pragmatic cogency, to use Malinowski's expression[56] (today we would say its "performative capacity"), was inversely proportional to the degree of its elaboration. What is at work, in sum, is a logic of de-ritualization. In contrast to the shaman's power, the *weikza*'s power and its effectiveness rely in the final instance on something that society is incapable of symbolizing, on something that, as the Buddha taught his disciples, language is incapable and must remain incapable of expressing: nirvana. If we still wanted to speak of symbolic effectiveness, the mechanism would have to be placed not at the physiological and psychological level of the patient, but at the level of the collectivity, because by means of the miraculous cure, the supramundane order embodied by the *weikza* and their action's success is made manifest and superimposed on the mundane order, which is represented by suffering and the community's inability to relieve it. It isn't so much that order is substituted for disorder. Order has rather been revealed to lie elsewhere, apart from disorder, which is the normal state of things and of the world. The community, confronted with suffering, is reminded of its impotence and of the single true way to overcome this suffering: to follow the path set by the Buddha when he attained Awakening, when he "succeeded." The affinity between curative action and religion becomes clearer if curative action is understood as an attempt at symbolization of the unrepresentable: spiritual perfection and the state of nirvana. It follows that establishing a contrast between practices with instrumental ends and practices with soteriological ends makes no sense. The *weikza*'s action, in the end, although it has a curative aim and is therefore instrumental (mundane), is endowed with a mystical signification and is therefore soteriological (supramundane).[57]

To hear the cult's disciples tell it, many are the miraculous cures brought about by the four *weikza*'s intervention. In every case, the doctors, who had abandoned all hope, found themselves speechless before what resembles a resurrection. But if neither symbolic effectiveness nor physiological laws can make the phenomenon comprehensible, how is it to be explained? How does a miracle happen?

SCIENCE COMES ONTO THE SCENE

Wednesday, August 20, 2003, early afternoon. Major Zaw Win, an eminent disciple of the four *weikza* who, three years earlier, first made me aware of the cult, takes me to see Doctor Sein Yi. An ex–vice minister, the Doctor has been living for several months in an apartment on the ground floor of a building for government officials in Yankin Quarter, north of the capital. A shed made out of sheet metal stands against the side wall of the building, on the side of the little court adjoining his apartment. The Doctor had it constructed so he could practice alchemy in it. He comes out of it now to welcome the visitors who have shown up unexpectedly—he doesn't have a phone. He receives us without fuss, dressed in an old *longyi* (a sort of long cloth skirt worn by Burmese men and women) and an undershirt of a certain age worn over a faded shirt.

The Doctor, like the Major, ranks among the oldest of the four *weikza*'s disciples, those called *thawaka,* from the Pali *sāvaka,* designating in Pali texts the Buddha's attested disciples, religious or lay. As in the army and the community of monks, length of service constitutes a hierarchical principle within the cult. It is a means of measuring the intensity of a disciple's believing and the depth of his or her relationship with the *weikza*. But it is not his seniority alone that grants the Doctor great prestige. He belongs, along with the Major, to the group of four living disciples who have participated in all the *weikza*'s life-prolonging ceremonies celebrated so far (in 1975 for U Pandita, 1989 for U Oktamagyaw, and 1994 for U Kawwida), major events in the history of the cult. As he was to say to me several months later, at the time of the cult's annual festival, when he wore pinned on his jacket two badges granted to participants in those ceremonies (he had lost the third): "See, I'm a two-star general!" Additionally, as a physician by profession, the Doctor is a person of learning (*pyinnya-shin*) and, still more significantly, a man of science (*theikpan-thama*). He has been, on top of it all, a man of power. In the 1970s and 1980s, he was given important responsibilities in the regional public health administrative structure. He then held the post of Vice Minister of Health for a time, before finishing his career as Director-General of the Department of Indigenous Medicine. Other persons of the first rank, including a head of state and a famous general, were disciples of the four *weikza*. That men in a position to blacklist the cult by declaring it out of line with Buddhist principles, thus bringing about its decline, should instead recognize and venerate the four *weikza* adds to the latter figures' credibility. Disciples place particular value on narratives of conversion to the cult on the part of political leaders. Despite believers' emphasis on individual experience and reflection, believing spreads just as much by social contagion. The public influence and celebrity of a cult's disciples help authenticate such-and-such a spiritual figure's ability to fly. Let us recall what his Burmese informant said to Melford E. Spiro: "If important people like U Nu [then prime minister] and U Kya [*sic*] Nyein [leader of the opposition party] and other officials and important people believe in him [the alleged *weikza*], then I'm prepared to believe too."

His remarkable professional career, with all the associated material advantages and symbolic gratifications it entailed, did not divert Doctor Sein Yi from his primary objective: to become a *weikza*. From the time of his retirement in 1993, he has directed all his efforts toward this goal. Wishing to accomplish Perfection in Renunciation (*neitkhama parami*), he left his home, an apartment downtown. He took up residence by himself, at first in a house on the outskirts of Yangon, in a quarter set up among former rice fields where lots were allocated to high officials for free, and then in this modest apartment, received in recompense for service rendered to the state. His wife visits him once a week. When he is not at this apartment, the Doctor is at the Energy Monastery, in Mebaygon, where he makes fairly long stays. During all these years, he has never stopped practicing meditation and alchemy. He considers himself ready, should occasion arise, to leave for the forest and live in solitude. Now in his seventies, the man is certain that he is on the point of becoming a *weikza,* soon to be able to "exit" and go live at Dragoness Mountain. The *weikza* U Pandita, whose nephew he was in a previous lifetime and so to whom he is the closest, has affirmed to him on several occasions that he will succeed. On the occasion of the most recent life-prolonging ceremony (in 1994), U Pandita gave him the monastic robe that he must wear at the time of his ordination, the final and indispensable stage before attaining his goal.

The combination of all these elements—social status, early engagement with the cult, participation in all of the life-prolonging ceremonies, his practice of meditation and alchemy, and acknowledgment of his accomplishments by the *weikza*—supports the Doctor's authority. When younger disciples do not know the answer to a question or do not know how to explain something, they recommend consulting him. By the same token, when they recount some episode in the cult's history, they mention that the Doctor would be able to provide more details.

The Major, the Doctor, and I seat ourselves in some old wood and wicker chairs in the little room that serves as the place to receive guests. The apartment is almost empty of furniture. The Doctor makes apologies: he has nothing to offer his visitors other than green tea and candies. It is not so much the modest sum he receives as a pension (3,000 *kyat* per month, a ridiculously small amount in light of the cost of living) that explains the simplicity of his surroundings. His two sons, who are prosperous businessmen, would be delighted to provide for him. One of them lives in the United States. He has invited his father repeatedly, without success, to join him there: his father tells him he will come once he has become a *weikza*, at which point he will not need to take a plane. As a matter of fact, as the Doctor likes to say about himself, he is a man of humble origins who has retained, despite the path his career took, a poor man's lifestyle. In his small apartment, he prepares his own meals, abstaining, like monks, from eating after noon. What's more, he has long practiced vegetarianism.

Alternating between English and Burmese, the disciple responds courteously and energetically to my questions. He is finishing up a work on the history of the cult, on the basis of a journal he has kept for decades. He has given a first draft of the manuscript to the very literate Major, who has polished the language. He is working on another book, titled *Do You Want to Become a Weikza?*

"It was in 1968.[58] I was living at the time in Pathein [principal city of the Irrawaddy Division, in the southwest of Burma]. I had gotten a letter from two friends. They were both high officials who had been trained in England. They worked in Yangon: one at the Ministry of Education, the other at the Ministry of Commerce. They were hoping that I would join them on a trip to the village of Mebaygon to pay homage to some *weikza* endowed with great supernatural potency.

I had put the letter aside without even responding. I was very busy: I had just been put in charge of the fight against malaria in Irrawaddy Division. Furthermore, I knew nothing of *weikza*. I am a doctor, a man of science.

My friends did not give up so easily. They wrote me a second time. And when I paid them a call in Yangon, they started in again on their campaign. I finally let them talk me into it.

As we were approaching Mebaygon, Bodaw Bo Htun Aung came down from the sky. He arrived gently, as though he was equipped with a parachute. But he had no parachute! He wanted to show me his extraordinary powers. He landed on the roof of the jeep, his legs hanging down. I touched his calves. He had skin and muscles, like a normal human being. 'So what were you thinking?' he asked me. 'Before I became a *weikza* I was an ordinary human being.'

Our driver wanted to put him to the test. He pressed on the accelerator. 'Instead of accelerating,' Bodaw Bo Htun Aung reprimanded him, 'you would do better to spread loving-kindness. You have no loving-kindness!' The *weikza* told him to stop the vehicle. He made us recite a formula for spreading our loving-kindness to living creatures. We were halfway between Minbu and Mebaygon. There were some thorny bushes by the side of the road. Bodaw Bo Htun Aung was barefoot; he walked through them. There was a pagoda about fifty meters away. He gave prayer beads to each of us and told us to go recite our beads seven times with the formula 'The Buddha has succeeded!' When we had finished, Bodaw Bo Htun Aung stated, 'You are true disciples of the Buddha.' He moved his arm along the length of his white habit. An apple appeared. He gave it to me. A second movement of his arm, another apple. He gave it to the son of one of my friends, telling him to cut it in two. But the boy had no knife. Bodaw Bo Htun Aung took the apple back and without the slightest effort cut it in two with his hands.

We left. After only about a few hundred meters, Bodaw Bo Htun Aung warned the driver: 'Careful. U Pandita is coming down from the sky.' The driver stopped. U Pandita landed. He was standing up, twenty meters ahead of the car. He called to me: 'Doctor Sein Yi, from Pathein, come here.' He knew my name! I was a little intimidated. I came closer, first to about two meters from him, then closer, and I prostrated myself on the ground. To tell the truth, it wasn't in order to pay him homage. I wanted to touch his feet and smell his scent. A perfumed odor emanated from his feet. 'You can smell my whole body if you want,' he said. That's what I did. It was the same: his whole body exuded a perfumed odor. It's because he's vegetarian and because he has practiced meditation intensively. He urged me to observe three moral precepts: not to steal, not to commit adultery, and not to use drugs or alcohol—I haven't drunk any beer since. He told me the story of his life, when he was born, how he had succeeded in alchemy and had become a *weikza*. That lasted about fifteen minutes. Finally, he explained that he would need my assistance for his life-prolonging ceremony. 'You're a doctor, and the ceremony is dangerous,' he said to me. I promised to help him.

U Pandita challenged the driver. 'Drive as fast you can. Let's see who gets there first!' The driver floored it and we got to Mebaygon in just ten minutes. When we got there, U Pandita was there, giving a sermon. The people present told us he had been preaching for ten minutes.

I stayed six days in Mebaygon. The four *weikza* showed me all sorts of extraordinary powers. They appeared and disappeared at will. They made bank notes proliferate. They made cabalistic figures appear on a bill by clapping it between their hands. Bodaw Bo Htun Aung even drank some mercury and then spat up two hundred alchemy balls. U Pandita predicted that I would make three pilgrimages to Bodhgaya [site of the Buddha's Awakening, located in the north of contemporary India]. That turned out to be true, and each trip was due not to my own wishes but to an official invitation. Science is incapable of explaining that. It's beyond science."

The logic that governs the *weikza* phenomenon is characterized by Burmese as being different from, and superior to, common rationality. In the world of *weikza,* universal truths are contradicted. Two and two do not necessarily make four, the sun may rise in the west, and an individual is capable of prolonging his life for several thousand years when at the very height of the scientific age (*theikpan khit*) no way has yet been discovered to make a person live for more than 120 years (the maximum length of a human life according to Buddhist texts). According to its adepts, *weikza* knowledge (*weikza pyinnya*) stands alone and distinguishes itself from scientific knowledge (*theikpan pyinnya*) by its lack of predictability. Someone practicing chemistry is certain of getting the same result by repeating the same experiment using the same elements. An alchemical procedure is on the contrary unpredictable, and its success is not repeatable simply through the reproduction of a recipe. But commensurate with how hard *weikza* knowledge is to obtain is how extraordinarily effective it is. Whereas science operates according to a long process of invention, modeling, and fabrication, *weikza* knowledge enables one to satisfy any desire at all, to produce any effect immediately. "The age of mantras (*mandaya khit*) will vanquish the age of machines (*yantaya khit*)," a monk who until recently visited the monastery of Mebaygon often tells his disciples—it is said that he himself has become an accomplished *weikza.* "One day, a piece of straw will be transformable into a wooden log."

In the many-faceted confrontation between science and *weikza* knowledge, particularly memorable is the image of Colonel Mya Maung challenging the four *weikza* by means of modern technology. The protagonist is no longer with us to bear witness, but his story is still told. The Colonel was a faithful disciple of the *weikza* and a proselytizing one. Because of his important position in government—he was at the head of Mandalay Division in the 1960s, before being promoted to minister in the early 1970s—and his tireless activity in the service of the *weikza,* he has become a much-cited figure in the cult, emblematic of its first stage when the *weikza* appeared in the house of Saturday's Son's in-laws, back when he was still a layperson and family man.

Colonel Mya Maung first heard about the *weikza* of Mebaygon after he was named commander of the Forty-Fourth Regiment, based in Minbu. He believed nothing of what was reported to him. He decided to go there himself to test, and confound, the so-called *weikza.* For this purpose he armed himself with a photographic plate of the sort that used to be put in cameras to fix the image. When he got to the Energy Center, the Colonel gave the unused plate to Saturday's Son, who put it on the Buddha altar. A séance followed, with U Pandita preaching through the medium. At the end of the séance, Saturday's Son gave the plate back to the Colonel, who went at once to have it developed in Sagu, the only city in the vicinity where it could be done. On the plate could be discerned an image of U Pandita.

By means of this photographic apparition, U Pandita gave proof of his physical existence, which, at the time of the séance, had been experienced by the Colonel only in a mediated manner and remained, in the eyes of the suspicious military man, only putative, not yet established. U Pandita showed at the same time that the *weikza* were capable of producing the same sort of results as those of modern technology; their power enabled them to create photographs in the absence of a camera, or rather in its place. The *weikza,* in sum, carried out a subversive act: photography, counter to its use for reproducing objective reality, had been used to make the invisible visible, to provide proof of the existence and power of precisely those beings that science, the basis for modern technology, rejects. In other words, science had not only been defeated but it had also been put in the service of the *weikza,* its power domesticated. With cameras' rapid spread in the 1980s, the demonstration found its equivalent in an inverted feat. If, during an appearance in the flesh of the *weikza,* a disciple tried to take a photograph without first having obtained permission to do so, the *weikza* would make sure the camera didn't work. They made the visible invisible in this way and shattered the principle of objective reality. Thus science and modern technology's challenge to the knowledge and power of the *weikza* is constantly reiterated and represented to better emphasize the superiority of the latter.

Notwithstanding, the Colonel continued to experience doubts. After all, he thought, this could be the photograph of an ordinary monk that got passed off as one of U Pandita. He visited all the monasteries in the vicinity to show people the photograph and establish whether there might not be a monk who resembled that person in the image. Only when he found no such monk did he come round to believing.

To the same degree that the apparition of U Pandita on a photographic plate in the absence of a camera strikes Burmese as credible, so does the idea of an official going from monastery to monastery, a photograph in hand, to question their occupants seem unthinkable. Such a procedure does not suit a man of his rank, a man who occupied an eminent position in the region and whom it is hard to imagine making a spectacle of himself in this way. Why does the course of his story now break with the hitherto rather scrupulously followed Aristotelian precept that states, "One should take the impossible that is likely over the possible that is incredible"?[59] We find ourselves no longer in the thick of the story, but rather in a necessary supplement before the expected outcome. What matters is not the content of the story but what it shows. It is no longer a matter of revealing the "objective" foundations of believing, which the wonder of the photograph has already established. What is needed is to emphasize that doubt persists in spite of substantial proof, that conviction is not immediate, that the future believer still resists believing. Only on this condition does his shift take on the dimensions of a conversion, establishing a radical and indissoluble attachment to the *weikza*.

Believing is a difficult phenomenon to measure, quantify, or describe. One can certainly say of a given disciple that he "believes a lot [in the four *weikza*]." Still it remains tricky to delineate a scale of believing. How to express, in these conditions—as the disciples themselves wish to—differences or nuances in the intensity of someone's commitment? How to make it clear that Colonel Mya Maung is not among the common mass of believers, that he is a very special believer? One does so by showing precisely, by means of the episodes of his conversion story, the strength of his original incredulity. His particular place at the center of the cult is determined and justified by this critical element of the drama. Thus it is not only that skepticism is the prior and necessary condition of believing. It is also the case that the initial degree of resistance to believing often indicates the future intensity of believing. Let us listen to the Colonel letting out the believer's last sigh, a while before his sudden death: "Even if the [*weikza's*] monastery were to be left with only one pillar standing [that is, fallen into disrepair due to the disciples' general disaffection], I would continue to revere Saturday's Son."

A number of the *weikza's* disciples keep a copy of the photograph, the first ever "taken" of U Pandita, in their homes. It also figures among those hung on a wall in the hall of the Monastery of Noble Success where the four *weikza* appear today. Not far from it is a photograph in black and white dating from the 1960s of Bodaw Bo Htun Aung standing on the hood of a jeep. Colonel Mya Maung is seated at the wheel in the background. The motif of a *weikza* landing on a vehicle, and remaining standing up or going on ahead of it in its path, recurs in stories about the *weikza's* feats. It constitutes a literal representation of the *weikza's* triumph over modern technology. Major Zaw Win—who served for a time under Colonel Mya Maung's authority and became through his good offices a disciple of the cult—drew my attention to the photograph during a visit to the monastery one October day in 2001. He explained that his superior had wanted to test Bodaw Bo Htun Aung's powers in a different way. Granted, the Colonel had driven at a reduced speed, but he could just as well have floored it. (For the purposes of the photograph, the vehicle was stopped.) On this occasion, the Major added,

Bodaw Bo Htun Aung, dressed in his usual white outfit, had taken on the traits of Saturday's Son, which he said was a customary feat on the part of the mischievous *weikza*: a number of photographs show him with the medium's looks.

In summary, the single law of *weikza* knowledge is that there is no law. As Doctor Sein Yi put it, it is situated "beyond" rational or scientific knowledge, beyond ordinary human comprehension. It is not apprehendable as an independent sphere of knowledge whose principles are amenable to study and decipherment. It exists only in opposition to the ordinary order of reality; it is linked to what is extraordinary (*htukya-, htuzan-*). Like a miracle, defined in the Occidental Christian tradition as a violation of the laws of nature, it can only be described negatively. As a result, a doctor or a man of science actually counts among the most qualified candidates for believing. His understanding of natural laws and his familiarity with examination and diagnosis make him competent to decide whether the facts under consideration lie beyond the possible. Of course, to say—as the believers do—that there is no law in the world of *weikza* enables one to refuse any effort to assign an order and logic to this world. The doubting observations of the incredulous are by that means rendered inconsequential. (How is it possible, some of them ask, for example, that U Kawwida could have carried out his life-prolonging ceremony in 1994—at the age of 1,026—when the maximum life span of a *weikza* prior to this ceremony was held according to widespread understanding within the cult to be 1,000 years?) However, *weikza* knowledge is opposed not only to scientific knowledge but also to magic knowledge (*hmaw pyinna*). In this perspective, science and magic both belong to the same domain, the domain of the mundane, as distinct from *weikza* knowledge.

Now this distinction has a long history. The Burmese term *theikpan*, translated today as "science," derives from the Pali term *sippa*. According to the Pali Text Society dictionary, *sippa* means "art, branch of knowledge, craft."[60] It can be found in many Buddhist texts. *The Book of the Discipline* (*Vinaya*), which discusses monastic rules, draws a distinction between two types of craft (*sippa*): "low crafts," held in lower esteem (pottery, weaving, etc.), and "high crafts" (arithmetic, writing, etc.).[61] In the *Jātaka*, the stories of 550 prior lives of the Buddha, the idea comes up often that a young prince or Brahman has finished his education once he has learned and mastered the Three Vedas and the eighteen "branches of knowledge" (*sippa*).[62] The latter are also called, in translations, the eighteen "sciences" or "accomplishments." No list of them is provided. According to *The Questions of King Milinda*, a dialogue between the Greek king of Bactria, Menander (Milinda in Pali), and the Buddhist monk Nāgasena, "the arts and sciences" (*sippa*) cover "the holy tradition and secular law; the philosophical traditions of Sānkya, Yoga, Nyāya, and Vaiseshika; arithmetic; music; medicine; the four Vedas, Purānas, and the Itihāsas; astronomy, magic, causality and spells; the art of war; poetry; the procedure for the transfer of properties—in a word, all of the nineteen [arts and sciences]."[63]

In these various uses of the term, one fact stands out: *sippa* refers in Buddhist dogma to all transmissible knowledge that can be acquired in a systematic manner, to all techniques that can be used in practical activity and allow someone to earn a living or to work in the world. They can thus be distinguished from knowledge and techniques intended to transcend the world. Supramundane knowledge, declares the *Brahma-gāla Sutta,* rather than learned must be "understood" or "realized," because it "is not to be grasped by mere logic."[64] The entirety of the *Sāmañña-phala Sutta,* a text said to reproduce the words of the Buddha, is built on the opposition between these two orientations. The point of departure is an enumeration by Ajātasattu, king of Magadha, of a list of trades or crafts (*sippa*), from horseman to arithmetician. The sovereign insists on the benefits obtained by individuals who engage in one of these activities and live a householder's existence: "They provide for their own needs, and for those of their parents, of their children, of their friends, in happiness and comfort. They make gifts regularly to ascetics and Brahmans, in order to raise themselves up, gifts that lead to rebirth in heaven, that contribute to happiness, that have felicity as a result."[65] Having made his presentation, Ajātasattu asks the Buddha about the benefits deriving from the way of life that he advocates in contrast: renunciation of the world. The Buddha responds by listing in order the benefits, starting from the most mundane and appealing to the senses—what an individual entering the monastic community gains in status or prestige—to the most supramundane and difficult to perceive. These benefits are the happiness linked to the conduct of a moral life; then accession to various kinds of supranormal knowledge (the possession of supernatural powers, *iddhi,* among them); and finally, the ultimate benefit, realization of the highest and most pleasing kind of knowledge that leads to nirvana.[66]

The Buddhist texts, in sum, designate two different orders of knowledge and accomplishments, opposed to each other and hierarchically arranged: mundane knowledge, which has no link to salvation, and supramundane knowledge, which is the gate of entry to nirvana. The Burmese notion of *theikpan* (*sippa*), taken today to be equivalent to the Western notion of science—covering the domains of physics, electronics, biology, and the like—has always had the same meaning, referring to something that can be taught or learned systematically but that remains little conducive to deliverance. By means of the opposition that they formulate between *weikza* knowledge and scientific knowledge, practitioners of the *weikza* path do much more than react to the trauma caused by the Burmese confrontation with Western modernity (to take up Spiro's thesis once again) or dodge the objections of the skeptical. Assimilating the *weikza*'s knowledge to that leading to nirvana, they reiterate an original distinction, fundamental to the definition and particularization of the religious domain. U Kawwida, head of the four *weikza,* puts it thus: "Today, *weikza* [knowledge] and mundane science (*lawki theikpan*) are rivals. *Weikza* knowledge no longer shines with the same light; science has risen above it. Everyone, from children on up, speak only of science. But let's wait and see if in the future the Buddha's doctrine, that is, *weikza* [knowledge] doesn't come to win out."[67]

I raised the question earlier of how to explain a miraculous cure if neither symbolic effectiveness nor the laws of physiology allow us to understand the phenomenon. How does a miracle happen? The question, all things considered, was poorly stated. In the Burmese context, a religious dynamic hinges on this reversal: a transcendent horizon, nirvana, characterized by its status as an absolute enigma, is capable ultimately of undergirding and orienting the entire social organization. As a consequence, precisely because of its inexplicable nature, a miracle gains its meaning and its value, distinguishing it from both magic and science. A miracle—an incomprehensible, ungraspable, unrepresentable event, whose operation escapes all attempts at explanation or formulation, whether scientific or magic (because a magic fact is, from a certain point of view, amenable to explanation and formulation, such that magic can be transmitted, taught, and practiced)— is indeed best suited to evoke this other reality, inaccessible and mysterious, that Burmese place at the summit of and apart from their world. Whether it consists of resurrecting someone who is almost dead or of a feat such as flying through the air, a miracle is the expression par excellence of the enigmatic logic that structures the Burmese religious order.

IN RETROSPECT: WHAT THE BUDDHA DID[68]

The year 544 before our era (according to Burmese "belief"). The Buddha, en route to Kusinārā, stops at the base of a tree. A traveler named Pukkusa notices him and approaches him; after greeting him, Pukkusa starts to praise the spiritual tranquility of those who have renounced the world. He makes reference to his teacher, Ālāra Kālāma, whose extraordinary power of mental concentration is attested to by this edifying fact: once when five hundred chariots paraded before him, the great man remained impassive, not even noticing the convoy. Such a feat, Pukkusa adds, inspired in him, its witness, an unshakable faith in Āḷāra Kālāma. The Buddha, clearly wishing to affirm his own superiority, replies by upping the ante. On one occasion, when he happened to be in a shabby hut, a storm took it down, killing two people and several beasts. A group of people arrived to take care of the victims. He asked one of them why they had gathered there. For although he had remained awake and conscious, he had not noticed the storm. Hearing this story, Pukkusa, won over by the extraordinary power of the Buddha, repudiates his teacher, Āḷāra Kālāma, and proclaims his faith in the Awakened One:

> "Lord, I reject the lofty powers of Āḷāra Kālāma as if they were blown away by a mighty wind or carried off by a swift stream or river! Excellent, Lord, excellent! It is as if someone were to set up what had been knocked down, or to point out the way to one who had got lost, or to bring an oil lamp into a dark place, so that those with eyes could see what was there. Just so the Blessed Lord has expounded the Dhamma [the law or doctrine] in various ways. And I, Lord, turn for refuge to the Blessed Lord, the Dhamma, and the Sangha [the monastic community]. May the Blessed Lord accept me from this day forth as a lay-follower as long as life shall last!"[69]

Fine. But in the course of this meeting and this dialogue, related in the *Mahā Parinibbāna Sutta,* a famous canonical text that describes the last days, the death, and the funeral of the Buddha, there is no mention of a presentation by the Master of his doctrine. Rather than having "expounded the Dhamma," the Buddha boasted of his powers, in a quite immodest manner at that, and this statement alone sufficed to bring about Pukkusa's conversion. It is later, following the gift made by his new disciple of two robes, that the Buddha delivers a sermon, after which Pukkusa takes his leave. Hence, this commentary of Thomas and Caroline Rhys Davids, eminent figures in Western Buddhology at the beginning of the twentieth century, on the traveler's declaration of faith: "This is a stock phrase constituting the final answer of a hitherto unconverted man at the end of one of those argumentative dialogues by which Gotama overcame opposition or expounded the truth. After a discussion of exalted themes it fits in very appropriately; here and elsewhere it is incongruous and strained."[70]

But what does it mean "to expound the truth," that is, the Teaching? Does the "argumentative dialogue" constitute the only way in which the Buddha or his saintly disciples can make the truth known and his listeners accept it?

Those Western scholars, such as the Rhys Davids, who in the second half of the nineteenth century set about translating and commenting on Pali texts—the ones containing the Buddhist doctrine to which Burmese adhere—discovered descriptions of, among other figures, men who fly.[71] Often, the scholars tended to deny or ignore their existence. They took these prodigious or miraculous feats to be legendary additions made subsequent to the earliest Buddhism. In their view, to an original Buddhism, sober and rational, was progressively superimposed a Buddhism steeped in the extraordinary and the supernatural, a magical Buddhism intended to glorify the Buddha and his teaching and to arouse the adherence of the faithful mass. Out of demagogic necessity, feats and miracles were grafted onto a doctrine that—this was pure conjecture on their part—was intended to be free of them. Buddhist texts were seen to bear the mark of this accretion. The method and final goal of Buddhological work was therefore to isolate the primitive and authentic layer of the religion amid the later additions and adaptations, following a procedure of a stratigraphic nature.

In this perspective, taken up by the sociologist Max Weber, on the supposed historical process in which Buddhism was popularized, the notion of "magic" refers, in a remarkably imprecise way, to all the "popular" practices that Buddhism as a doctrine would reject, but which it was, despite everything, constrained to incorporate in order to become established in society. To survive, Weber conjectures, the monks would have had no choice but to resign themselves to using their supernatural abilities. They would have been forced to satisfy the mundane expectations (good health, prosperity, etc.) of the faithful to assure their own material support. But in the original, "primitive" Buddhism the mechanism of believing would have been of quite a different nature: rational and intellectual. "The typical form of Buddha's teaching," writes Weber in *The Religion of India,* published in 1917,

> is the Socratic dialogue, by which the opponent is led through a considerable argument to a *reductio ad absurdum* and then forced into submission. Neither the short parable, the ironic dismissal, or the pathetic penitential sermon of the Galilean prophet, nor the address resting on visions of the Arabic holy leader find any sort of parallels to the lectures and conversations which seem to have constituted the true form of Buddha's activity. They address themselves purely to the intellect and affected the quiet, sober judgment detached from all internal excitement; their factual manner exhausts the topic always in systematic dialogical fashion.[72]

Weber took his place in a lineage including not only the Rhys Davids but also and above all the eminent German Buddhologist, Hermann Oldenberg, who saw in Buddhism a religion stripped in its essence of all numinous features. "Here and there [in the canonical texts] there is inserted a story of some wonder which rises in no way above the level of quaint and tedious miracles," notes Oldenberg in a classic work of 1882 on the life of the Buddha and his works. The German scholar makes this evaluation after having offered, by way of example of a Buddhist conversion story, the translation of a passage from the *Book of the Discipline* (in Pali, the *Vinaya*). In this episode, the elders of the eighty thousand villages of the kingdom of Magadha are invited by the king, who has just given them an audience treating of mundane affairs, to approach the Buddha to receive his teaching on the matter of transcendental questions. Once in his presence, they lack the attentiveness required to benefit from listening to the words of the Master. The Buddha orders the saintly disciple who is helping him, Sāgata, to execute a series of feats. The disciple raises himself very high in the air, where he walks, stands, sits, lies down, emits smoke and flames, disappears, and reappears. He then prostrates himself at the feet of the Awakened One, saying, "My Master, Sire, is the Exalted One; I am his disciple." The elders are fascinated. "Truly this is glorious," they think to themselves. "Truly it is wonderful: if the disciple is so exceedingly mighty and exceedingly powerful, what will the Master be!" The Buddha then has only to deliver his teaching to them, the episode concluding with their conversion.[73] Now, in the absence of Sāgata's performance, would the visitors have believed in the Master and laid much store by his teaching? Was it therefore justified for the eminent Buddhologist to disqualify men who fly as incarnations of "extravagant creations of a boundless imagination"?[74]

A contemporary of Hermann Oldenberg, Émile Senart, a brilliant and ingenious scholar, started early on to put this way of conceiving Buddhism into question.[75] Still, it fell to Paul Mus, in the 1930s, to give the problem of method in Buddhology its most remarkable formulation. Countering the desiccating approach of Oldenberg and his epigones, which amounted to disfiguring Buddhism by reducing its content to the dimensions of a type of Western philosophical thought of the nineteenth century, Mus meant to restore to the religion its true nature, to "restitute, at the antipodes of scientific objectivity, the magical and religious mentality of the time, in a word [people's] ideas."[76] This restoration took the form of exploring the themes as well as the mental and ritual operations specific to "Indian thought," a fertile field in which, he, like Senart, claimed Buddhism was conceived.

Mus focused on certain feats and miracles pertaining to the Buddha's person or particular points in his teaching, as enacted in the texts or represented in iconography, that he, Mus, took to be modes of symbolic representation. When the Master is described as having taken seven steps immediately after his birth without touching the ground, with lotus flowers or some covering coming between the mundane plane and the physical manifestation of the great person at the behest of the gods, it is his transcendent nature that is figured, suggests Mus.[77] However, to make sense of this figuration, Mus goes on, it does not suffice to claim that the marvelous is a graphic representation of canonical teaching; that the texts, far from catechizing only in an abstract mode, use, along with iconography, a figurative rhetoric by illustrating doctrinal principles with miracles or wonders; and that a commentator must work hard to decode the metaphorical language of the supernatural on the basis of its theological references. That is because, as it happens, symbolism does not reflect the content of dogma in a simple and straightforward manner: it precedes it. Although we find early on, in the Pali texts or in artistic representations, the image of the feat of the seven steps, Mus points out that the principle of the Buddha's transcendence does not receive dogmatic statement until the rise of the Mahayana (Great Vehicle) Schools. So, marvelous facts cannot be taken only as a means of expressing doctrinal ideology. Miracles and wonders do not expatiate, out of a symbolic entailment or pedagogical necessity, on a preexisting theological discourse. Rather, collective representations anticipate dogma, the latter coming to confirm or, on the contrary, attack the former when these have already become established on their own. The extraordinary is not secondary to the doctrinal norm; it prepares for it and lives its own life. According to Mus, there is a very ancient Indian tradition of royalty, identifying the monarch with a god, to which ordinary Buddhists quickly turned to think about and represent to themselves the person of the Buddha, without troubling themselves with conceptual considerations or distinctions.

With Mus, we enter into the Buddhists' imaginary, the intellectual and cultural mainsprings of their representations. In inscribing this imaginary in the *longue durée* of Indian civilization, the brilliant author of *Barabudur* turns away (without freeing himself entirely) from the all too seductive chimera of trying to reconstitute an epic of the historical Buddha and his original teaching, in favor of the study of collective representations and their functioning. When Mus speaks, like Oldenberg, of "imagination," he gives to it and to its operations a fundamental role in the fashioning of the Buddhist religion.[78]

Truth be told, Mus does not always shy away from speculating about the life and work of the Buddha, even if the topic, unresolvable, interests him little.

When he does do so, he supposes that early Buddhism—the Buddha's Buddhism—must have been "relatively unreligious," and consequently he confirms Oldenberg's vision of the person of the Awakened One and of his original teaching: a doctrine of salvation, in Mus's summation, professed by an itinerant spiritual master who "appears to have taught people how to act and think, rather than how to believe or above all how to worship."[79] He reproaches the German Buddhologist only for having confused what we can legitimately suggest, in a hypothetical manner, about the reality of Buddhism at its birth, with what the Pali sources, after the event, tell us about Buddhism: in other words, for having ignored a number of elements at the heart of these sources in order to reduce them to the expression of the austere soteriology at Buddhism's origin.

If we take all their perspectives together, it seems as though the first Western commentators wanted to preserve Buddhism's singularity by refusing to men who fly a primordial place in the religion's origins and development, a religion based ultimately, in the view of each and every one of these scholars, on reason. Anthropologists who study contemporary Buddhism are not in a position to indulge themselves in this way. Men who fly are sometimes just about all their interlocutors have to offer them; men who fly make up the bulk of anthropologists' material. Hard then to give them the slip! Study of the cult of the four *weikza* should thus lead us to question the pertinence of the early Buddhological vision of primitive Buddhism.[80] Anthropologists, *pace* Oldenberg and Mus—both of whom see in the Buddha's transcendence a development subsequent to the Buddha's life, and both of whom, although to different degrees, operate on the basis of an axiom of religious evolutionism that treats the history of Buddhism as the gradual metamorphosis (denaturalization for the one, maturation for the other) of a doctrine into a cult—can instead suggest, on the basis of their observation of Buddhism at work, that it is unthinkable that the Buddha, in his lifetime, would have aspired to show the way to salvation without having at the same time affirmed and construed his transcendence by means of the demonstration of his supernatural powers. The two Buddhologists' sin is a lack of good sense, which is to say, an excess of "imagination"! If the Buddha ever existed, his superhuman character was inherent to his role. To win over his first disciples, the Buddha must have done and must have known what every spiritual founder does and knows from the outset: that he must display his powers and be regarded as extraordinarily potent. Just as much as a rational interpretation of suffering and as an explanation of how to liberate oneself from it, the Master must have offered miraculous relief from suffering in this very world. It was in demonstrating by means of miracles and wonders his capacity to dominate the mundane order that the Buddha could convey the possibility of surpassing this order, of the existence of a supramundane order, and of his capacity to show the way to the latter—saying things with deeds, as it were. Instead of a performative utterance, we have an expressive performance. If language contributes to bringing about reality ("I now pronounce you husband and wife . . ."), a miracle or wonder contributes to expressing a reality that cannot be stated. In the Buddhist context, it is the signifier par excellence of the religious fact.

Such a perspective, suggested by the study of the Burmese cult of the four *weikza,* seems to correspond at least to a degree to that of certain contemporary Buddhologists who distance themselves from their predecessors' representations of Buddhism. If John S. Strong wisely sticks to a Paul Mus–like approach in his recent biography of the Buddha by emphasizing the symbolic relationship of miracles reported in texts to the Master's doctrine,[81] others are happy to let themselves get dragged into committing the much decried sin of speculating about what the historical Buddha could have been and done. Reginald A. Ray, seeing in the life and work of the Buddha as described in texts, a paradigm of Buddhist sainthood, distinguishes various constituent "themes" of this paradigm on the basis of the study of the classic biography of the Buddha attributed to the poet Aśvaghoṣa.[82] Figuring among the thirty-five themes he identifies is the "possession of supernatural powers": "The Buddha, as a result and essential complement of his realization, possesses supernatural powers. . . . As depicted in Aśvaghoṣa's text, the Buddha's supernormal powers are used in service of his compassion, chiefly to teach and convert others."[83] These powers include *iddhi,* a word Ray translates as "magical powers": flying through the air, touching the sun with one's hands, making multiple copies of one's body, and the like.[84] Having determined on the basis of the text the Buddha's paradigmatic qualities, Ray wonders, "How closely does this 'paradigmatic Buddha' correspond to the actual 'Buddha of history'?"[85] To which he responds:

> It may be suggested here—and this is a point that is gaining increasing acceptance in buddhology today—that in approaching Buddha Śākyamuni, it is invalid and finally impossible to separate, as some have tried to do, the man from the myth. Western and modernist notions of a demythologized individuality standing apart from and independent of symbol, cult, and legend have no relevance for the early Buddhist case. Gautama, in his own time and in subsequent times, was able to be the Buddha precisely because he was understood to embody, in an unprecedented way, the cosmic and transcendent. Far from being incidental to

who he was, myth and cult defined his essential person, for his earliest followers as for later Buddhists. Thus we arrive at the seemingly ironic position of affirming that we likely come closest to the historical Buddha precisely when we take the legendary and cultic idiom of his hagiographical tradition most seriously.[86]

Two points spring to mind if we read this programmatic statement in light of what the cult of the four *weikza* has to teach us. First, even as he deems the Buddha's supernatural powers the "result" of his spiritual perfection, and even as he recognizes the importance of these supernatural powers to the Buddha's identity, Ray nonetheless continues to follow a long Buddhological tradition in describing some of these powers (the *iddhi*) as "magic."[87] Yet labeling them in this way does not do justice to the Buddhist distinction between magical potency and mystical potency. The terminological confusion persists even among those scholars who wish to distance themselves from the vision of Buddhism that informs it. Second, despite himself, Ray remains blinkered by a perspective in which the person of the Buddha derives from his disciples' and devotees' cult-based and mythical (or legendary) construction of him, a perspective that fails to grant the Buddha an active role in this construction. More specifically, it isn't merely that supernatural powers are the "result" of the religious figure's spiritual perfection, which is the Buddhist view. It is also the case that the Master's spiritual perfection is the result of his supernatural powers. There is a circular relationship between spiritual perfection and supernatural powers such that demonstrating the latter is indispensable to laying claim to the former, which is otherwise not amenable to proof. It is by means of demonstrating the possession of supernatural powers that individuals prove the credibility of their claims to spiritual perfection, quality that those claims would otherwise lack.

Such a circular relationship between spiritual accomplishment and supernatural powers, which the cult of the four *weikza* makes clear, escapes the attention of another Buddhologist, one who, like Ray, seeks to fill in our representation of the Buddha with material more in keeping with what the Master could have been and could have done. "Surely," writes Donald K. Swearer in his book on the consecration of Buddha images in Thailand, "from the outset the Buddha was venerated as a powerful holy man capable of miraculous feats, not just after Buddhism expanded, became institutionally complex, developed devotional rituals, and embellished stories about the Buddha into a mythology."[88] For Swearer, there is no point in pitting an original Buddha against the Buddha as he is conceived of by today's Buddhists.

The Buddha that emerges through the medium of the image becomes a grantor of boons, and the Buddha's teaching about nonattachment falls victim to an obsessive preoccupation with sacred objects revered for their protective potency and economic value.

Are we, then, witness to two oppositional forms of Buddhism—an "original" monastic worldview of high moral philosophy and spiritual practice versus a thoroughly compromised, if not debased, tradition of magical expectation? Such a dichotomy is the projection of the logical mind uncomfortable with the incongruities within religious thought and practice, and the creation of Buddhist apologists whose relatively narrow view of a nontheistic, rationalistic Buddhism appeals to the modern mind. But the lived tradition of Buddhism, like all classical religions, is not so tidy. It teems with paradox, myth, legend, and symbol not so easily rationalized into a logical system. The seeming oppositions and paradoxes found in the Buddha image consecration ceremony reflect a dialectic at the very core of Buddhism between the ideal of an ultimate personal transformation and the need to address the entire range of life experiences bracketed by birth and death. This dialectic is reflected in distinctions that permeate the tradition between the mundane (*lokiya*) and transmundane (*lokuttara*), and applies to the person of the Buddha himself: human and supernatural, teacher of the *dhamma,* miracle worker, grantor of boons. Indeed, the *Mahāparinibbāna Sutta* incorporates these several views of the Buddha in a single text and exhorts the Buddha's followers not only to honor the *dhamma* but also to venerate the Buddha's bodily remains (*sarīradhātu*).[89]

Although we can only welcome the writer's principled position concerning Buddhism and the person of the Buddha, we must nevertheless ask whether it makes sense to see the Buddha as simply combining "various personae"[90]—"teacher of the *dhamma,* miracle worker, grantor of boons"—or it might instead be more to the point to see these "various personae" as interconnected features of a single "persona." In other words, the link between the mundane and the transmundane (or supramundane) isn't simply a matter of a "dialectic" but rather one of co-construction and coalescence. Manifestations of the Buddha as a grantor of boons are not there simply to satisfy "the need to address the entire range of life experiences bracketed by birth and death." Far from being a simple antithesis or a statement contradicting "the ideal of an ultimate personal transformation," they make this ideal real and creditable—they make the supramundane. Rather than "teem[ing] with paradox, myth, legend, and symbol not so easily rationalized into a logical system," the "lived tradition of Buddhism" displays an unimpeachable logic and rationality.[91]

FLYING MEN, BELIEVING AND THE ANTHROPOLOGIST: AN ULTIMATE ADMISSION OF INCOMPETENCE

For at least 2,500 years—that is, since the Buddha's time—the *weikza* tell us, the drama of believing, bound up with the question of salvation, has been mounted and repeated, and their monastery, located though it may be in an anonymous village in Central Burma, is one of the places where its contemporary staging takes place. Lending an ear to their truth, taking at their word these beings who identify themselves with the Buddha, we have been able to recover, little by little, the full significance of that extraordinary incident: Bodaw Bo Htun Aung's apparition flying in the air, an expression of the *weikza*'s supramundane character and his superiority over the magic and scientific orders. Thanks to them, we have been able to recognize in men who fly one of the foundations of Buddhism since the time of its origin, and thereby helped banish the idea of a Buddhist exception on the subject of the supernatural. The latter idea, however, is not only linked to the history of the West's relation to this religion, which some have wished to erect as a model of reason (which means, paradoxically, that putting Buddhism in a different light amounts to reducing its alterity and strangeness). The responsibility for it also rests in part with Theravadin Buddhists. Although they have always recognized the place of believing in their religious attitude, they have also worked to create and maintain the illusion that believing was of secondary importance in, if not absent from, their religion. At the same time that they have defined Buddhism and the sciences as distinct and hierarchically ordered forms of knowledge, they have emphasized the supposedly rational, if not scientific, nature of Buddhism. At the same time that they have scattered men who fly into their stories, they have made it possible for the scholar to ignore them. "True" Buddhists, the Theravadin Buddhists tell us, know nothing of believing. Rather, they study, they practice, they discover, they realize. Nevertheless, the Theravadin Buddhists also inform us that the same Buddhists have a thirst for "the huge." They ask not only to understand but also to believe. They are therefore ready to let themselves be carried into an alternative order of reality or, more exactly, to an order that contradicts ordinary reality or goes beyond it; it is an order of the extraordinary—an order at the heart of which the notion of objective reality turns out not to apply. In the domain of believing, there exist multiple realities, realities that cannot and must not be universally shared. To conclude that the logic of believing immunizes the phenomenon against skepticism would come down to reducing the believer's argument to a simple defense mechanism, when it is an entire discourse on fate and election that is actually put into play, an entire exercise of differentiation and individualization that operates beyond beliefs. When a person appears on a street corner, anyone in the vicinity can see that individual. But when Bodaw Bo Htun Aung appeared in the sky that day in 1998, only Yan Shin and his family saw him, not the others seated in the back of the little van.

But let us not fool ourselves. Although it appears that we have covered a certain distance from our point of departure, the anthropologist remains incapable, in the end, of getting access to the extraordinary; he remains stymied. He is still unaware of how to believe. No matter if Bodaw Bo Htun Aung flew into the monastery from several sides at the same time, if relics proliferated infinitely in perfume bottles, even if the *weikza* worked still more extraordinary wonders, the anthropologist's attitude would remain the same. Therein lies no doubt the strange, if not to say tragic, condition of the anthropologist: he observes, he studies, he draws conclusions, but he is incapable of believing and as a consequence he does not act, condemned to live vicariously, through the lives of others. Is his quest motivated by an intellectual wish to understand believing or by the need to make up for its absence?

2 Being a Disciple, Fashioning a Cult

A DISCIPLE AND HIS PARAPHERNALIA

Sunday, August 24, 2003, 5:00 a.m. The driver and I enter the yard in our car, in the middle of one of the capital's residential areas, not far from Inya Lake. It is still dark. A faint light can be seen in the front room. Major Zaw Win is waiting, ready to go.

"The Buddha has succeeded!" Stepping jauntily, despite his seventy-seven years, into the car, the disciple pronounces the four *weikza*'s motto and then comments to me, "It's our passport for the trip." Wearing a cloth skirt (*longyi*) and a thick yellow shirt over a sweater, he is wearing his customary faded gray Bireley's cloth cap. Around his neck hangs a string made up of 108 prayer beads. It was given to him by the chief of the four *weikza*, U Kawwida, in 1967. It was the Major's first meeting with the *weikza* or, more precisely, with their medium. The latter was staying in Mandalay, and Colonel Mya Maung had invited the Major and his wife to attend a séance. On the appointed day, the couple took a car to the Colonel's official residence, located within the walls of the former royal palace of Mandalay. The vehicle had just stopped at the steps in front of the house when some coins suddenly fell on the car's roof. The Major got hold of two twenty-five-cent coins. Their host, having come down to greet them, invited them up to the first floor. There, in front of the Buddha altar, stood a man of about the same age as the Major (who was forty-one) with short hair, wearing a turban: he was Saturday's Son (at that time still a layperson). There were a fair number of people in attendance. "Let's invite the *weikza!*" the medium soon said. He turned toward the altar and prostrated himself before the Buddha, his hands clasped together in a gesture of homage. Suddenly his turban fell off. He turned back to the audience. A *weikza* had possessed him and was greeting the Colonel. It was U Kawwida. "Major Zaw Win, how are you doing?" asked the *weikza* before telling the visitor to come closer. Under the control of U Kawwida, Saturday's Son took off from around his neck a string of 108 wicker prayer beads, new in appearance, that the Major had not noticed until then. He gave it to him while the *weikza,* speaking through his intermediary, said, "Do not give, sell, or exchange these precious prayer beads under any circumstances. Disciple, the more you practice meditation using these beads, the more they will shine, and you will slowly discover the power of these prayer beads."

Soon after, a golden ring set with an energy ball popped out of the mouth of the medium, who took it in his hand. U Kawwida called to the Major's wife. "Try it on," he ordered her. "If it doesn't fit, give it back to me. Avoid wearing it when you go to impure places [the toilet] but otherwise keep it with you always! This ring provides protection from all dangers, even from bad karma of ineluctable consequences [*upithsaydaka kan,* which provokes violent death]." The Major's wife put the ring on her finger. It fit perfectly.

U Kawwida then delivered a long sermon: he invoked the Buddha, his Teaching, and the Community of Monks. Members of the audience donated money, robes, incense sticks, and candles and asked for the *weikza*'s help—some for the fulfillment of a wish, some for the solution to a problem. "Venerable, accept me as a close disciple (*dabyi ayin akhya*)," begged the Major for his part. The term *ayin akhya* names a blood relation (a biological son as opposed to an adoptive one) and so indicates, by extension, proximity or intimacy among individuals. The four *weikza* could from then on make use of the Major as they wished. The new disciple had, in his own words, "entrusted his body to the *weikza*"; he had entrusted his life to them as a gift.

According to U Kawwida, the Major's string of prayer beads, similar to ones he still hands out to people on the occasion of his appearances, contains remarkable powers. In the case of an evil spell (*payawga*), it suffices to use it to encircle the victim's head to break the spell's effects. If a baby cries ceaselessly, sprinkling the infant with water poured over the prayer beads will chase away the supposed assailant, often a ghost (*thaye*). When traveling through an unsafe area, twirling the prayer beads in the air while reciting the formula of the Nine Supreme Qualities of the Buddha immunizes one against danger.[1] The Major takes this string of prayer beads with him whenever he goes on a trip to protect himself from whatever mishap might befall him. He recites the beads, too, when practicing meditation. (Reciting one's prayer beads is one of the most common forms of meditation practice in that it allows one to attain a certain degree of mental concentration.) Not every day, however. To these prayer beads are allotted Monday, the birthday of the chief of the four *weikza,* and Sunday, the day of success, because it refers, according to the Burmese system of correspondences, to the letter *a,* the same one with which the verb *aung,* "to succeed," is written.[2] On Tuesday and Thursday, the days of his birth and that of U Pandita, respectively, the Major practices with a second set of prayer beads given to him by U Pandita. A third set, presented to him by Bodaw Bo Htun Aung, is for use on Saturday, the birthday of this *weikza,* and on Wednesday, a day considered in Burmese astrology to be linked to Saturday. For Friday, finally, is reserved a fourth and final set, purchased on a recent pilgrimage to Bodhgaya, the site of the Buddha's Awakening.

Thus the Major's devotional time is arranged in a weekly cycle relating to the greatest of the *weikza* (the Buddha), to three of the four *weikza* of Mebaygon, and to himself. This cycle, uniting him to the figures of the Master and his stand-ins, reflects his personal fate's inscription in the Buddhist order and makes apparent his ultimate aspiration, the horizon of a disciple's long career: to become a *weikza* and attain nirvana. The Major's aspiration receives daily expression by pairing the shifts entailed by linking the days of the week to different prayer beads with the unchanging formula he repeats in every instance. For no matter which string of beads he uses or on which day, the formula the disciple recites as he moves one bead after another through his fingers remains the same: "In paying homage to the Buddha, called the Perfect One, may I attain success!" A combination of Burmese and Pali terms, this formula was taught him by U Pandita. Still, the realities of life have to be taken into account. The family home is full of activity. Most of the Major's children, some of them married and with children of their own, live with him. It is often difficult for this disciple, who is much in demand, to apply himself to the saying of his beads. He contents himself, at such times, with murmuring this formula or one of the Buddha's eleven great discourses (*payeik*) while he is being driven somewhere in a car.[3] In this way, at least his mind doesn't err, and no negative thought, a source of bad karma, arises.

A ring sits on one of the Major's fingers. He wears it on his right hand. When he eats (which is done with the right hand), he puts it temporarily on a finger of his left hand (impure because it is used to clean oneself after defecating). The "jewel" set in the ring consists of a small metallic ball, like the ring, of a dark yellow color: this ball of energy (*datlon*) was made by the *weikza* using an alchemical process applied to mercury, one of the noblest of metals but also one of the most difficult to manage. The Major received the ring from U Pandita, a *weikza* with whom his family is specially connected: the Major's wife, who died three months ago, was the mother of the future *weikza* in a previous life. The ring figures among the amulets the *weikza* produce for their disciples with the aim of supporting their well-being and their personal success. These amulets are termed *asaung* in Burmese, "guard, keeper, watchman." When the Major is unoccupied, he takes the ring off his finger without thinking and rubs it and the ball with his fingers in a compulsive gesture. The more brightly the ring shines, the more potent it is thought to be, the ball of mercury producing a greater protective and beneficent energy. The work of making the object effective that the *weikza* started is carried on by this regular rubbing on the part of the Major. And this ceaseless rubbing is not without resemblance to the action of passing the prayer beads through his fingers to accompany a recitation that is also intended to foster success. These are intensely tactile activities that one can hardly fail to recognize: rubbing, polishing, touching, and tapping are just so many gestures that follow from a science of power in which the *weikza* and their disciples are deeply enmeshed, the science of the production and transmission of success energy (*aung dat*).

The Major's equipment is not confined to these two tangible elements, prayer beads and ring. These elements are complemented by several other, invisible ones. The entire set makes up a sophisticated panoply that is an integral part of his person, constituting a shell at once protective, discursive, and distinctive: at the same time that it functions as a shield, the disciple's equipment materializes, condenses, and recounts his relationship with the four *weikza* and their medium.

Were one to continue to make an inventory of the Major's gear, one would find in his wallet little laminated photographs of the four *weikza,* pictured individually, along with a small plastic packet containing a sheet of copper, with rounded corners, measuring about three centimeters by three. Cabalistic diagrams (*in*) are inscribed on both sides of the copper sheet. On one side is the standard diagram: a square with four boxes, and one letter (*sa, da, ba,* or *wa*) written in each one of them. According to the Major, each letter is the first in one of the four lines of a Pali verse that he glosses as follows: "(*sa*) The Buddha possesses the power to see into the future or for thousands of kilometers in space. (*da*) The teaching preached by the Buddha can bring peace of mind and makes it possible to obtain nirvana. (*ba*) The strength of the Buddha is equivalent to ten times the strength of the king of the elephants, Hsaddan [an incarnation of the future Buddha Gotama featured in one of the stories of his previous lives]. (*wa*) May the Buddha grant me all of his strength and his protection!" The Major has not come by this verse from the *weikza;* he has instead drawn it from Buddhist writings and works on the *weikza* path. On the other side of the copper sheet, a diagram made of intertwined letters traces the Pali word *arahan,* "the Perfect One," an epithet of the Buddha. The Major owns a second copper sheet, identical to this one, that he keeps on his domestic altar. One was given to him by U Pandita, the other by U Kawwida—he doesn't remember which came from whom.

Also to be found in his wallet are two minuscule statuettes of the holy Shin Thiwali, given to him by the *weikza*. Shin Thiwali is a disciple of the Buddha, famous for his ability to attract offerings. He is venerated as a patron both of abundance and of good fortune (*lat kaung-*).[4] The first statuette, which is two centimeters high, is made out of bamboo. The second, a little over one centimeter, is carved out of a black wood used in the making of charms (*thitka, Pentace burmanica*).

The crucial element in this portable collection of a man who has, let us be clear, nothing of the eccentric about him, is the Major's ball of energy. It is about the size of a large marble. When he takes it out of his house, he wraps it up in cotton (to prevent scratching), then puts it inside a small, opaque plastic container. The container is attached to a strap, also made of plastic, the sturdiest of materials, which he hangs around his neck. This pendant of a special sort is then hidden beneath his shirt.

The Major's ball is unusual inasmuch as it is not the product of an ordinary alchemical process. For a long time, the Major was not interested in alchemy. In the late 1980s, his older brother and he decided to try their hands at it. Alchemy is the most common and most respected means for becoming a *weikza* or for obtaining certain of the extraordinary powers (*theikdi*) characteristic of *weikza*: to be invulnerable, to be able to transform metals into gold, to live without drinking or eating, to walk on water, to fly, and, of course, to prolong one's life.[5] Three of the four *weikza* of Mebaygon have attained their condition—have "succeeded" (*aung-*, or *theikdi pauk-*)—through alchemy. Many disciples try hard to follow in their footsteps. They work to increase the potency of their ball, engaging in alchemical practices at home or at the Mebaygon monastery when they get the chance. The Mebaygon monastery is a good place for alchemical pursuits. It is pervaded by the energy of success produced and spread by the *weikza*. Isn't it called the "Energy Monastery" (Dat Kyaung), and its outbuilding the "Site of Success" (Pauk Chaung)? People also speak of the "Energy Center" (Dat Zakhan), where communication with the *weikza* takes place. The monastery is the prime place of localization, of manifestation, and of distribution of the four *weikza*'s energy (*dat*). Let us therefore abandon the Major for a moment and, like a *weikza*, transport ourselves to the place where the energy of success is given and received, in order to learn a bit more about these curious balls and the art of their making.

A REFUGE FROM THE BITTERNESS OF THE WORLD

The monastery is pleasant at this time. During the monastic season of retreat, from July until October, the *weikza,* three of whom are monks, do not in principle make any appearances. They remain in their invisible and fabulous realm, Dragoness Mountain, where they devote themselves to meditation and alchemy. Their medium, Saturday's Son, spends the season of retreat in a monastery in Mandalay. Thus for a quarter of the year, "the Energy Center is closed," according to the standard expression, and visitors are quite rare.

Most of the sixteen monks who live at the monastery, some in the Dat Kyaung, some at the Pauk Chaung, do not practice alchemy. (Nor do the three nuns. Alchemy is a manly skill, in keeping with the idea that only men are susceptible of attaining a high degree of spiritual accomplishment, which is what success in alchemy implies and demonstrates.) They display no interest in the *weikza* path and say so without hesitation. Often having taken on the robe at an advanced age, between fifty and seventy, they have not, for that matter, obtained the kind of religious education that would allow them to take on some of the duties that fall to a monk (rituals, sermonizing, and teaching). Most of them former workers in the oil fields of Minbu, where the village of Mebaygon is located, they have simply and unceremoniously taken themselves out of the world and its bitterness, but not without having paid it tribute by way of suffering, sometimes heavily. They consider it time to ensure themselves a satisfying rebirth, either as a human or in one of the gods' heavens, thanks to the merit that their religious life and their contribution to the *weikza*'s work should produce. Furthermore, the monastic robe is potent: wearing it protects you. It attenuates the ravages of fate that befall some people who, victims of an evil spell cast by some envious person, suffer personality disorders or repeated misfortune. For these men of little standing, the *weikza*'s monastery is a safe harbor. They benefit by a sort of right of asylum in exchange for guarding one of the many buildings in the two compounds, which fill up once a year, at the time of the celebration of the Festival of Success, held at the full moon of Dabodwe, sometime in February.

If these disciples do not play a prominent role in the cult's activities and do not seek one, their presence at the Energy Center is not without import. It is significant that Bodaw Bo Htun Aung's entrance on the scene, opening every séance in which the *weikza* appear, takes place during the collective recitation that, at this monastery as at all the others in Burma, gathers the religious residents together every evening about 7:30 or 8:00 p.m. Seated in the space reserved for them—an alcove, slightly raised, at the front of the hall in front of the altar to the Buddha—the monks chant several classic texts from the Buddhist corpus, always the same ones, without pause for a half-hour. The start of their recitation signals the imminent arrival of Bodaw Bo Htun Aung. Visitors must come upstairs and sit in the hall to attend the séance. Those who are unaware of the rule or choose to ignore it to spy on the *weikza*'s coming are pressured by lay assistants to rejoin the assembly. Bodaw Bo Htun Aung's sudden appearance in the window on the left side of the alcove does not interrupt the recitation. The *weikza* waits until it is finished before starting to speak. He remains silent, close to the window, takes a seat in one of the preacher's chairs, or circulates among the members of the audience to transmit to them energy of success by slapping them on the head and back. Once they have finished their duty, the monks remain in place. Theoretically as affected as the visitors by the *weikza*'s teaching, they stay there until the end of the séance. They would be easily forgotten, what with the darkness in the hall and the row of preacher's chairs that form a screen as long as attention is focused on the *weikza,* were it not for Bodaw Bo Htun Aung or U Pandita addressing them at intervals, putting a question to one of them, remonstrating another, or asking for their collective assent. After an hour or an hour and a half, the average time a séance lasts and the last *weikza* leaves, the monks, who have not budged, observe a brief rite of reciprocal absolution, a standard procedure. Each one of them speaking in a low voice to a colleague of greater seniority, they ask that minor infractions of monastic discipline committed during the day past be erased. The moment at which, this act accomplished, they stand up and leave the hall marks the end of the séance, allowing the public to disperse.

The séance plays out in front of the monastic community formally gathered together, and it begins and ends with two emblematic ritual manifestations of this community. The monks fulfill the modest but necessary function of extras. They represent the monastic community in the midst of the cult and attest thereby that all of this takes place, without the slightest possible doubt, in a monastery, no matter how unusual the activity may be, and that the cult as a consequence concerns the ongoing development of Buddhism and Buddhists, no matter what the skeptics say. They assume this walk-on part with neither regret nor irritation. Knowing themselves to be, and wishing themselves to be, ordinary men, they aspire to nothing more. Their situation nevertheless appears doubly paradoxical. While having them live in the world of *weikza* in a troubling manner—they live in the midst of it but declare themselves indifferent to it, and some even seem not to believe in these *weikza*—they are passed off as something they aren't quite, if one considers their minimal religious competence. We will make no further acquaintance of them, willingly granting them what little they seek—anonymity and peace.

THE ART OF SELF-FASHIONING

There are other people at the monastery, however, both monks and laypeople, who have come there not just to arrange for a good rebirth or in search of a retreat but also and above all in a quest for energy of success.[6] They do not balk in the slightest at our intrusion in their lives, quite the contrary. Among them is the most obsessed of these disciples, whom we find patching up his alchemist's bellows. It must be said that the tool has come in for rough treatment, because of the intensive use to which it has been put as a result of the man's grand ambition: to become a *weikza*. The monk willingly stops his work when he sees our interest in what he is doing, taking up in passing a wrinkled old cigarette and drawing a big breath without thinking to light it. His ordination name, U Thakkara, is rarely used at the monastery, where many are identified and named according to the name of their place of origin or their ethnic group, a common practice that nonetheless makes the population of the Energy Center a microcosm, although incomplete, of the nation as a whole. Here he is known as Monk Taungtha, after the name of his natal town, near Myingyan in Mandalay Division, and sometimes also as Monk Thamanya, after the name of a famous religious site in Kayin State where he donned the robe and lived before coming to take up residence in Mebaygon. The man is as thin as a rail. Already a vegetarian, he stopped eating rice, the basic component of the Burmese diet, two years ago. He eats noodles, vegetables, and fruit. By means of this ascetic regimen, Monk Taungtha aims to acquire one of the typical abilities of *weikza,* the capacity to live without eating or drinking (*ahara theikdi*).

His lodging is a small, one-room building, built in the southwest corner of the paved yard that surrounds U Pandita's cave, at the Site of Success. The "cave" (*gu*) in question consists of a square building inside which U Pandita underwent the trial by fire in 1975. This area of the yard, defined by a wall, marks approximately the space where the disciples took up positions during the ceremony. Under no circumstances were they to leave this space, at the risk otherwise of causing the failure of the whole undertaking and bringing about everyone's death, including that of the *weikza*. Other life-prolonging ceremonies have taken place at the Site of Success, for U Oktamagyaw in 1989 and for U Kawwida in 1994, each one requiring the construction of a new "cave," and buildings have sprung up around them. But U Pandita's cave remains the high point of the cult, the epicenter of the formidable energy that emanates from the *weikza*. The place, "a success ground" (*aung myay*), is propitious for the practice of alchemy, as is, more generally, the whole complex made up by the Energy Monastery and the Site of Success.

But what a difficult and uncertain practice! It is demanding and thankless as well. Monk Taungtha himself says so—and he speaks from experience. It has been nine years since he renounced the world, tiring of his bachelor's life as the driver of his family's transport vehicle. He was thirty-one at the time, he tells us, and was weary of the lay condition where all is thirst, an infinite and senseless race for the still better, a rage for still more—the curse of desire and its permanent dissatisfaction from which no one escapes, even if he is the most powerful man in the country and so in principle the one whose desires are most fully satisfied. Becoming a monk meant ceasing to race, living day to day, relaxing the taut rope of desire. So speaks Monk Taungtha, although minus the literary affectation of the above, which must be blamed on the author's reflexes. But hardly had he loosened the ties that bound him to this entangling world when he embarked on a new and still more all-consuming quest. An ironic reversal? No, because in the eyes of this man who discovered alchemy shortly after his ordination, at first as an interested observer before throwing himself into it heart and soul, it is no longer a question of thirst but rather of aspiration; no longer a question of unassuageable desire, but rather of accomplishment. To speak of a wish to become a *weikza* in terms of desire would be to mistake the true nature of the endeavor, which is to approach nirvana, the realm where desire disappears and, with it, suffering. We should be clear: the man knows that he is a very long way from his goal, and in the end he doesn't care much about being so far away. The quest for nirvana is not a matter of waiting and contemplating the world, but rather the basis of and yardstick for action.

Even though alchemy is an instrument of salvation, only a small number of individuals—at most a few laymen or monks per village or urban neighborhood, and invariably male—actually enter into its complicated time- and wealth-consuming pursuits. Yet these people's fervor and determination are startling. Furthermore, despite the limited number of its practitioners, it turns out that almost all Burmese are familiar with alchemy. Although the history of its first appearance and subsequent development in the country is unknown, Burmese date its practice as far back as the medieval kingdom of Bagan, which they consider foundational to both Burma and Burmeseness. In this way, alchemy is inscribed among the sources of Burmese Buddhist civilization.[7]

Monk Taungtha makes his first steps as an alchemist in a monastery at Thamanya, where he works under the guidance of an older, experienced monk who has nevertheless not yet "succeeded" (*aung-*). He must begin by making a "*dat* ball" (*datlon, dat* naming a material or the energy that it contains, *lon* labeling objects of a round shape). This metallic object constitutes the material starting point of alchemical work. Monk Taungtha wants a ball of mercury (*byada-lon*), more precisely a ball made up primarily of mercury, which is the usual type of ball used by alchemists. An iron ball (*than-lon*) also makes it possible—but with greater difficulty—to reach the *weikza* state because, an alchemist explained to me, iron contains a good deal of mercury. Other metals, such as copper, lead, silver, and zinc, are also used, whether singly or in combination, to make balls. However, these balls would contain very little mercury. Once an alchemist has worked to fashion such relatively weak balls, they are put to use as amulets (*asaung*) worn on the body, usually on the finger or neck, as protective objects. Otherwise, these combinations of metals may be used to make gold. The "path of gold" (*shwe lan*), as opposed to the "path of amulets" (*asaung lan*) and the "exit path" (*htwetyat lan*) or "path of extraordinary powers" (*theikdi lan*), which leads to the *weikza* state, arouses both scorn and fascination. As the "eating path" (*sa lan*), it signals a desire for wealth, a major obstacle to the quest for nirvana. Those Burmese seeking to disqualify the practice of alchemy as a way to reach salvation will state that alchemists are really only interested in making gold. Still, the path of gold appeals to many. These various alchemical paths, although ordered hierarchically, are actually more complementary than mutually exclusive. The same person might practice several of them, and achieving success in the most elevated, most difficult, path would mean enjoying mastery of the others: such a person would be able to make both gold and potent amulets. Someone believed to have become a *weikza* or his disciples may thus claim that he can make gold and may even attempt to demonstrate it concretely to claim success.

Monk Taungtha first prepares an alloy of lead, silver, and bismuth. Putting this mixture in contact with liquid mercury causes the mercury to solidify. Referring to the transformation that it causes, this alloy is called *htun,* a substantive derived from the verb and spelled the same way, labeling a change in property or state. It is said that, by this means, "the *dat* changes" (*dat pyaung-*): the mercury's material or structure is modified.

The alloy is prepared in a utensil essential to the practice of alchemy, the *lon,* a crucible of white clay in the shape of a thick pipe with a bulging end and a separate cover. It is in this type of receptacle that alchemists put their ball to submit it to fire's effects: the so-called ball is not therefore round, but rather flat on top and rounded below, molded after melting to the crucible's shape. (There is no standard size for a ball. The flat top of a ball measures, as a general rule, between five millimeters and two centimeters.) Producing crucibles is in itself quite a complicated matter. Their makers offer as many as nineteen different models, numbered in ascending order of size from zero to eighteen. The most common series stops at twelve. The standardization is far from perfect, with the same model number corresponding to different sizes from one manufacturer to another. To select the crucible best suited to the size of their ball and to the planned procedure, alchemists go by their own visual estimate as much as by the number written on the outer surface of a crucible. The covers are sold separately: they do not always fit snugly the crucibles for which they are intended. These tools, crucibles and covers alike, are available in shops selling Burmese medicines and in goldsmiths' shops, the other realm of activity in which such tools are called for. There are no shops dedicated to the sale of alchemical materials.

Monk Taungtha coats the crucible with a layer of mud, soil with adhesive properties from a termite mound mixed with water. The heat of the hearth will harden this covering and protect the crucible from direct contact with the fire, which might otherwise break it. Once the crucible is ready, the monk inserts eighty grams of lead, sixteen grams of silver, and sixteen grams of bismuth. He puts the cover on it. The latter remains accessible and removable; it can be removed to observe what degree of fusion has been obtained and, if necessary, to add ingredients in the course of alchemical operations. (If no other ingredients need to be added, the alchemist works with a "closed crucible" (*lon peik*), the crucible and its top being covered with mud.) Monk Taungtha puts the crucible in the middle of a terra cotta hearth. The hearth, which has the appearance of a pail with thick sides, is connected with a tube to a manual bellows. Air enters the hearth through either one or four holes. The crucible is positioned relative to the air vents in varying ways, as a function of the degree of heat one wishes to apply to its contents. Three positions are possible, depending on whether the jets of air are directed at the base, the middle, or the top of the crucible, with the heat diminishing in each case. They are named the "fire that hits the butt" (*hpin taik mi*), the "fire that hits the waist" (*kha taik mi*), and "the fire's flame" (*mi shan mi*).

Alchemy is first and foremost an art of fire. According to some of its practitioners, its name, *aggiyat pyinnya,* means "the science of the art of fire" (*aggi,* derived from Pali, means "fire," *yat* an "art," and *pyinnya* a "science," a kind of knowledge or expertise).[8] Even if interpretations vary as to the exact meaning of different expressions linked to alchemical practice, fire is always at the heart of its conceptualization. "To engage in alchemy" can be expressed in at least three ways: "to practice the art of fire" (*aggiyat hto-*), although some people translate the phrase as "to blow on the fire" (*hto-* being a verb with many definitions); "to work the bellows" (*hpo hto-*), with reference to the alchemist's prototypical gesture, this phrase also being sometimes translated as "to blow on the fire" (*hpo* naming both the bellows and the hearth and, by metonymic extension, the fire); and finally, "to play with fire" (*mi kaza-*), as others play with cards or checkers (*mi* is the Burmese synonym of the Pali *aggi*). To know and understand fire—to know how to interpret the color of its flame, to regulate its intensity, and to decide how long to use it—is the alchemist's primary skill. Monk Taungtha will soon learn this the hard way.

Preparing an alloy, however, requires no precautions or competence in handling fire. It is enough to melt down and bind the alloy's component elements to each other. After the crucible is placed in the middle of the hearth (stood upright on a pile of ashes) and the charcoal poured in, the fire is lit and then stoked with the bellows. Several hearthfuls of charcoal are consumed before reaching the temperature at which the metals can be fused. From time to time, with the help of long tongs, Monk Taungtha removes the lid to take a look. When the metals have been fused together, he takes the crucible out of the brazier and pours its contents into a small bowl. The alloy, which solidifies, must remain slightly warm and a little soft. Monk Taungtha works a well into its center and pours into it sixteen grams of heated mercury. The mercury, on contact with the alloy, absorbs some of its elements. It cools and becomes firmer. All that remains to do is to scrape it free and reclaim it.

There would be no point asking either Burmese alchemists, Monk Taungtha included, or this anthropologist about the chemical principle that makes mercury solidify in this process. The alchemists know the procedure—there are a number of others—but not the atomic reaction it brings about, to which they are in any case indifferent. The anthropologist is out of his depth. As a matter of fact, until he undertook the practice and study of Burmese alchemy, he was unaware that mercury—the only metal that is liquid in its normal state—is theoretically impossible to make solid (unless placed at −39°C)—that doing so, in other words, goes against nature and is fairly extraordinary. But what is at issue here is not whether the practice of alchemy is based in part on the laws of chemistry and whether it should be understood as a proto-science. Our purpose is rather to understand alchemy in Burmese terms, in the language of its practitioners. This language stands as the antithesis of abstract scientific formulas. The keywords are instead life and death or, more precisely, death and life. What is a Burmese alchemist actually hoping to achieve? He endeavors, through a long process of his ball's transformation, to make of it "dead matter" (*dat thay-*): the ball should become so strong and so resistant that its weight suffers no alteration, no matter how high the heat to which it is subjected—this despite the fact that it is in the nature of mercury to evaporate easily. Once he has succeeded in this first step, the alchemist then strives to "revivify" (*pyan shin-*) the ball. He will obtain at the end of this process a "ball of living mercury" (*byada-shin-lon*), which grants its possessor access to the *weikza* state and, with this access, the certainty that he will arrive, eventually, at nirvana. To put it another way, the ball must escape the law of change and impermanence that conditions all existence and attain eternal life, perfect and all powerful. The ball must pass through a death that is one only in name—but this name in itself indicates how necessary the passage is—in order to get beyond it and accede to an exceptional durability and force.

After the preliminary stage of the ball's creation has been completed, the long and difficult process begins of transforming the material to bring about its "death." Acutely aware of the nature of their quest, practitioners compare this progression toward "death" to the process of life, indeed of human maturation. They invoke the image either of gestation in the womb (from a shapeless fetus to a fully constituted baby) or of a child's growth (from birth to adulthood) or of the entire course of a life (from conception through adulthood by way of birth). A ball whose material is dead—that is, no longer negatively affected by exposure to fire—is deemed "ripe" (*yin-*). The metaphors and terms that practitioners use indicate that the ball is seen as a living being whose development must be fostered.

This development implies not only maturation but also purification (*than-sin-, hpyusin-*). The ball must be rid of the metallic elements that have been mixed with it in order to obtain a mercury that is at once solid and "pure" (*sinkye-*). The ball must be purified, say some alchemists, just as individuals wishing to attain spiritual perfection (enlightenment) must strive through meditation to eliminate the mental impurities that stand in the way of their quest. Thus, the elements mixed in with the mercury are sometimes called *mala,* a term derived from Pali, naming the three principal sources of mental defilement (greed, hatred, and delusion). In fact, the two processes, purification of the ball and purification of the individual, are often assimilated: the practice of alchemy is taken to be a form of Buddhist meditation. This is all the more significant because the practice of meditation is said to be, in addition to the strict adherence to Buddhist precepts of morality, a condition for succeeding in alchemy and attaining the *weikza* state. More precisely, it is concentration meditation (*thamahta*), supposed to produce extraordinary powers through mental absorption and purification, rather than insight meditation (*wipathana*), supposed to lead to enlightenment through the understanding of the three marks of all existence (impermanence, suffering, and selflessness), that is linked to alchemy and the *weikza* path. Just as someone practicing concentration meditation (*thamahta*) fixes attention on an object or phenomenon or endlessly repeats a single phrase in order to become oblivious to the enticements of the outside world, so the alchemist fixes his attention on one aspect of his activities. This may be the fire in the hearth, in a procedure evocative of the meditative technique of concentrating on fire (*mi kathaing*). Or it may be the movement of the bellows, resembling the process of breathing (inhalation and exhalation) that lies at the heart of one of the most common Burmese meditative techniques. Ideally, then, alchemy brings about an individual's purification much as meditation does, at the same time as it purifies the ball's material. Furthermore, the two processes, spiritual for the alchemist and physical for his ball, are linked. On the one hand, someone who can "catch his mind" (*seik hpan-*)—that is, control his senses and his desires—has no difficulty, according to alchemists, "catching material" (*dat hpan-*): mastering the alchemical process and preventing the mercury's evaporation. On the other hand, the fact that alchemy constitutes a meditative technique enables its practitioner to obtain a certain degree of mental concentration (*thamadi*), such that he releases a kind of force that is conveyed to the ball like a wave. This force, produced by the alchemist's spiritual condition, increases his ball's power.

Fire lies at the heart of the dual process of the ball's maturation and purification. Subjecting the ball to fire means instilling it (*thwin-*) with the specific energy that fire releases. Heat (*tayzaw dat*), literally, "fire's property" or "fire's energy," penetrates the ball and strengthens it (*in-a hpyay-*). It increases its material resistance while enhancing its "potency," its "efficacy" (*aswan* or *anithin*). The procedure is not without risk. Instead of strengthening the ball, excessive heat can cause the mercury to escape or evaporate (*dat htwet-*, "the *dat* leaves") from a ball that is too "tender" or "young" (*nu-*), spelling failure. The practitioner must be capable of interpreting the color of the flames rising above the hearth: their variations indicate the reactions, otherwise indiscernible, taking place in the ball. The difficulty lies in finding the precise temperature that will enhance the ball without causing the loss of the mercury and the particular energy it contains. Borax (*letkhya*) is used to prevent such a loss. Added in little bits to the crucible containing the molten ball, it looks like a burst of snow that then liquefies and spreads over the bottom of the material without mixing with it. It "covers the material" (*dat hpon-*), preventing evaporation; it "keeps the *dat* under its control" (*dat htein-*). Its placement on top of the ball probably explains this notion of borax's insulating property: when the crucible is taken out of the hearth and its contents have cooled and hardened, its side is broken and on the inside is found the ball with its top, flat, surface covered with a solid layer of borax, which can be removed by filing.

Fire, moreover, makes purification possible by supporting matter's transformation (*dat pyaung-*). It melts the ball prior to the introduction of purifying elements, called *hsay* (drug, medicine, potion). Among these, borax is used the most frequently. In the course of the smelting, borax draws and absorbs the "impurities" or "filth" (*anyit akyay*) mixed in with the mercury. (Saltpeter and sulfur are also used for this purpose.)

In light of its double function, both insulating and purifying, borax is often defined with reference to the human constitution, which according to the Buddhist conception is a combination of mind (*nan*) and body (*yok*). Borax is the spiritual authority of the ball, controlling its physical body and bringing about its changes. Alchemical theory distinguishes more generally between two classes of elements: the nine bodies (*yok-dat*), metallic materials susceptible of entering into the composition of a ball, and the nine, or sometimes twelve minds (*nan-dat*), materials susceptible of acting on the ball.[9]

A ball is "bathed," to use the alchemists' figure of speech, on a regular basis, once again with the aim of transforming its material. The molten ball, poured out of the crucible into a bowl, is immersed in a substance said to be nourishing and purifying (*kan yay laung-*, "to water with a strengthening liquid"). Honey, milk, melted butter, crude oil, pig's grease, sesame oil, coconut oil, sugar cane juice, and lemon juice are the liquids of choice. The procedure endows the material with a more perfect consistency: in some people's telling, it makes the material softer, but more numerous are those who say, on the contrary, that it makes the material harder. It makes the ball shine, a supposed sign of purity.

Of such is the alchemist's routine: close contact with fire, experiments on matter, a quest for purity, and a spiritual practice. This is the regimen followed by thousands of practitioners, adepts of the *weikza*'s path, who strive to strengthen and purify their ball until they obtain a "dead" one. A "dead" ball, one that has undergone a significant change of state and is thus ripe, inalterable, and made of pure mercury, confers on its possessor several of the ten extraordinary powers characteristic of *weikza,* such as invulnerability (*kaya theikdi*) or the ability to make others love you (*piya theikdi*). Now the overwhelming majority of alchemists are far from having reached this stage and, to be blunt, never will. The next stage, which consists of "revivifying" the ball, remains the sought-after, if never attained, goal. Nevertheless, the way forward is clear.

A "dead" ball, state the alchemists, taking up for another purpose an analogy already put to a different use, is only matter (*yok*). To give it life, it is necessary to join to it a spiritual component (*nan*), in the same way that human life is possible only through the coupling of matter and mind—here once again, the ball is equated with a living being. To "instill spirituality" (*nan thwin-*) in the ball, one must "nourish" (*kyway-*) its body, formed and mature, with metals whose energy (*dat*) it is now capable of taking on and that will increase its force without modifying its weight. Those metals are, primarily, and, in this order, silver and gold. They are sometimes given the eloquent labels, respectively, of "matter for someone who has entered into the stream" (*thawtapan-dat,* the term *thawtapan* naming one of the four states leading to nirvana) and "nirvana matter" (*neikban-dat*). The ball and the nutritive substance are placed in a crucible that is hermetically sealed before being positioned in the hearth and heated with coal and bellows. In the course of the smelting, the ball absorbs its food. The operation is repeated several times with silver, then with gold. The ball will become sated. Taking on no more substance, when exposed to fire it will begin on the contrary to "give up" or "vomit" (*an-*) material, in the form of a dust deposit at the base of the crucible. These "ashes of energy" (*dat pya*), also called "ashes of gold" (*shwe pya*), a golden or white powder, are very much sought after. They have the power to solidify mercury; more important, when mixed with honey in order to be ingested by people, these ashes keep them in good health or cure their diseases, prolonging their lives. Discharging these ashes is a sign that a ball has become "living" (*shin-*), and its possessor has succeeded (*aung-* or *theikdi pauk-*). By eating the ashes, by holding the ball in his mouth, or simply because of his success (conceptions vary on the matter), he reaches the state of a *weikza;* he will enjoy a long life. He then "exits," leaving the world of ordinary humans to go live at Dragoness Mountain or in one of the *weikza*'s other fabulous realms. He does so either by "exiting alive" (*ashin htwet*)—that is, vanishing into thin air—or, far more commonly, by "exiting dead" (*athay htwet*); that is passing away only apparently and continuing his life invisibly.

Among many stories prized by alchemists, one relates that a monk from Meikhtila in Central Burma, having succeeded, was persuaded by a man from England to sell him his ball of energy. This man took it back to England and entrusted it to a laboratory in order to find out the nature of its power. But the expert chemists never managed to identify the elements making up the ball. The point is that a living ball is the essence of matter: it represents a principle of irreducibility and indissolubility, a principle of permanence.

For months on end, Monk Taungtha devotes most of his time to what is only the very start of this never-ending alchemical process; namely, to endow the ball he has been working on with a sufficient degree of firmness. The ball, although solid, remains soft: it cannot withstand so much as a pair of scissors. Monk Taungtha subjects it to fire (with some borax) to firm up the material. In April 1995, he undertakes a three-week expedition around the country to practice alchemy at famous religious sites where accomplished *weikza* who have already "exited" have left their mark and where he hopes to capture their *dat* or beneficent energy. He goes north from Thamanya. After going to Shwezayan Pagoda (Thaton), the domain of Alantaya (founded by a monk in the vicinity of Thaton), he proceeds to Kyaikhtiyo Pagoda, Shwedagon Pagoda (Yangon), Shwesandaw Pagoda (Pyay), and Myat Thalun Pagoda (Magway). He stops at Shwesetdaw, a pilgrimage site about sixty kilometers from Minbu. It is now May 1995; the life-prolonging ceremony for U Kawwida, much talked about, took place the preceding December, and the traveler hears about the four *weikza*. He proceeds to Mebaygon, where he pays homage to the *weikza* and engages in the practice of alchemy with his ball inside the monastery compound. The alchemical equipment there is rudimentary and little looked after. The bellows, in poor condition, are not properly positioned, such that Monk Taungtha, seated too close to the hearth, gets burned. After five days, he leaves for Mount Popa, a necessary stage in any aspiring *weikza*'s career. He practices alchemy at the very spot where the famous U Paramawunnatheikdi, the great monk of Popa (Popa Hsayadaw), born in 1931 and "exited" in the early 1990s, had done so.[10]

Back at Thamanya for the annual monastic retreat (when monks may not absent themselves from their home monastery for more than seven days at a time), he continues his pursuits. Alas, after a full year's determined efforts and considerable expense—his well-off family pays for the utensils, the charcoal, and other materials—he meets with failure. Monk Taungtha still knows nothing of fire, which he fails to manage properly. His ball's material has evaporated; there remains too little to hope to make anything of it. A cruel disappointment, this makes our apprentice alchemist deeply despondent.

Alchemy is an inexact science, and it is because it is such that it makes sense to Monk Taungtha and to the rest of its adepts. Its characteristic operations constitute a scenario endlessly replayed, with only minor variation, for days, months, or years at a stretch, with no guaranteed outcome. The outline of the plot remains the same, but its end result remains uncertain. Despite its orderly and methodical character, alchemy is not a systematic procedure for matter's transformation. Its basic rules and operations provide no formula for success; they leave open the specter of experimentation. Monk Taungtha bathes his ball in crude oil when someone else would have used lemon juice; he opts for a "dry" method (*lon khyauk*), the ball being exposed to fire with no additive, when someone else would have added borax. Not only do the chosen methods vary from one alchemist to another but their understandings do as well. If many conceive of the alchemical process as consisting of two stages (the ball's death and resurrection), others consider a "dead" ball as representing full and unqualified success. Although bathing a ball is common practice, any given alchemist may count it only among the methods for making gold. For some, borax both insulates and purifies; in the eyes of others, it is really only effective as an insulator. And so it goes. It all comes down to the fact that trying, as here, to come up with a synthesizing account of alchemy amounts to betraying its nature—and betraying its practitioners in the bargain.

Above all, alchemy is a complex and unpredictable game with several rules. A practitioner's success depends on the unforeseeable conjunction of several factors whose respective contribution and efficacy turn out to be unknowable yet essential. Alchemy, in the Burmese context, is better deemed an indeterminate art rather than an esoteric one. Alchemists practice alone or in groups according to circumstances, but their activity and their formulas are in no respect secret. No initiation is required to gain access to alchemical knowledge. Yet, without being esoteric, alchemy is indeterminate because its general workings and the formula for its success remain indiscernible.

Among the factors that affect the alchemical process must be included not only the spiritual state of the practitioner but also his karmic state (the two being linked). The latter depends on, among other factors, his personal store of virtue capital (*parami*). An individual who "is in possession of virtue" (*parami shi-*)—that is, who has accumulated a kind of positive force by the practice of moral perfection through all of his successive lifetimes—is favorably positioned to succeed in alchemy.

Another fundamental element weighing on the alchemical transformation of matter is the configuration of the planets and stars at the time when someone engages in its practice. Granted, not all alchemists agree about this point. Some think the planets and stars have no influence; a great majority, however, believe they do. According to Burmese belief, power (*aswan*) inheres in the position of the heavenly bodies, such as the nine planets (*gyo*) and the twenty-seven constellations (*netkhat*). Their position at any given moment produces a more or less propitious force. Thus, one takes care to "choose the [right] moment" (*akha yway-*) to undertake an endeavor: lay the first stone of a building, become ordained as a novice or monk, marry, plant rice, build a house, dig a well, lend or borrow money, and so on. There are calendars put out each year by astrologers' associations indicating, in light of the progression of the stars, what days are auspicious and inauspicious in general, as well as which days are propitious for particular undertakings (often including mention of a precise time of day, hour, or time slot). For greater precision or assurance, people turn to the services of an astrologer (*baydin hsaya*): these people are numerous, working out of their homes or in stalls set up along the walkways leading to pagodas. A specialist of this sort relies on a complicated calculus that takes into account the date, day, and hour of a client's birth—the position of the planets and stars at the time of an individual's arrival in the world inflecting the whole of his or her fate. The astrologer uses such information to reckon the most propitious moment for accomplishing the intended action.[11] Alchemists, for their part, have no acknowledged method to decide the most favorable moment for the practice of their art. Certain alchemical treatises, one sometimes hears, provide instructions to this effect, but in point of fact, no one consults them. Practitioners admit without embarrassment to knowing nothing of the movement of the stars. They hope that the alchemical process and the astral forces will converge spontaneously (*netkhat mi-* "to capture [the force] of the planets and stars"). To a certain extent, alchemy is practiced haphazardly. At the Energy Center, the haphazard nature of things is somewhat attenuated by the fact that the disciples attribute to each day of the week a specific influence on alchemical projects in relation to the system of correspondences commonly known within the cult (the *weikza*'s birthdays, the day of success [Sunday], etc.). People also rely on the recommendations provided by the *weikza*, who, as their name suggests, "know": the word *weikza* derives, we should keep in mind, from the Pali *vijjā,* "knowledge."

To hear Monk Taungtha and his peers tell it, such are the enigmatic workings of alchemy, subject to the influence of determining forces whose effectiveness is random: while one practitioner can work at it obstinately for decades without arriving at any conclusive result, another may, in an extreme case, make a successful ball on the first try, with no prior experience, simply because of the lucky convergence of a set of favorable factors and actions at the moment he makes his attempt. No one can possibly know in advance what the result will be, because the undertaking is so completely shot through with uncertainty. Everyone has a chance at success and owes it to himself to give it a try.

Alchemy, in other words, makes sense as a particular modality of the Burmese discourse concerning the play of fate, its complex logic and indecipherable shifts and the possibility of pitting oneself against it and deflecting it. Every individual development, it reaffirms, is ordered by powerful forces, such as karma and the energy of the stars, over which people have no control and whose operations are unfathomable. At the same time, there is nothing inevitable about the making—one might better say the alchemy—of fate. There inheres within it a range of possibilities, and it is incumbent on each person to strive to bring about the best of them.

An alchemist's ball, insofar as it functions as a potential condenser for a good fate, as an instrument for its crystallization, is susceptible of prefiguring an individual's future, anticipating his success. But should the disparity between the ball's power and the state of its alchemist owner then turn out to be too great, the ball eludes the alchemist in one way or another. Doctor Sein Yi began practicing alchemy at the start of the 1980s with a ball of mercury that U Pandita had put in his hands. In 1989, this disciple, Vice Minister of Health at the time, left on an official trip to Japan. He relates that during his stay there, his ball, which he kept in the pocket of his shirt, fell out, landing in a toilet bowl. He thought it was lost. But it splashed like a rocket. He took this to mean that it had "succeeded" (aung-).[12] On his return to Burma, he reported the incident to one of the weikza, who then confiscated the ball. If he wanted to be a weikza, the disciple needed to bring about the success of a ball of his own creation, which he then started to do. Confiscating the ball was intended to prevent the ball's disappearance. A ball in the possession of an individual who is not at a sufficiently elevated spiritual level risks getting stolen by one of the creatures in the service of the Evil One (Man Nat), a deity opposed to Buddhism. These creatures, demons called tanaw bilu and alawaka bilu, try hard to bar the path of aspiring weikza by stealing their ball. In other cases, a ball disappears of its own accord, as it were: it rises up above the alchemical hearth and vanishes into thin air. Lieutenant-Colonel Thein Han, an eminent disciple of the four weikza, saw his ball rise into the air above the alchemical hearth and disappear. This can happen because a ball has its own will, its own desires, its own reactions, all of which point once again to its character as a living being. If it "hungers for fire" (mi hsa-), it will desert the domestic altar or the little bag hung around someone's neck where it is kept. That individual will find it again next to the alchemical hearth, clearly demanding heat. If it is put someplace inappropriate or impure (ma than bu), for example close to a woman's clothes, or if an individual of doubtful morality should hold it in his hands, its surface will become coarse or it will darken. The same will occur should its owner be lacking in Buddhist virtue, becoming angry or entertaining an evil thought. Should the opposite be true, the ball will on the contrary shine more brightly. The alchemist's ball, in other words, shows or even imposes the proper path. It constitutes an ideal representation of what an alchemist must do, be, and become.

Inasmuch as it is in line with the Burmese conception of fate, alchemy speaks, and with some acuity, of the perspective of a radical resolution, a sudden and total liberation that the ball's success would make possible. In the midst of all the extraordinary powers that would come en bloc, the ability to fly most fascinates aspiring *weikza*. It should no doubt be understood as the expression of liberation's imaginary. An old dream of childhood supported by stories, heard early on, about the time of the Buddha or about certain contemporary spiritual figures, flying means releasing oneself from all limits and all conditioning. The flying man par excellence is the monk thought of as a saint (*yahanda*), someone who has succeeded in breaking free of desire and breaking the servitude of life in society. This condition of both physical and social weightlessness does not result in an absolute exteriority vis-à-vis the world, however. Becoming a *weikza,* for Monk Taungtha and his fellows, means working for the temporal and spiritual salvation of others, as well as ensuring one's own—as though it would be impossible to imagine liberation in terms other than of ties, the position simply inverted, from protégé to protector, from prisoner to liberator.

What to do? In October 1995, Monk Taungtha, burned by his failure, decides to return to Mebaygon, to the Energy Monastery, to ask the four *weikza* to help him make a new ball. The four *weikza,* in particular Bodaw Bo Htun Aung and U Pandita who have "succeeded" and have "exited" with a ball of mercury (*byada weikza*), are endowed with the power to solidify the willful metal. During a séance in which the *weikza* appear in the flesh, Monk Taungtha informs U Pandita of the failure of his attempt and addresses a plea to him for help. At the following séance, the *weikza* invites him into the small room in the front right corner of the hall. Monk Taungtha has brought the necessary materials: a number-two-sized crucible, sixteen grams of mercury, and a little bit of borax. The *weikza* grips the crucible and rubs his finger around the inside of it. He applies a few ashes of *dat* (*dat pya*) to the utensil's inner surface while infusing it, by virtue of his touch, with power (*theikdi tin-*). Monk Taungtha does not know the origin of the white ashes; probably, he suggests, they are produced at Dragoness Mountain by subjecting a "successful" ball to fire. The important thing is that they are obtained from the four *weikza*. That fact alone assures their efficacy. The *weikza* then pours the mercury and the borax into the crucible, before telling Monk Taungtha to go heat everything up. The disciple leaves the hall where the séance is taking place and goes down to the rear of the monastery compound while the séance continues. He places the crucible into an alchemy hearth. There is no need to cover it with mud, because the heat will be relatively moderate.

After he has filled the hearth with charcoal, burned it, and then done this a second time, Monk Taungtha takes the crucible out, waits for it to cool, and breaks it open. Scraping off the outer layer of borax reveals the now solid ball, which he returns to present to the *weikza* and to the audience, evidence of the feat that has taken place. Monk Taungtha stays another week at the monastery to practice alchemy with his new ball. After that, he will come back twice a year, remaining each time for about a month, before moving there in 2001.

Eight years have passed since his ball's manufacture, during which time this disciple has worked to improve it, spending from twelve to fourteen hours a day at his alchemical work in periods of intense activity. For a long while, he neglected to protect himself from the heat of the fire: his sight has suffered as a result. He has now taken to wearing welders' goggles when he is working. A wall of the building where he lives at the Site of Success is lined with bags of charcoal, about ninety of them, thanks to the financial support of his parents and of some donors. He likes to say that the first thing you need to do alchemy is money. It is not unusual for an aspiring *weikza* to suspend his activities for a time due to a lack of funds. When using bellows, Monk Taungtha consumes as much as a bag of charcoal each day—thus, in combustible material alone, an outlay of close to twice the daily wage of an agricultural worker. What's more, at Mebaygon, he has to nourish his ball from time to time, at the *weikza*'s instruction, with silver or gold, costly materials. (The ball is not yet "dead," but simply by virtue of the fact that it was made with the help of the *weikza*, it has quickly reached an advanced stage of development, people say, and these feedings are still good for it.) Monk Taungtha keeps his ball in the pocket of his monk's sash. He says it is best to keep it close to one's body. Even if the ball, for the time being, does not contain any tangible power, nevertheless it keeps its possessor in good health and protects him from accidents. Still, there remains a long path to follow.

Wishing some respite, Monk Taungtha devotes himself to making balls of lesser importance—of zinc, copper, and silver—to distribute among his relatives and other donors. He uses the so-called ascetic's fire method (*yathay hpo*) because it is what ascetics make use of in the solitude of the mountains and forests. It consists of letting a ball heat up slowly in a hearth without using bellows. Although this method leads to only limited results, it has the advantage of being relatively less time consuming. A hearth burns for several days in front of the entrance of where Monk Taungtha resides, on the ground of success of U Pandita's cave. For convenience, Monk Taungtha feeds it charcoal rather than sticks, the only combustible material available in the forest. Every so often, he removes the crucible containing an alloy of zinc and copper from the fire, lets it cool, and then plunges it back into the middle of the fire. To speed up the process of transformation, he uses a bellows but only occasionally, because he fears that excessive heat would make the metals' *dat* evaporate. The alloy takes the form of a bar about the length of a person's little finger; he intends to cut it into ten equal parts to make as many amulets.

Committed and indefatigable, Monk Taungtha has revamped the equipment available at the monastery of the four *weikza,* where he has established himself as the alchemy specialist. Whenever a ball of mercury is produced with the help of the *weikza,* he goes with the disciple who received it, guiding him from the séance hall to the alchemists' hearth. Generous with both his time and his skills, he happily puts himself at the disposal of disciples wishing to practice alchemy at the monastery, supporting them in their uncertain endeavors for days and nights at a time. He finds it fulfilling, he says, to be a master (*hsaya*). And he takes on the master's role with both verve and good humor, fostering the practice of the art of fire at the monastery by dint of his presence and his personality.

Monk Taungtha intends to resume work on his principal ball with the *weikza's* help. Without masters, he emphasizes, success is impossible. The *weikza* are omnipresent in the practice of alchemy among their disciples. Their success-granting energy pervades the monastery, and many are those who, when they visit Mebaygon, work ardently on their ball, some of the keenest among them having come for just that purpose. The *weikza* intervene as well when their disciples practice where they normally live, assisting their success. Monk Taungtha, like the others, shows his ball to U Pandita, to Bodaw Bo Htun Aung, or to Saturday's Son to obtain success-granting energy and recommendations on how to proceed (with borax or "dry," using a high heat or a moderate one, bathing the ball in one medium or another). Sometimes, the *weikza* take a ball with them to Dragoness Mountain. They keep it there for some time to subject it to treatments that their disciples do not know but that increase its power. The ball serves as a receptacle and storage cell for the beneficent energy of the *weikza.* Furthermore, the four *weikza* are alone in a position to provide the mysterious plant seed that, according to the doctrine professed at Mebaygon, must be fed to the ball in the last phase of its resurrection to bring about its success. The *weikza* indeed know where to find this seed called *ywayhpyugyi,* a term that probably derives from the name of a tree, the *ywaygyi (Adenanthera pavonina),* a type of mimosa common in Burma (*hpyu* means "white").

The action of the four *weikza* is especially visible because of their regular appearance in the flesh. Yet other *weikza,* although they do not appear in the flesh, intervene equally actively to favor the practice of alchemy. They send messages to the practitioner in dreams or in visions during meditation sessions to guide him in his practice. They may also express themselves through a medium whom they possess (which the four *weikza* of Mebaygon do in addition to their appearances in the flesh). A *weikza* moreover communicates some power that supports success to the practitioner or his ball.

To recapitulate: in its most widespread and most advanced form, the form that leads to the condition of a *weikza,* alchemy proclaims itself an art of synthesis. Rather than demarcating a strict sphere of thought and action, it gathers up and integrates logics and procedures; it pursues its ends by means of understandings and techniques deriving from what are in principle heterogeneous registers. There are many examples of how alchemy telescopes registers in this way, but three suffice here. First, alchemy relies on empirical observations yet inscribes them in an analogical mode of thought. Thus, it is no accident that mercury should be the metal chosen as the means for gaining access to the condition of a *weikza*. Its remarkable singularity—as the only liquid metal—makes it suitable for evoking an extraordinary being like a *weikza*. In addition, mercury offers, on a material level, a challenge analogous to that taken up by an aspiring *weikza*. To produce at normal temperatures a pure, solid, and inalterable mercury, and to gain access to superhuman powers, including immortality, amounts to reversing the normal course of nature and, most notably, overcoming the principle of impermanence. Second, alchemy links physics and mysticism: the material transformation of the ball takes place under the influence of fire and under the influence of the alchemist's spiritual state, both of which are conduits of energy. Third and finally, alchemy appears to be guided by an experimental method, and yet its successful outcome turns out to be determined by forces outside the treatment of matter.

This art of synthesis, however, is oriented and addressed to the individual. Beyond its ultimate objective—reaching nirvana—which grounds its legitimacy, the practice of alchemy touches on different elements of personhood, physical and metaphysical, and so on an identity and development of the individual of which those elements are the foundation and the driving force. On the one hand, alchemy plays on analogies and interactions between the actions performed by the practitioner on the material of his ball and the constitution of his biological and spiritual being. In this respect, it resembles a procedure for an individual to produce himself. On the other hand, alchemy incorporates the action of forces— karmic, astrological, supernatural (the *weikza*)—influencing an individual's present and future, forces that the practitioner seeks to turn to his advantage. In this respect, it resembles a procedure with which an individual can produce his own fate. Alchemy appears to be a form, religiously defined and socially meaningful, of self-fashioning.

Thus, the practitioner doubles himself in his ball, which he keeps and works on throughout his life. The ball is likened to a living being, even to a person, and as such is susceptible to benefiting from the influence of the planets and stars. The practitioner must, with the help of fire, assure its growth and purify it, in the same way that someone who is embarked on the path to nirvana increases his spiritual force and purifies himself by various ascetic and contemplative practices. He must then feed the ball with active substances. He does all this to cause the death of the ball's matter—that is, to render it inalterable—and then make it live once again, in the manner of the aspiring *weikza* who strives to get beyond death and to free himself from the law of impermanence in order to prolong his life. The evolution of the ball materializes the process by which one becomes a *weikza*. When the ball "succeeds," so does its owner.

Not only do the alchemist and his ball progress in concert but they also reinforce each other. In the alchemists' words, the internal *dat* (*adwin dat*), namely, the individual's *dat,* and the external *dat* (*apyin dat*), namely, the ball's *dat,* are linked; they penetrate and influence each other. This interrelation can be represented in an unmediated fashion by effecting a transfer between the two: to benefit from his ball's power, an alchemist can place it momentarily in his mouth or drink a liquid, most often green tea, in which it has been immersed. He will, by this means, become less and less vulnerable to sickness, accidents, and attacks. Nonetheless, the fact that there may exist a disparity between the ball and its owner, the former succeeding when the latter remains a long way from his ultimate goal, shows that the object does not constitute a simple replica of the person. The ball can prefigure the individual's intended accomplishment, providing a model for it. In the end, the alchemist's ball represents a living double of the person, one in which it is possible to project and look at oneself in the present or future, and on the basis of which, above all, it is possible to work long and hard on the self—which explains alchemists' fascination with their ball and their deep attachment to this object. Thus throughout the alchemical procedure, a strong bond of participation is established between the alchemist and his ball, a bond of identity and interdependence at the same time.

The practice of meditation, to which alchemists frequently liken their activity, also enables one to work on the self by introducing a reflexive distance between individuals and their sensations and affects, their being. But it does not produce the sort of objectification of the practitioner in a material double that he can take as the subject of his experiments by observing its transformations, that he can use as proof of his own accomplishments, and whose condition he is free to discuss with others. In addition, the ball, in light of its materiality, makes the individual's power and the diffusion of that power more concrete. An alchemist can immerse his ball in water or green tea and give the liquid, with its protective and curative virtues, to those close to him. External to the person but tied to him, the ball is an instrument for producing, for fixing, and for distributing power. Whereas meditation leads, in its ultimate stage, that of insight, to the disintegration of the very idea of self (because it leads to the realization that the individual has no essence, such as a soul, but rather is made up of temporary assemblages and states), alchemy is a reification of the self, a self made into a thing. Yet these two ways of removing oneself from the self are more complementary than mutually exclusive: alchemy, once again, is a means, a paradoxical one certainly but a means nevertheless, of gaining access to salvation; that is to say, to the understanding of the three marks of all existence: impermanence, suffering, and selflessness. Alchemy, like concentration meditation, makes the individual a master of the self, which appears as a prelude to the breaking down of the self through insight.

If alchemy is a form of self-fashioning and if it is underpinned by the idea of participation between the practitioner and his ball, still one cannot say that there occurs within the intimate being of the alchemist a revolution similar to that supposed to occur in the material of the ball. There is no need to state (after the manner of Mircea Eliade) that the alchemist undergoes an internal metamorphosis following from a (hypothetical) affective experience comparable to that of a boy who has undergone an initiation ritual's trials.[13] It suffices to understand that the ball's development and that of the alchemist are conceived as linked and that the association is culturally recognized and so endowed with social efficacy, thereby enabling the alchemist to construct an identity in the midst of the community. The self of which I speak in the expression "self-fashioning" is not an ontological self, but a social self (that is, the self the individual imagines for himself, the self he presents to others, and the self others see in him, the three being bound together). To claim the opposite would be to get caught in the snares of alchemical conceptions.

All of the operations specific to alchemy, from the doubling of the individual by the making of a ball to judging the degree of the ball's progressive development, including the various treatments to which the ball is subjected, take place in one way or another with the support of a third element, the *weikza*. Apart from the *weikza*, assert the practitioners of alchemy, there is no salvation. The *weikza,* figures placed by the community above ordinary people, reduce the uncertainty inherent in the practice of alchemy by dispensing a knowledge and an energy that allow the process of transformation to take place successfully. They act as a means for channeling the forces of fate, thereby improving their outcome. Their function is at the same time to support and validate every disciple's work on himself, as given material form in his ball.

To act on oneself through the agency of a double and to see this action made effective and legitimate through the mediation of collectively recognized figures, the *weikza,* are, in sum, two touchstones of the Burmese practice of alchemy as conducted by the four *weikza's* disciples and by its Burmese adepts more generally.

HOW TO PRODUCE ENERGY OF SUCCESS

Major Zaw Win, faithful and fervent disciple if ever there was one, was actually denied the possibility of engaging in this major art of self-fashioning by the *weikza,* his masters. When he and his older brother, in the course of a séance, informed U Kawwida of their wish, the chief of the *weikza* discouraged the project. "You two brothers are not the sort whose chest will withstand the heat [that the alchemist's hearth will give off]." In other words, karmic conditions for the two brothers were not such as to foster success in such an enterprise. The path to Dragoness Mountain was not, however, barred to them—not for the Major, at least, who could reasonably lay claim to access to the *weikza's* realm in light of the remarkable services he had rendered. But he would need to find a different mode of access.

However, the desire to have a ball of energy continued to work on the Major, who was, it must be said, cruelly disappointed by U Kawwida's decree. He discussed it with a specialist in Burmese medicine, Kyaw Khaing, who had participated alongside him in U Pandita's life-prolonging ceremony in 1975. A number of the four *weikza's* disciples work as therapists. They come to Mebaygon Monastery to draw on an energy that will shore up the effectiveness of their treatments, no matter what type of cure they practice: medical remedies, cabalistic diagrams, the pronouncement of a formula to make an illness disappear. Many take the *weikza's* energy, which they transmit, as the basis of their power. A hardened practitioner of alchemy, Kyaw Khaing explained to the Major that the fire and bellows method was not the only means by which to produce a ball. Another method consisted of mixing mercury and silver powder with a little water—at a moment identified by the *weikza* as propitious—and then putting the amalgam, with a mud-like consistency, on the domestic altar to the Buddha and waiting for it to become solid.

Having requested and obtained U Kawwida's assent, the Major set to work making a ball using this method. The result was far from satisfactory. The ball was long and not spherical, with holes marring its surface. The Major gave it to Bodaw Bo Htun Aung, who took it to Dragoness Mountain. When the *weikza* gave it back to him a week later, the ball's appearance had changed. It was round, smooth, and shiny. How had this transformation been accomplished? The disciple does not know: he had never asked himself the question. Whatever the case, he could now think of himself penetrating the palace of the glorious Burmese king Kyanzittha in order to enjoy the favors of his daughter, much like the Indian prince Panaikkhaya once did. Panaikkhaya, as the Major tells the story, possessed a ball of this type. Once, he put it in his mouth and flew to the kingdom of Bagan. After making himself invisible, he reached the princess's room. He had a pleasurable moment there, before leaving just as sneakily as he had come. Smitten, he wished to make a second visit to the young woman. But as he traveled through the air in the direction of the palace, he crossed paths with Shin Arahan, the holy figure famous for having permitted the reintroduction of orthodox Buddhism into the kingdom of Pagan. In speaking with him, Shin Arahan informed Panaikkhaya that he was returning from the princess's wedding! The lover was so surprised and so shocked that he opened his mouth wide, dropping the ball. At that very instant he fell down and died.[14]

Rather than an "energy ball of Panaikkhaya," a common label for this sort of ball conceived without recourse to fire, the four *weikza* recommend to their disciples that they speak of a "sun-sun energy ball" (*ney thurein datlon*). Indeed, for the four *weikza* language is not neutral. More than an instrument of description, signification, and communication, it represents a constitutive force, an energy operating in the making of the world. Words, formulas, and turns of phrase affect, as much by their content as by the uses to which they are put, the ongoing development of beings and things: they hold a particular influence, among all the elements that fashion reality and orient its movements, whether propitiously or pejoratively. The *weikza,* in other words, have a dynamic conception of language.[15] The dramatic story of Panaikkhaya, which hardly fits with the atmosphere of success that they wish to establish, cannot serve as a reference for an object as essential as an energy ball. In the same way, between the two possible spellings, and therefore pronunciations, of the word for disciple, *dabyi* (တပည့်) or *dabe* (တပဲ့), the *weikza* recommend the use of the first. It invokes an idea of completeness (the verb ပြည့်), whereas the latter evokes (because of the verb ပဲ့),

on the contrary, a break, a tear, and, by extension, a separation between masters and disciples.

This principle of an effectiveness inherent in the means, no matter what the end sought, does not apply only to language. Various actions, beyond their immediate implication or meaning, are also considered to be vehicles of an intrinsic potency, whether lucky or unlucky. Such a conception, although it constrains both behavior and practices, is the basis of a permanent project of modeling the real. Even if the *weikza* in one incident or another gesture toward a fate in the face of which they declare themselves impotent, at the same time they never stop manipulating ways of speaking and acting in order to exert a beneficent influence on the course of things. In fact, nothing is more characteristic of the world that they construct together with their disciples than this formidable intensification of the superstitious function.[16] The term "superstition" is to be taken not in its original sense—the worship of false gods—but in its colloquial use as a receptive awareness toward fate's signs. Every individual, tending to attribute a logic to the playing out of his or her life, is inclined to read and to decipher in the world as experienced signs of the future, indications of good or bad fortune, while at the same time trying hard to act on that future by producing influential signs on his or her own part. Even if this is related to the belief in magic (in the neutral sense of the term), this superstitious orientation must not be confused with it. Magic implies the existence of an agent socially qualified to take charge of its procedures—a magician—whereas the work of superstition is, on the contrary, everyone's business and everyone's practice. Magic consists of a knowledge that is constructed, elaborated, formalized, and explicit, whereas the work of superstition relates more to a sensibility, one little reflected on. A natural disposition, the superstitious function is more or less elaborated in different societies, giving rise to diverse notions and actions. In Burmese society, particularly in the cult of the four *weikza,* it is drawn on a good deal and is therefore always in operation.

Out of this relation to a world ruled by intense activity of the superstitious function follows the notion of *ateik. Ateik* means "past," "presage," or "omen" and "future." A basic element in the cult's existence, the notion manifests itself in two ways: when the *weikza* identify things as being good or bad omens (*ateik kaung- / ateik ma kaung bu*), and, above all, when the *weikza* and their disciples carry out actions that, producing beneficent energy, are aimed at putting the immediate or more distant future under favorable auspices (*ateik lok-*). As it happens, the phenomenon of the omen matters less as a resource for discerning what is supposed to happen than as an instrument with which to alter this fate. It matters not so much because it makes it possible to foresee the future as because its workings suggest a means of acting on that future. Thus happens an overturning and over-coming of omens: whereas some phenomenon was supposed to appear unexpect-edly in order to prefigure a conditioned future, people instead generate it themselves in order to condition that future; whereas the relationship between the omen and what it announced was supposed only to be a symptomatic, not a causal, one, people instead confer on it an active power in the coming to be of the expected reality, the force of an efficient cause.

"Doing an *ateik*" (*ateik lok-*), an operation for the construction of reality that amounts to producing a leavening agent for success, is so common a practice among the four *weikza* and their disciples that it has become second nature. When it came time for the *weikza* to decide the most propitious moment to hold U Kawwida's life-prolonging ceremony in late 1994, they chose a Saturday. At the same time, they labeled this day unlucky. The paradox was quickly resolved, the *weikza* clarifying for the benefit of their disconcerted disciples that by this means they were undertaking an *ateik*, based on a verbal conceit. The term that names a day as unlucky, *pyatthada*, is close to that of the expression *pyatpyat tha-tha;* that is, to accomplish something "without hesitation, with resolve and preci-sion," a characterization that, when applied to the organization and execution of a ceremony, would guarantee its success. At the time of the ceremony, Saturday's Son asked Htu Aung in particular, among some three hundred disciples present, to sit in the first row. His name evokes an extraordinary (*htu-*) success (*aung-*). The construction in 2001 of a small building in wood and bamboo on the Energy Monastery's grounds to accommodate a nun who had come to live near the *weikza* was accompanied by a double *ateik*. The *weikza* had the building built on the southeast side of the compound, the Tuesday side; that is, in a direction and with reference to a day that they deemed as acting favorably on the country's general welfare. They also required that the construction be financed by a gift linking Doctor Sein Yi and Major Zaw Win, both "sons of Tuesday" (born on a Tuesday), to one another. Each of them made a contribution to the tune of 90,000 *kyat*—thus a total of 180,000 *kyat,* in a double reference to the number nine (1+8=9), lucky number par excellence in Burmese numerology.

To do an *ateik* consists in this way of inscribing an action in a temporal, spatial, numerical, or linguistic order in such a way as either to place the object of this action under the umbrella of a beneficent energy or to produce beneficent energy without that action having any other object. The days of the week, each one corresponding to some letters and to a planet; the eight cardinal points that are linked to the days of the week (Wednesday is divided in two); the numbers, letters, and words that refer to ideas—these constitute so many semantic coordinates of action, so many wheels with automatic effects on the inner workings of energy's machinery. The *ateik* procedure obtains its value and its meaning not as a performative operation but as a prospective one. It does not make a reality arise immediately, by means of a gesture or a pronouncement (something that, incidentally, the *weikza* are capable of doing). Instead, in supporting and influencing the course of fate, it contributes, laboriously and cumulatively, to the production of a reality, whether the fate of an individual, of a community, or of the nation. It concerns a long-term productive effort seeking to charge the atmosphere with positive energy, to generate an ideal order where everything prospers and succeeds.

Exemplary of this ceaseless generative activity and its workings is the choreography of Bodaw Bo Htun Aung's appearances. The various demonstrations of supernatural potency that punctuate his sermons, in addition to proving that he is a "real" *weikza,* also constitute *ateik* in most cases. Together they form a sequence that produces success energy, whose logic and meaning Bodaw Bo Htun Aung or U Pandita—the latter almost always appears after the former—never fails to bring up at one point or another. In addition to the literal interpretation of the various scenes of this sequence, which attest, for Burmese spectators, to the authenticity and amplitude of Bodaw Bo Htun Aung's extraordinary powers, an anagogical reading is added that makes every movement of this figure an evocation of the reality that the four *weikza* work to bring about.

Here is Bodaw Bo Htun Aung flying into the hall of the building that serves as the venue for his appearances, aptly called the "Monastery of Noble Success." He arrives through a window located in the northeast corner, the *Sunday* side. This spectacular entrance is followed by falling coconuts and candles, which fall among the members of the audience as though tossed by an invisible hand. Having addressed those in attendance for a moment, Bodaw Bo Htun Aung tells a chorus of young women, sitting in the middle of the audience, to recite in two directions—that is, two times—the Leavening of Noble Success (Aungdawmu Ateik):

> "May all the beings of the land of men and of the land of divinities *to the east* immediately enjoy physical and spiritual delight, may they be delivered from poverty, may they be wealthy, may all their needs be satisfied! May they succeed, may they succeed, may they succeed! May they reach the condition of *weikza!* May all their wishes be granted! May they possess the ability to make what they wish happen! May they obtain extraordinary powers! May they accomplish all their plans! May they reach nirvana!

Thanks to the sublime loving-kindness that we distribute presently from the Energy Center of Noble Success, may the whole world be at peace! Succeed, succeed, may all succeed!

May all the beings of the land of men and of the land of divinities *to the west. . . .*"

As the chorus begins its recitation, Bodaw Bo Htun Aung goes back the way he came, flying out the northeast window to reappear a few seconds later through the door of the small room located in the southeast corner of the hall, on the *Tuesday* side. He preaches once again before inviting some of the members of the audience to follow him into the smaller room. During the time they pay homage to the Buddha statue there, Bodaw Bo Htun Aung hails the chorus and invites them to recite the Leavening of Noble Success in three directions. He then flies out of the room's window. Less than twenty seconds later he pops up at the rear of the hall, in the *west* (the Thursday side), carrying one or two coconuts that he has borrowed from some lucky people in the audience who were able to get them when they fell. This choreography in three movements—in which only entries into the hall, and not exits, are significant—outlines the points of a triangle inside which are included the Buddha altar, the representatives of the monastic community, and the audience, thus depicting Burmese society in its entirety, on whose behalf the *weikza* exercise their generative activity.

An exegesis of these different movements is always delivered by one or another of the *weikza* in exactly the same formulation, which the audience understands despite its extreme concision. But we, ignorant of the Burmese idiom of the production of success energy, have no choice but to try to unpack this elliptical commentary. Bodaw Bo Htun Aung, the audience is informed, comes "from the *Sunday* side in order to foster the peace and tranquility of the country." Indeed, the expression "to be at peace, to be tranquil" (*ay-khyan-*), begins with the letter *a,* which corresponds to Sunday and to the energy of a specific planet, the Sun.

After his first exit, the *weikza* reappears "from the *Tuesday* side in order to foster an abundance of rice and oil." The names of these basic elements of the Burmese diet, *hsan* and *hsi,* respectively, are both written with the consonant *hsa,* linked to Tuesday and the energy of the planet Mars.

Following his second exit, Bodaw Bo Htun Aung comes back "by the *west* side to foster the coming of a king supportive of religion in Burma" or, as is often said more vaguely, "to foster an increase in the number of people capable of supporting religion and teaching the Buddhist doctrine in Burma." It is the direction (the west) and not the day (Thursday) that matters in understanding the point of this final movement. It refers to a well-known prophecy concerning the return, from the west, of the Prince of the Universe, Setkya Min. The young man, son of King Bagyidaw (r. 1819–1837), became the focus of popular hopes for the recovery of the kingdom after the humiliating treaty of Yandabo (1826), at the end of the First Anglo-Burmese War. At the time of his birth, in 1820, the Brahmans officiating as astrologers at the court had predicted that he would reign over the universe, whence the imposing name bestowed on him. He was also known by the title of Prince of Nyaungyan, after the name of the region that his father granted him to "eat." But when Bagyidaw's younger brother seized power in 1837, he had his nephew assassinated along with other claimants to the throne. They were drowned—it was forbidden to make royal blood run. Setkya Min, wrapped in a velvet bag, was thrown into the Irrawaddy River. Now the rumor spread that the Prince of the Universe was not dead. He was said to have been rescued from the waters by the *weikza* Bobo Aung, who had "gone out alive" some years before. And the Prince would reappear one day from the west to establish peace, concord, and prosperity in Burmese society, putting an end to the Buddhist religion's decline (which intensifies in proportion to the distance in time since Buddhism's founding, more than 2,500 years ago). Setkya Min, whose coming is hastened by the combined efforts of all the country's *weikza,* will find among them crucial help in his task of reforming and developing the religion. In waiting for the prophecy finally to be realized, "he who will be king" (*min laung*) lives, with some *weikza,* in an invisible place near Bodhgaya, the site of the Buddha's Awakening, where he devotes himself to the practice of meditation.[17]

A while back, the explanation the *weikza* gave of Bodaw Bo Htun Aung's final movement—his return to the monastery's hall from the west—mentioned the name of Setkya Min, whose reappearance they hope to hasten. The outfit he will don, the mount on which he will ride about (a royal elephant), along with a copy of the Buddhist canon engraved on gold leaf—are these not already held in waiting at Dragoness Mountain? Today, in place of the prince's name the more allusive label of "king supporter of religion" (*thathana pyu min*) has been substituted. That is no less evocative, for most Burmese, of the coming of the Prince of the Universe. But the reference to the famous person is often blurred, replaced by the simple evocation of "individuals capable of supporting religion." This is because, reflecting an inherent feature of Buddhism that places at some indeterminate time the establishment of an ideal order produced jointly by a royal figure and a spiritual one—a feature that some scholars are inclined to deem millenarian— the reference to the Prince of the Universe can, in the world of the *weikza,* be so pregnant with meaning as to become heavy with immediate political implications. The expected but hazy and distant horizon that this imagined ideal order represents becomes, as here, the focus of efforts to hurry its attainment, efforts susceptible of being regarded as so many oblique criticisms of the existing order or even calls for its overthrow. All evidence suggests that the *weikza* have forsworn making explicit mention of the Prince of the Universe in order to avoid laying themselves open to accusations of sedition, particularly in light of a local religious struggle that causes some monks, envious of the cult's success or opposed to its orientation, to label it as a cover for the development of subversive political activities.

Having said that, what then, among all of Bodaw Bo Htun Aung's movements, can we make of the coconuts and candles that fall on the audience after his arresting entrance onto the scene? Coconuts, whose name begins, like the term *aung-* (to succeed), with the letter *a,* are impregnated with the *weikza's* energy of success. A struggle to grab them follows their fall. Bodaw Bo Htun Aung, when he flies out the window of the little room and comes back from the west, carries one or two of these coconuts in order to foster the arrival of the Prince of the Universe. The candles, in furnishing light to illuminate the disciples' path, whatever it might be, also procure them energy of success. However, beyond their character as bearers of success, don't coconuts and candles prefigure the rain of precious stones (*yadana mo*) that, to hear the prophetic stanzas with which the *weikza* stock their sermons, will rain down on the country when the reign of prosperity begins?

All of the above—Bodaw Bo Htun Aung's movements, the chorus's recitation, the miraculous rain, and the prophetic stanzas—already do much in the realm of energy production. It remains for the *weikza* to offer their disciples instructions on how to make energy of success on their own. Either Bodaw Bo Htun Aung or U Pandita communicates these instructions without fail in the course of their sermons, not without having first informed their listeners that they appreciate the limits of the latter's spiritual capacities. "Friends in the Teaching [of the Buddha], if you are not in a position to go practice meditation in a meditation center, do not at least let the flowers on your home's Buddha altar wilt!" they exhort their listeners before transmitting the instructions in question, which concern the composition of a floral offering for the domestic Buddha altar. The instructions are not delivered in one go, but rather are pronounced bit by bit in the course of a dialogue with the audience in the interrogative mode—a conventional Burmese preaching interactive style that the *weikza* are fond of and that helps enliven sermons even as it facilitates the assimilation of their contents:

"Members of the audience, no matter what the problem is, don't you want its solution (*pyaylehmu*)?"

"Yes, we do, Venerable," the audience replies in unison.

"Seven branches of the Eugenia tree (*thapyay*)," advises the *weikza* concerning the offering's first ingredient. (The two terms, *pyaylehmu* and *thapyay,* both contain *pyay,* which as a verb means "to be resolved.") "Don't you want good things (*kaunghmu*)?"

"Yes, we do, Venerable."

"Seven branches of *Mesua ferrea* (*kankaw*)," recommends the *weikza*. (The verb *kaw-* means "to have the chance, to enjoy a lucky moment.") "Don't you want success (*aunghmyinhmu*)?"

"Yes, we do, Venerable."

"Seven coconut palm fronds (*on*). Three times seven makes?"

"Twenty-one, Venerable."

"Add three small branches of *Crataeva religiosa* (*khantet*)!" (The verb *tet-* means "to rise, to progress.") "Doesn't that make twenty-four?" asks the *weikza* with reference to the twenty-four elements of the canonical text, the *Pahtan.*

"That is correct, Venerable."

"With the exception of an aluminum can [because the name of this material, *dan* (အဋ္), is pronounced exactly the same as the word for wound or punishment (အဏ်)], you can use any kind of container [to put the offerings in]. Put twenty-four spoonfuls of water in the container. And recite the twenty-four elements [of the *Pahtan*]. Buds will sprout on the *Crataeva religiosa* branches. That's energy of success! You will have energy of success, you will have energy of success! So, don't stop reciting the twenty-four elements. Your home will be peaceful, your business will go smoothly, you will be safe from danger!"

To those even only a little familiar with the superstitious activities of the Burmese, these instructions will be hard to distinguish from those that astrologers provide their clients wishing to influence reality. Indeed, "to do an *ateik*"—the phrase is the *weikza*'s own, it is not used outside the cult—is nothing other than a common procedure for producing one's fate, the *dat yaik dat hsin*—given a new name in the hope, probably, of removing its quite obvious character as "mundane knowledge" (*lawki pyinnya*), so without any link to nirvana as its objective. The instructions, in either case, are described as bearers of success energy (*aung dat*). The only difference, but it is not an insignificant one, is that the energy produced according to the *weikza*'s instructions has a general effect, whereas the *dat yaik dat hsin* actions have a precise aim. You want to win a lawsuit, shut out other candidates for a job, increase your business's clientele, or bring about an inconstant husband's return? Consult an astrologer who will determine the appropriate procedure on the basis of a complex system of correspondences specifying the effects of connections (*hsetsathmu*), of affinity (*meik*, "friend"), or incompatibility (*yanthu*, "enemy"). According to a respected astrologer in Mandalay, the phrase *dat yaik dat hsin*, which labels this type of effort, combines two possible types of operations that are sometimes confused. *Dat yaik*, "to hit with energy" (the translation is tentative), is used to make something go away. You need to sell a car quickly? You need, in other words, for the car (*ka*) to leave (*htwet*-)? The letter *ka* corresponding to Monday, and the letter *hta* (the initial consonant of *htwet*-) to Saturday, you must use *khantet* (*Crataeva religiosa*) leaves—that is, *kha* for Monday and *ta* for Saturday—fifteen of them, a number that refers to Monday. At the appropriate time, slap these leaves against the car while saying, "May the car leave quickly!" The expression, "the car leaves" and the *khantet* plant share, or so explain the astrologers, the same principle, the same energy (*dat*), which is what makes the action effective and what makes "the car leave." This is, of course, only one of a thousand and one possible devices for ridding oneself as quickly as possible of the car, strategies that can be elaborated on without limit. Inversely, *dat hsin*, "to get ready with energy with a view to obtaining some result" (this translation is equally tentative), is used to make something come, to get something. Your business is doing poorly; your customers are few? Purify yourself by bathing; then get yourself an umbrella that you will donate, as you open it, to a monk walking in the street who is coming from the west and heading east. Every monk possesses a certain spiritual potency (*hpon dago*) that he can direct to the benefit of his lay donors. The umbrella offers protection. Opening it just before handing it to the monk makes the karma bloom (*kan pwin*-), the good fortune bloom (*lat pwin*-). Coming from the west, the equivalent of the rear, and going east, to the front, means getting first place, being among the winners.[18]

For Burmese, the *dat yaik dat hsin* operation does not involve the supernatural. It is, on the contrary, completely natural (*thabawa*). Just as—to take up images used by our astrologer, who admitted to having wondered for fifteen years about the nature of the effectiveness of this procedure, on the basis of which he makes his profession—clapping your hands makes a noise, or gasoline lights when you get near it with a match, without our knowing exactly what mechanisms bring about those effects, by the same token the *dat yaik dat hsin* maneuver consists of setting in motion objects' properties, particularly literal ones (ones inhering in written letters), thereby releasing their intrinsic power or energy. The *weikza*, for their part, lend this procedure a mystical character by linking their intervention, crucial for its effectiveness, to it. They introduce transcendence into the most mundane of activities.

GETTING BEYOND DEATH

The name "sun-sun energy ball" given by the *weikza* to the ball in Major Zaw Win's possession names the method used to fashion it. At the same time, it evokes the immense energy that emanates from it, putting it on a par with that of the great star. The Major exposes his ball to the sun all day on his house's balcony, the sun's energy warming and activating the mercury, making it work. At night, he puts the ball in a glass of water that he places on the altar to the Buddha; cooling it in this way gives the material greater consistency. Subjecting the ball to this thermal process on a daily basis, alternating heat and cold, helps increase its potency. The Major often takes the ball in his right hand and rubs it while silently reciting the same formula that he recites when he fingers his prayer beads: "In paying homage to the Buddha, called the Perfect One, may I attain success!" He feeds the ball with sheets of gold leaf; they are applied on its surface with a little mercury, which aids the absorption of the precious metal's powder. In addition, whenever he gets the chance, he presents the ball to one of the *weikza* or their medium. They hold it in their hands for a few minutes or even put it in their mouths to infuse it with power. Benefiting from all these different inputs of energy, the ball slowly changes color from silvery to gold. The more this solar radiance takes hold, the happy alchemist explains, the more the ball gains in potency and the more it assures the lengthening of its owner's life.

For, let us say once again that, even though the Major does not make the claim out loud and does not advertise the fact, he hopes to become a *weikza*. He knows and acknowledges, with all his characteristic modesty, that he remains a long way from this goal. Unlike his friend Doctor Sein Yi, he still lives with his family. The time he spends at his practice—reciting his prayer beads and working on his ball of energy—is limited. But this does not gainsay the fact that becoming a *weikza* is his overriding ambition. This dearly held hope has stayed with him through all his years of service to the four *weikza* and their medium, thirty-six years to be precise, during which time he has never failed them.

Figuring among the services he has rendered them is his contribution to the organization and execution of the three life-prolonging ceremonies that have already taken place: U Pandita's in 1975, U Oktamagyaw's in 1989, and U Kawwida's in 1994. In each case, the lives of the *weikza* and of the disciples involved were put on the line. There is also the famous "hand grenade affair." Bodaw Bo

Htun Aung rarely fails to mention this incident in the course of his sermons, and when the Major is present, the *weikza* calls on him to testify to the veracity of the facts. "Major Zaw Win, wasn't a hand grenade once thrown [at us]?" "That is true, Venerable," the disciple responds, sitting near the front. One evening in the late 1970s, some men burst into a séance in full swing and threw a grenade from the entrance to the hall. The projectile hit a column in the hall. It fell on the head of a child, who was slightly injured, and then it fell to the floor and rolled a bit without exploding. The Major, taken back to the time some thirty or forty years earlier when he was on the frontlines in combat territory, rushed to grab the grenade and throw it outside through one of the windows. Later, he told the authorities about the incident, orally and then in writing, in the vain hope that they would undertake an investigation.

It was never learned who was responsible for this failed attack. Some attribute it to communists in the village who loathed the *weikza,* whose monastery was frequented by highly placed political figures. Others accuse U Zawana, the monk who lives at the edge of the village. Known to be jealous of the success of the *weikza* and their medium, he has caused them a number of difficulties. The disciples liken him to the Evil One (Man Nat), who tried his best by all means available to prevent the Buddha from attaining Awakening and spreading his teaching. U Zawana, in this scenario, would have recruited a small group of individuals to perpetrate the attack. Actual responsibility for the attack nevertheless matters relatively little with respect to the meaning that the incident has taken on in the cult's history as the *weikza* and their disciples choose to formulate it. Basically, the "grenade affair" counts among the events of an epic cycle. It enters into a representation by means of which the four *weikza* depict themselves, and are depicted, as heroes of the Buddhist religion, stoically confronting the attacks of their adversaries as they pursue their project. This incident belongs to the category of "disturbances" or "disruptions" (*ahnaung ashet*). The expression designates phenomena of either human or nonhuman origin (they may be caused by evil spirits) that threaten at all times to make the *weikza*'s undertakings fail. At those times when preparations are being made for a life-prolonging ceremony, as well as when it is taking place—climactic moments in the life of the cult—this disorganizing menace is thought to become particularly intense. This threat generates in response a heightening of the superstitious function, with an increase in activities among the disciples for the production of beneficent energy. Everyone finds their place in the *weikza*'s odyssey, because everyone contributes, to whatever extent they are able, to the support of their heroic march, even to the point of risking their lives for and with them. It is a collective epic whose most indefatigable participants—among other disciples, Hpay Myint (author of the standard reference work on the *weikza,* which first appeared in 1972), Major Zaw Win (editor of a substantial supplement to this work in its 1990 edition), and Doctor Sein Yi (who wrote two unpublished manuscripts on the cult)—have wished to be its chroniclers, convinced as they are that they are taking part in a tale of greater import and worthier of collective memory than that taking place and being recorded in the ordinary course of the world's affairs.

Also numbering among the Major's credits is his role as lay assistant to Saturday's Son. When he is staying in Yangon, the *weikza*'s medium is put up at the home of a long-time friend of the Major, Myo Lwin. This man of Chinese descent, soon to turn seventy, has a large and comfortable house in which one room is reserved for Saturday's Son. Myo Lwin is not, however, quite up to the task of taking care of a monk. Therefore the Major moves in during the medium's stays to serve him according to the rules, and with all the formal respect due a monk.

The Major's staunch devotion matters importantly to his identity as a disciple. The stories the *weikza* recount in their sermons—Victorious and I have drawn up an inventory of twenty-five of them—sketch out this identity. Whether the stories refer to the past lives of the Buddha, to the era of early Buddhism, or to the centuries of Burma's Pagan dynasty or they are presented as a timeless parable, their protagonist is often neither the Buddha nor a saint nor a monk nor even a pious king, but rather one or more ordinary laypeople. And in any case, even if the stories put the Buddha, a saint, or a monk at the heart of the plot, the point of their adventures is less to glorify that person than to edify the audience by pointing out the path of virtue. It is also to arouse veneration for the *weikza* by means of an apology that either extols believing or describes the dreadful fate of skeptics. These stories represent and teach a way of imagining a lay model of virtue that does not amount to an imitation of the monastic ideal. They institute a paradigm of virtuosity distinct from the monastic model.

Since the 1950s, the time when the cult of the four *weikza* was born, Burma has experienced a spectacular expansion in the lay practice of meditation.[19] Yet this phenomenon, which elevates the layperson to participation in a practice and an experience theoretically reserved to the monk in search of salvation, has not spread to the entire population. The demanding practice of meditation requires doing violence to oneself. For most of those drawn into it, meditation's spread has only added a scheduled supplement to the course of their lives: contemplative practice takes place during brief stays—ten days or so, once a year—at one of the meditation centers specializing in its teaching. Without denying the fundamental place and superior value of meditation in the Buddhist path of deliverance, the four *weikza* make an effort through their sermons to sketch an image of the layperson that is not the negative obverse of that of a monk. They shift attention from the spiritual virtuosity of the world-renouncer toward the ethical virtuosity of the man or woman in the world, through the creation of a distinctive lay ideal. Gratitude toward one's parents, donations, loving-kindness toward one's own people and toward others—in sum, moral virtue and its benefits, both immediate and eventual—in contrast to the agonies to be undergone by those who do not evince this attitude, are at the heart of their teaching, which is both accessible and expressive. Disciples can discern in the *weikza*'s stories the model of a lay greatness whose version of religiosity is applicable to their own daily lives. Are these disciples, for all that, more virtuous than other people in the end? Impossible to say. But to be a disciple of the *weikza* implies putting oneself in the service of this ideal, which is already saying quite a lot.

Thus the Major, in light of the relationship he has formed with the *weikza* and their medium, one based entirely on believing, can hold out fond hopes of becoming a *weikza*. Note, however, that it is not a matter of attaining the state of a *weikza* by the usual path, via success in one of the techniques specific to aspiring *weikza* (alchemy, cabalistic practices, etc.), then followed by "exiting" from the world and the cycle of rebirth. What the Major hopes for, in contrast, is to see himself "called" (*khaw-*) by the *weikza* to live with them at Dragoness Mountain at the moment of his death. There, he will devote himself to the *weikza*'s path while awaiting the reassembling of the Buddha's relics, the ultimate phase of the Buddhist era and the time for obtaining entry to nirvana.

To be called? This unusual possibility that the Major is counting on is one that he himself helped substantiate. The long supplement that he wrote for the 1990 edition of Hpay Myint's work, ninety pages out of a total of close to five hundred, deals with the life-prolonging ceremony for U Oktamagyaw that had just taken place. It includes a brief biography of this *weikza,* the only one among the four names that sounds familiar to Burmese ears.[20] U Oktamagyaw is a famous historical figure. Yet the *weikza* never recount his biography in the course of their sermons, as they do in the case of U Pandita or Bodaw Bo Htun Aung. What is fundamental about him is his fame as a great religious scholar. If the figure of U Kawwida, born in the year 968 of our era, refers to a historical moment of religious and political reform—according to Burmese chronicles, the reintroduction of orthodox Theravadin Buddhism in the kingdom of Bagan in the middle of the eleventh century—U Oktamagyaw embodies the function of preserving this orthodox Theravadin Buddhism. He possesses a wide-ranging knowledge of the canonical texts thought to contain the authentic teaching of the Buddha. When he comes (he appears only occasionally), he has a solemn bearing, delivering a short sermon on Buddhist morality in an august tone. Even though a fairly large distance separates him from the disciples, and even though they make few references to him in their conversation, he is nonetheless an indispensable figure in the cult's overall structure: he is the guarantor of its orthodoxy. U Oktamagyaw counterbalances Bodaw Bo Htun Aung's excesses—his boastfulness and informality—without vitiating them. The four *weikza* do not try to produce a harmonious image: on the contrary. Even if the dominant "line" (*laing*), according to the word of English origin that Burmese use to name the different orientations in their practice of Buddhism, is incontestably that of the *weikza* (*weikza laing*), the economy of the whole relies on the counterpoint, the juxtaposition of different religious lines that are partly dissonant while also complementary. The Burmese understanding of religious lines, which makes it possible for anyone to situate and classify any individual's mode of spiritual engagement, is based on a system of oppositions: the path of scriptural study vs. the path of meditative practice; the path of concentration meditation vs. the path of insight meditation; the *weikza* path vs. the path of insight meditation. Yet the four *weikza* partially escape this manner of classification, which is one of the features that distinguish this cult from other *weikza* cults and from manifestations of other types of religious orientation that are more homogeneous in their content and their forms. Or, rather, they rearticulate and transcend this classification. The four *weikza* constitute, one might say, a polyphonic ensemble.

If therefore U Oktamagyaw, in light of the irregularity and brevity of his appearances and of the little mention he gets in the disciples' discourse, appears to be almost a figure of secondary importance among the four *weikza,* still he cannot be likened to what is called, in the realm of performances, a "supporting role," a character whose raison d'être is to make the main stars look good. He occupies a central place, in his own right and in equal measure. It is not insignificant that the *weikza,* at the end of the great scholar's life-prolonging ceremony, asked the Major to produce, in addition to a detailed account of the event itself, a biography of the illustrious figure, as though they wished to make up for a lack. To "produce"? Indeed, when the Major asked U Oktamagyaw to relate his story so he could put it in writing, the *weikza* was content to mention the title of a work tracing out his life. The disciple had only to find himself a copy and draw inspiration from it to come up with an adapted version. The Major's task, in other words, consisted of making the identification complete and incontestable of one of the *weikza* appearing in the flesh in the village of Mebaygon at the end of the twentieth century with the famous religious savant of the fifteenth and sixteenth centuries. There was nothing obvious about this task. The historical U Oktam-agyaw (1453–1542) was not considered a *weikza;* far from it. With the exception of this particular cult, he is absent from the universe of practitioners of the *weikza* path.

The Major bought a copy of the work in question, a classic biography of the great monk that was written by a royal minister. He acquired a second biography, more recent, which he judged less satisfactory and which he did not end up using. He proceeded by selecting those elements from the earlier work that seemed to him fundamental, and so worthy of being reported. Scrupulously, he notes at the end of his account that the authorized biography of U Oktamagyaw ends with the great man's death. However, he goes right on to remark that this death is not the actual end. U Oktamagyaw was not cremated, as is customary for monks, but was placed in a tomb. U Pandita then came looking for him to take him to Drag-oness Mountain, the *weikza's* realm, where he still resides.

Why call Oktamagyaw, who appears in no way linked to the *weikza* path? No explanation is provided. The *weikza,* the Major told me, have remained silent on this point. The disciple supposes that it was a matter of welcoming a scholar who could bring the benefit of his remarkable knowledge to the many *weikza* of Dragoness Mountain, who are themselves little concerned with scriptural stud-ies. In any case, in his text the Major describes in just a few lines U Oktamag-yaw's incorporation into the cult. He acts as though it was self-evident, as though this way of becoming a *weikza* followed a customary procedure, one it would be superfluous to comment on. To be called is treated in the same way in which every monastic biography includes a reference in conventional terms to the subject's ordination ceremony, without the need for any reminders of the origins and pro-cedures of this ceremony nor for any insistence on its effectiveness—the fact that it transforms a lay person into a monk.

That what is, in the field of religious representations, actually a revolution can be presented as obvious fact shows how much being called is ingrained in the cult of the four *weikza.* As the initial and distinctive feature of the cult, the *weik-za's* appearances in the flesh have reduced the distance that, otherwise and in principle, separates "exited" *weikza* from ordinary men—the former establishing communication with the latter through dreams, visions, or possession. If the four *weikza* travel the path in both directions, from Dragoness Mountain to the human world and back, why would they not be able, with the help of their formi-dable powers, to take one of their disciples along? Why would they not be able to convey the most zealous of them from an apparent death to resurrection, fulfill-ing in this way the role of psychopompos in reverse? Gaining access to the *weik-*

za's domain represents neither a mundane nirvana (material and moral well-being in human life) nor a supramundane one (spiritual perfection and definitive deliverance from the cycle of existence). It opens onto a third condition in which, even though one has escaped reincarnation and enjoys the assurance of salvation, one must nevertheless continue to make an effort. Although it is a physical space, Dragoness Mountain belongs to none of the thirty-one planes of existence set out in Buddhist cosmology. It is assimilated to this cosmology without being incorporated into it. To be called amounts to acquiring an extra-cosmological condition, outside the cycle of reincarnation: getting beyond death.

Mingyi Sein Hlaing, who was a high government official in the 1950s before he founded a business in Yangon, played a major role in the cult for two decades, from 1957, the year he first encountered the *weikza,* until 1977, the year of his death. On the occasion of U Pandita's life-prolonging ceremony, he was accorded the privilege of throwing the first of the three medicinal balls bringing about the *weikza*'s regeneration through fire. He practiced alchemy daily. He hoped to "exit alive" (*ashin htwet-*), to be called to Dragoness Mountain before meeting his own death. Thus he appealed to the *weikza* on the grounds of the fidelity he had shown them and the help he had given them, urging them to make his wish come true. He related to them as he would have related to a business partner. On the day of his death, he tried by a final move to force the *weikza*'s hands, pressing them to pay off their debt toward an indefatigable disciple. As though he sensed his end was near, he got up that morning at 4:00 a.m. and, after asking his wife for a glass of water, seated himself, his energy ball in his mouth, ready to "exit." In vain! A few moments later, he succumbed, apparently due to a heart attack. His body was placed in a closed tomb in a cemetery in the city of Mawlamyaing. Saturday's Son, at the *weikza*'s instruction, went to the tomb on the sixty-sixth day after his death (in accordance with the age of the deceased). At 11:00 p.m.—there are eleven fires (greed, hate, delusion, etc.) that burn in every individual and that must be extinguished in order to reach nirvana—the medium lit two candles, one at the dead man's feet, the other at his head. He dug the ground to bury a piece of copper on which a cabalistic diagram had been drawn. All of this had been conceived to help Mingyi Sein Hlaing "break the ties" (*than-yawzin hpyat-*) that still bound him to the living. Soon after, the *weikza* announced that they had summoned their disciple, in the same way that they had called U Oktamagyaw. Removed from the process of reincarnation and invisible to ordinary people, Mingyi Sein Hlaing practiced meditation for another eleven years in four pagodas located in different parts of the country, before attaining the status of a *weikza.*

"Breaking the ties": the expression means renouncing the world in order to enter the monastic community. So to be called by the *weikza* requires, if not becoming a monk, at least taking on one of the monk's obligations: to be an individual who has detached himself from his family. Such is the price of salvation. This requirement is congruent with the Burmese Buddhist conception that sees in renunciation of the world a parameter of spiritual accomplishment. By the same token, just as an applicant at the time of his ordination is asked whether his parents have assented to his decision, and even, although this is not imperative, that his wife has done so too, so the rupture implicit in the departure for Dragoness Mountain is allowed only on the condition that it has been consented to by those most directly affected. One night in September 1997, U Kawwida and Bodaw Bo Htun Aung appeared in the flesh at Doctor Sein Yi's house, in the suburbs of Yangon. Bodaw Bo Htun Aung, addressing the disciple, offered him the chance to come live at Dragoness Mountain. In 1980, the Doctor had already had a foretaste of the happiness that awaited him if he accepted: while he had donned the robe temporarily and had undertaken a pilgrimage to Shwesetdaw, the *weikza* invited him to visit their extraordinary realm. In the huge cave inside the mountain, the Doctor relates, stand thousands of pagodas. Some were donated by disciples of the cult. One, U Pandita revealed, was the Doctor's own donation in the course of a life in which he was a cousin and principal general of the great king Anawratha (in the eleventh century of our era). The Doctor didn't leave empty-handed. He brought back 1,500 relics of the Buddha, which he gave away so that they might be encased in various pagodas. Seventeen years later, he was offered the chance to obtain permanent accommodation among the *weikza*. But ever since he had given up conjugal life, his wife had visited him weekly. On this occasion, she begged him to decline the offer. One of their sons was getting ready to leave for the United States, and a number of other problems remained to be taken care of. Too many things still bound the Doctor to the world. He stayed behind.

How many of these disciples are there who, prisoners of their ties to their relatives, have missed the tremendous opportunity to be called to Dragoness Mountain while they are still living? One thinks immediately of Ba Yi. The leader of Mandalay's disciples aspired, as have others, to escape death and "exit alive." He spoke of this wish explicitly with the *weikza*. Because here is what the four *weikza* are: the visible and direct manifestation, in the flesh, of venerable and potent beings who, however human their origins, were nonetheless hitherto beyond immediate reach, beings with whom one is only now in a position to engage without anyone else's intervention. No longer is communication with them necessarily mental and spiritual or achieved through the intermediary of posses-sion. They are now a physical presence; they can be seen, touched, and addressed. No longer does there stand an absolute divide between the realm of mortals and that of immortals. Now a bridge has been established between the two, and with it a relative familiarity among those on either side of it. The fact that some people, on their first encounter with one of the four *weikza* and in the same way as Doc-tor Sein Yi himself, couldn't restrain themselves, despite the incongruity of the gesture, and touched the feet or calves of the illustrious person to establish his true physical nature, says much both about the strangeness of the figure of the *weikza* and about the unprecedented sensory experience represented by the appearance in the flesh of a *weikza* who has "exited." Through the cult, the properly religious movement of distancing and separating, of removing, to which the figure of a *weikza* is subject, is completed and compensated for by an inverse movement of approaching and relating, of interweaving. In the relations between the mun-dane and supramundane spheres, a dialectic is established between a breaking into different planes and their rejoining.

Of humble origins—a sidecar driver, he had eventually acquired a dozen of these vehicles, living off the rent he charged for their use—Ba Yi became the principal representative of the cult in Mandalay in the 1980s. Anyone wishing to learn about the *weikza* and how to pay them homage went to him to find out. Ba Yi had not gotten beyond primary school. Nevertheless, he "knew how to speak"; he could impress people with his speech, and his visitors, no matter their status, acknowledged his superior skills. People gathered at his modest home to discuss and test each person's spiritual potency. Each sat facing the altar to the Buddha, a glass of water placed in the palm of his hand. If the liquid formed bubbles, as if under the influence of some strong stimulus, it was a sign of a high degree of men-tal concentration. From time to time, Ba Yi gave his friends some extraordinary water (*theikdi yay*) to drink; this was water he had infused with power.

The *weikza* wanted to summon their distinguished disciple when he was still alive, but the explicit authorization of his wife and his son were required. Hadn't people seen family members bothering the *weikza* relentlessly to send back to the world a relative called prematurely? At the time, Ba Yi's son was working in Japan. His parents having no telephone, it was impossible to get his agreement. When Ba Yi died in 1999, at the age of seventy-three, from throat cancer—the *weikza* had, by virtue of their power, pushed back the fatal occasion by two or three years—his cadaver was laid out for three days. It emitted no odor and his appearance remained fresh, as if the distinguished man were still alive. In accordance with the wishes of the deceased, his remains were placed in a tomb with four tiny holes, one on each side, in a funerary arrangement specific to *weikza* who "exit dead" (*athay htwet-*). The holes reflect a *weikza*'s ability to leave the tomb in order to continue his life. Seven days after the burial, Saturday's Son asked Ba Yi's wife to see if any odor emanated from the remains through the holes; no, none whatever. Later, some disciples from Mandalay who had assisted Ba Yi, went to the cemetery. They may have bribed the warden to break open the tomb, or they may have contented themselves with looking through the holes. Whatever the case may be, the conclusion remains the same: Ba Yi's body was no longer there. The disciple had been called to Dragoness Mountain. The *weikza* confirmed this by announcing that Ba Yi was with them. Years later, endowed with the title of Noble Grandfather (Bodaw) granted to lay *weikza*, the former sidecar driver possessed one of the cult's disciples for several months.

WOMEN EMPOWERED

The *weikza*'s vocation for rescuing beings (*thattawa ke-*) leads to an original development in the cult of the four *weikza*. Rescuing beings is, first and foremost, the project accomplished by the Buddha, during his lifetime, when he revealed his teaching. Applied to the *weikza,* it is understood to mean that they work for the salvation, both temporal and spiritual, of their disciples. A *weikza* helps his disciples to confront life's dangers (sickness, accidents, material difficulties, etc.) and guides them on the path to deliverance. At the Energy Center of Mebaygon, this salvational vocation has been expanded to such an extent as to claim that *weikza* are beings endowed with the extraordinary power to snatch people away from the inevitable—impermanence and death—and transport them to a marvelous realm where, almost immortal and therefore protected from the aleatory nature of the cycle of existences, they are assured access, when the time comes, to nirvana.

But let us not decide too quickly that things have drifted all that far from the mainstream. In spite of its apparent eccentricity, such a means to salvation—one we might describe as "elective"—remains linked to Burmese Buddhism as a whole and its Theravadin foundation. We are, no doubt, at the farthest limit of its range, where many Burmese would refuse to venture. People who have never been to Mebaygon are completely unaware of the possibility of being called. Informed of it, they contest its validity, much as some of the four *weikza*'s disciples do, for that matter. In Buddhism as conceived by Burmese, there is no Savior in the strict sense of the word. People pass through the stages of spiritual perfection by means of their own effort and commensurate with the virtuous acts they had carried out during previous lives. Progress on the path to nirvana and its eventual attainment are seen as the fruit of work (*kyin-,* "to practice"). Even if someone's masters support his or her quest for salvation, the possibility of achieving a spiritual revolution as a result of an external intervention is inconceivable. Yet, to be called, either at one's death or—even more astonishing and vastly more difficult—while still alive, amounts to "exiting" the cycle of existences thanks to a connection a person has made with the four *weikza.*

But this connection is phrased entirely in the idiom of Burmese Buddhism. It is seen as the product of a complex of influences conjoining one's virtue capital (*parami*) and a chain of relationships over a number of lives, not necessarily successive ones (*pahtan hset*). Proximity with the *weikza* is interpreted as a consequence and re-actualization of a relationship in one or several previous lives—as, in other words, the continuation of a karmic interdependence (which is the meaning of the phrase *pahtan hset*). To be called constitutes both the continuation and the crowning of this relationship. Given that this phenomenon is bound so closely to Buddhist understandings, by what right could we separate it again, as though it were up to us to judge its orthodoxy? A religion is not a closed and rigid corpus of dogmas and practices. It is a system of potentialities that, while defining an ideal or a goal, leaves open the range of ways of getting there. So there are sure to be surprises left in store.

Mya Nan Nwe was a rich Chinese woman of Mandalay who, in her later years, had rid herself of almost all of her possessions and had distributed the proceeds of their sale among several monasteries. She had moved to the Energy Center of Mebaygon to live near the *weikza.* She did not practice alchemy, but she ingested cabalistic diagrams. Endowed with an iron constitution, she died suddenly after fifteen years of residence at the monastery, in April 2002, while walking in the southeast corner of the monastery's grounds; that is, Tuesday's corner. It is in this direction that the *weikza* depart at the end of every séance, when they leave the hall through the little room located to the right of the altar to the Buddha. This is the direction in which Dragoness Mountain lies and the direction that the way leading to it takes. The *weikza* did not take long to confirm the rumor that Mya Nan Nwe had been called. The disciple, buried in the village cemetery, now spends pleasant days at Dragoness Mountain.

She has been joined there by Kyin Myaing. The latter, also of Chinese descent, was one of the four living disciples, along with Doctor Sein Yi, Major Zaw Win, and Lieutenant-Colonel Thein Han, who had taken part in all the life-prolonging ceremonies already performed. She was the only woman invited to participate in U Pandita's ceremony in 1975, in the company of thirty-five male disciples. This was a signal honor of which she showed herself worthy: during the ceremony, her children recount, she kept Saturday's Son inside the ceremonial circle when the medium, under the shock of the explosion and the reach of the flames following the lighting of the pyre, was backing out of it. Had Saturday's Son crossed that line, U Pandita and all the participants would have died. Her action explains the affection the *weikza* bore his disciple.[21] When she was seventy years old, U Pandita offered to call her to Dragoness Mountain. Kyin Myaing refused, wishing to remain with one of her daughters, who was unmarried. She died in December 2003 at the age of eighty-three. After her death, her body was exposed for three days, neither showing any sign of decomposition nor emitting any nauseating odor. She was buried in a cemetery in Yangon. At the time of the Festival of Success two months later, in the middle of a packed séance in the hall of the monastery, U Oktamagyaw announced, in the presence of two of Kyin Myaing's four children, that the disciple had reached Dragoness Mountain. He lectured her children. A fight had arisen concerning the division of their mother's estate: the wealthier ones appeared to be trying to minimize one brother's share. U Oktamagyaw explained that Kyin Myaing had asked him to pass along this message: peace within the family needed to be restored as quickly as possible so that nothing would disturb her in her retreat and so that she might devote herself to her spiritual development. The *weikza* made the two children, both in their fifties, promise to act according to their mother's wishes. Kyin Myaing's son and daughter were not the least bit disturbed by being admonished publicly in this way. The incident demonstrated the privileged attention that the *weikza* had always bestowed on the family. It is by no means rare for the *weikza* to enter into the private affairs of their close disciples. Doing so is part of the relationship that makes of these disciples the *weikza*'s sons and daughters (*weikza tha thami*).

Thus the four *weikza,* not content merely to develop a new path to salvation, matched this accomplishment with a complementary innovation: the possibility of a woman attaining the status of a *weikza* by being called to Dragoness Mountain. When that possibility is put to Burmese, in particular to those who are practitioners of the *weikza* path, they say that a woman is capable of becoming a *weikza*—in principle, certainly. In actual fact, the overwhelming majority, if not the totality of practitioners of the *weikza* path, are men. Furthermore, no one knows of a *weikza* of the feminine gender, and as a result, no woman is venerated by people in the manner of Bobo Aung, Bo Min Gaung, Bo Paukhsein, the four *weikza* of Mebaygon, and the like.[22] This state of affairs fits with the Burmese gender hierarchy, established on a Buddhist foundation in accordance with the idea that spiritually women are relatively weak. Some nuns state that they are pursuing a religious life in order to accumulate merit and obtain a good rebirth—that is, as a man—which would permit them to make their way toward nirvana. It is no doubt true, they say, that in the Buddha's time some women attained spiritual perfection. But we are no longer living in the Buddha's time, and without their knowing why this should be so, it appears to these women that such an accomplishment is impossible today, even for a nun. They make this observation without any bitterness or anger, as though it was a simple fact, bound to a given order whose foundations it would occur to no one to question, let alone challenge.[23] It is true that the very same move by which they acknowledge masculine superiority—stating their aspiration to be reborn as a member of the other sex—removes them de facto from men's domination. For a woman to renounce the world is not only to affirm her desire to become a man; it is also to shy away from marriage and the domestic condition or even to evade it completely. If nuns are subject to the authority of monks, this turns out to be much less burdensome and arbitrary than masculine authority as exercised at home. Yet it remains the case that, for women to renounce the world amounts, on an ideological level, to confirming men's superior spiritual capacity, to the extent that being a nun means expressing the hope to be reborn as a man.

Constraints imposed by Burmese Buddhist ideology are, in sum, overcome in two complementary ways by means of the cult of the four *weikza*. The cult undermines both the monopoly held by monks on access to salvation and the principle of women's relative spiritual incapacity. What's more, the path of salvation that the cult opens up, as compensation reserved for certain elite disciples who are "called" after their death, will undergo *in fine* a remarkable extension. Once Bodaw Bo Htun Aung's life-prolonging ceremony has been carried out and Saturday's Son's "exit" accomplished, the *weikza* will call all of their disciples to Dragoness Mountain. They will not have them come one by one but all at once, "like a fisherman catching fish in a net." All the disciples will have to do will be to close their eyes to be transported to the *weikza*'s realm, where they will meditate and practice whatever specialty (alchemy, etc.) they choose in order to reach, like the *weikza* before them, a near-immortality.

This means that, instead of being something obtained by only a few rare virtuosos, obtaining the status of a *weikza,* and then reaching nirvana, becomes a possibility, even a certainty, for all. At the same time that the four *weikza* sketch this mirage of universal deliverance, they seek, by virtue of their energy-producing activities, to bring about in human society a condition of general felicity under the governance of the Prince of the Universe. Thus the idea of salvation operates at two levels in the cult's framework. Salvation arrives by access to an ideal space *outside* of society and at the same time by the construction of an ideal order *within* society: a disciple hopes to be called to Dragoness Mountain just as he expects good fortune and happiness in his present life. No contradiction arises out of the coexistence of these two inverse movements, one pulling toward the beyond, the other rooting about here below. They are two sides of the same coin, made up out of what inheres in a Buddhist life. Their conjunction crystallizes the condition of *homo religiosus*.

THE LIFE OF MAJOR ZAW WIN

Our trip in the company of one of the cult's longest serving and most eminent disciples has hardly begun, and we have already wandered far afield! While we were getting carried away along our own path, from the practice of alchemy to the unusual path of salvation opened up by the four *weikza,* traveling along the route of their tireless activity in pursuit of the energy of success, Major Zaw Win has quietly taken his seat in the front of the car to the left of the driver. I am sitting in back. We are leaving for Mandalay, where we are to meet Saturday's Son. More precisely, the Major is accompanying me in order to introduce me to the *weikza*'s medium. As for the driver, he is an old friend of mine. A placid mechanic in whose garage work moves along at a slow pace, he has already gone along on several of my expeditions, as much to see the country and meet people as for the (modest) payments he receives.

The car sets out along the immense Pyay Road that runs from south to north through Yangon. The Major's lips are moving slightly: the disciple is reciting in an inaudible voice canonical texts known for their prophylactic efficacy (*payeik*)—this in addition to the indispensable "passport" for the trip's good outcome, the formula "The Buddha has succeeded!" Like so many others, the Major draws water from all springs, maximizing the forms of protection he calls up, much as a state builds its national defense. There's no being too careful when it's a matter of preventing the possible onslaught of fate's forces.

It's the rainy season, and we have chosen to travel to the city of Pyay and then along the Irrawaddy River: this route is longer, but it is less often affected by the torrential rains than the country's central axis. Two hours after we leave the city, we pass close to a village that was the site of a double tragedy. In 1942, at the age of sixteen, the Major had joined the Burmese army just at the time it was about to turn against the Japanese occupation. One of his superiors, a colonel, took advantage of a village woman. His bosses learned of this and sent the man a condemnatory letter. Humiliated, he committed suicide.

The Major sticks to retelling the facts; he adds no commentary. Why recall this particular incident? That a ranking officer should be reprimanded for having violated a young woman and that the shame drove him to kill himself: this says much about what the Burmese military was like—the nature of its values and the degree of its discipline—at the time of its origin. It also draws a sharp contrast with what it has become after more than forty years leading the country. To remember is to speak of the present. In the contrast that he is suggesting between the army of those years of struggle for independence and the army of today, there is no bitterness on the Major's part. He makes only a simple observation on power's inevitably corrupting effect. "Those who are in power want to keep it. They use their authority to favor their friends and hurt those people they don't like. It's the same everywhere, it's not something specific to Burma," he was to say on another occasion. "Politics is the dirtiest thing in the world."

The man speaks from experience because he was thrown into the middle of the power structure instituted by General Ne Win after the 1962 coup d'état. The course of the Major's career sounds like a parable about the history of the Burmese army, an army that knew well how to defend the nation's unity but understood so poorly that its relative success at this mission, for which it has been and remains today duly recognized, did not authorize it to monopolize power. After the war, in 1945, the Major rejoined the Burma Air Force as a technician in telecommunications. At the start of the 1950s, he participated in the fight against Kuomintang troops, who had fled to Burma after the communist victory in China.

It was the custom at the time to send brilliant young officers to England for training. The Major went for the first time in 1952–1953 for a training course in military aviation, then for a second time in 1957–1958 to improve his knowledge of telecommunications. In between those stints, in November 1956, he married a woman living on the same street he lived on in Yangon, a woman whom he would cherish his entire life. Both were of mixed blood (*kabya*). The Major's father was a Chinese man from Canton who came to Burma to work in the textile trade and got established there after his marriage to a woman from the group called "the Shan from Pyay" (some of whose ancestors, originally from the Shan Hills, had migrated to the city of Pyay, in the middle of Burma, and had married Burmese). The couple opened a Chinese porcelain store in Yangon. They spoke Burmese at home. The Major was the fifth of six children and went to a Burmese school. His wife, for her part, was born to a Sino-Burman father and a Mon mother; she, too, spoke only Burmese.

This history turns out to have striking parallels with the story of Bodaw Bo Htun Aung, which is certainly of interest to those among the cult's disciples who are of Chinese or mixed ancestry but who, for the most part, know no language or cultural idiom other than Burmese. Bodaw Bo Htun Aung, his biography relates, is the son of a Chinese man who, exiled from his country, married a woman of mixed Sino-Shan origin who lived in the region of Kyaiklat in Lower Burma (in what is today Irrawaddy Division). In spite of his origins and the Chinese element in his parents' names, the future *weikza,* who was born at the start of the nineteenth century, was given a Burmese name, Saw Htun Aung, after his childhood nickname, Hsin Saw. ("Bodaw Bo" means "Noble Grandfather," a common label for a lay *weikza.*) As a young man, he married a Burmese woman by whom he had one daughter. His Chinese origins came up again at the time of a potential marriage for his daughter. To explain Htun Aung's upset in the face of such an eventuality, the biography notes the Chinese custom by which a couple lives with the husband's family, causing the separation of a father from his daughter.[24] Both Bodaw Bo Htun Aung's story and his very being, in sum, refract the considerable heterogeneity of Burmese society and the strength of the combinatory formula that the society generates to accommodate this heterogeneity. They point to both the country's irreducible ethnic diversity and the ways in which that diversity is countered, which is through the relative reduction of cultural differences by means of their aggregation into a whole that articulates and transcends them. (But no room is made in the story for religious difference: Hindus, Christians, Muslims, and practitioners of spirit cults who also make up part of this society are all absent.) Bodaw Bo Htun Aung's Burmanization is made complete and crowned by his accession to the status of a *weikza,* a uniquely Burmese type of figure. And doesn't the Major aspire for that very same status of a *weikza?*

At the start of the 1960s, the Major was posted to the Burma Air Force's base in Meikhtila (Central Burma). Six years later, his superiors chose him to become a cadre in the Burma Socialist Program Party (BSPP), the single party created by General Ne Win's regime, all of whose supervisory positions were entrusted to the military. He took a six-month course at Mingaladon, in the capital city's suburbs, along with 255 other officers. They were instructed in grand ideologies ("from the Romans to Napoleon Bonaparte"), international politics, Burmese politics, and the BSPP's doctrine.[25] His critical distance—"obviously, they taught only what was to their advantage; they didn't talk about the bad things they were doing"—did not prevent him from finishing first in his class. That honor propelled him to an eminent position, Secretary of the Security and Administrative Committee of Mandalay Division. These ad hoc committees, chaired by military men, substituted for the governmental institutions in place before 1962.[26] From 1967 to 1972, the Major, freed from his military obligations, took charge of supervising the political, economic, and social administration of Mandalay Division's thirty-five townships. It was at this time that he and his wife became disciples of the four *weikza,* spurred on by Colonel Mya Maung, President of Mandalay Division's Security and Administrative Committee.

The years following 1962 had seen the state take control of much of the Burmese economy, nationalizing the most important industries, banks, export and import sectors, and rice trading, as well as creating "people's stores" that were supposed to provide for people's basic needs from then on. These measures threw the country's economy into disarray, and the shortage of basic goods, including rice, in a country that had been the world's largest producer of that commodity, caused immediate and intense resentment. It was in this context that a businessman of Chinese descent arranged, in 1969, to have bags of rice transported by river from Yangon to Bagan to feed his workers. The police, working on a tip, searched the boat. The businessman was accused of illegal trafficking, arrested, and put in prison. One of the businessman's close friends contacted the Major, asking him to get the accused out of this tight spot. The Major went to Bagan himself. Having investigated the ins and outs of the affair, he was convinced that the businessman had not intended to sell the rice on the black market. He used his authority to free the man. Afterward, the Major, displaying an attitude that is at the very least highly unusual in a system where corruption was and remains a normal way of doing things, refused on principle to accept any compensation. As a result, the man whom he had helped, prevented from freeing himself of this debt, has continued to this day to consider himself obligated to him. Nevertheless, despite the esteem and friendship he felt for the Major, for a long time this man had no interest in the four *weikza.* Looked at from the outside, it all seemed like a thorough mix of deception and tall tales. But at the beginning of 1976, shortly after the life-prolonging ceremony for U Pandita, he asked if he could accompany the Major to the Energy Center. It went precisely as it was supposed to. Giving up all resistance after years of skepticism, the businessman became a disciple of the cult, a disciple so fervent that the *weikza* gave him the name of Khyeik, by which he is known to people at the monastery. *Khyeik* means "safety pin," a reference to the way in which the disciple, for a time the owner of a factory producing these items, attached himself to the *weikza:* like a safety pin pinned to their robes. It also means "fish hook," the man having drawn a number of Burmese of Chinese descent to Mebaygon. To others, he is Myo Lwin.

As Secretary for Mandalay Division, the Major was obliged to obey his superiors' orders. When an action he was urged to take struck him as unjust, he tried hard to mitigate the damage. On two occasions, after examining the cases of innocent people who were to be imprisoned, he resolved to exonerate them. His punishment for doing so came down swiftly. In 1972, he was thanked for his service and sent back to the Air Force to serve as an instructor.

Yet the Major was not yet done tasting the bitterness of this world. In 1975, he was called on to judge certain people who had taken part in the demonstrations the previous December, following the death of the former Secretary-General of the United Nations, Thant. Thant died in New York, and his body was repatriated to Burma. General Ne Win, it was said, was jealous of this intelligent and educated man and refused to grant him, despite his stature, a state funeral. This treatment aroused the populace's wrath, particularly among students, who seized the occasion to express their hatred of the regime.[27] Eight special courts were convened, each consisting of three members, to pass judgment on those people presumed to have caused the riots. The Major took part in Court Number Four, along with one of his superiors and a Party cadre. They were to pronounce a verdict in the case of a famous monk who was much revered by Thant during his lifetime. The monk had demanded that a memorial in honor of the deceased be constructed. The three judges acquitted him. This decision angered General Ne Win. He ordered that all cases from then on be taken up and adjudicated at a higher level, such that the courts were constrained in their decisions to follow decrees issued at this higher level.

Following this incident, the Major requested permission to leave the army. He was only fifty years old, so this was well ahead of the age of mandatory retirement. But he had served for more than three decades and felt quite worn out. Leaving the army, however, was no easy thing, because doing so was perceived as a defection, if not treason. The Major asked for the four *weikza*'s support. In 1977, he received permission to retire with the full pension due an officer of his rank, 600 *kyat* per month. He and a friend went in on a business venture making bottle caps and other metal parts. The business failed, and they lost a considerable sum of money. Several years earlier, in recognition of his service during World War II, the government had awarded him an honorific title and a commercial space at a market in Yangon. His wife took charge of the market space to sell tobacco and candles wholesale. They acquired a second stall at the same market. From then on, they busied themselves running these two stores.

One of the Major's seven children—in addition to the five born to them, the Major and his wife had adopted two little girls when he was posted to the air base in Meikhtila—has remained unmarried. Nor does he work. On my visits to the elderly disciple, I notice in the course of our conversation this son wandering through the house, a smile on his lips. Thirty-four or thirty-five years old, the man sometimes speaks to me in incomprehensible bits of basic English. The first time this happened, his father said, "Please excuse my son; he is not normal." I thought it was a matter of a slight congenital disability. Things turned out to be more dramatic—and more Burmese too. The boy was doing fine during his childhood and adolescence. He entered the university and was studying botany. In his second year, his fiancée, who came from the town of Taungngu (Central Burma), went home to her family for the academic holiday. A Burmese man of Indian descent tried to woo her. The young woman, irritated by this suitor, called to her lover for help. He was working at the same time he was pursuing his studies, but he asked for a leave from work and traveled to Taungngu. When he returned, he had lost his mind. No one ever learned what had happened. The Major's wife saw the young woman once or twice, but learned nothing from her. Ever since, he has wandered endlessly through the house, half-distraught, half-blissful.

At the time when the son returned, the Major submitted his case to the *weikza*. They are known for curing evil spells that make people sick or mad or even kill them, caused by someone's envy or animosity. People take a relative or a friend whose behavior has become strange to the Energy Center in Mebaygon to show them to the *weikza*. The latter, whether directly or through Saturday's Son's mediation, take on the task of lifting the spell. It is enough for them to pronounce the formula "The Buddha has succeeded!" or to wave a dragon-headed stick along the victim's body. This treatment is accompanied by a recommendation to stay for a time at the monastery. But when the Major presented his son to the *weikza,* they pronounced themselves unable to act on his behalf. There was nothing to be done, because what had struck the young man was fate's most potent blow in the face of which the *weikza* themselves, despite their extraordinary power and their tremendous energy of success, sometimes had to submit: King Karma, absolute monarch if ever there was one. The son "was paying for a bad deed committed in a previous life" (*wut kyway hsat-*); he had to settle a heavy karmic debt. The *weikza* said nothing more. The Major does not know what his son did to deserve such distressing retribution. The young man has in any case been protected from the most dire of his affliction's consequences. He would have died, his father states, had the *weikza* not at least protected his physical well-being.

FASHIONING A CULT

We have passed Pyay. We reach the town of Aunglan, "Sign of Victory," at about 11:30 a.m. There's no use looking for Aunglan on a map of Burma. During Ne Win's reign (1962–1988), people say, opponents of the regime chose the place, whose name signaled success, to start a revolt against the government. The revolt failed, and the authorities, anxious to discourage any new impulse to rise up against the government, renamed the town Myayde—"Buried"—by which it is identified on maps to this day. Burmese nonetheless continue to call it by its old name.

Leaving the town, the Major tells the driver to stop at a modest building located on a rise. This is U Thilasara's monastery. The Major had met the monk previously at the Energy Center of Mebaygon. He had introduced him to me a few days before, during a trip U Thilasara was making to the capital. The three of us had seated ourselves in the large room on the second story of the Major's house containing the household altar, which was decorated with photos of the four *weikza* and the cult's motto, "the Buddha has succeeded!" U Thilasara sat with his back to the altar, cross-legged, on a mat. He did not sit at the center of the mat, as though he was leaving the spot vacant for its legitimate occupant, who was about to appear. To every question that I put to him, he first responded with another question, a procedure I took to be a rhetorical habit. "How to explain things with the greatest possible clarity?" the monk asked in a loud voice. He paused for several seconds, as though searching for inspiration, before launching into a free-flowing account based on a metaphor intended to make intelligible what seemed disconcerting or problematic to me. From time to time, he stood up and, leaving the mat behind, went to sit briefly on a chaise lounge placed on one side of the room. His response complete, he would go back to this original place. I hardly noticed this movement back and forth, as I strained to grasp what the monk was explaining. U Thilasara used an obscure idiom, expressing himself in a literary and image-filled Burmese that I struggled to understand.

After our meeting, I took him back by car, and the monk then clarified the meaning of his strange behavior. In the course of our conversation at the Major's, with neither of us realizing it, U Kawwida, the leader of the four *weikza*, had possessed him. The space left empty at the center of the mat marked the involvement of this invisible but present third element in our exchanges. When he wished to give his own opinion, U Thilasara left the mat, where he was possessed, and went to sit on the chaise lounge, where he regained complete mastery of himself. So throughout our conversation, the monk had subtly oscillated between possession and de-possession, between a loss of self and a return to self, passing from one state to the other by simply moving about the room. If, on the one hand, U Thilasara's off-center position on the mat signaled U Kawwida's separate existence, didn't his free movement from one place to the other, from one order of reality to another, mean on the other hand that the monk was taking on two identities, that he was both U Thilasara and U Kawwida? Rather than displaying his ability to be possessed, wasn't U Thilasara representing his capacity for duplication?

The monk's movement back and forth should not have surprised me, because it suggested what anthropologists claim the right to suppose: U Kawwida speaking through U Thilasara's mediation was nothing other than U Thilasara changing into U Kawwida. Figuring out who U Kawwida is and, more generally, who the four *weikza* are amounts to sorting out what individual experiences—those of U Thilasara and of others—and what collectively held logics give rise to and sustain this phenomenon of duplication. The empty spot at the center of the mat indicates the enigma in need of solution, but with this one difference: unlike in the case of a spirit (*nat*) or other cults of *weikza* who have "exited," the spot is not bound to remain empty. The four *weikza* appear in the flesh; they can be seen and touched. This difference, in the end, best expresses the need for them to exist.

U Thilasara, forty-four years old, became a novice at the age of eight in a monastery in the town where he was born, Myan Aung, in Irrawaddy Division. Four years later, he fell ill. He doesn't remember what the illness that he had was. U Kawwida, who was unknown to him, appeared to him in the flesh at midnight one night. The *weikza* used three fingers to take a pinch of salt and told him to swallow it. The novice felt better. U Kawwida took him to the Energy Center of Mebaygon. U Thilasara has no idea how. He was transported to the Site of Success: that's all he knows. There were two buildings or "caves" (*gu*) there that had been used in the life-prolonging ceremonies, one for U Pandita's, the other for U Oktamagyaw's. U Kawwida took the novice to U Pandita's cave and instructed him to practice meditation. He handed him a white circle made out of cardboard to focus his mind on. U Thilasara explained that this is a meditation technique called *kathaing* (*kasina* in Pali) that enables a practitioner to achieve intense mental concentration. During the forty-five days he continued to meditate inside the small building, the novice ate only one plain banana, given to him by U Kawwida. Later, the leader of the four *weikza* explained the special interest he took in him: U Thilasara had been his disciple in a previous life.

After his meeting with U Kawwida, U Thilasara left for Mount Popa, a site often frequented by aspiring *weikza*. (It was there that the famous Bo Min Gaung "exited" in 1952.) He meditated there for three years. Then the head of the four *weikza* encouraged the novice to pursue his studies. Without scriptural knowledge, his spiritual path would become perilous. An unschooled monk who meditates and experiences some vision will think, mistakenly, that he has achieved a remarkable degree of insight (*taya ya twa-*, literally, that "he has reached the Teaching or the Truth"). A learned monk will know how to think reasonably about this type of experience, as it is described in the texts. U Thilasara started a course at one of the most celebrated monastic study centers in the country, the Maha Gandayon in Amarapura, on the outskirts of Mandalay. He stayed there eight years, until he had obtained the rank of Master of the Teaching (*dammasariya*), an honorific title bestowed on those who have successfully undertaken the entire cycle of monastic studies. He taught for a time, then returned to the intensive practice of meditation, taught once again, and finally took up the position of head of this little monastery in Aunglan.

One might be surprised, in light of U Thilasara's early and extraordinary meeting with the head of the four *weikza,* that when the monk recounts the major stages of his life, U Kawwida should disappear from his story, except when he intervenes to direct the young man toward the path of study. As a matter of fact, the part about his meeting with the *weikza* was probably made up on the spot, ex nihilo. It would be hard not to notice the inconsistency, a striking one in fact: U Pandita's cave was constructed in 1974 and U Oktamagyaw's in 1988, whereas the events narrated by U Thilasara are supposed to have taken place in 1972. Put on the spot by the anthropologist to explain his very special relationship with U Kawwida, U Thilasara has improvised the story out of whole cloth. But that story, in his eyes and those of other Burmese, has nothing of the improbable about it.

U Thilasara's monastery was named "Weikza Theikdi Kyaung" by its founder, his predecessor. This ambiguous name suits its current occupant. It means both "Monastery of the Weikza's Extraordinary Powers" and "Monastery of the Accomplishment of Knowledge." The building is made out of ordinary wood, not teak. It was rebuilt and enlarged three years ago, but looks like it is a hundred years old. It provides shelter for four monks and one novice. Among them, only U Thilasara has been to Mebaygon. Because he is the head monk, the other residents are de facto disciples of the four *weikza;* they are placed under their protection.

The Major has given U Thilasara word that he will be visiting along with the anthropologist. U Thilasara cannot stay with us very long. During the three months of the season of monastic retreat, the monks of the sixty-four monasteries in Aunglan township take turns delivering daily sermons. Today it is U Thilasara's turn, and he is getting ready to leave for the place where the sermon is to be delivered.

The monk shows his visitors a water tank, nearing completion, that will hold 108 gallons (about 500 liters); it will serve the monastery and houses in its vicinity. The Major and his wife have financed the greater part of the project. According to U Kawwida's recommendation (mediated by U Thilasara), the principal donors were to be a couple made up of one person born on a Tuesday and another born on a Saturday. The Major and his wife fit this specific combination and offered to support the undertaking to the tune of 350,000 *kyat*. The tank was erected at a place specified by U Kawwida.

The Major, the driver, and I go up to sit in the monastery's main hall. U Thilasara takes up a book he has gotten from his bookshelf for my benefit. The monk wants to go back to a question that I had raised during our previous meeting, one concerning the definition of a *weikza*. The book contains the collected sermons of a famous preacher, Shwesetdaw U Thayzawbatha. In one of these sermons, the preacher provides not a definition, strictly speaking, but rather a classification of the different types of *weikza*. He distinguishes among four types: the *zawgyi*, who has mastery of the art of medicine and flies in the sky and underground; the *zawgi*, who practices yoga; the *gandayi*, who has the power to disappear and reappear at will; and the *weikzado*, who has succeeded at a specific technique, namely, alchemy, the cabalistic arts, medicine, or the recitation of mantras. U Thilasara notes this point: if a scholar of U Thayzawbatha's ilk speaks of *weikza*, then the *weikza* path clearly constitutes an orthodox phenomenon, entirely consonant with Theravada Buddhism. To U Thilasara, for that matter, the distinctive sign of an aspiring *weikza*, as compared to an ordinary monk, is not his achievement in any of the techniques U Thayzawbatha mentions: U Thilasara doesn't practice any of them. An aspiring *weikza* is marked by an intense commitment to the pursuit of nirvana and by the huge and prodigious effort he sustains for the entire duration of his quest. This spiritual radicalism takes the form of an assiduous practice of meditation.

The Major listens without reacting. Three years earlier, when he first met me, he had described the *weikza* phenomenon as a composite one. The *weikza*'s path, he had explained, linked two complementary elements: the attempt to prolong one's life and the practice of meditation in the way that the Buddha had taught. The first element—the avoidance of death—is, the Major noted, absent from Theravadin doctrine and makes the *weikza* phenomenon distinctive within

Burmese Buddhism. Uncovering its origins would require looking in the direction of Tibet, where many adepts of the *weikza* path have appeared.

I peer about the humble monastery's main hall. Nothing suggests the relations that the place's master enters into with U Kawwida (and only U Kawwida, because U Thilasara almost never mentions the three other *weikza,* making of their chief his only link to the cult). The bare altar to the Buddha contains no photograph of the chief *weikza,* let alone of the other three or Saturday's Son. I remark that I am surprised by this absence. There's no use cluttering things up with unnecessary signs of veneration, responds U Thilasara. People who make a great show of such things on their altar do not necessarily follow the teaching of the four *weikza*. Still, there is a little statue placed prominently in front of the altar that looks like a *weikza*. That, U Thilasara explains, is U Weikzadhara, alias Bo Paukhsein ("Grandfather Axe"). The monk gives me a gift, a tattered copy of a booklet published by a lay disciple at the time of the apparent death of the celebrated *weikza,* who "exited dead" in 1965.[28] But he avoids all discussion of the subject. The Major's presence is not conducive to explanations. Over the thirty-six years that have passed since his encounter with Saturday's Son, this loyal disciple has never—despite all the *weikza* and aspiring *weikza* that swarm throughout Burmese society—venerated any *weikza* other than those of the Energy Center of Mebaygon. To justify his loyalty, the Major has recourse to one of the military metaphors he is fond of using. Burma, he is in the habit of saying, is divided into several military regions, each one under the command of one officer. It's the same for the *weikza*. Many groups exist, living in different domains: Dragoness Mountain for the four *weikza* and their disciples, the Great Forest (Mahamyaing Taw) for others, Mount Zinkyai, and so on. Each of these places represents a kind of regional command. But altogether they form one and the same society, the society of *weikza,* whose members share a similar aspiration: to prolong their lives and reach nirvana at the moment the Buddha Gotama's relics are reassembled. (In truth, one set of *weikza* and aspiring *weikza* do not concern themselves with this moment, but rather focus on the much later epoch when the future Buddha, Metteyya, is to appear.) Along with this horizontal organizing principle of the *weikza*'s world comes a vertical one. Just like in the army, a general-in-chief has to coordinate and direct the whole ensemble of regional commanders. U Kawwida is this general-in-chief. For the Major, as for the rest of the cult's disciples, the hierarchy ranking all of Burma's *weikza* should be based on the criterion of age. Now U Kawwida was born in 968 (the year 330 in the Burmese reckoning). Not only is he vastly superior to Bobo Aung, born in the eighteenth century, to Bo Min Gaung and to Grandfather Axe, both born in the nineteenth century, but also to Shin Eizagona, considered the apical ancestor of *weikza,* whose story places him in the Bagan period (1044–1287).[29] The Major gives no thought to turning to other *weikza* when he has the chance and the privilege of paying homage to the most eminent of them all.

The Major knows that U Thilasara's devotion to the four *weikza* is hardly so exclusive. The Major would like to keep a clear hierarchy in place, a rigorous account of the distribution of roles and power within the cult—in brief, an orthodoxy. In his view, only Saturday's Son, chosen originally by the four *weikza* as their medium, can be possessed by any of them. All those—and there are several among the monks and laypeople participating in the cult—who claim to be possessed by the four *weikza* in the same way and to the same degree as Saturday's Son are usurpers. Thus the Major prefers to pretend to be unaware of some of U Thilasara's claims. Several times in conversation with me, he has named Grandfather Axe or Bo Ming Gaung as the monk's masters, rather than U Kawwida. In fact, when U Thilasara speaks of U Kawwida, and even when U Kawwida speaks through U Thilasara, the Major sees Grandfather Axe or Bo Min Gaung. This substitution is only one of the features of the implicit agreement between them, made up of a play of appearances, of deliberate misunderstanding, and of the unspoken, that makes possible the exchanges between these two men—exchanges that the glaring contradictions in their respective relations to the four *weikza* would otherwise make unsustainable.

A similar agreement controls the relationship between the Major and me. In the course of our many discussions and excursions, the Major never puts to me the one question that really matters to him: "Do you believe [in the four *weikza*]?" Interlocutor, assistant, or intermediary by turns, but never inquisitor, he is careful not to force me to make the impossible choice between believing and not believing. I, for my part, avoid saying anything that would undermine the fragile fiction that I am a believer in the making. The Major and I act as though, like others more skeptical still, I am prolonging my period of observation of the cult before joining it and writing an appropriate work on the *weikza.* A great many things can be said, clarified, and accomplished on the condition that this bit of obscurity remains. Within the framework of this hardly fortuitous encounter and relationship between two men on a quest, none of us of will put the other on the spot.

Such a valuable fiction comes at a price. The Major's disinterestedness, his support for and participation in the anthropologist's project, out of which he does not seem to expect the usual result (that the anthropologist become a disciple of the cult), create a debt that the anthropologist, unless he becomes a believer, can never clear. Worse, the anthropologist will aggravate matters by reporting in his work information that the Major would have preferred that he keep to himself. When I returned repeatedly to the dramatic story of his son, the beleaguered Major guessed that I was planning on making some use of this story. He asked me not to mention the matter in my study nor, for that matter, to allude to his personal history in general, which in his view had nothing to do with the cult. Another time, the aging disciple expressed a more general anxiety. Having spoken with so many people and collected such different accounts—sometimes critical toward the four *weikza*—could I still distinguish between what was true and what was false? Writing an article, the Major explained, requires having a clear objective and sticking to it. If an author expresses contradictory opinions, the reader soon gets lost. So it is essential to present "the truth." The Major also worried about the unflattering picture of Burmese Buddhism that my work might offer foreigners. Were readers to come away from it with a lack of respect for Burmese religion, the help he had given me would turn into a negative act, with predictable karmic consequences over the course of his future lives. Yet the anthropologist is certain to break faith with the Major; there is no denying that fact. What to do? The anthropologist must either abandon his vocation, or he must betray the Major.

A singular trio this, one has to say, made up of U Thilasara, the Major, and the anthropologist—the first two speaking without quite communicating, while the third one carefully records what they tell him, to use when the time comes, soon enough, for him to betray them. All three of them are fashioning the cult.

A FABRICATED WAR AGAINST A CHIMERICAL PERIL

U Thilasara, whom a layperson has come to fetch in a car, goes off to deliver his sermon. The Major and I await the return of our driver, who has gone to get lunch. In the course of our conversation with the monk, an enormous man, very well dressed, came and sat on the floor a little bit away. It would appear that he is a person of some note in the neighborhood whom U Thilasara has invited to keep us company in his absence.

The Major starts a polite conversation. He declares himself delighted to learn that Buddhism flourishes in the good city of Aunglan. It's all very well and good to be tolerant, he says, but you have to admit that there really is something not quite right about Muslims: their sectarianism, their exclusivity. A Muslim man, the Major states, is authorized to marry four women, who must be Muslim or willing to convert, and their children are Muslims. Buddhists, in contrast, leave everyone at liberty to follow his or her own religion. The Major speaks without spite, in a tone suggesting objective observation. The other man agrees fulsomely. Yes, all these Muslims are a worry. Just look at Aunglan: there are three mosques here. The Muslim religion is gaining ground all over Burma. One city is an exception, he notes, because it has succeeded so far in preventing the construction of a single mosque: Kyaukpadaung. The people of Kyaukpadaung are tough, the Major and his interlocutor both agree. Hasn't the city grown rich over the past few years thanks to its inhabitants' business sense, while the rest of the country is in a big slump?

I keep quiet. There is nothing surprising about the Muslim menace coming up as a spontaneous subject of conversation and an area of sure mutual agreement between two Burmese Buddhists. For the 90 percent of the national population that is Buddhist, it is not inconsequential whether a non-Buddhist is Hindu, a practitioner of a spirit cult, Christian, or Muslim. There is a gradation in degrees of religious difference that determines the degree of someone's Burmeseness.[30]

A month later, the first question I will put to a disciple of the four *weikza* who is of Indian descent and whose family has lived in Burma for three generations will be about the date of his conversion: when did he make the switch from Hinduism to Buddhism? Such a question is one of the queries that, given the density, strangeness, and sometimes the disorderliness of people's stories, can provide an anthropologist a brief respite. It asks for no more than the statement of a date. The anthropologist can calmly write this down in his notebook before launching into a discussion about the causes and circumstances of this conversion, one in which the four *weikza* will no doubt have played a role. As expected, at 12:30 p.m., Victorious and I will have found Hsami at one of his two betel stands, located on adjacent streets in downtown Mandalay. These are wooden sheds resembling all the others that dot the country's towns, with the one difference that his stands are more attractive and better stocked. Assisted by his wife and daughter, the owner sells areca nuts, betel leaves, cigarettes, cakes, drinks, and candies. A cigarette lighter for the customers' use hangs by a string. The enterprise is modest, without a doubt, and Hsami has to get up at 5:30 a.m. to ride his bike the eleven kilometers into town, only getting home at close to 11:00 p.m. The man gives himself only one day off a month, except for when the Festival of Success takes place. Then he closes up shop and takes himself off to the Energy Center in Mebaygon.

But Hsami has known much more difficult days. His family was poor. His father died when he was thirteen. He started work as a dockworker, the first of any number of petty jobs. When he married a Hindu woman in 1981, he had one tiny betel stand. The following year, because his wife was suffering from asthma, they went to see a specialist in Burmese medicine whose treatment turned out to be quite effective. The therapist told them about the four *weikza*. Saturday's Son, who was spending the monastic season of retreat in Mandalay, often came by the home of a pair of his disciples, a married couple, to conduct séances in the late afternoon. Hsami went to attend such a séance. There the medium was possessed by U Pandita. The *weikza* announced that Saturday's Son was leaving the next day for Mebaygon: he asked Hsami to go with him. At the Energy Center, U Pandita appeared in the flesh. "Watch over me, Venerable!" Hsami begged him. "I will watch over you; it is my responsibility," the *weikza* stated. To watch over someone (*saung shauk-*), an essential mission of the *weikza*, means to protect and support a disciple in all areas of his life (health, family, business, travel, and, of course, spiritual practice). Hsami had brought along a brand-new bottle of perfume. "We are going to make some relics appear in the bottle," U Pandita said. Ordinarily, the *weikza* would put the bottle on the altar and the chorus of young women would call on the Buddha, or he would hit the bottle with both hands. But Hsami wanted to be convinced; he wanted to make sure that no doubt remained in his mind. He insisted on keeping the bottle in his own hands, an effrontery that stunned the audience. U Pandita took up the challenge. The *weikza* placed himself in front of the Buddha altar and proceeded to make a recitation lasting a good ten minutes. Bodaw Bo Htun Aung was present, and when U Pandita was done, he told Hsami to check the bottle. Nine relics had appeared. "Nine, that isn't good; ten would be better!" proclaimed Bodaw Bo Htun Aung. He took the bottle and struck it with both his hands. A tenth relic appeared. Hsami has saved the bottle, placing it on his household altar. Strangely, pressing the bottle's aspirator produces no perfume, as though the relics were retaining the fragrance.

On average, Hsami came back to Mebaygon three times a year. Having less work at that point gave him the time to do so. The four *weikza* supported their disciple as they had committed to doing. Hsami and his wife had trouble conceiving a child. Bodaw Bo Htun Aung promised them a son on the condition that the child, when he was old enough, would undergo a novice's ordination and stay temporarily in a monastery, like any Buddhist boy. The child was born in 1988. Five years later, his ordination was celebrated at the Energy Center. In the meantime, one day in 1991, Saturday's Son visited Hsami at his home, a tiny room that the disciple rented. "You live here? So buy a house!" exclaimed the monk on seeing the pitiful dwelling. Hsami smiled: he didn't have the means to do that. His family lived from day to day. But the following year his sales increased so dramatically that he bought a little house on the outskirts of Mandalay. Soon he opened a second stand.

Hsami will have taken Victorious and me to a pagoda close to his stands. He often goes there at noon to say his prayer beads. There's little business at that time of the day: the heat keeps people off the streets. The pagoda is a vast enclosed space, with a number of pavilions sheltering Buddha images scattered about its inner court. We will have seated ourselves on the concrete slabs surrounding one of the pavilions, where there is no risk of anyone interrupting an interview that promises to be easy. Hsami will be cheerful and affable. Nonetheless, without any malice, simply because he sees the world differently, in reaction to the question I pose he will exclaim as though taken aback, "Converted? But Hinduism and Buddhism are the same thing!" Victorious, too, who will already have assisted me for some time and will have therefore taken the measure of my interest in Buddhism, will add—because he too will be flabbergasted by my ignorance— "Yes, of course they're the same. Didn't you know?" No, I did not know. Furthermore, to say so will obliterate a distinction that I thought was obvious. Hinduism and Buddhism are the same thing? My interlocutors would not have confused the two religions. Rather, it goes without saying that one can be both Hindu and Buddhist at the same time. The two religions, they will explain—determined as they will be to shine some light on things for the anthropologist, who will appear stunned and indeed be quite shaken—are based on the same principle, that of retribution: a good action entails a future benefit, and the opposite. And they both advocate the practice of meditation, although they use different techniques. Meditation consists of concentrating the mind on a divinity, in one case, or on one's own bodily and mental sensations, in the other. Knowing almost nothing about Hinduism, whether in India or Burma, I will hardly be able to sustain a conversation that will take on the features of an earthquake. Some will say that the point is already spelled out in books; many have stigmatized the Western observer's restricted vision, narrowed by Christian preconceptions, according to which an individual can only have one religion. But it is one thing to read something in books and it's quite another to experience it in real life. Disoriented, I will create a diversion, shifting the conversation to the firmer and more familiar ground of the cult of the four *weikza*.

If it is possible to be both Hindu and Buddhist at the same time, the Muslim religion, in contrast, is thought of as the furthest point of otherness, where there is not just difference but also incompatibility and even a latent state of war. The great majority of Muslims are descendants of the wave of Indian immigration that supplied colonial Burma with civil servants, with businesspeople and usurers, and with laborers—all of them docile. The Indian presence being associated with the British presence, tensions mounted after World War I. These led to two series of anti-Indian riots in the 1930s. Those of 1938 targeted Muslims particularly. Nationalists grew alarmed at the growth in mixed marriages and the requirement that Buddhist women who were party to such marriages convert. Today, the idea is widespread among Buddhists, although unsubstantiated by the facts, that there is a worrying growth of Islam in Burmese society, said to be due to Muslims' aggressive proselytizing. An appalling popular fury comes down on the heads of Muslims periodically, bringing about beatings, if not massacres, looting, and mosque burning. Such violence has long offered an outlet for the population's political and economic frustrations. But there is more to the relation of Burmese Buddhists to the Muslim religion and to Muslims than a scapegoating reflex. At least the cult of the four *weikza* reveals another aspect of this relationship.

The four *weikza* are described by their disciples as great converters of Muslims. The conversions that can actually be credited to them, however, are few. Only one example is named when people allude to the *weikza*'s sterling record in the collective fight against the Muslim religion: the conversion of the figure whom the disciples of the cult refer to as Kala Mya Than. The term *kala* labels people of Indian descent and, by extension, foreigners. In this instance it serves a commemorative function, because it indicates the man's previous religious alterity and its diminution at the hands of the *weikza*. Diminution and not elimination, because Mya Than, as an emblematic figure and practically the only convert won over by the *weikza,* must remain a Muslim who became a Buddhist (or a formerly Muslim Buddhist). His first encounter with the *weikza* took place in the 1960s, at the home of Colonel Mya Maung, who was introducing the cult to the Major and many others at the same time. Mya Than, a bicycle repairman, had come along with his friend Ba Yi. At the séance, U Pandita possessed Saturday's Son. He told the two companions that they had been royal officials in the Bagan era (1044–1287) and had shown themselves to be his loyal donors. (U Pandita "exited" at the end of the thirteenth century.) There was nothing of chance about their meeting with him; they were all of them caught up in a chain of relationships.

But Ba Yi and Mya Than were not won over by this first experience. A year later, they had an opportunity to go to the Energy Center of Mebaygon, to the house where Saturday's Son lived with his family. Bodaw Bo Htun Aung appeared in the evening. After his sermon, he came down from the house using the stairs. The two visitors found it odd that a so-called *weikza* would use the ordinary way out. They wanted to follow him but he disappeared. When looking for him failed to turn him up, a voice called to them from the house. It was Bodaw Bo Htun Aung. "We are real *weikza* and have come to support the religion, by means of Saturday's Son," he declared. Despite this display, Ba Yi, called on to become the leader of Mandalay's disciples, remained skeptical. He continued to observe the cult for another three years. Mya Than, for his part, was a believer from this first visit at the Energy Center. On returning from Mebaygon, he became a Buddhist, accomplished by repeating a simple formula, that of taking refuge in the Three Jewels. He had been completely transfixed by the *weikza*'s teaching about the path to nirvana, he will tell me to conclude his account of his famous conversion—an account, however, in which all that mattered was the supernatural potency of the *weikza*.

It is of no consequence, in the eyes of the cult's disciples, that when Mya Than first entered into relations with the four *weikza* and their medium he already wanted to convert to Buddhism and, ready to take the step, had entered under his own steam into a phase of Buddhist religious study. What matters is that he had not yet converted and was socially identified as a Muslim. Were one to forget that fact, the prefix attached to his name would serve as a reminder.

The disparity between the rarity of actual conversions attributable to the four *weikza,* presented as though obtained through fierce struggle, and the importance the conversion motif takes on in the rhetoric of the cult's disciples shows that in this peculiar war what matters is less the direct confrontation with the enemy than the propaganda addressed to one's own troops. It seems as though Buddhists sought to give a human face to a worrying shadow, which they fashioned according to their own wants, and projected it on Muslims. The fantasizing relationship of Buddhists to Muslims serves above all to keep the former in a state of permanent war: a war they carry on with themselves. Isn't it the case that, by means of this imaginary Muslim menace, Buddhists see their religion as in peril, even close to getting swallowed up completely, thereby persuading themselves of the necessity for everyone to engage in its defense and so allowing for the active perpetuation of Burmese identity? In this war, which is considered one only to them, they reveal their haunted fear of the decline of the practice of Buddhism in society and their anguish at a possible collective inability to face up to it. This fear and this anguish, knowingly maintained, are so strong that they induce paranoid fantasies, a method of self-perpetuation based on a pathology in which collective violence becomes a foundational part of the community. The image of the Muslim results from the Buddhists' own anxiety that they externalize and magnify to fight against it.

To work, the segmentary mechanism of a Burmese Buddhist identity, in which opposites at one level combine at a higher one, must finally hit up against an absolute difference, that of the Muslim, the negative point at which all Buddhists agree and come together. In the midst of this reproductive device that combines a collective artifice (to remind oneself constantly of the possibility of one's own disappearance) and a projective mechanism (to make manifest—to give a name and a face to, to identify—that possibility), Kyaukpadaung is mentioned as Buddhism's last stronghold, highpoint of the resistance against a chimerical peril. And the four *weikza* become war heroes, because heroes are needed for this fabricated war, in which fictive aggressors, although defeated from time to time, still see their existence spared, as though better to fulfill their original function: to serve as a specter for Buddhists.

WHEN YOU'RE IN TROUBLE

Beyond Aunglan, the countryside changes. The road to Pyay is punctuated by towns, villages, vehicles, and people. After three hundred kilometers, the distance from Yangon to Pyay, in which the scenery is desperately flat, the ground becomes hillier. The rice fields give way to bushy areas or nonirrigated fields (for growing beans, sesame, peanuts) where the human presence becomes less noticeable. A strange calm sets in. The road, narrower from now on, is little used; there are few towns. The climate changes too. The wearisome tropical stickiness that envelops the southern part of the country is gone, and as the humidity diminishes, the air becomes healthier and more breathable. We have reached Central Burma.

It is about 5:00 p.m. when the three of us, having skirted the town of Magway, reach the area surrounding the Dying Peacock streambed. We must cross it to get to Yenangyaung, where we plan to spend the night. A row of vehicles blocks the way to the streambed. The driver stops the car at the back of the line. The Major and I go to find out what's going on. The line is two or three hundred meters long, made up of group taxis, buses, and commercial trucks, as well as a few private cars. Things quickly become clear: the dry streambed has become a river. A crowd of travelers, massed on the bank, is waiting. A dog has slipped and fallen into the water. Several times over, it looks like it will be carried off by the current and sink. Every time, it resurfaces, struggling to get back to the bank. The animal's plight arouses a certain liveliness, even gaiety, among the idle observers. People talk about it, they laugh, they exclaim, as they watch the animal struggling between life and death in the water. Forgotten are the Buddhist virtues of benevolence and compassion, of which Burmese at times like these seem completely lacking in their altogether human cruelty. The dog finally manages to get back to the bank, and the entertainment is over.

On the other bank, seven hundred meters away, can be seen an identical column of stopped vehicles. There is no way a bridge could be put in here. The ground is too prone to shifting; the bottom is only sand. The inhabitants of the village who live on the bank don't complain, because they make their living in part on the basis of this fact. When there is a heavy rain during the rainy season, in no time the dry arroyo turns into a raging torrent. For the first few hours, crossing it is out of the question. But when the force of the floodwaters begins to subside, owners of tractors in the village tow the vehicles of travelers in a hurry across, for hefty fees. Others wait patiently to cross, for cheaper fees. Yet they, too, require the villagers' help. Only the latter know the sands well enough to guide a vehicle across without it getting stuck in the mud. People know better than to annoy these masters-for-a-day, with their muddy legs and ragged clothes, by making it appear that they want to argue about the price demanded. The local men are said to have the malicious habit of getting the vehicle of any stingy person stuck in the mud straightaway, forcing the owner into the hands of the tractor owners, who will charge them a good deal more.

The water rose at about 3:00 p.m. We hope that the waters will recede quickly. Some vehicles, towed by tractors, succeed in making the crossing. The driver, anxious not to damage our car, is reluctant. It is getting dark. We turn back to spend the night, not in Magway, but on the opposite shore of the Irrawaddy, in the town of Minbu, a few kilometers from the Energy Center of Mebaygon. The Major and I know of a guesthouse in Minbu authorized to put up foreigners. We had stayed there during our previous trip, two years earlier, when having left Yangon on a bus in the late afternoon, we had gotten to Minbu before dawn the next day. Once we had gotten ourselves settled at the guesthouse, it had been necessary to make known to the authorities the presence of a Frenchman and to explain the reason for his stay: a visit to the *weikza*'s monastery. Minbu lies outside the tourist circuit, so a foreigner's arrival there is noteworthy. The village of Mebaygon, furthermore, is located in the midst of an area of oilfields developed by the state. The Major, prudent and possessed of a highly developed sense of discipline, wished to observe the official formalities and rules to the letter. But when we got to the Immigration Office to announce our intentions, we were informed that it was now forbidden for foreigners to visit Mebaygon. The person in charge of the office claimed to have received a directive in this regard. He acted as though he was looking for it among his files. In actual fact, the directive did not exist. As we discovered later, two Germans, having been granted long-term visas to practice meditation, had spent a night at the *weikza's* monastery without informing anyone. Had any sort of incident occurred during their stay, a ton of bricks would have come down on the heads of the local authorities, unleashed by their superiors. The person in charge of the office was going to make sure to keep himself covered. Nevertheless, it was difficult to present his interlocutors with a firm and definitive refusal. At the start of their meeting, the Major had made known his identity. His military rank put the official in a predicament. He tried to sidestep matters by asking the visitors to give up their plans on their own, while stating that, should they persist in their intentions, he would yield to the wishes of the most potent local authority, the Secretary of the Minbu District Peace and Development Council.[31] Seeing that we were ready to try our chances in that corner, he thought he could dissuade us by assuring us that in any case going to Mebaygon would be a waste of time: Saturday's Son was away on a trip. The Major, aware of that fact, explained that we had come not to see Saturday's Son but rather to present monk's robes to the head of the four *weikza*, U Kawwida. "U Kawwida is dead," the official retorted abruptly.

As a general rule, the people of Minbu, like those of the village of Mebaygon and those of the oilfields, do not believe in the four *weikza*. Those who do believe in them, it is customarily said, come from far away. And people quote the proverb, "A village's cows don't graze on the grass nearby"; that is, they go looking for it elsewhere, as though it were better there. In light of the difficulties that morning, the Major had recourse to one of the four *weikza's* favorite parables: the image of a pond covered with lotuses whose pollen attracts bees from afar while the frogs who live there fail to make any use of it. They are happy simply to make a racket croaking. And when the surprised bees question the frogs about this, they respond, "Making noise is good enough for us!" For the cult's disciples, incredulity is the child of moral turpitude. If people nearby do not believe, it is due to their depravity, incapable as they are of following the precepts laid down by the *weikza*. A significant dividing line is drawn in this way. The people of Minbu, of the oilfields, and of the village of Mebaygon, are placed in the despised category of "drinkers of alcohol." Sensing themselves surrounded by immorality, if not irreligion, the *weikza's* disciples think all the better of themselves and become all the more resolute in their commitment. One might say that the local incredulity surrounding the cult contributes to its development: far from undermining the disciples' convictions, on the contrary it enhances their devotion.

However, I saw that the bureau chief's cutting remark put the Major, always so calm and affable, into a rage, his face turning red with anger. In a tone that betrayed the strength of his feelings, he pointed out that he had been going to Mebaygon since 1967 and had paid homage to U Kawwida on a regular basis. He invited the insolent miscreant to come observe with his own eyes the existence of the venerable *weikza*. The way the official then looked at his interlocutor left no doubt as to what he was thinking. Only his status spared the Major from being treated like a gullible old fool. The bureau chief ended the meeting by grabbing a file and starting to read it. The Major and I took our leave. As we made our way in a horse cart to the offices of the Peace and Development Council, hardly five minutes from that of the Bureau of Immigration, the silent Major rubbed frenetically the little energy ball mounted on the ring he wore on his finger. He prayed wordlessly to the four *weikza* to help assure the successful outcome of a highly uncertain endeavor.

The Secretary of the Peace and Development Council received us immediately. He was in military attire. He, too, had the rank of major, but he was much younger, only about forty or forty-five. On seeing his pudgy face and arrogant look, I thought all was lost. The Secretary listened to the Major who, although he was speaking practically to a subordinate, expressed himself with his customary humility. How many times had I seen him, despite his age and social position, speak in this way to some poor soul whom we came upon in the course of our wanderings? The Major evinced a modesty and respect toward manifestly inferior individuals that were astonishing in a society in which status hierarchies are so strongly marked. "Please don't be annoyed, and I may well be wrong, but . . ." he would say when about to make a remark or voice an opinion in the course of a conversation he had taken up with a scruffy-looking peasant, a sidecar driver, or a fruit seller. How could they be annoyed? For even if the Major's behavior had been proud and scornful—which it was not in the least—his age alone would command a certain deference, even if only superficial. His manners were such as to disarm the most irascible and to banish all vulgarity. The worst loudmouths quieted down in his presence and responded to him in a civil tone. Paradoxically, there was something a little indecent about his demeanor. The Major refused to play the role that he had by rights come into, and I was sometimes embarrassed for him because of this humility, when everyone expected a certain formality, even haughtiness, on his part.

I said not a word during the entire meeting. You would have thought it had nothing to do with me. Two worlds were meeting up. The Major belonged to the first generation of officers, those who had taken part in the resistance to the Japanese occupation, had experienced firsthand the highpoints in the Burmese army's past, and furthermore—and this mattered—had been trained abroad. His interlocutor incarnated the new order, from the period of Ne Win's listless regime and the period after the coup d'état of 1988, when the army brutally reasserted its power over the country. These officers had never been outside the country's borders. Their status had also been devalued as a result of a massive wave of promotions to the ranks of major, colonel, and general after 1988. To be a major in the 1960s and to be one in the first decade of the new millennium did not mean the same thing, and the Secretary knew it. He might well be made testy by the sudden appearance in the fiefdom in which he ruled of a man who symbolized a glorious—but long gone—era.

When the Major had finished explaining the aim of our project, without failing to mention his rank and the official compensation he had received—an honor granted by the government to World War II combatants once they reached the age of seventy-five—the Secretary picked up his telephone, an old black model that graced his almost bare desk. He wished to ask some questions of the chief of the Immigration Office. He also probably wanted to put a bit of a pause in the course of the conversation. The situation was delicate and he was hesitant about what path to take. The Major was not throwing his weight around, but it was quite possible that he still had connections entrenched in the army. The Secretary would be in deep trouble if he displeased his superiors. Doubly careful, he authorized his guests to go to Mebaygon for the day without giving them a pass for which he could be held responsible. "Success!" the Major exclaimed once we were out on the street.

Two years later, the same owner of the guesthouse welcomes the Major and me warmly. Yet he cannot put us up. Tension is at a peak in the town. Four days earlier, three soldiers deserted after having been slapped either by their superior or his wife—no one knows which—taking their arms with them. They have taken refuge on an island in the middle of the river, directly facing Minbu. The incident has attracted a lot of attention, with rumors reaching all the way to Yangon. Cases of mutiny, in a country in the hands of the military, are rare. The day before, the island was attacked and two of the deserters killed; the third managed to escape. The authorities in Minbu are on edge. No foreigner can stay in the town. We must make a U-turn, cross back over the Irrawaddy River, and go to Magway. The guesthouse owner recommends a guesthouse not far from the bridge that can accommodate foreigners.

Run-down and dirty, the Rolex Guesthouse, as it is called, has little appeal. We are up and on our way at 7:00 the next morning. I am getting anxious. The difficulties and obstacles are piling up, and I worry that the trip, for which I am in a certain respect responsible, is going badly. I do not, however, make my feelings known. For his part, the Major, on whom this series of incidents could very well start to weigh, seems serene, possessed of his usual composure. Yet it will soon become evident that in his case too, this lack of concern is only a facade.

When we get to the streambed, at about 7:30 a.m., we come upon the same line of vehicles as the day before. The stream has almost entirely disappeared. There remains only a slight flow and patches of water here and there, but the ground is muddy and full of potholes. A bus has gotten stuck about thirty meters from the bank, stopping traffic. Villagers have attached several tractors to the bumpers to pull it to the bank. On the other side, many vehicles are waiting. Once the bus gets pulled out, the cars get taken across one by one to avoid a traffic jam and a mess of vehicles getting stuck in the mud, which could be disastrous—the weather looks threatening. The tractor drivers have worked all night without taking a break and will keep on working for most of the day. We notice some cars crossing about three hundred meters downstream. A narrow stretch of sand, which only lighter vehicles can navigate, hives off from the main road leading to this ford's entry. We decide to take this route, which will spare us a long wait. As insurance, we ask for the help of villagers equipped with a tractor. Once the cables connecting the tractor to the car are in place, the towing begins. But hardly have we gone two hundred meters, before we've even reached the entrance to the ford, when the tractor stops cold. It is out of gas. In the thick of the struggle, no one had thought to check the tank. We are still close to the village, five minutes by foot from any house, even the farthest one away. A man goes off in search of fuel.

After waiting a half-hour, the Major reaches under his shirt to pull out the ball of energy hanging from his neck. He starts rubbing it compulsively with the fingers of his right hand. After an hour, the man reappears with a can of gas. We ask no questions, nor show signs of irritation. We are at the tractor driver's mercy.

It remains to get the tractor going again. A good deal of comment has been made about how difficult it is to restart an engine after it has run out of gas. Everybody joins together to push the vehicle, except for the Major, who keeps rubbing his ball of energy. Once, twice: the engine roars. The streambed is crossed without further difficulty. The sands behind us, and with his serenity restored, the Major proclaims enthusiastically, "The Buddha has succeeded!"

A POTENT MEDICINE

Mandalay is not an attractive city, but it is a pleasant one. Traffic is less congested than in Yangon: people get around by bicycle or motorcycle. The numbered streets and their arrangement in a grid make it easy to orient yourself. The Yasa-gyo Monastery, where Saturday's Son has spent every Lenten season since the 1980s, is located at the end of Twenty-Second Street, a few steps from the Ir-rawaddy River. Surrounded by a yard and a wall, the building is in the middle of a complex of about fifteen independent monasteries. On the ground floor, in a large, dark, and gloomy room, lives a destitute-looking monk in his seventies. His older brother was a disciple of the four *weikza* and had invited their medium to live with him whenever he came to Mandalay. In 1996, after his brother's death, the younger brother ceded the monastery's property to Saturday's Son, judging that the latter's considerable number of lay supporters better positioned him to take care of the building.

Saturday's Son lives on the upper floor of the monastery. The hall is a vast open space, with a little room to one side that serves as the monk's bedroom. In the middle of the hall sits a glassed-in cabinet containing a television set and a tape recorder. When the Major and I arrive, on Tuesday, August 26, 2003, the medium is sitting on a chaise lounge watching a comedy show on DVD. The Major pays him obeisance by prostrating himself, then introduces me. Once the conversation has gotten going, I ask the monk to recount how he met the four *weikza* and became their intermediary fifty-one years earlier. As he responds, Saturday's Son rubs the Major's energy ball in his hands. His remarks move from subject to subject. The Major intervenes from time to time to clarify or comment on a particular point. Taking advantage of a moment when the con-versation pauses, he makes Saturday's Son a gift in his own and his wife's name. It is the first time the Major has seen Saturday's Son since the loss of his wife three months before. Overcome with emotion, he starts to choke up. It is five minutes before he is able to recover his good humor. When the time approaches to end the meeting, he speaks once again of his late wife. Saturday's Son explains that he was much affected by the death of his disciple. "They say the *weikza* have called her. Is it possible, Venerable?" asks the Major, bursting into tears. "Or is it possible that she has been reincarnated as the guardian spirit of a pagoda's trea-sures (*thaik*)?" "I don't know," Saturday's Son responds. "Only the *weikza* could tell you."

Meanwhile, the driver has come upstairs. He has sat down on the floor to-ward the back of the hall. Seeing that the Major and I are preparing to take our leave, he asks Saturday's Son for some of the *weikza*'s medicine. The medium gets up and goes into his bedroom. He comes back holding in his hands three little cones with flat tops, about two centimeters in height and of a reddish-brown color. The Major, the driver, and I get one each. Simply licking the cone with your tongue is enough to incorporate its substance, which has both prophylactic and therapeutic benefits: the range of its effectiveness is virtually universal, protecting and healing someone from all ills. The medicine contains energy ashes, derived from the *weikza*'s alchemical practice as well as from the pyres of their life-prolonging ceremonies.

"You're really lucky!" exclaims the Major, regaining his good cheer as the three of us go down the outside staircase. "This medicine is very potent." He goes on to explain how it made it possible to cure his wife's cancer. She was about forty years old when the illness first appeared. The doctors removed her left breast. The *weikza* gave her one of these cones. Three years later, the cancer reappeared. It was necessary to remove her right breast. Once again, the *weikza* gave her a cone. Then, for thirty years, nothing, the Major emphasized. His wife's death was caused by heart problems, not cancer.

Similarly, the Major attributes his own longevity and vigor to the four *weikza*'s support, particularly in the form of the medicinal cones and fortifying materials—energy ashes, fruit—that they distribute. He takes chemical medicines—tonics ("made in the U.S.," he points out with pride) and pills that prevent hypertension, facilitate digestion, or reduce soreness. Were a serious health problem to arise, he would decide, as his wife had, as other of the four *weikza*'s disciples would, and as Saturday's Son himself (hospitalized several times over) would, to be treated with Western medical science—"English medicine" (*ingaleik hsay*), introduced during the British colonial era. But this medicine is worthwhile only from a social perspective because of its cost. And it costs a lot, a huge amount relative to Burmese means. Anyone coming back from a stay at one of the private clinics, a type of establishment that flourished in the 1990s, making up for the dramatic inadequacies of the public health network, has just one tale to tell: how much money he or she has spent. The acknowledged and sought-after effectiveness of Western medicine makes no sense to the Burmese; treatment takes place with no, or very little, affinity with Burmese understandings. Treatments, although definitive on the organic level, are perceived to be incomplete. In the face of an event that overwhelms the individual and those close to him or her, Western medicine does not make it possible to pronounce anything meaningful, either about the original cause of the illness or its resolution. "The doctors said it was a case of cancer," grumbled Ba Yi's wife about his death in 1999, which took place in a Mandalay hospital. "But we don't know anything about that."

Medical science, for all its esoteric terms and methods, provides no help when it comes to interpretation. You cannot "believe" in doctors and their science like you can believe in a *weikza* and his power. In short, treatment does not restore the order of things, because it remains in large part incomprehensible to the sick person and to those close to him or her. Thus it is that disciples of the cult so often tell the same story about sickness and its treatment. Onto the recounting of their stay at the hospital gets grafted that of an appearance by one of the *weikza,* either to the patient or to relatives, which precedes and clarifies the eventual recovery. The *weikza's* mediation is necessary for the outcome; it makes it possible to articulate a suitable discourse and formulate an explanation. That mediation is then taken to be effective, no matter the actual result. Yes, Ba Yi died of throat cancer, but the *weikza* extended his life (*athet hswe-*) by several years before bowing to fate. Yes, the Major's wife has departed this world, leaving her husband distraught—but the *weikza* had granted her a thirty-year reprieve.

A similar logic prevails in the relations between personal enrichment and veneration of the *weikza.* Several disciples of the cult whose business affairs have prospered are reputed to have been "supported" (*ma sa-*) in their business dealings by the four *weikza.* I would look at the phenomenon in reverse order. It isn't the *weikza's* intervention that fosters someone's enrichment, but rather their getting rich that impels them to attribute their wealth to intervention on the *weikza's* part. Getting rich, in addition to the material security that it provides, gives rise to an inexplicable difference and, by that fact, a lack of meaning, just as much as getting sick and then regaining one's health do. Interpretation with reference to karma is insufficient to bring a full measure of social value to dramatic events in an individual's life. Linking these events to the actions of an authority situated on a supramundane plane not only makes them communicative and legitimate but also extends the range of their meanings. People do not get well thanks to the *weikza,* although relations with the *weikza* explain and exalt that recovery. People do not get rich thanks to the *weikza,* although relations to the *weikza* explain and exalt that material gain.

THE FRAGMENTS REASSEMBLED: WHAT IS THE CULT ABOUT?

So our trip ends here, at the foot of the stairs of the Yasagyo Monastery, with the Major, the anthropologist, and their driver contemplating the tiny cones of *weikza* medicine. What have we learned? What have the events and contretemps that have punctuated the journey and what have the various people we have met up with taught us about being a disciple?

The tie that binds the four *weikza* to their disciples follows from a conception of humans as beings who suffer from a deficiency of vital strength. The mortal condition and the torments and uncertainties of life, as well, are both a manifestation and an effect of this deficiency. The same defect affects the *weikza,* although to a lesser degree, because their lives, too, although remarkably long, are finite. The principle that underlies the whole set of the cult's practices is to make up for such a lack of vital energy by looking to produce more of it.

In the idiom of the cult, the word *dat* labels this generic vital energy.[32] In its primary sense, the word refers to the four elements (*dhātu* in Pali) that Buddhist physics defines as the fundamental components of matter: earth, fire, water, and air. These elements are also thought of in terms of their properties: solidity, heat, liquidity, and mobility, respectively. More generally, *dat* concerns a thing's "essence" or "quality."

The word *dat* enters into a number of phrases, often relating to the idea of strength or energy, including *atwin dat* ("internal power" or spiritual strength), *akya dat* ("the power to hear," that is, to perceive the *weikza*'s voices or those of other invisible entities), *dat-hsi* (fuel), *dat-a* (electric power), and *dat-khe* (battery). Relics obtained from the cremation of the remains of a Buddha or of a saint are their *datdaw,* their "noble essence or energy," remaining beyond their death. (It is not an accident that these relics' principal attribute is their ability to bring about miracles and wondrous feats: supernatural potency is part of the essence of spiritual perfection.) Furthermore, Burmese medicine understands sickness to be caused by a disequilibrium in an individual of the combination of the four material elements, due to an insufficiency or a surfeit of one of them. It seeks to reestablish the harmony among them by acting on the body's organs on the basis of remedies with specific properties: this food or preparation will induce heat in the body (*apu dat,* "hot principle"); another, cold (*a-ay dat,* "cold principle").[33]

Used in a variety of ways, the notion of *dat* amounts to a principle that conveys a force: it is an energetic principle. For the cult's members, this principle takes the form of "energy of success" (*aung dat*), a source of vitality, of success, of plenty. Producing such energy—the primary preoccupation of the four *weikza* and their disciples—is accomplished by techniques as diverse as practicing meditation, doing meritorious acts, engaging in alchemy, drawing and consuming cabalistic diagrams, tattooing, and making use of lucky symbols. And the success sought after touches on all areas of life. It means, for one disciple, being able to conceive a child; for another, being successful in business; for a third, being healthy—when it isn't all of those things for the benefit of one and the same person.

Buddhist ideology, of course, considers all forms of life as permeated with suffering. Rather than the promise of happiness in one's present life or the hope of a marvelous life after death, it offers the means of escaping the cycle of rebirth. This means of escape, the quest for nirvana, is nonetheless so demanding that it is reserved for a tiny minority of spiritual virtuosos. Thus it hardly responds to the aspirations of the many people seeking "success." The figure of the *weikza* and the practices and the objectives of the *weikza* path are one solution, if not the only solution, to this difficulty. The *weikza*'s path institutes a quest for happiness and immortality linked to the quest for nirvana. Obtaining the *weikza* state prolongs life even as it frees it from the suffering that inheres in it, because it banishes sickness and the fear of death. It guarantees being able to be present for a Buddha's appearance, when the time comes, and so gaining final deliverance. With the *weikza* path, the quest for "success," which is a quest for energy, claims to be the foreshadowing of and precondition for realizing nirvana. By making the quest for success a means for reaching nirvana, the *weikza* path expands the possibility for accession to nirvana yet without devaluing it. Because if the *weikza* path satisfies the shared aspiration for success, it implies the practitioner's total commitment—a commitment, precisely, of one's entire life.

Being a disciple of the four *weikza* amounts to plugging oneself into the energy grid of which they are the source. Just as customers of an electric grid receive a current that they are incapable of producing themselves and that they pay for, so the disciples receive the *weikza*'s energy of success, which they pay for, one might say, with their gifts and their contributions to the life-prolonging ceremonies. They then "take energy of success" (*aung dat yu-*) that the *weikza,* who possess an exceptional ability to generate it, "give" them (*aung dat pay-*). The distribution of energy goes in only one direction. Reciprocity is impossible and indeed negated: what the disciples offer is not equivalent to what they receive. This impossibility and negation of reciprocity are congruent with the dualism between mundane and supramundane levels that determines the whole *weikza* phenomenon. Ordinary people, suffering a deficit of vital energy, rely on a category of extraordinary beings to make up for this deficit. They rely on beings who are superhuman inasmuch as they have managed to mitigate, for themselves, the human insufficiency of vital strength.

Unable to produce an energy equal to that of the *weikza,* the most zealous and most advanced of their disciples operate as relays or channels for the diffusion of this energy. In spite of the idea that Saturday's Son is alone qualified, from a karmic point of view, to be their medium, many are those who are possessed by one or several of the four *weikza,* multiplying the number of points in the country where their formidable energy is exuded.

Just as much as they seek to receive energy of success, disciples are concerned to store it up and make it bear fruit. Portable objects make it possible to stock a certain mass of energy that the *weikza* provide initially, enabling one to work on increasing it and suffusing one's own body with it. These objects, which serve as amulets, are at the same time receptacles for an immaterial principle and the means for its symbolization: they contain *dat,* with which they are identified. The energy ball (*datlon*) is queen among them all because it makes it possible to represent, through its changes in form, consistency, color, and weight, the process of energy's accumulation and also to direct that process. However, the vital force that the various artifacts tied to the cult release is not immediately tangible. Some sort of event, such as a physical affliction, is necessary for this force to manifest itself in a meaningful way, at least in the view of the disciples.

When it comes to the four *weikza* taking charge of their disciples' fate, the actual benefits, which are not evident, matter less than the feeling people get of being in relation with a transcendent authority, one that conveys both meaning and power. We must tread carefully here. Disciples of the cult though they may be, Major Zaw Win, Doctor Sein Yi, Monk Taungtha, and all their peers have no better a life, one any less subject to the vagaries of misfortune and despair or one any less tumultuous, than that of other people. To borrow their word, they do not "succeed" any more than others. But their experience of disorder, of life's joys and miseries, is transformed by the fact that the activities they undertake under the *weikza*'s protection and encouragement enable them, if not to master, at least to believe they exert some influence over their fate—not to undergo the foreordained passively but rather to act within the constraints of their own destiny—in the hopes of eventually achieving the status of a *weikza* and reaching the fabulous realm of Dragoness Mountain, the disciples' enchanted horizon.

Thus the word "fate" should not be understood in a strictly tragic or determinist sense. In fact, there is no Burmese word equivalent to the word "fate" understood as *fatum.* Instead, there is a cluster of notions and practices, one that refers in turn to a specific conception, a Burmese idiom of fate that surpasses any simple framework of the foreordained, of fatality. This conception does not represent fate under the single aspect of an independent and sovereign power, fixing in an irrevocable fashion the course of lives and events, a power whose action is discernible only after the fact. It would be a mistake to equate the notion of karma (*kan* in Burmese) to such a univocal understanding. Reference to karma does function as reality's ultimate explanatory principle. But even though it is conceived of as a kind of recording and processing device tracking an individual through successive lives, karma does not actually suggest an ineluctable mechanism whose programmed unfolding no one could impede. Karma combines several active forces that do not proceed in a single direction in a coordinated fashion. The generic idea of karma encompasses, without integrating them into a coherent whole with respect to its dynamic or its determinism, the following: an individual's store of merit (*kutho*) and demerit (*akutho*); the accumulated virtue capital (*parami*); particularly bad acts committed in previous lives (which generate a violent karmic retribution, called *wut kyway-*); ties of interdependence among people across their lives (*pathan hset*);[34] and other notions Burmese use to label fate's powers. Added to this complex of forces is the power of the stars, which is positive or negative according to the moment. Bonds of affinity and contradiction among all these forces are in the end unknowable: they are not even thought about or conceptualized. Instead of a system, fate presents a set of possibilities. It thereby offers everyone a chance, with the help often of others (such as the *weikza*), to act on the karmic and astral process to foster their better realization or to correct the negative effects of this process. Significantly, Burmese identify one particular type of bad karma, called *upithsaydaka kan* (from the Pali adjective *upacchedaka*, "destructive"), whose two features are, first, that it is inevitable and unstoppable, and second, that it causes a violent death and a cruel rebirth in hell. With this single exception (but here again, some claim, as the four *weikza* do, that they are in a position to make available an amulet of such potency that it provides protection even from this dreaded kind of karma), it is possible therefore, as Burmese put it, "to make bad karma disappear" (*kan hpyauk-*) or "to avoid" it (*kan shaung-*), just as it is possible to improve one's karma in the interests of immediate needs, such as professional or academic success. It is possible, in brief, to produce one's own fate.[35]

The Burmese Buddhist conception, in sum, suggests a tension between fate's uncontrollable and sovereign powers, whose action is of an almost mechanical nature, and the means that people put into play, either individually or collectively, to support, direct, or on the contrary neutralize the action of these forces. This conception, rather than seeing fate as at once arbitrary and meaningful in its inevitability, assimilates it to a flexible process in the constitution of one's personal development.[36] Fate's work is placed at one and the same time both beyond the reach of and in the hands of every individual, while being thought about at the scale of the cycle of rebirth. In other words, to restate the same proposition in the form of a general rule: the more a society looks on its members' fate as subject to numerous and powerful forces, the more it falls back on providing them with tools to prevent or reverse fate's course. Studying the cult of the four *weikza* allows us to observe that this work of constructing reality is sustained by a theory of energy, one that conceives the course of the world and of lives as moved by contrary forces, lucky and unlucky, that people must capture, produce, or counter.

3 The Possessed

HOW IT ALL STARTED

Monday, June 30, 1952, ninth day of the waxing moon of Waso, in the year 1314 of the Burmese era.[1] The day is drawing to a close. A large crowd has gathered both outside and inside the house of Police Inspector Nyein, in Minbu. People have come to hear Gyan, or rather U Nareinda. The *weikza* suddenly emerged in the young woman's life six months earlier, putting an end to the illness—disquieting menstrual disturbances—that had been afflicting her. Since that time, he has possessed her on a regular basis, delivering sermons through her, his intermediary, with the aim of furthering the Buddhist religion. After listening to one of these sermons, Nyein, much taken with the *weikza* teaching, has invited the medium to Minbu. Gyan, *alias* Weikza Gyan, is staying at the Inspector's home, designated for present purposes as a place for preaching.

Outside, among the people unable to get inside because of the size of the crowd, is a young man, twenty-six years old, suffering from a strange and terrible malady. Htun Yin recently married a young woman from the village of Mebaygon, just a little way from his own village. But shortly after the wedding was celebrated, with the young man now living at the home of his parents-in-law—well-off farmers—his belly started to swell alarmingly. Soon Htun Yin was unable to eat normally. He started coughing and spitting up blood. With his condition worsening, he was hospitalized in Minbu. His belly was filling with water, the doctor explained, before attempting to drain it, to no avail. An operation was called for. Two of his relatives—his wife and his uncle—were asked to sign a document releasing the institution from all responsibility in the case of his death. They reached the hospital in the late afternoon. The doctor had already gone. Htun Yin, terrified by the idea of an operation, chose to sneak out of the hospital with the help of his wife. On their way home, they heard U Nareinda's sermon being broadcast by loudspeaker. They rode their oxcart to Inspector Nyein's, took their oxen out of harness, and sat at the rear of the audience, the density of the crowd ruling out any hope of getting inside the house.

Htun Yin pays little attention to U Nareinda's teaching. Preoccupied by his illness, he has come to the event to ask the *weikza,* through his intermediary, Gyan, for medicine (*hsay*) to save him. A monk comes down the house's stairs, accompanied by a layperson dressed in white. Htun Yin, thinking they must be disciples of U Nareinda, prostrates himself on the ground before them and then voices his plea:

"If you have good medicine that can make your disciple's suffering disappear, give it to me, I beg you, Venerable."

"Well done, well done!" the monk responds in acknowledging the homage rendered. "May you be of good health, may you be of good health! The malady that has attached itself to your body, Saturday's Son, has made serious inroads. But you have now met the great monk, U Pandita, and you no longer need have any fear. Your illness will disappear; you will regain your good health. I ask you to give your word. Disciple Saturday's Son, we will make a contract. When you have recovered, just as the *weikza* U Nareinda possesses Gyan to preach and support the Buddhist religion, in the same way we will possess you in order to support it in whatever ways are needed. Are you willing to be possessed and to support the religion for five years with us? If the answer is yes, we will make your illness disappear. You will be able to engage in virtuous acts with us and obtain a very special merit . . ."

While the *weikza* continues, reiterating the terms of the contract he is proposing, Htun Yin thinks about it, hesitant and perplexed. At this point the layperson dressed in white, Bodaw Bo Htun Aung, intervenes: "Disciple Saturday's Son, not everyone gets a chance to be possessed and to support the religion. It's because the great monk and you have engaged in virtuous acts together in previous lives that the *weikza* are offering you this opportunity today. You have no reason to refuse!"

Htun Yin, imagining what awaits him should he drive the two figures off, accepts the bargain. He commits to serving the *weikza* and the religion for five years. U Pandita gives him a bit of medicine that he must ingest at once. The medicine has an extraordinary scent and taste. The *weikza* gives him a second dose. He is to take it the next day, at 5:00 p.m., standing upright facing northeast, while focusing his attention on the Three Jewels and thinking of U Pandita.

"Disciple Saturday's Son, your illness will come out of your body and leave you in peace. Don't worry. The *weikza* will watch over you. May you be of good health, may you be of good health!"

After U Pandita says these words, the two *weikza* both disappear from the spot. Only real *weikza* endowed with great supernatural potency could disappear into thin air like that, thinks Htun Yin to himself. Remarkable, too, is the fact that when the *weikza* came down the stairs of Nyein's house, as well as for the whole time they were speaking, no one in the crowd seemed to see or hear them except for the young man and his wife. Relieved, Htun Yin and his relatives go back to Mebaygon.

When it gets to be 5:00 p.m. the next day, Htun Yin takes the *weikza* medicine as per U Pandita's instructions. Two hours later, he feels something getting big in his stomach. In front of his flabbergasted relatives, he vomits up a cow's tongue, some hair, and clots of blood. He also suffers diarrhea. Yet he doesn't seem to be in pain. He has a very pleasant night. The next morning, his look of good health astonishes and delights his loved ones.

The following Friday, at about six or seven in the evening, the voice of an invisible person—Bodaw Bo Htun Aung—can be heard in the village of Mebaygon. The *weikza* invites the villagers to come to the home of Pan Aung and Hpwa Kywe, Htun Yin's parents-in-law, to listen to the teaching of a monk named U Pandita. People flock to the place. The house and surrounding area are filled with people, in spite of the fact that Pan Aung and his wife have no idea what's going on. Once the crowd grows impatient and starts to grumble, an unknown voice springs from Htun Yin's mouth:

> "I, the great monk *weikza* U Pandita, have come from Dragoness Mountain where I live to support religion in the country of men. Starting today, I will preach by possessing Saturday's Son as I am doing now. Pay no attention to Saturday's Son's physical appearance. Saturday's Son is like a radio receiver and we, the *weikza,* are like the broadcasting station . . ."

THE PATH TO MEDIUMSHIP

Fifty years later, Saturday's Son remains the four *weikza*'s "radio receiver." Rather than being able to communicate and converse with them, the medium, through possession, serves as the vehicle of their speech and their power. Possession by a *weikza* features neither special attire nor music and dance. It is notable for the lack of dramatization; in any case, these features are by no means necessary for its implementation. The medium is not an interpreter; he does not personify, body and soul, the beings who possess him. Rather, he passively relays the "transmissions" he captures. Only the timber of his voice and the register of his speech change, and even those supposed changes sometimes grow faint. Thus there is no

need for him as an individual to be initiated into possession by learning to behave in accordance with the genre's rules.[2]

It remains nonetheless true that in everyone's eyes Saturday's Son, rather
than representing a simple transmission channel, embodies in the course of a
possession one or another of the four *weikza*. He is no longer himself but rather
the *weikza,* speaking and acting in the first person. The metaphor of the radio
broadcast, so dear to the *weikza* path's practitioners, actually seems too conve-
nient not to appear suspect or at least in need of close study. It masks a remarkable indeterminacy about the actual mechanism by which possession by a *weikza*
takes place, an indeterminacy that highlights the difficulty in imagining the phenomenon in any practical sense. Two expressions are used to name this process.
The first, *nan kein-,* "[the *weikza's*] mind resides," raises a number of questions to
which Burmese respond evasively, vaguely, and contradictorily, if they respond at
all, admitting freely that they do not understand how something they are so familiar with works. In what part of the medium's body does the *weikza* reside?
The term "resides" suggests a kind of permanent possession: does the *weikza* reside
there continually? If, as all readily agree, the medium loses all self-control and
awareness at the moment of being possessed, by what means does a *weikza* achieve
this ascendancy? In the fashion of a horseback rider, sitting astride and guiding
his mount? By some kind of substitution, the *weikza* mind abrogating that of his
medium? Or—and this would appear to contradict the idea that "the mind resides" but does correspond to the followers' favorite image—in the manner of a
radio broadcast, the *weikza* sending waves from afar that his medium receives
and passes along?

Similar uncertainties surround the meaning of the other phrase used to describe possession by a *weikza: dat si-.* This second phrase is favored by the four
weikza of the Energy Center of Mebaygon because it can be applied more restric-
tively. *Nan kein-* lends itself to confusion, members of the cult explain: it can be
used just as readily to refer to possession by the guardian spirit of a pagoda's trea-
sures (*okzazaung*), although such a being is inferior to a *weikza*. Yet the expression *dat si-* raises just as many questions as the other phrase. *Dat* can be translated
as "quality," "essence," or "energy." This leaves obscure the nature of what passes
from the *weikza* into the medium at the time of possession. For that matter, the
verb *si-* means "to flow" or "to ride," and interpretations oscillate between the first
and the second of these possibilities. A *weikza* is conceived either as a spiritual
substance that penetrates ("flows") into the medium or as a rider who mounts him.
The perplexity that the phrase *dat si-* induces only intensifies in light of the fact
that it can allude to different modalities of *weikza* manifestations. If, in the cult

of the four *weikza,* it refers to possession in the strict sense (with the individual's loss of consciousness), in other *weikza* cults it points to a subtler phenomenon, such as inspiration or the conveying of some power.

For a long time, I struggled to make my interlocutors describe and specify the way possession worked. But no shared model, no systematic representation came of this. I was obliged to conclude either of two things: that possession was a mechanism that took many forms, despite the fact that Burmese made no distinction among the different kinds of possession a *weikza* might bring about, or that people's inability to account for the workings of so widespread a phenomenon pointed to a blind spot meaningful in its own right. My quest for an account of possession's physical processes turned out to exceed the natives' understandings on their own ground: it urged them to be consistent and describe the process in mechanical terms. My undertaking was bound to fail, because it took my interlocutors at their word and tried to force their metaphors back to their literal meanings. The trope of radio transmission is not a concrete and faithful representation of a physical reality, which would consist of communication from afar via waves sent by a transmitting station. Thus it actually obscures more than it illuminates by distancing the object it describes. Its very transparency exposes it as the illusion of an explanation, rendered in mechanical terms, of a phenomenon of a different nature. Granted, the image of the broadcasting station does suggest both a certain exteriority and a certain centrality in a *weikza*'s relationship to the human world, as well as his ability to enter into communication with it via the intercession of his medium or "radio receiver." But it tells us nothing about the workings of possession, which it objectifies unduly. We must look for these mechanisms elsewhere, where they can be found, putting aside the distorting mirrors that indigenous formulations offer up. The physical modalities of possession actually have no life of their own. When indigenous thought theorizes them—for example, when it treats the medium as a transmitting station, thus an object-being—it is less to suggest a physical process per se than to say something about the meaning of possession, of which physical modalities are a derivative expression.

That said, what was supposed to last five years has stretched out indefinitely, and a simple farmer, almost illiterate, has been at the center, if not quite at the very start, of one of the major Burmese religious phenomena of the second half of the twentieth century. It is by virtue of the length of his career as a medium and the degree of his fame that Saturday's Son differs from his contemporary, Gyan. At the start of their remarkable trajectories, both suffer an affliction, consisting of some disorder in the body's excretory functions: in the one case, amenorrhea, in the other, a swelling of the belly caused by an accumulation of water. The illness comes on at an age—twenty in one case, twenty-six in the other—when society enjoins them to enter into adulthood, meaning in Htun Yin's case his marriage shortly before he falls ill. Might the biological phenomenon of blockage and retention express resistance or, at least, some difficulty in the face of a transformation required by the flow of time and, with it, the stages of life? The cessation of menstruation especially suggests such a denial of femininity's attributes and the generative role at issue at this stage of life.

In any case, the stories about Gyan and Saturday's Son—because, of course, we are dealing with stories developed in written or oral form after the fact, with all the further elaborations they call for, rather than events I have observed myself—utterly defeat Western medical science, a science of organic reason. In Gyan's case, "English medicine" is never even brought into play, the malady deemed beyond its competence from the very start; in the case of Saturday's Son, it is represented in the person of a hospital doctor, but after an initial setback, he proposes to perform an operation that will put the patient's life in danger. Because the cause lies elsewhere, so does its cure. The physiological disorder is only a symptom, a consequence and a manifestation of a problem of a different order. In one case, people speak spontaneously of a curse; in the other, even though no explanation is formulated, what the poor man vomits up (hair, etc.) reveals the source of his suffering.

We should note nevertheless that, although the idiom of sorcery plays a part in the scenario, it plays only a minor role. The diagnosis of Gyan's ailment is not based on any divinatory procedure; it is a simple conjecture, with those close to the young woman attributing her troubles a priori to some envious person's malicious acts. Admitting that fact does not imply going on to attack the actual person suspected of having caused the illness, even were people to make the effort to identify who it might be. Taking a different tack, people focus their efforts on neutralizing the curse by overcoming its hold over the victim. It isn't that the rhetoric of sorcery is little developed in Burmese society—far from it. Rather, it does not act as misfortune's ultimate explanatory principle. When accounting for misfortune and when fighting against it, the logic of fate and the principles of its fashioning prevail. Behind sorcery—which, like organic problems, is only a symptom—lies the original cause of illness, which is karma. Whatever lot one suffers, it follows from one's karma—particularly one's degree of morality and of mental concentration—being weak, which makes someone vulnerable to attack. In other words, if sorcery constitutes an autonomous field in the Burmese system of representations, with its various beliefs and practices, this autonomy is relative:

a sorcerer's or a witch's power to do harm is contained within limits set by Buddhist ideology. And once the responsibility for an affliction lies just as much with the person suffering it, then undoing the misfortune requires acting on his or her person as much as on the aggressor. Counter-sorcery is partly a struggle with fate, a fight to defend oneself from it and to redirect it. Thus a man whose erratic behavior suggests that he is the victim of a powerful curse may well enter the monastic community, where the merit and spiritual strength that a monk's condition produces will protect him from the spell's most noxious effects.

Therefore, the idea that the time at which Gyan and Saturday's Son first suffer from their ailments has some relevance, because it is the disquieting time of a person's passage to adulthood, has nothing about it that Burmese would find unacceptable, even if they never put it this way. But much like a hypothesis of sorcery, it cannot be taken as the final explanation. The difficulties individuals have reaching the status of an adult, along with whatever personal crises may follow, stem in the end not from their psychology but from their karma. Thinking that you could put an end to some disorder by acting exclusively on the psychic level would amount to taking the effect for the cause and would spell certain failure. The Burmese system of representations ties the misfortune, in the final analysis, to a karmic etiology, rather than a social one (envy or jealousy that gives rise to a sorcerer's attack), a mental one (psychological problems), or an organic one (physiological problems). Any therapy, therefore, includes a decisive, more or less elaborate, treatment of a person's fate. The *weikza* are, indeed, potent correctors of a person's fate, which they put right and improve with such help as their medicine.

Yet we see that for Gyan, as well as for Saturday's Son, the end of suffering is a beginning. The person who has been delivered from misfortune adds to its resolution the claim of being the vehicle for a collective salvation. Both of these figures assert that their cure was brought about when they entered into a privileged relationship with one or more *weikza,* relationships marked by a contract whose terms could be summarized as follows: "You will be saved if you are willing to save others in turn." (The idea of being saved includes, in accordance with the ambiguity of the Burmese verb *ke-* to which it corresponds, both a temporal and a spiritual register.) The affliction provides the opportunity to reveal a vocation. Reference to sorcery serves to set in motion a drama of quite a different import. It brings onto the scene the *weikza,* who have no part in causing an affliction's torments. Unlike a spirit (*nat*) who, when it "catches" someone to make him or her its medium, shows itself by causing illness, a *weikza* is not, as a general rule, a source of misfortune. He is thought of as an agent for good. Thus an attack of sorcery is significant in this respect: reference to it shores up impressions of a *weikza* as a guardian of good fortune, of success, of prosperity. Rendered as the paradigmatic opposite of a sorcerer, a *weikza* can be seen or rather can be imagined as the agent of salvation par excellence.

In contrast to the way the scenario usually plays out, therefore, the end of Gyan's and Saturday's Son's respective illnesses does not mean the end of the story. The initial episode is essential, in that it proves the efficacy of the *weikza* intervention and provides a prototype for the cures that follow. Yet it is not enough, because in Burmese society someone who has been cured does not by virtue of that fact earn the power to cure others in turn. In fact, neither Gyan nor Saturday's Son has any particular qualification, positive or negative, that would set them apart from others. Both figures practiced Buddhism in the usual way, nothing more. Neither one nor the other had shown any interest in the *weikza* path or shown any special spiritual calling. Whereas a career as a saint, by way of comparison, requires considerable personal effort and a long delay before achieving its aim (which is, to say, recognition), being possessed by a *weikza* is socially effective almost immediately. It brings about a wondrous transformation wherein the most ordinary and anonymous of villagers is metamorphosed into a preacher and thaumaturge, and a hero of the Buddhist religion. No need, it turns out, to detach oneself from the world, to have entered into the religious life, to have practiced meditation and ascetic rigors. Neither Gyan nor Saturday's Son would have been capable of submitting to such a regimen. In sum, the phenomenon of possession by a *weikza* is remarkable in that it enables an individual to attain, without bothering with any preparatory stages, a certain religious virtuosity—one that in theory, of course, does not depend on him or her, but that nonetheless does implicate the person in part by the very way that possession takes place.

So it is no surprise that, when someone who has been elected affirms that fact, he or she is treated with inquisitorial suspicion. Think of Gyan facing a group of experts known for their religious learning, no fewer than four monks and four laypeople, gathered together one day in May 1952: they are tasked with deciding whether a *weikza* is possessing the young woman. They listen to U Nareinda's teaching and question him about certain aspects of the monastic disciplinary code in the interest of determining his identity. Whether these erudite figures have been assembled at the request of the *weikza* in order to erase all doubt or whether they have been called at the behest of witnesses who find the phenomenon perplexing—versions differ on this point—it is true that the entire matter is treated with the utmost circumspection, particularly by those whose authority is confounded by this sudden emergence on the religious center stage of an individual with no credentials whatsoever and, what's more, who is both young and a woman. At the same time, other monks, certified exorcists, struggle to counter the witch who they are convinced has taken control of the young woman. Their efforts are ineffective but significant: they demonstrate how much denial first meets the claims of the possessed.[3]

Think, too, of Saturday's Son—in his case events take place two months later, in July 1952—whose uncle, a monk respected by the local populace, does not choose to believe that his nephew who can barely read and write and who has a well-earned reputation as a rowdy could have been elected by the *weikza*. Saturday's Son, the uncle is convinced, is under the control of a female guardian spirit of a pagoda's treasures, an *okzazaung*. She "sticks" (*kat-*) to the young man and will soon cause his death in order to draw him close to her in her realm. She says she is a *weikza,* but she fools no one. Having taken the matter up with a number of exorcists, the uncle has recourse to the services of one of them. Maung Lay is a practitioner of the "lower path" (*auk-lan*), or so he is described in the story: it is a discrediting credential. He cures people by calling on the help of nonhuman entities that support him by means of their power to expel the spirit disturbing the patient.[4]

Maung Lay prepares an offering for these entities. The offering includes a piece of cotton cloth of nine arm-lengths, money in the sum of nine *kyat,* candles, and tea leaves. When it is ready, the exorcist calls to the spirit causing the trouble and orders him or her to possess Saturday's Son in order to enter into a dialogue. His summons has no effect. Saturday's Son smiles. Impotent and increasingly shamed in front of his audience, Maung Lay grows impatient. He threatens the spirit in all possible ways. At this moment, Bodaw Bo Htun Aung, taking possession of Saturday's Son, speaks to the exorcist and the audience: "All right. I, Bodaw Bo Htun Aung, have come in order to rid you of doubt. We are *weikza* and not, as you think, sorcerers, spirits, or pagoda guardian spirits. So how is it that you expect to cure Saturday's Son?"

Maung Lay, who is doubtful about the identity of the speaker, responds that he will give the young man three doses of medicine to cure him.

"Fine," replies Bodaw Bo Htun Aung. "I'm not afraid of swallowing this medicine. But taste a little yourself first. Everyone should taste medicine he has prepared first, isn't that so? When you have taken some, I'll take some, too. Trust me! If I didn't, wouldn't you think that I was afraid of you and your medicine? Go ahead. Take a bit of your medicine!"

Impossible to beat a retreat, Maung Lay does it. Saturday's Son then swallows the three doses that the exorcist hands him.

"Good," says Bodaw Bo Htun Aung, "I have taken your medicine. Now you must take some that I am going to give you."

Maung Lay falls apart. He argues confusedly that he is not ill and has no need of any remedy. His cowardice makes him lose face. He decamps.

That is one among many tests to which Saturday's Son submitted, Hpay Myint notes as he concludes his telling of this story, although some were so barbarous that decency prevents him from mentioning them. Just as attributing the future medium's initial illness to an act of sorcery generated an opposition between the sorcerer and the *weikza* so as to emphasize more the beneficent nature and salvational function of the latter, by the same token, bringing up suspicions of a dangerous possession (on the part of a witch or a harmful spirit) that requires treatment (as for an illness) underlines the positive nature of possession by a *weikza,* a propitious possession that is best left to take its course. The story develops out of a play of oppositions in such a way as to throw the figure of the *weikza* into sharper relief.

A GENIUS WHO KNOWS NOTHING

There is more to what might be called a primitive incredulity—the community's initial mistrust if not denial in the face of possession by a *weikza*—than the necessity of objecting on principle to an individual's extravagant claim that he or she has, without so much as a nod to the usual preconditions for taking on an eminent religious role, suddenly become the incarnation of a spiritually accomplished being. To say as I have that "when someone who has been elected affirms that fact, he or she is treated with inquisitorial suspicion" already constitutes something of an abuse of language from the point of view of those who respond to that claim. What the community puts to its inquisitorial process—what it scrutinizes, interrogates, tests, evaluates, what it even forces to undergo outrageous efforts at repression—is the entity it has not yet identified who is possessing someone, not the one being possessed. The hypothesis that someone is faking, the idea that an individual would feign possession, that he or she might not be speaking under the control of another entity, is not considered. There is no doubt as to the authenticity of what is happening. What is in doubt is what the original source of the incident might be: *weikza,* spirit, or witch. Thus the problem is not to determine whether the possession is real but how to interpret it. This leads to a confrontation between the community and the possessed, the former consenting to acknowledge the phenomenon if and only if the latter submits to the required collective examination and verification.

Put another way, the show of initial skepticism characterizing the community's reaction is not a means of objective evaluation, a demand for proof: the community itself comes up with that proof by means of the test to which it puts the possessed. Instead this display of skepticism is a way to impose a definition on the situation: the possessed is the object of an extraordinary phenomenon in which he or she takes no active part and exercises no control. The possessed is neither liable nor authorized to decide on the meaning and validity of this phenomenon. For possession by a *weikza* to be recognized as such, for it to make sense, two conditions must be met: the complete absence, on the part of the possessed, of all personal responsibility in and mastery over the experience being undergone and the collective accreditation, if not appropriation, of that experience. Were it only a matter of possession by a spirit or a witch, the accreditation might be limited to a few people close to the victim. An exorcist would take matters into his hands, and the issue would not be in doubt. Here, however, exorcism is useless. It falls to the community—that is to say, to each of its members—to decide on the nature of the phenomenon by subscribing or not subscribing to the claim of possession by a *weikza*.

It is significant that one of the points most often made both by himself and by others about Saturday's Son concerns the resistance the medium has put up throughout his life against possession by the four *weikza*. It appears that it is essential even at this late date to reaffirm constantly that the possessed is only the instrument of another's will, the intermediary of a power beyond his own. Poor Saturday's Son! That he was a pleasure-seeking young man, with a penchant for drinking, eating, having a good time, and joking around is emphasized in all accounts, to the point of appearing to be the most prominent of his character traits. Those accounts also insist on his having shown no interest whatever in religion and barely being able to state the Five Precepts. The sudden appearance of the *weikza* meant an entirely new way of life for him, both constraining and challenging. Séances left the young man exhausted, so much so that he tried, in contravention of the terms of the contract he had made with his masters, to evade the obligation to undergo them. Whenever disciples brought a perfume bottle for the *weikza,* through their medium intermediary, to perform the feat of making Buddha relics appear, he would make the bottle disappear. The *weikza* were not fooled, and each time Saturday's Son was struck with an invisible club or violently shaken. One day, pushed to the limit, he took an article of clothing from a woman in labor and put it on his head. Cause for a devastating soiling, this gesture should have made him repugnant to the *weikza*. No use: the article of clothing caught fire, supernaturally as it were. The feckless young man grumbled even at having to say his prayer beads every day, as the *weikza* required of him. Incapable of concentrating, he tried to get out of this duty. He would go for a stroll, chatting with people in the village, or go watch a cockfight—in spite of his age, he preferred the company of the young to that of adults. On his return, there was no escaping a good clubbing.

The medium found the restrictions and privations imposed by the *weikza* burdensome. The *weikza* disapproved of his smoking, especially on formal occasions. When Saturday's Son ventured to light a cigarette in the presence of a disciple, an invisible hand grabbed it out of his mouth. Above all, the vegetarian *weikza*, hating the smell of meat, forbade Saturday's Son to eat any. Sometimes the desire was too great, and Saturday's Son tasted some savory meat dishes. He would get sick immediately and vomit up what he had eaten.

To better control their medium and to make of him a worthy representative, the *weikza* tried constantly to get him to take on a monk's robes. Their first attempt, in the mid-1960s, failed: Saturday's Son disrobed after three years. His attachments to his family and to the joys and liberties of lay life were too great. A few years later, in 1973, approaching the time of U Pandita's life-prolonging ceremony, he yielded to the *weikza* wishes and at the age of forty-seven took on the robes once again. The monk who presided over his ordination, U Pyinnya, was the head monk of the village's main monastery. He had rights over a very large property, and he granted Saturday's Son the use (not the ownership) of a part of it. This was where the building in which séances took place from then on, the Monastery of Noble Success, was built. Furthermore, Saturday's Son received as a gift a large lot bordering that of U Pyinnya that his father-in-law owned. Here were built other buildings: a large preaching hall and several residence halls. Their placement on the latter lot made it possible to avoid litigation with U Pyinnya's disciples and legal heirs, who retained the rights over the initial parcel, after his death in 1992. One of those heirs, U Zawana, succeeded his great-uncle in 1966 to become the head of a monastery at the other end of the village, where he lives to this day. The other heir, U Thondara, runs a meditation center neighboring the *weikza* monastery. (U Pyinnya's monastery, which was falling apart, was demolished.) Thus the village of Mebaygon has three monasteries, the *weikza* having strained relations with the other two.

Saturday's Son was overjoyed in 1980, one of his daughters relates, when he learned that he had been summoned to an inquiry that was part of the government's big project to purify the monastic community.[5] At last he could return to lay life. The *weikza*, this time, could do nothing about it. Alas! When a committee of monks questioned him to check his knowledge of the fundamental rules and principles of monastic life, one of the *weikza* possessed him and answered all the questions correctly. Still, the 1980 reform had a clear impact on the cult. In light of his status as a monk, Saturday's Son was forbidden to become possessed. If previously possession was enough to motivate an evening's séance at the Monastery of Noble Success, from now on the appearance of the *weikza* in the flesh took precedence. In other circumstances, however, when Saturday's Son visits disciples of the cult—that is, in a private context—he continues to be possessed.

This ability to become possessed is not tied, from the Burmese point of view, to any event or development in the present life of the medium. It results from his karma, particularly his relations, in one or more past lives, with the *weikza* who has elected him. Eight lives ago, Saturday's Son was the nephew of U Pandita and helped him attain the *weikza* state. He disposes of enough *parami,* as a result, to be his medium. (A person's *parami,* made up of his past virtuous actions, orients his fate, including his accomplishments in the religious domain.) Mediumship's origin is cast back to a previous life, and the medium, as a person endowed with a conscience, with his or her own will, does not exist. The medium is not a subject but a pure object: this is the very axiom of mediumship. No one, for that matter, cares about him or her as a person. Whereas a holy man can take pride in one or even several biographical texts that retrace his spiritual trajectory—signs of his future accomplishments appearing at a very early age—whereas, in other words, the community develops a story about such a man's greatness, a medium stands out by virtue of his colorlessness. His story begins with the appearance of the *weikza*. Once the latter's identity has been established, what matters is becoming aware of the *weikza's* biography, his achievements, and his teaching.

Nothing needs to be known about the medium, other than a few facts necessary to situate him or her in Burmese society. As a matter of fact, the book about U Nareinda provides no information whatsoever about Gyan; what has been reported here was learned from her by the anthropologist. Attributing an instance of possession to a *weikza* means negating the individuality of the possessed. In the very act of acknowledging and validating the fiction that the person produces, the community takes it away from him or her, denying to that individual both authorship and authorial control. A medium is deprived of the chance to fashion his or her own aura. The individual's work, including any idiosyncratic variations, is drawn back into the collective act that provided the initial material, and in contrast to the case of a holy man, the community prevents any focus from being placed on the individual. By the same token, no initiation or rite separates the medium from the common run of people: he or she enters into no special society and takes on no special identity. To be accepted in that role, someone who is possessed by a spirit (*nat*) must be ritually married to the entity who has taken hold of him or her and then learn the art of possession (namely, dances) under the direction of a master, before embarking on a medium's career path, which is marked by stages and hierarchical titles. In contrast, someone who is possessed by a *weikza* is crowned with the title of medium ipso facto, in spite of him- or herself and without any further specifications.

It appears, in sum, that being elected by a *weikza* is thought of as arbitrary: anyone else could be in the place of the possessed, on the condition of having been linked to the *weikza* in a previous life, a condition anyone could have potentially fulfilled. It seems, further, as though the election necessarily affects the people least likely to be taken as an object—a young woman, a rowdy boy, neither of them given to any particular religious zeal. And no special arrangements modify the social condition of the possessed. On the contrary, people seem determined not to grant any such privileges. "Saturday's Son knows nothing," the cult's disciples say. "It is the *weikza* who are knowledgeable." The medium follows right along. Despite his eminent role, he continued, until his entry into the monastic community, to play the simple villager, tending his fields and together with his wife raising six children. At the same time that the external and passive nature of possession is emphasized, so, too, is a principle vis-à-vis the possessed whereby the medium is individually irrelevant and socially undistinguished. Everyone, including the medium, makes his or her discourse and attitudes adhere to this principle. All evidence suggests that the collective use made of possession requires depicting the possessed as a protagonist despite him- or herself, as someone of the most ordinary sort. This is because the individual serves as the loudspeaker for shared values and aspirations (the defense and promotion of the Buddhist religion, the salvation quest), gathered up in the collective creation that is the figure of the *weikza*. The medium exists to serve as the group's interpreter: he or she speaks for all and can take no personal credit for doing so.

It is at this price of an individual's self-effacement in the process of enacting possession that the medium can express his or her cultural genius, although not recognized for itself. By cultural genius, I refer to the affinity between an individual's personality and a prominent feature of the culture to which he or she belongs—in this case possession by a *weikza*. This affinity turns out to be so strong that an individual finds naturally and even urgently, in the implementation of that cultural feature, a social raison d'être. Like everyone else, Gyan and Saturday's Son were imbued from earliest childhood with the beliefs, values, and religious themes that provide the content of Burmese culture, including knowledge and practices relative to the *weikza* path. A singular aptitude then enabled them to go beyond ordinary uses of this shared competence, taking charge of it and delivering a spectacular, extemporaneous performance. No one pushed them into the path of possession nor, for that matter, the *weikza* path. There is no teacher or institution that could have prepared them for such an accomplishment, none that could have developed their talent. No doubt, their cultural genius bursts forth all the more resoundingly—the outburst is all the more dazzling and its impact all the greater—for its having been in a way neglected and ignored. But as it happens, the construction of self, the means by which an individual becomes fully him- or herself, proceeds through the construction of the group, by the reproduction and development of its identity. That is why the immediate dispossession undergone by the possessed takes place with his or her active consent. Minds and attitudes join together to make sure that the cultural genius of the person who displays it be denied from start to finish, because it is unthinkable that a single person's voice might monopolize collective speech.

"Voice of the *weikza,* voice of the people," one would be tempted to say. This helps explain a fact that seems at first glance surprising. The *weikza* path (*weikza laing*) and the path of insight meditation (*wipathana laing*) are conceived as two distinct "lines," as two different, if not to say opposed, pathways to nirvana. The first operates through a quest for supernatural powers via the practice of concentration meditation (*thamahta*) and techniques like alchemy or the cabalistic arts. Its adepts work to construct things: they apply themselves to the process of formation, to becoming, to growth (*ahpyit*), as is evident in their wish to prolong their lives. The second articulates with the realization right here and now of the truths taught by the Buddha by dint of the practice of the contemplative method of insight. Its adepts seek to deconstruct things, keeping their attention on the process of degradation, impermanence, and destruction (*apyet*) and striving to make themselves conscious of it. The two different paths inform antithetical approaches to relations with the world, a relation of investment and active transformation in one case, of retreat and contemplation in the other. (This does not mean that the practitioner of insight meditation has no influence over the course of things.) Yet Gyan, in the fullness of her twenty years, combines with undeniable success possession by a *weikza* and teaching about insight meditation. But the fact that the voice of a young village woman should arise to spread, in the name of a *weikza,* the practice of insight meditation at a time—the 1950s—when the nation was made aware of this practice by a vast state effort to promote the Buddhist religion should hardly be surprising, if we see in the mechanism of mediumship a way for the community to give itself a representative and an interpreter.[6] Gyan was of her time and, through possession, made of herself the voice of the era by enabling the people of the region of Sagu—farmers, businesspeople, or officials—to mount the stage in the great postcolonial project of revivifying Burmese Buddhism.

It becomes all the more understandable, moreover, that the *weikza* phenomenon should worry the political authorities. In addition to giving rise to cults around figures to whom are attributed supernatural abilities and who are liable to provide a focus for intimations of rebellion against the powerful, when the phenomenon takes the form of possession, it is the means of expression for collective speech. The medium's assumed vacuity and absence of responsibility make the mechanism's effect unopposable. Even if one medium's activities are curtailed, that does not mean muzzling the collective speech: another or even several others will appear if circumstances and social pressure require it, without it being possible to predict where the threat will arise. The political authorities, as their own representatives sometimes explain, as do the adepts of the *weikza* path, do not promote the cult of the *weikza* for fear that it would lead to general disorder. If everyone—farmers, soldiers, and so on—relied on the *weikza* and their power to make their way, no one would work anymore, and the country would go to wrack and ruin. Yet the disorder the people who make these remarks have in mind is not actually economic. It is the disorder that arises, in the eyes of the government, in the expression of a collective will located anywhere other than at the heart of the state.

Finally, the meaning of incredulity also becomes all the more understandable. This attitude amounts to denying a medium the ability to express him- or herself in the name of the community. Everyone is free to accept or reject whoever claims to take charge of collective speech. But should someone not yield to this particular claim, that same person will yield to another. It follows that *weikza* cults and mediums proliferate, which is to say that sites for the articulation of collective speech abound. This dispersion, which allows anyone so disposed to become a vehicle of collective speech and anyone who wishes to do so to participate in its elaboration, corresponds to a pluralist regime of believing. Every individual enjoys the sovereign right to believe or not believe, and no representative—*weikza* or medium—is in a position to maintain or to be granted a monopoly on speech or power. Burmese, it seems, would refuse to believe in the phenomenon of *weikza* if they were all obliged to believe in one and the same *weikza*. It's as though the society sensed that its survival as a community depended not only on its cultural unity—a unity of beliefs, including that in *weikza*—but also on the development of divisions within that unity. It is as though the society demanded and fostered, by a kind of self-defensive reaction, a fragmentation of believing, a diversification of expressions of collective speech. Difference would then be essential to unity, as the society well knew and, consequently, assured. But who has ever had access to the thinking of a society—let alone its intentionality? One could be forgiven for doubting that the anthropologist should have found such access and explored it in a monastery in Central Burma—as well as for greeting with skepticism and circumspection his explanation for the fragmenting of believing, grounded as it is in an organicism well known for its teleological tendencies.

AT THE POINT OF CONTACT BETWEEN THE HUMAN AND THE SUPERHUMAN SPHERES

It is certainly said of Saturday's Son that he "knows nothing." Yet it is also said of him, and this by the same people, that he "knows," that he is almost, if not in fact, a *weikza*. The nondescript character of a medium amounts to an element of his or her identity. Yet what people say about a medium puts just as much emphasis on the singular nature of his or her person and closeness with the *weikza*. The figure of the medium, the role of intermediary, is conceived by means of an ontological duality, a paradoxical identity: a medium is at once an ordinary person and a superman. Therefore we should refine our earlier representation of the appearance and status of this figure, so as to avoid rendering things too simply and only emphasizing the medium's social insignificance.

At the beginning of their visitations, the *weikza* found it inappropriate that the young Htun Yin, given the eminent function that he was going to assume, retain his proper name. The name they chose, "Saturday's Son" (Sanay-tha), can be applied to anyone born on that day. It was necessary to avoid having people confuse the distinguished representative of the *weikza* with the anonymous villager he had been hitherto, yet to do so without separating him from the community. In 1973, at the time he entered the monkhood—an event that involves giving up one's lay name and adopting a title conferred by the monk who presides over one's ordination ceremony—Saturday's Son became U Tilawkeinda, "Governor of the Three Worlds." But this title, significantly, is rarely used by the cult's disciples. They are more likely to say Sanay-tha Hsayadaw, "great monk Saturday's Son" (the word *hsayadaw* is the title conferred on the head monk of a monastery), as though something of his lay identity still remained. Those unfamiliar with the cult speak of the "possessed monk" (*dat si hpongyi*). Such appellations reveal the particular status of the figure: if a monk can become a *weikza*, it is unusual, shocking even in the eyes of some, that he become possessed. Possession is judged incompatible with a monk's condition because it reduces the monk to a neutral and passive role, while positing the existence above him of another reality and will—whereas he is in himself and through his own efforts an embodiment of the Buddhist doctrine.

By combining in the same person the medium's role and the monk's identity, the four *weikza* have introduced a typical expression of lay Buddhism into the heart of monastic Buddhism. They have brought off a masterstroke that is also a power move. A similar shake-up followed Gyan's possession by U Nareinda: for as long as the *weikza* was present, the young woman was invited to officiate at a monastery, which is, to say, to take on the de facto role of a monk in the teaching of Buddhist doctrine. It's true that both she and Saturday's Son were possessed by one or more *weikza* monks, so it is logical that they would occupy monastic ground. But that is just it: Saturday's Son has never been a monk like other monks. Lacking sufficient knowledge to assume the ritual responsibilities that fall to a monastery's head monk, he participates in no religious recitation or ceremony, even at the Energy Center. He could have acquired the necessary knowledge over time, but has not bothered to do so. The second-in-command at the monastery, U Sandima, represents him at ceremonies. Originally from Irrawaddy Division where he owns his own monastery, and a monk since he was twenty years old, U Sandima is a placid man now approaching sixty. By virtue of the length of time he has been a monk, he is higher in the religious hierarchy than Saturday's Son. Nonetheless, he is considered his subordinate, due to the prestige associated with being the *weikza* medium. Is it indeed this status that induces Saturday's Son to keep clear the difference between him and other monks? Or does his attitude stem from a blind resistance to the monastic condition and its constraints? The two explanations are not mutually exclusive. In any case, the medium does not take part in monastic commensality, a sign of and the principal manifestation of the monastic community's unity: no matter what the circumstances, he takes his meals alone. Thus taking up residence at the monastery does not bring about the normalization of the status of the possessed. This status seems irreducible to the monastic state, because the medium's abilities surpass those of an ordinary monk. The medium is the transmission channel for the speech and power of a being much superior to a monk. More precisely, possession by a *weikza* creates a relationship of oscillating inadequacy: the medium, because he or she becomes possessed, is at the same time both less than a monk and more than a monk.

The cult's disciples, with proof in hand, all attribute extraordinary abilities to Saturday's Son. Here is Major Zaw Win picking up an album of black-and-white photographs. Two are dated January 14, 1977. At that time the *weikza* wanted to offer their medium a chance to make an irrefutable show of his powers. Saturday's Son was to spend eleven days closed up in U Pandita's cave, in the Site of Success, during that time eating only one single banana given him by the *weikza*. The period of his confinement had been set in order to produce a leavening of success. It would help Saturday's Son put out the eleven fires that consume every person and impede their spiritual progress.[7] The *weikza,* as per their habit, combined a demonstration of supernatural potency with an effort to influence the course of fate.

The building's door had been sealed at the time of U Pandita's life-prolonging ceremony, in December 1975. Saturday's Son got inside by going through a hole eleven inches (twenty-eight centimeters) in diameter placed in one of the walls. His performance made a big impression. Several disciples, including Doctor Sein Yi and Lieutenant-Colonel Thein Han, stayed at the monastery for the entire eleven days, taking turns guarding the cave. The Major, having attended the start of Saturday's Son's confinement, returned to Yangon. When he got there, he got a phone call from Kyin Myaing that made him go straight on to her home. Saturday's Son was there, sitting on a chaise lounge! The medium visited several other disciples. He was seen at Kyaikhtiyo and at Shwesetdaw, two major pilgrimage sites separated from each other by a distance of 500 to 600 kilometers. On the twelfth day, the test's final one, a large crowd was waiting outside the cave. Saturday's Son's family members, worried that they would find the medium dead after such a long fast, were crying. The entrance to the building was opened with sledgehammers by two disciples—one of them was the Major who had come back for the occasion. Saturday's Son appeared, fit as a fiddle. In spite of this display, the medium reaffirmed his lack of agency. To a witness of the feat who asked him how he had managed to be in two places at once, he responded, "I don't know. I found myself in these different places without knowing how."

In the Major's view, Saturday's Son is already 90 percent a *weikza*. For Doctor Sein Yi, it is 50 percent. How can someone become a *weikza* without having practiced alchemy or meditation? People explain that Saturday's Son has the requisite *parami:* the virtuous acts that he carried out in earlier lives pre-positioned him for a remarkable future. Furthermore, the *weikza* have been transmitting energy to him for decades. His organism has evolved. He needs less and less food to live. He is said to be in possession of one of a *weikza*'s ten characteristic powers, the power of satiety (*ahara theikdi*), which enables him to survive without eating—a sign of progress toward immortality. In any case, phrasing these evaluations in percentages shows that the medium has something of the *weikza* about him without being assimilated to them. Possession implies ontological compatibility and even continuity, but not identity. Actually, the cult consists only of so many mediations pieced together, so many intermediaries bound together hierarchically, from the four *weikza* down to the most ordinary of their disciples, passing through their medium and all those who serve, to whatever degree, as relay stations for their energy. The four *weikza,* although they are at the cult's source, are not located at its actual point of origin. It is the Buddha, the most inaccessible figure, who is located there. Consequently, the cult community should be thought of less as a vertical structure with four levels—Buddha, *weikza,* medium, and disciples—with a break between each level, than as a concentric structure, in which every step toward the nucleus means a greater energy capacity. There is no break in continuity among the levels because all, from the Buddha to the simple disciples, share a basic human nature. Saturday's Son, given his remarkable status, constitutes a level all his own, which is, moreover, located at the midpoint. The medium is both enveloped by the circle of disciples—outside of which he is of no significance—and stands as an indispensable point of communication between them and the *weikza* or the Buddha. He is the principal agent and the principal actor in the cult. His singular condition is defined entirely by the ambiguity intrinsic to his position, at the point of contact between the mundane and supramundane, the human and the superhuman, spheres.

The two ways of imagining the cult's community, a vertical structure or a concentric one, constitute schematic projections of the ways, very different in the end, that possession by a *weikza* can play out. They are the poles of a continuum along which could be situated the entire set of possession cults relating to one or more *weikza.* The difference stems not from the modalities of possession, which are always much the same: no costumes, no music, no dances, simply speech. Nor does it stem from the identity of the one or more *weikza* responsible for making the possession take place. Some *weikza* have a particular character—this one is known to be surly, say, which translates into a brusquer tone—but all *weikza* say pretty much the same thing: that one must venerate the Three Jewels, behave morally, and so on. The difference lies in how mediumship is conceived by those concerned, in what the role of a medium entails. Representing a cult as a vertical structure reflects the most elementary situation from the native point of view: the break in levels between the *weikza* and the medium is marked; the medium is a passive intermediary for the *weikza,* disposing of no power of his or her own and sharing nothing of the nature of those who possess him or her. The medium offers no resistance to becoming possessed and is the sole representative of the *weikza* within the cult. Such is the case for the *weikza* U Nareinda and his medium Gyan. We might well speak of a simple structure of possession, a system of relations whose elements assume distinct identities and enter into clear-cut relations with each other.

The complex structure, in contrast, shows much more indeterminacy. The medium is an ambiguous figure, separated only indistinctly from those entities who possess him or her and endowed with certain powers about which one is never sure whether they are the medium's own or are conferred by the *weikza* for a particular occasion. This medium is depicted as rebelling against the role that has befallen him or her, as if to offset the effect of ambiguity. Furthermore, others in the cult are susceptible to playing the role of transmitter for the *weikza*'s speech and power, such that the singular nature of the medium's role has a tendency to dissolve. In the simple structure, the medium remains from the native point of view a pure object of possession; in the complex structure, the medium also becomes its subject, through the reaffirmation of his or her individuality and through a reappropriation and what might be called a "re-personalization" of possession.

The evolution from one structure to the other is probably a matter of time. The longer that possession lasts, the more complex its structure becomes and that of its accompanying cult along with it. The cult of the four *weikza* has in a sense reached this process's fulfillment. The cult has given birth to the idea that possession could take place at any time and imperceptibly. This phenomenon is called *dat win-:* "the essence or the energy [of the *weikza*] enters [the medium]." This is what happens when Saturday's Son responds to a disciple who asks him for advice about his energy ball or when he makes some recommendation to some disciple. In the end there is always a possibility of confusing the speech of the medium with that of the *weikza,* a confusion implicating the source of this speech. Just as the *weikza* tend to become confused with the Buddha, the medium tends to become confused with the *weikza.*

A HOPELESS STRUGGLE

People say that a major obstacle has so far prevented Saturday's Son, already in large part a *weikza,* from "exiting alive" to reach the fabulous domain of Dragoness Mountain: his attachment to his children. Four of them live in Mebaygon, one on the site of the family home (that belonging originally to the medium's parents-in-law), the other three on plots bordering the Energy Monastery. The remaining two live in Minbu. Several of them maintain strong bonds of affection with their father, who has now become a grandfather. Even if they play no role in the cult, they are often seen at the monastery, just as Saturday's Son is often seen going to their homes to pass the time and see his grandchildren.

The four living in Mebaygon own some of the most beautiful houses in the village, built of durable materials rather than bamboo or wood. The income they receive from the farmland they have inherited from their parents or have acquired themselves does not suffice to explain this wealth. In other words, a not negligible portion of the gifts made to the *weikza,* gifts intended to support their religious activities, are enriching the medium's children. The houses make the surprising fact clear that Saturday's Son appears in no way concerned to hide this appropriation of the cult's money. He might even be thought to wish to make a display of it. So you would have to be blind not to notice what is happening—and the disciples are not blind. Yet although the relations between Saturday's Son and his children constitute a recurrent motif in commentary about him, that commentary does not involve a denunciation of this diversion of the cult's funds. I never heard any comment along those lines. The disciples are, quite the opposite, pleased to emphasize the medium's human failings, incapable as he is of breaking his ties. The disciples reaffirm in this way the condition sine qua non for accession to the *weikza* state and Dragoness Mountain: renouncing the world, a world that, for everyone, begins with his or her family circle.

The ultimate sign of Saturday's Son's attachment to his family came in December 2005, when the medium ceded ownership of his monastic complex to his children. The move was legal. Two major categories of monastic goods are recognized in Burma: personal goods, which belong to a monk by private title, and collective goods, which are the property of the monastic community as a whole. The monk makes use of the former as he likes, but he is only the user and manager, in the name of the monastic community, of the latter. However, a monk in possession of personal goods can only transfer them to others during his lifetime, because customary law does not grant the religious the right to bequeath goods. Should a monk fail to make a gift of his personal goods before his death, they fall automatically, on his death, into the possession of the monastic community: they become collective goods. This explains Saturday's Son's action, because the grounds of the Energy Monastery (except for the plot whose use was granted him by U Pyinnya) and of the Site of Success, along with the buildings located on them, belong to him personally. This gift was, however, exceptional, inasmuch as it benefited laypeople, his children, and not a monk. Furthermore, said laypeople are not the ones who financed the buildings' construction or provided for their upkeep. Saturday's Son's children will thus enjoy the right to name a new head monk when Saturday's Son and U Sandima, who manage the monastery jointly, are no longer, for whatever reason, in a position to perform their functions. By transforming the site of the cult into his family's patrimony, the medium has denied the disciples all control over the future of what they themselves have helped establish. Saturday's Son's disappearance will mean the end of the cult, something that everyone knows from common experience even if no one ever says so.

It would appear that both openly redistributing part of the cult's funds to his children and ceding ownership of the Energy Center to them constitute ways for the medium to get his revenge for the all-consuming role that has been imposed on him. These flagrant demonstrations of Saturday's Son's attachment to his family look like a sign of his refusal, despite his being possessed, to be totally subsumed in the collectivity. They are all the better tolerated by virtue of the fact that they touch only on the material domain and so do not put into question the principle of his being so subsumed. The outcome of the game was determined long ago—the fight was hardly fair. Has there ever been such a thing as happy possession?

IMPERMANENCE, SUFFERING, AND SELFLESSNESS

Should you have a chance to go to Burma today, go to the village of Letkhotpin, near Sagu. Gyan spent the greater part of her life there, in a bamboo house, modest but clean, where she lived with her family. U Nareinda possessed his medium for nine years, from 1952 to 1960. Never once did the *weikza* appear in the flesh. He made no direct display of his supernatural powers, even though he gave Gyan the ability to lift spells and to neutralize the poison of venomous animals. He did not oblige the young woman to follow any strict regimen in her life. His essential activity consisted of teaching the practice of meditation through the voice of his medium. Then, believing his mission accomplished, he withdrew and returned permanently to his realm, Brown Mountain. He announced his departure well in advance, asking that a group of monks note down his teaching. This was done, and in 1959, the cult's disciples published at their own expense a work of more than three hundred pages identifying the *weikza* and providing transcriptions of his most important sermons.[8]

After U Nareinda's departure, Gyan, who had moved into her natal village's monastery, returned home. She took up her place again as though nothing had happened. U Nareinda had promised to take care of her, and indeed, her family's affairs—farming and eventually rice trading—prospered for a while, although there was nothing resembling opulence. Gyan married late, at the age of thirty-six.

She never knew what she had preached. She kept a copy of the book on U Nareinda and his teaching, but the medium barely knew how to read.

From Letkhotpin, go to the village of Paygon, some three kilometers farther out in the countryside. At the entrance to the village, you will find the Yadanabonpyan Monastery, where Gyan officiated. An uninformed visitor would suspect nothing of the phenomenon that put the villagers in such high excitement in the 1950s. The monastery, ravaged by time, has been rebuilt. The current head monk, about forty-five years of age, did not experience the period of Weikza Gyan. No photograph of the medium attesting to the episode has been kept. There are still some buildings where people lived in solitude in order to practice meditation. They have gone unused for decades and are in complete disrepair.

Gyan herself is no longer living. She died due to heart problems at the age of seventy-three in May 2005. She received Victorious and me graciously a year and a half earlier, on our first trip to Letkhotpin. A lively woman, she related her story and lent us the book in which she hardly appears. She died in the hospital in Minbu. She was buried in the town cemetery, without fanfare, without even so much as a gravestone, her family having experienced some serious reversals after an earlier period of prosperity.

Having made this visit, continue on your way to the village of Mebaygon, about fifteen kilometers away. Gyan never made it as far as Mebaygon. She had only heard that one day during a sermon a certain Htun Yin, who was ill, wanted to ask for U Nareinda's help, but was prevented by the size of the crowd from doing so. There is a good chance that when you get to the Energy Center, Saturday's Son will not be there. Both of his two drivers will assure you that the man rarely stays in one place for long, despite his eighty years. Either he stays at his other monastery, in Mandalay, where he meets the many disciples who live in the city, or he is in Yangon to discuss some project under way with Major Zaw Win, Doctor Sein Yi, or other people. Or he may have gone off on a trip to some other part of the country, to Mawlamyaing, say, or Loikaw, at the invitation of an important monk, of a family, or a group of disciples.

You will not have wasted your time in coming, however. There is always some lay resident of the monastery ready and willing to show you the sights. You will gaze at the three pagodas and numerous other buildings, including the Monastery of Noble Success where the *weikza* appear. You will be taken to the Site of Success, with its buildings that were used for the *weikza* life-prolonging ceremonies. If your guide is feeling talkative and if you show an interest, he will tell you about the old days, before Saturday's Son entered the monastic community, the great days of Colonel Mya Maung. Don't forget to take a look at the photographs hung on the walls of the Monastery of Noble Success, including that of Bodaw Bo Htun Aung strutting about the hood of a jeep, with the Colonel at the wheel. Egg your guide on a bit and he will take you to the edge of Mebaygon village, to the house where Saturday's Son lived when he was a layperson and where the *weikza* appeared in the flesh. In those years—the cult's golden age in the eyes of the disciples—the medium sometimes edified the audience with a concrete representation of the Buddhist theme of impermanence. He would reproduce the three visions that, according to the tradition, induced Prince Siddhatta, the future Buddha, to renounce the world in order to embark on the quest for enlightenment. His body would first appear completely decrepit, his features sunken: this was Old Age. Then he seemed weak, blood dripping from his nostrils and his mouth, pus coming out of his ears: this was Sickness. Finally, he fell down lifeless: this was Death, certified by Doctor Sein Yi, if he was there, checking the figure's pulse to make sure that his heart was not beating. When the medium came back to life, he would find the audience—thinking him gone for good—in tears.

Brilliant Saturday's Son! How many elements of the universe of Burmese *weikza* has he introduced or revised by means of an identity that, unlike Gyan, he has never been able or wanted to give up? Consider the almost unprecedented phenomenon, the appearance in the flesh of *weikza* who have already "exited." Consider, too, the appearance of Buddha relics in a perfume bottle or the richly elaborated life-prolonging ceremonies for the four *weikza*. How many roles has he had to assume? Head of a farming family, medium, monk, *weikza* (meaning taking on the role of one or another of the four *weikza* when possessed, and of two of them, Bodaw Bo Htun Aung and U Pandita, when they appeared in the flesh). An uneducated peasant, Saturday's Son has turned out to be at the start and at the heart of one of the most durable and most important cults of contemporary Burma. But keep in mind that he will never be recognized for all of this, that his seminal role in all that he has invented, constructed, and brought about will never be acknowledged, because, both by definition and on principle, the possessed does not belong to himself.

In the end, it is perhaps his daughter who provides us the best key to understanding the man. Her father's pleasure and ambition in life, she asserts, have been to make other people happy.

4 In Quest of Invulnerability

A DEMONSTRATION OF INVULNERABILITY

Tuesday, January 27, 2004, 8:00 a.m. The monastery's Willys jeep starts right up. The driver keeps it in good repair. Not that it is an antique: there are practically no original parts left in it. In the course of its repairs the jeep has been refurbished with parts found hither and yon or imported from India. A "miscellaneous" (*supaung satpaung*) model, remarks the driver wryly. In any case, Burmese do not have a taste for antiques. They are fans of new cars, preferably of Japanese make, of which they have long been deprived. Only a few foreigners, especially Anglo-Saxon veterans of World War II, take an interest in the fate of these jalopies. If the monastery's jeep receives such solicitous attention, like so many others that keep on going after more than fifty years of good and loyal service, it is because cars remain such rare and costly items. The country is not in a position to produce its own vehicles on a mass scale. And imports are subject to a quota, a policy of whose rationale no one is aware. Some think it must be to limit traffic problems in Yangon, the capital having experienced its first traffic jams after a period of economic opening in the mid-1990s. Others think that government officials create the dearth of cars on purpose, in order to be able to sell the few import licenses they control at a very high price. Most people don't know what to think. They resign themselves to keeping track of the market, one of the only ones in the world in which, due to the disparity between the supply and the demand, a vehicle, old or not-so-old, loses no value over time and may even increase in value.

The jeep passes beyond the monastery compound's walls and then leaves the village of Mebaygon. Great-Master Aung Khaing, sitting in the car's front seat, asks the driver to stop at the Site of Success. Wearing dark glasses and with his hair slicked back, Aung Khaing sports a large khaki military jacket made in the People's Republic of China: the words "US Army" appear on its upper pocket. Hanging open, it reveals something of a potbelly, a sign of the man's relative wealth. He has the unmistakable air of a private first class at the head of his meager troops: Myint Hsway, who, sitting next to Aung Khaing on the front seat, takes on the role of deputy for this trip; five young men, about twenty years of age, who, equipped with two swords and a long bamboo rod, are squeezed into the back seat along with Victorious and me. Aung Khaing did indeed once serve in the military. He fought against communist insurgents and made it to the rank of sergeant. Of Arakanese origin, from the west of the country, he married a woman in the east, at Loikaw, capital of Kayah State, where he was stationed. He stayed on there after doffing his uniform in 1975. Were one to credit his story—although few people actually go so far as to believe everything he says about his past—he enjoyed a brief period of prosperity while working in the wholesale comestibles market, but his business then foundered because of the ex-soldier's excessive faith in and generosity toward his partners. His wife now has a small business in Loikaw while he concerns himself with religion, having been, as he puts it, "called" to Mebaygon in a dream by the four *weikza* in the late 1970s, shortly after his business went under.

Aung Khaing did not provide this biographical information to me, toward whom he long demonstrated a deep distrust. He revealed it to the soup seller at the market near Mebaygon village. She expressed surprise, with all due respect, at the way that he guzzled his soup, having seen him wolf down a second bowl just as avidly as his first. It was a habit that had stayed with him from his life as a soldier, he said. When you were getting ready to go into battle, there was no lingering over a meal. The soup seller was unaware that her customer, a regular at her shop, had been in the military. Aung Khaing drew out his explanation by telling how he had come from the fields of battle all the way to Mebaygon. I happened to be present on this occasion—we had set out together to purchase food supplies for lunch at the monastery—and was careful to make mental notes of the bits of information divulged in this way. I learned later that "Aung Khaing" was not the man's real name. The name belonged to a famous disciple of the four *weikza,* who had played a prominent role in U Pandita's life-prolonging ceremony in 1975, but withdrew from the cult soon after as a result of a misunderstanding. The name "Aung Khaing" is of a propitious character: *aung* means "to succeed," and *khaing* "durable, solid." The disciple's withdrawal meant the discontinuation of the favorable influence that he bore. This was liable to throw monkey wrenches into the energy works that sustained the cult's smooth functioning. The *weikza* thus endowed our ex-soldier with the name to make up for the loss of their ex-disciple.

When there is no possibility of confusion, Aung Khaing is called "Great-Master" (Hsayagyi, also "Great Leader"), an epithet Burmese use to address or refer to any superior of great age and high rank in the hierarchy of a group or institution. At close to age sixty, Aung Khaing has become the head of the Tactical Encirclement Group (Setka Byuha Ahpwe) for Kayah State, one of the regions where this organization, which arose out of the cult of the four *weikza* and is dedicated to the promotion of Buddhist virtues through the practice of martial arts, recruits the greatest number of its members. Although no records are kept, people estimate that between 1,001 and 1,500 people have entered the group in this state.

When we get to the Site of Success, the driver stops the jeep in front of a court surrounded by a wall. In the middle there stands a small rectangular building of several square meters: U Pandita's cave. It is in this building that the *weikza* successfully underwent the trial by fire in 1975. It is good for the five boys, who are getting ready to enter combat, to tread this "ground of success" (*aung myay*) beforehand. The glorious kings of the past, Bayinnaung (r. 1551–1581) and Alaunghpaya (r. 1752–1760), did so, Victorious points out to me. When they were about to enter into warfare, they led their troops to walk on a pagoda's "ground of success" to increase their chances of victory. In 1920, a group of students did the same at Shwedagon Pagoda before launching a strike protesting the university's rules, a famous event in the struggle against British colonial domination.

The group takes off their shoes and enters the court, passing under an arch formed by a double Bo tree. Once they are inside the building, the boys kneel while Great-Master lights three candles and some incense sticks on an altar on which stands a small statue of the Buddha. Myint Hsway gives each of the boys a piece of folded paper, which they hold tightly in their fists. A cabalistic diagram (*in*)[1] has been sketched on each piece of paper; it is the same diagram they ingested for the first time several years earlier when they joined the Tactical Encirclement Group. It is the "diagram of knowledge" (*pyinnya in*), also called the "basic diagram" (*muyin in*), the "diagram of prowess" (*swanyi in*), the "diagram for showing one's extraordinary powers" (*theikdi pya in*), and the "diagram of the [eighteen] sciences" (*ahtaratha in*). In an atmosphere of great solemnity, Myint Hsway, using both hands, takes the first boy's arm, stretched out toward the altar to the Buddha. As the master, and acting in the name of the boy who ranks only as an ordinary member of the group, he proceeds to make a declaration of truth (*thitsa hso-*). This widespread practice consists of facing an altar to the Buddha or a pagoda, stating the nature of a meritorious act one has already done or one is about to carry out, and then explaining the benefit expected in return. Myint Hsway gives the pronouncement an unusually violent tone, as though an impetuous force was possessing him and was about to explode.

"O Noble Master Buddha of infinite glory, perfections, mind and potency! We, the sons of the noble master Buddha, render you homage [regularly] by reciting our beads according to the formula of the Buddha's Nine Supreme Qualities, starting with *arahan* [the first quality] and through to the last, *bagawa*.

If that is the truth, thanks to the potency of the noble master Buddha may we become good and noble individuals who might possess the eighteen sciences of the accomplished individual and show their extraordinary powers to the people of the 101 populations;[2] may the great monks U Kawwida, U Pandita, U Oktamagyaw, and Saturday's Son [*alias*] U Tilawkeinda, as well as Bodaw Bo Htun Aung, who live at Dragoness Mountain, the 84,000 *weikza*,[3] and we ourselves, may we give homage to the Buddha at the time of the reassembling of his relics and gain entry to nirvana, O Buddha!"

When Myint Hsway finishes this recitation, the boy whose arm he is holding seems to be carried away by some uncontrollable force. He trembles and his body contracts, as if a potent energy were invading him. Myint Hsway having let him out of his grasp, the boy thrusts two or three convulsive blows into the air before putting his hand to his mouth and swallowing the piece of paper. He regains his composure. The four *weikza* of Mebaygon along with the other *weikza* who oversee the martial arts have transmitted to him their energy of success to support and protect him in the trial that awaits him: this morning he and his fellows must demonstrate their invulnerability in front of university students of Magway, the regional capital, thereby inspiring them to become members of the Tactical Encirclement Group.

After the procedure has been carried out for each of the boys, Myint Hsway stands near the altar to the Buddha. He holds in his hands a glass of water and a piece of paper on which a diagram has been drawn—one that is reserved for masters. He murmurs the following phrases on his own behalf:

"O Noble Master Buddha of infinite glory, perfections, mind and potency! From this day, from this date and from this hour, from the moment I ingest this diagram, may I convey many gifts together with all the *weikza* and share the merit therefrom, may I together with them spread veneration of the Three Jewels among the 101 populations, may I become a man full of perfections, O Master Buddha!

From this day, from this date and from this hour, from the moment when I ingest this diagram, may I become a noble and extraordinary individual who can show his power and teach the eighteen sciences of the accomplished individual to the people of the 101 populations, O Master Buddha!

From this day, from this date and from this hour, may I make the martial arts group, Tactical Encirclement Group, prosper, O Master Buddha!

From this day, from this date and from this hour, from the moment when I ingest this diagram, may I become a good and noble individual who makes Myanmar [Burma] known to the world, O Master Buddha!

And from this day, from this date and from this hour, may all the *weikza* watch over and protect me, O Master Buddha!

From this day, from this date and from this hour, may they teach me still more profoundly the eighteen sciences of the accomplished individual, O Master Buddha!

May I, a disciple of the Buddha, be granted the ten extraordinary powers!"

Once he has finished this recitation, Myint Hsway swallows the diagram with water. The ritual ends with a collective proclamation, a leavening of success:

"The Buddha has succeeded, the Buddha has succeeded, the Buddha has succeeded!

The Teaching [of the Buddha] has succeeded, the Teaching has succeeded, the Teaching has succeeded!

The monastic community has succeeded, the monastic community has succeeded, the monastic community has succeeded!

The Buddha's disciples have succeeded!

One and all have succeeded!"

The jeep sets off again, but does not travel for very long. Leaving the town of Minbu and approaching the Irrawaddy River, which must be crossed to get to Magway, which is located on the opposite bank, the engine shows worrying signs of overheating. The driver parks by the side of the road to fill up the water tank. He starts up again, glancing nervously at the hood from time to time.

As the jeep approaches the immense bridge that spans the river, Great-Master makes a show of saying "Success!" It is a matter of maintaining the good fortune that has been obtained so far in the trip. It is also a matter of keeping the troops' spirits up: the boys are nervous about the upcoming demonstration. In the middle of the bridge is one of the billboards with white writing on a green background that decorate towns and roads throughout the country. The regime in place since the military coup d'état in 1988 makes use of these billboards to display its dictates and slogans: "The Four Political Objectives," "The Three National Causes," "The People's Desires," and so on. On this particular billboard appear, in Burmese, the words, "Toward a new nation, modern and developed." The bridge was one of a number of great infrastructure construction projects. It was finished in 2002, accompanied by the government's customary self-glorification for its actions on behalf of the country's development. "It's a good sign [*ateik,* or catalyst for success, that is, a formula stating what is hoped for in the future, this statement itself fostering the realization of that reality]," notes Great-Master about the inscription. "Previously, it would have been necessary to cross the river in a boat, a long and complicated endeavor. With the bridge built, everything has become easier. Our group [the Tactical Encirclement Group], too, strives to raise Myanmar to the level of a great nation, by supporting religion and making the country renowned throughout the world for its Buddhism."

In spite of the driver's fears, the jeep reaches Magway without incident. The vehicle soon enters the university campus. The driver parks at the entrance to a vast, bare court, in the middle of which stands a house. Here lives Professor May Aung, head of the Physics Department and a faithful disciple of the four *weikza*. The single-story brick house is modest. There are three rooms in a row: a foyer that also serves as the living room and contains a television set, to the right a bedroom, and to the left the Buddha's room with the domestic altar. It is in Buddha's room that the professor invites his visitors to be seated. The pale walls are decorated with many photographs of the four *weikza,* along with a photo of Aung Thaung, founder and leader of the Tactical Encirclement Group.

Great-Master sits down on a wooden bed propped up against a wall. The others find places on the floor. The host and his wife bring in plates of food— fried snacks, sticky rice, rice with chickpeas—which are presented to Great-Master and then passed around among the others. It is barely 9:00 a.m., and the professor has told his students to come at 9:30. To pass the time, Great-Master reviews the Tactical Encirclement Group's objectives for the benefit of Victorious and the anthropologist. The first is to seek out and reassemble the *thakiwin min-myo,* the members of the royal clan of Sākya, the Buddha's clan of origin.

The expression *thakiwin min-myo* means several things, notes Great-Master. The *thakiwin min-myo* are first of all those who were related to the Buddha in one of his many lives. They are also those who have received and accepted the words and teaching of the Master during his last lifetime, that of the Awakening. Finally, they are those who venerate the Three Jewels and observe Buddhist precepts today. Another goal of the Tactical Encirclement Group is to spread the practice of martial arts. Martial arts, Great-Master declares, constitute one of the eighteen sciences (*ahtaratha hseshit yat*) that flourished in the Buddha's time. These sciences also include equestrianism, archery, mathematics, and writing. The group's activities have been initiated thanks to the active support of the four *weikza* and under the direction of Aung Thaung. At this point, Great-Master draws the attention of Victorious and the anthropologist to the photograph of the leader hung on one wall. A ray of light emanates from Aung Thaung's left hand; it is none other than the light of Arimetteyya, the next Buddha, Great-Master explains. Aung Thaung is a future Buddha, and this light signals his perfection. Great-Master declares himself very pleased by the presence of the anthropologist and his companion. He is counting on them to write articles and make the Tactical Encirclement Group known to people abroad. The group aims to foster universal peace by spreading veneration of the Three Jewels and observance of Buddhist precepts. Its members are virtuous individuals who wish to show the world the right path. It is important to bear in mind, Great-Master adds, that if the group uses martial arts, it is for self-defense, not for aggressive purposes. He notes in conclusion that the *weikza*'s power is such as to protect people even from atomic weapons.

At 9:20 a.m. a group of about twenty-five students arrives. Others are still expected. To entertain the students who have come early, the professor puts on the video of an earlier demonstration performed by the Tactical Encirclement Group at an official event. It includes scenes of a boy sticking a sword into a young girl's chest. The sword bends; the girl is unharmed.

It is past 9:30 a.m., and Great-Master gets his combatants ready. He gives each one a little folded-up piece of paper with the same diagram that they ingested in U Pandita's cave. He then approaches the altar to make a "declaration of truth":

"*Weikza* U Kawwida, U Pandita, U Oktamagyaw, Bodaw Bo Htun Aung, Aba Bobo Aung, Aba Bo Min Gaung, Great Monk U Tilawkeinda, Great-Master Aung Thaung, the 80,000 [or 84,000] *weikza* and us, disciples of the Buddha, we together support the religion, O Buddha!

By virtue of the truth of this declaration, give us the power of speech [*hnok swanyi*, the ability to convince and seduce others], the power of the mind [*seik swanyi*, the ability to guess others' thoughts], and the power of the body [*ko swanyi*, invulnerability], along with the ten extraordinary powers!"

The five boys repeat the declaration. Their bodies shake, filling up with the energy transmitted by the *weikza*. They swallow their pieces of paper. They pay homage to the Buddha, then to Great-Master, who pronounces this wish: "May you support the religion with success!" The boys also prostrate themselves before Myint Hsway.

Outside, the students are waiting. There are about fifty of them, the great majority of them young women, squatting on one side of the large courtyard of hard-packed earth. A wooden table and chair have been set out facing them, with a space left for the demonstration. Great-Master takes his place in the chair. The professor stands a little ways away.

In the Buddha's room, Myint Hsway gives the boys his last instructions. "Don't worry; we're only going to do a basic demonstration, elementary moves, mostly with bricks. It'll go like the program we decided on last evening. [A rehearsal took place under his supervision the evening before at the monastery.] And above all, when you're doing your demonstration, fix your mind on your masters [the *weikza*]."

Great-Master stands up to introduce the Tactical Encirclement Group to the students. He explains that at the foundation of the group and of the "knowledge" (*atat pyinnya*, or *pyinnya*) that they are spreading stand the four *weikza* of Mebaygon. Had the Burmese had the benefit of such knowledge at the time of the British invasion (in the nineteenth century), they would never have been defeated and colonized. Spreading this knowledge means making sure the Burmese are never again reduced to "servitude" (*kyun bawa*, literally "a servant's life or status"). The group's two goals are to reunite the members of the royal clan of Sākya and to teach the eighteen sciences that flourished at the time of the Buddha. Its three fundamental precepts are morality, mental concentration, and personal dignity.

The first combatant appears. He salutes Great-Master and then the audience. After making a number of thrusts into the air with his arms and his legs, he lies down on the ground. A brick is placed under his head, like a pillow, and two others on his forehead. Myint Hsway approaches him, armed with a sledgehammer. Letting out a terrible cry that emphasizes his exertion, he lands a powerful blow on the bricks on the boy's forehead. The bricks break. The boy stands up, not even stunned, and salutes the audience. That is only possible, Great-Master explains to those in attendance, because the young man observes the Five Precepts, which grant him a specific strength: the "strength of morality" (*thila swanyi*).

The second combatant comes forward. There are salutations once again. He is carrying a sword, which he swings about in the air. He puts its point up against his windpipe and, using the handle, pushes forcefully. The sword bends in two. The sword gets passed around among the spectators to dispel all doubt as to the metal's hardness. At the same time, Great-Master, to make the performance even more impressive, reminds people that the trachea is a very delicate and very tender spot. He says, "This happens because the sword reveres morality. So rely on morality!"

The third combatant's turn has come. He is holding a long bamboo club with which he makes a number of moves. Great-Master points out that it is a technique intended for self-defense and not for aggression. The boy lies down on his side, so that one of his temples rests on a brick set on the ground; two bricks are set on top of his other temple. Myint Hsway comes forward with his sledge-hammer. The boy possesses both morality and mental concentration, Myint Hsway states before striking him with the same blow and same cry as earlier. The two bricks on top break.

The next combatant proceeds to perform using two swords, which he twirls about in the air. He puts one of them aside and sets the other one upright on the ground, with the point against his chest. He pushes it with his body. The sword bends in two. On Great-Master's order, he opens his shirt, making it clear that no form of protection lies beneath it. His chest shows no ill effects.

The fifth and last combatant, after several strenuous thrusts into the air with his arms and legs, undergoes the brick test: two bricks on his head and Myint Hsway's sledgehammer blow. Everything that has been seen, Great-Master informs the audience, draws on only an elementary level of skill.

The demonstration has lasted about twenty minutes, and when it's over, Great-Master speaks to the students. He reaffirms that no trickery has been used, and he urges those who would like to be endowed with a power similar to that of the combatants to join the group, whose three fundamental precepts he repeats. He preaches to the young people as well, urging them to pay homage to the Five Objects of Veneration (the Buddha, his Teaching, the Monastic Community, Masters, and Parents): otherwise, they risk being reborn in hell. The students disperse, leaving the courtyard without having asked a single question. They had come to please their professor, who will soon grade their exams. They seem to have been little moved and hardly impressed.

Great-Master and his troops return to the Buddha's room, where they are served some snacks. The professor's daughter, seventeen years of age, wishes to "take the knowledge" (*pyinnya yu-*). Her parents are already members of the group. Myint Hsway puts a folded piece of paper in her hand—the diagram of initiation is drawn on it. He extends her arm toward the altar to the Buddha and recites the prescribed formula:

> "O Noble Master Buddha of infinite glory, perfections, mind and potency! From this day, from this date and from this hour, from the moment I ingest this diagram, may I together with all the *weikza* convey many gifts and share the merit therefrom, may I together with them spread veneration of the Three Jewels among the 101 populations, may I become an individual full of perfections, O Master Buddha!
>
> From this day, from this date and from this hour, from the moment when I ingest this diagram, may I become a noble and extraordinary individual who can show his power and teach the eighteen sciences of the accomplished individual to the people of the 101 populations, O Master Buddha!
>
> From this day, from this date and from this hour, from the moment when I ingest this diagram, may I become a good and noble individual who makes Myanmar [Burma] known to the world, O Master Buddha!
>
> May I, a disciple of the Buddha, be granted the ten extraordinary powers!"

The young woman swallows the piece of paper. Two bricks are immediately put on her head; Myint Hsway breaks them with a blow of the sledgehammer. The young woman, from now on endowed with the "extraordinary power of the body" (*kaya theikdi*) or invulnerability, has felt nothing. To complete the "knowledge" she has received, she will have to ingest the same diagram once a day for the next eight days (thus nine times in all, on nine successive days). A second candidate, the professor's factotum, wishes to join. The procedure is repeated. Every new member must make a gift of 5,000 *kyat* (equal to the cost of ten meals at an ordinary Burmese restaurant). Part of that sum pays for the expenses of the masters who spread word of the group and its "knowledge"; part of it is given as gifts to the four *weikza* or to the group's leader, Aung Thaung.

The jeep starts right up. As the vehicle is leaving the university grounds, Great-Master pronounces one last, satisfied "Success!" People joke. The atmosphere is more relaxed than it was on the way there. The boys go back over their performance and the spectators' reactions; they congratulate themselves on having attracted two new members. They recall the success of the preceding demonstration, which took place several days earlier in front of a regional military regiment. The commander was so interested that he invited the boys to come back again.

On the road, the jeep makes a brief stop in the town of Minbu: Great-Master invites his troops to have some tea before going back for their midday meal at the monastery.

FIGHTING WITH AND AGAINST ONESELF

What enemy are the young and fiery recruits of the Tactical Encirclement Group fighting against? This is a strange form of combat that sets boys to striking the air because there is no one there to receive their blows, that has them turning their own weapons against themselves because no one is there to attack them, and that has them getting hit with a sledgehammer wielded by their master because no one is there to hit them with it in his place. The essence of their performance, in the demonstrations they give in various parts of the country, consists of proving not so much their bellicosity as their invulnerability. But invulnerability to what? What invisible adversary are they defending themselves from?

These five boys reflect a segment of the male membership of the Tactical Encirclement Group, those members who go about giving demonstrations and spreading the "knowledge." They are as yet unmarried, often out of work, and uncertain about their future. Not having stayed in school, they help out their farming or petty trader families on an occasional basis. They are, in a word, vulnerable. They are particularly vulnerable to alcohol, a vector of masculine sociability and a way to fill up the empty stretches, to make the time go by, the time that weighs so heavily on them. The ethic of the Five Precepts, the moral charter for Buddhist laypeople, prohibits its consumption. Among men, especially young bachelors, observing the rule is actually the exception. It would be only a slight exaggeration to say that in the village, women go to the monastery, men go to the bar. But joining the Tactical Encirclement Group implies giving up alcohol. Individual morality conditions the obtaining of invulnerability. Relatedly, this power is not acquired once and for all: it disappears automatically on any infraction of the group's rules. Any untoward incident in the course of a demonstration, such as a sword penetrating the flesh when pressed against a part of the body instead of bending, will be interpreted in this way, and suspicions will focus on drink, the most common form of backsliding.

The boys give up alcohol and give up violence as well. Paradoxically, the invulnerability granted the members of the group is a way to domesticate their violence. Far from authorizing the use of force in a raw and destructive form, granting someone invulnerability circumscribes violence's manifestations and transforms its effect. As Great-Master never tires of repeating, the power of invulnerability is an instrument of self-defense and not of aggression. One of the group's rules, deemed fundamental by its members, prohibits killing any living creature. This is, in fact, the first of the Five Precepts. From this point of view, a Buddhist one, an individual's propensity toward violence results from his vulnerability to affects (aggressiveness, spite, envy, pique, etc.). Invulnerability is acquired by mastery of the self and signifies the progressive disappearance of all desire for violence. To state it as a formula, the more nonviolent an individual becomes, the more he becomes invulnerable. Physical invulnerability follows from mental invulnerability.

Thus absorbing the initiatory diagram does not in itself suffice to confer invulnerability. Doing so allows someone to enter into communication—this is what is indispensable—with the four *weikza* of Mebaygon, who are at the origin of the group and are the source of the effectiveness of the "knowledge" its members spread, and with other *weikza* (unidentified) who watch over martial arts practitioners. "It's like putting in a telephone line," Myint Hsway explains. "And every time you ingest the diagram, it's like you're telephoning the *weikza*. You let them know where you are and you ask for their protection." Absorbing the diagram repeatedly also makes it possible to accumulate "strength" (*aswan*). This absorption is thought about as though it was a kind of nutrition, as though it was literally an incorporation, an individual's power increasing as he keeps ingesting copies of the diagram.

But to take full effect, the *weikza*'s support and the increasing physical resistance that follow from regular absorption of the diagram require the individual to develop morally and spiritually. Just as the "knowledge" acquired is effective and persists only insofar as certain rules of conduct are respected, so the degree of invulnerability attained is a function of the degree of someone's spiritual accomplishment as defined by Buddhist logic. The power of invulnerability is imagined in terms of a continuum—being more invulnerable or less so—rather than as an opposition—all or nothing, being invulnerable or defenseless. The more someone adheres to Buddhist precepts and works at developing a capacity for mental concentration by reciting prayer beads (conceived of as a form of meditation by Burmese Buddhists), the more one's power of invulnerability will intensify, manifesting itself in more and more extraordinary performances, to the point of sawing one's tongue with a sword or—although occasion has never yet arisen to exercise this ability—diverting missiles launched against Burma. Everyone in the group emphasizes that there would be no use ingesting diagrams without cultivating morality and mental concentration, that only these qualities, in other words, make it possible to metabolize invulnerability—transforming little pieces of paper bearing esoteric inscriptions into a source of potent, vital energy. Self-mastery, mastery of the senses, is the basis of invulnerability, and it is with oneself that combat must be engaged. The true representative of invulnerability, for that matter, is not the man of war but the spiritual virtuoso, the saint who has subjugated desire, triumphed over the passions, and no longer needs assistance to defend himself from himself, from others, and from the world. Characteristically, a saint offers unhesitatingly to have his head cut off, and the person who attacks him exerts himself in vain. However, is there any point expecting everyone to attain such perfection? So it falls to the collectivity to cobble together some basic safety net for the most vulnerable among its members, those who remain prisoners of a fate that society itself has helped manufacture. This safety net is offered them but not without asking of them that they make some effort to enjoy its protection.

Thus the young recruits of the Tactical Encirclement Group fight with and against themselves, negotiating by means of the instruments at their disposal the fraught passage to manhood. This is a time of uncertainty, of indeterminacy, when a young man must release himself from parental authority yet is not yet himself a parent or even a husband: it is a time when he must find his own place. It is also a time that may continue indefinitely. Myint Hsway's story, as it gets told in the group, speaks of this time, with its agonies and their long-sought relief. The man who now distributes a salutary diagram for ingestion was in the past an inveterate drunkard. In his village, in the region of Aunglan, he had a well-earned reputation as a rowdy. As a bachelor—which he remains, at close to the age of forty—the young man drank constantly. Not a single soul trusted him because of the many stories he had made up to wheedle out of people whatever tiny amounts of money he could to satisfy his love of drink. But one day, having gotten himself good and drunk, the intemperate young man went to sleep it off on a nearby hill, known in the past to have been frequented by holy men, both ascetics and monks. And there he received in a dream, sent by some *weikza* who had lived there, a winning number for the Thai lottery: 361. (People in Burma bet on the last three digits of the number that gets drawn in Thailand.) He was skeptical about all this. But what would it cost to try? After many fruitless efforts, he managed to persuade someone he knew to lend him a small amount of money to play the lottery. He bet on the number and won. At this point a monk from a neighboring village spoke to him about the four *weikza*. The debauched man decided to use his winnings to go to Mebaygon. He paid homage to the *weikza* at the Energy Center. He also attended a demonstration of the Tactical Encirclement Group and asked to take the "knowledge." It was Great-Master Aung Khaing who initiated him. Myint Hsway "was delivered" (*kyut-*): the same expression is used to describe reaching nirvana. When he returned to his village and described the extraordinary things he had seen in Mebaygon, people thought he was delirious, that alcohol had made him lose his mind. But in the years that followed, Myint Hsway spread the "knowledge" so well that the region of Aunglan became a bastion of the Tactical Encirclement Group.

The group's recruits offer proof to themselves, as well as to others, by means of their spectacular demonstrations that their struggle proves victorious. As for Great-Master himself, he tells anyone who will listen that his ambition is to govern the country for five years in order to reform its drunks and drug addicts. Therefore it is hardly surprising that the feats of our group of invulnerable young men should have resonated so little with the students of Magway University. The audience was made up almost entirely of young women, who are better protected from the dangers of idleness. Students do not float aimlessly about; they are bound by their studies, by the rhythm that those studies impose on their lives, by the social fabric that those studies create, by the future that those studies enable the students to imagine for themselves. It would be a mistake to suppose that belief in invulnerability presents any substantial affinity with some "popular" mentality or culture, whose content would turn out to be hard to define in any case. Rather, invulnerability becomes relevant and truly meaningful only in specific situations, in this case that of young men who left school early and are now spinning their wheels. Made fragile by their situation, these young men are removed, and remove themselves, from the world's grip in order to be protected from its corrosive effects. They are not deluding themselves when they believe themselves invulnerable: their involvement with the Tactical Encirclement Group, which inoculates them against devastating threats, does indeed confer on them a kind of indestructibility.

The group members' double renunciation, of both alcohol and violence, brings with it no loss of virility. As if by way of compensation for their self-imposed denial of certain traits thought appropriate to their gender and to their situation, these young men simultaneously reaffirm their virile nature by means of what they put on display in their demonstrations: the art of war. Yet they implement the warrior function in an original way. They must confront without attacking, fight without being violent, and win without doing battle—because they are not ordinary warriors but the "Buddha's soldiers" (*hpaya sittha*). The demonstration of invulnerability must alone suffice to disarm the adversary. What can the attacker do, in the face of invincible combatants, other than yield to the advantage of their superior strength? That at least is the anticipated result of the demonstrations the group organizes. If the adversary of our invulnerable young men turns out to be invisible and absent from the field of battle, it is not only the case that these boys are fighting themselves. It is also the case that their true opponent occupies not the field of operations but the place of the spectator. The latter, watching the martial performance, is expected to experience catharsis, a purging of his or her passions made possible by the emotions and feelings that the performance arouses. The demonstration of invulnerability, a discourse directed to spectators on the subject of their own vulnerability, is intended to convince them to enter the group and to live in moral accord with their society.

Joining the Tactical Encirclement Group, according to our invulnerable young men, means taking a "right path" (*lanzin hman-*), a "good path" (*lanzin kaung-*), and avoiding the fate of an "evil boy" (*lu-zo*), one who does nothing but drink (or worse), talk (about the vain matters young people talk about), fight (sometimes steal)—someone who represents a source of problems or concern for the community. It means becoming an accomplished individual, an aspiration that the recurrent reference, whether in these young men's recitations or their conversation, to the eighteen sciences (*ahtaratha hseshit yat*) further emphasizes. The phrase evokes the canonical period, the era of the Buddha's successive lives. In stories about these lives that Burmese monks recount to illustrate their sermons, such-and-such a young prince or Brahman is described as having acquired knowledge of the eighteen sciences, a conventional way of indicating that he has successfully completed a well-rounded education. In addition, a well-known episode in the last life of the Buddha, the life in which he attained Awakening, has him called as a sixteen-year-old prince to provide proof of his competence in the eighteen sciences in order to gain the confidence of members of his group—the Sākya—who are reluctant to give him their daughters in marriage. The prince must show his mastery of archery, taken to be emblematic of the entire set of eighteen sciences. The knowledge of these sciences, as it happens (but which happens for a reason, because it concerns the Buddha's own person), is a prerequisite for attaining the married state.[4]

Classical texts provide several lists of these eighteen sciences, drawn from scriptural sources.[5] None of these lists, which vary somewhat in their content, include the martial arts. Still, Great-Master is not mistaken when he counts martial arts among the eighteen. What exactly the field of eighteen sciences covers matters less than what the phrase suggests. Just as we think of the formula $E = MC^2$, whose sense few people grasp, as the symbol of the Einsteinian revolution, so do Burmese refer to the eighteen sciences to evoke the figure of the accomplished individual, the individual educated in all domains required for adult status, the cultivated and honorable individual, as such an individual lived in the canonical era. The phrase "the eighteen sciences" is for that matter easier to use than an equation. Alluding to a content that is both vague and accessible, it can be invested with a variety of elements, including the martial arts. Rather than reflecting an aspiration to the mastery of specific kinds of learning, the constant invocation of the eighteen sciences by the Tactical Encirclement Group's members corresponds to a way of indicating the desire to make of them worthy and respectable individuals, similar to those of the golden age. In this respect, the group's two goals, reuniting the members of the Sākya royal lineage (the Buddha's lineage of origin) and the diffusion of martial arts, look like two faces of the same coin: the price of (re)constructing an ideal order. For a community established on this double fiction—proclaiming all of their own as equally noble and equally invulnerable (this second ploy preventing anyone from being able to harm anyone else)—what else could follow but unity, peace, and harmony?

But we know what comes from such projects. The desire for an ideal order, for a perfect humanity and perfect solidarity, gives rise to horror and servitude. Only a society liberated from this myth, a society disabused of such desires, produces some measure of liberty. Does feeling glad, then, that no one in Burma has any intention of satisfying Great-Master's burning desire to be given control of the country break with the usual convention that would have the anthropologist carefully avoiding passing any negative comment, however slight, on the people who, willingly or not, put up with his or her presence? This is not to say that Great-Master himself stands outside the great edifice of servitude that the Burmese have experienced for more than a half-century, since the year, 1962, of General Ne Win's coup d'état. It is only that Great-Master occupies a tiny and anonymous role, one that is hard to notice against the immense facade of the state's power and of its institutionalized tyranny. Will we ever be in a position to account for servitude's invisible architecture?

Putting political science aside, at least the kind that draws up lists of traits of various systems (democracy, fascism, communism, etc.), we need to undertake a consideration of the economy of servitude, to focus on the social and cultural ideas, facts, and gestures that bring about subjugation. To understand how the cloth of tyranny gets woven, it is not enough to show the power of violence, to dissect the techniques of absolute power, to deconstruct official myths and images—although doing so is already a considerable task. To undo the mesh of subjection, it is necessary to look into the midst of what constitutes the collectivity to discern the unrecognized places where the bonds of servitude are joined, where forms of subjugation are fashioned without even being noticed. We need to move from a reflection on the immediate basis of tyranny to the machinery of alienation, understood as the ethnographic study of the social and cultural logics that result in the creation of both a collective identity and servitude.

The Tactical Encirclement Group's activities are, of course, to be analyzed in and for themselves, and we will not fail to do so. Yet looking at the ideas conveyed by some of the group's members in the name of the group makes it impossible to avoid the question of how such activities contribute to the dynamic of tyranny. Doesn't the Tactical Encirclement Group represent not only a safe haven for some boys adrift but also one of the many places where the free and inexorable movement toward servitude occurs?

THE MAN WHO WAS TO BE A CROCODILE, NOT A PIECE OF WOOD

Aung Thaung, the founder and leader of the Tactical Encirclement Group, was born in the village of Kyungyi in the region of Myan Aung, south of Pyay, at the border of Bago and Irrawaddy Divisions. He still lives there, now sixty-six years of age, surrounded by his wife, about a dozen years his junior, and his three children, two sons and a daughter, all of them unmarried. His house, a grand structure only recently completed, replaces that of his parents—he was their eldest son. It is the only house in Kyungyi made entirely of durable materials (the others are made out of bamboo, wood, or bricks and wood). He is a wealthy farmer, the most well-off farmer in the village. He has gradually acquired fifty acres of land (as compared to the average farmer's three to ten acres), on which are planted corn, tomatoes, peanuts, and pulses. He also owns about fifteen head of cattle and about a dozen cows. Active and enterprising by nature, Aung Thaung is now prevented from working because of pain in his knees, which forces him to use a cane when he walks. He has so far resisted suggestions that he be operated on, because, he says, the pain is not constant. He is happy just to take medicine for it. He keeps a little basket containing an array of medicines, both Burmese and "English," close at hand.

Aung Thaung spends most of his time in the main room on the ground floor of his house. This room serves as the warehouse for his farm's harvests, as the dining room, and as the living room. In the evening, a small television can be turned on thanks to a solar panel, a startling device introduced by the man of the house into this village without electricity. An imposing domestic altar takes up one wall of the room. Richly decorated, it consists of a statue of the Buddha sitting on a golden preaching throne, along with three small statues set out behind glass: in the middle, a statue of the Buddha in copper, given to Aung Thaung by the four *weikza;* to the Buddha's right, another statue of the Buddha—this one protects the house from fire—made from wood of the double Bo tree from the Site of Success; and to the Buddha's other side, a statue of Shin Thiwali bought by the family, this saintly disciple of the Buddha abetting prosperity. On the wooden posts closest to the altar are arranged a number of photographs of the four *weikza* and one of Aung Thaung, the one most often seen in the possession of members of the group, in which a ray of light can be seen to radiate from the leader's left hand. A wooden bed has been placed against the far wall, perpendicular to the altar. It is meant for the *weikza,* who stay there when they come to visit, invisibly, their distinguished disciple. The oldest of his children, who is close to thirty, sits on this bed for hours at a time, reproducing cabalistic diagrams based on numerous models of Aung Thaung's design. People say he often recites his prayer beads the whole night through, a sign of an intense capacity for mental concentration, much like his father's.

On the house's upper floor, a spacious room, almost empty, can house a hundred or more people. This is where people who have come to consult Aung Thaung in search of a cure are put up. This is also where members of the group sleep when they come to visit. They come on a regular basis, individually or in a group, to pay their respects to the leader (respects that come with a gift) and to get diagrams from him. During their stays, they assist him with his patients. And once a month, Aung Thaung receives a delegation sent in turn by one of the regional branches of the group, according to an order set yearly. These delegations include bastions of the group in Lower Burma, in particular places located along the Yangon-Pyay-Aunglan axis (Letpandan, Gyobingauk, Zigon, Aunglan). But people come from much farther away as well (Mogok, Loikaw). Money is collected beforehand among local members of the group about to make a visit. Once the delegation has arrived, it organizes a donation in the group's name, in that of the founder, and in that of the branch it represents: a meal is offered to thirty-nine monks from the area, each one from a different monastery. If it is the appropriate time of year, from March to May, the delegation sponsors an ordination ceremony for local boys who will become Buddhist novices and spend some time at a monastery, as is customary for Burmese adolescent males.

The monthly donation ceremonies do not take place at Aung Thaung's home. They happen instead at the monastery he has had built a few steps from his place on the site of the village's old monastery. In 1946, following exceptionally high flooding of the Irrawaddy River, its banks, which protected the village and its fields, collapsed. The village was moved almost in its entirety two or three hundred meters away from the river, so as to avoid the risk of being completely submerged during the next annual spate of the river. (All the same, the area is submerged during the rainy season, when people get about by boat.) Only those villagers, including Aung Thaung's family, living at the easternmost edge of the old village, the part farthest from the river, were spared having to move. It was in this area that the monastery was located. It was taken down and transported so that it could be set up once again at the entrance to the new village. In the 1980s, Aung Thaung conceived of the project of setting up a monastery in the original location. The village, made up of four or five hundred houses, could support a second (or even a third) monastery, as often happens in Burma. Construction, financed entirely by Aung Thaung, started in 1987 and was completed twelve years later, in 1999. The leader intended a complementary restoration of the ordi-nation hall, a pavilion without walls. Nevertheless, once he was ready to invite a monk to take up residence there, he faced a setback. People objected, claiming that creating a second monastery would lead to a split in the village. Monks in the area to whom Aung Thaung turned pronounced themselves to be of the same opinion. He had to give up his plan, despite a sizable investment and many years of effort. The intended monastery was renamed as a library (*pitakat taik,* "build-ing for canonical texts")—a modest piece of furniture on the upper story con-tains some volumes of the Buddhist canon—and its financial sponsor had to abandon claims to the prestigious title of "monastery donor" (*kyaung daga*). Un-occupied ever since, the building is opened once a month, on the occasion of the ceremony organized by one of the group's branches. Aung Thaung, to whom many disciples attribute extraordinary abilities and in whom some even see a fu-ture Buddha, has thus failed at what some altogether ordinary villagers, made rich by farming or commerce, have succeeded in doing. As a matter of fact, the power of the founder of the Tactical Encirclement Group does not derive from the villagers' wishes, which can counter it. But if his power does not arise out of the community in which he has lived his life, where does it come from?

In 1318 of the Burmese era (1956–1957), recounts the person with whom we are concerned, when he was about eighteen and was helping his family in the fields, two famous *weikza,* Bobo Aung and Bo Min Gaung, appeared to him to teach him the "knowledge of the cabalistic arts" (*in pyinnya*), including the rules one must follow to ensure the efficacy of diagrams.[6] They made sketches of several designs for him to see, so that he could reproduce and use them. Acquiring this extraordinary skill did not actually change anything about Aung Thaung's life: unaware of his mission, he made no use of the "knowledge." But the context in which this skill he didn't know what to do with was delivered to him is not without significance; indeed it is meaningful in two respects. Although Aung Thaung pretends to forget the fact, it is difficult not to stop and note that the year 1318 (1956–1957) corresponds to the 2,500th anniversary of the religious era founded by Gotama Buddha, the era that began with the death of the Master and is supposed to last 5,000 years. Burma had just regained its independence (in 1948), and U Nu's government was relying on Buddhism as the mainstay of the country's national identity. The anniversary year, celebrated with great pomp, was marked by the organizing of a council to revise and purify the entirety of the Buddhist canonical texts. It was hoped that the event would inaugurate a new golden age of Buddhism and good times, at last, for Burmese society, after the trials of the colonial period and World War II. These years saw an efflorescence of *weikza* cults (that of Mebaygon was born in 1952). *Weikza* and their intermediaries were expected to support the renewed expansion of the Buddhist religion. The two *weikza*'s revelations to Aung Thaung, as he recounts the incident, should be linked to this dynamic.

The revelations took place, furthermore, in his late adolescence, at the time of his passage to manhood. Aung Thaung showed clear signs of personal trouble at this point in his life. He behaved strangely, and withdrew into himself, even while showing himself capable at times of a shocking brutality and frankness. He would address himself rudely to some older notable, who was usually treated with deference, because the latter had behaved inappropriately, or to some monk for having violated the prohibition of eating after noon, one of the fundamental precepts of the code of monastic discipline. He behaved so erratically that for three years villagers considered him mad. At just the time when the ordinary course of life would have led him, like anyone else, to become a full member of the community, the young man took himself to the community's margins to highlight its pretenses, rejecting the rules of the game that he should henceforth have made it clear he both respected and was worthy of. Distancing himself from the village community but without leaving the field, like a body in orbit—wasn't this the first sign of a singular history? Indeed the young Aung Thaung's apparent madness, instead of indicating his descent into the abyss of mental illness, prefigured and prepared the way for his making his way free of—his surpassing—the run-of-the-mill order of things.

Something else came to suggest and then confirmed his exceptional fate: Aung Thaung remained a bachelor. He wasn't to marry until the late age of thirty-five, at the very time (a little before or a little after?) of his encounter with the four *weikza* (in 1973–1974) who were to make clear to him his mission and set themselves up as his masters. A striking coincidence this, making it possible to resolve both the mystery of a skill whose application its possessor did not grasp and the impossibility of becoming a man of parts because he could not or did not know how to submit to the conventions of social life and marry a woman with whom he might set up a household.

We find, in other words, the conjunction of an experience, a skill, and an encounter that enables Aung Thaung to offer others—those who in their turn are lost or delayed on their way—a means to forge a path to manhood. But they must pay a price: they will have to control their thoughts and their bodies, put up with the whims of the masters they have chosen for themselves, and even give up the right to speak before finally being able to enjoy that right while filled with the exhilarating feeling of becoming men. During the demonstrations of invulnerability in which they are featured, the boy members of the group are silent. Not a word, not a sound, not even a gesture suggest what they are thinking or feeling. Their subjugated minds and bodies have already suffered a prior violence in the form of the renunciation of the world and a degree of subordination they have had to accept—a violence they seem to have called down on themselves at their own behest and taken on with pride and that now, at the time of the demonstrations, neutralizes the violence they are undergoing. Nothing, absolutely nothing, escapes their lips, even as their master doubles the shock of his sledge-hammer's phenomenal blow with a resounding shout. A blow and a shout that provide an image, it is tempting to think (at the risk of interpretive excess), of both the potent organizing strength that has subdued them and the terrible destructive strength that they have by the same token avoided and against which they are now immunized. A blow and a shout, in other words, that reveal the substitution not of order by disorder but rather of one arbitrary imposition by another, the displacement of an individual's servitude (his subjection to his passions) by a collective one (his subjection to the group). Having consented to being made subject, these boys will soon be masters in their turn, even being able to draw the initiatory diagram and give it to people to ingest, to reveal the secret, the great secret, the one that makes you invulnerable, that makes you a man, and that consists of learning, sometimes painfully, that no deliverance comes but at the price of a new servitude.

Thus the anthropologist must widen his gaze. It is not enough for a boy to have gone through the customary rite of passage, the novice's ordination (*shin pyu-*) followed by a temporary stay at a monastery, to make a man of him. That rite of initiation only turns a boy into a prospective man. On a personal level, its effect is virtual rather than existential. The rite grants an individual social recognition as being in a position to gain adult status, and particularly to marry, but makes no guarantee that he will really be able to do so. There remains a long path for him to follow, and obstacles to confront. And because the collectivity joins in to light the way on this dark and hazardous path to manhood, we should enlarge our perspective beyond rites of initiation (which anthropology privileges to an almost inordinate degree) to focus our attention on procedures, less visible and more limited, that foster that passage and make of boys men in actual fact, not just in name. We should also focus our attention on the people who make use of those procedures, as they take on the delicate function of escorts, of makers of men.

But here we have gone far ahead—in too great a hurry no doubt to lay out and make sense of all the facts—when the singular fate of Aung Thaung remains only on the verge of being realized. For a long time, the man took no advantage of his knowledge of the cabalistic arts. Around 1335 (1973–1974), or nearly twenty years after this knowledge was transmitted to him, the four *weikza* "called" him (*khaw-*). They used their powers to bring about his visit to Mebaygon. At the Energy Center, the *weikza* U Pandita, appearing in the flesh, posed the same question to the visitor three times over, and three times over Aung Thaung responded in the same way:

"Great Disciple, what have you come here to ask of us?"

"I seek knowledge (*atat pyinna*) that would let me regenerate the religion of the Buddha, Venerable."

"And as for what concerns the worldly domain (*lawki*), what do you want?"

"I want nothing, Venerable."

The second question's formulation implied that Aung Thaung's wish was going to be granted, if it had not already been. It is not clear on what basis the man tells us what he believes himself to be indebted to the *weikza* for: the simple activation of a skill already acquired or the transmission of that skill itself. The ambiguity points to the tension and the conflicts about his status: between dependence on the four *weikza* (a source of legitimacy), on the one hand, and an affirmation of the autonomous nature of his power, on the other.

Later, after several more visits, U Pandita revealed to the disciple what his mission was. He informed him as to the use he was to make of the extraordinary "knowledge" whose agent he had been elected to become: "You must teach young people so that they will behave morally. When you meet your parents [with whom you have been linked in one or more previous lives and who will become your disciples], I will tell you your biography [your previous lives] in detail."

Encouraged by this mandate received from the *weikza*'s own mouth, Aung Thaung reflected on how to fulfill his mission. He thought to use or was incited by U Pandita to use (our man makes varying statements about this too) the martial arts (*thaing*). Promising young people invulnerability—bodily power (*kaya theidki, ko swanyi*)—and the possibility of displaying it if they remained virtuous in their conduct would bring them to the religion. The idea, Aung Thaung goes on to say, was to revive the practice of the eighteen sciences, emblematic of the accomplished individual at the time of the Buddha, the best known of which is archery.

Thus it fell to Aung Thaung to counter the supposed decline of the religion among young people, to lead them to a greater respect for the Buddhist precepts and to a greater morality, in a society in which order and continuity are understood as resting first and foremost on how closely people adhere to the system of Buddhist values. His mission fit into a salvational program that had led the four *weikza* to accept and treat drug addicts and alcoholics at the Energy Center. Significantly, it was not so much young people in general, but rather young men who were deemed morally and religiously deficient and for that reason were the special target of the undertaking. Young women are denied any rite of passage analogous to a novice's initiation and are also denied the monastic vocation: women have not had the right to higher ordination for many centuries. They are thought and think themselves incapable of reaching nirvana in their life as a woman and are condemned, as a result, to strive to be reborn as a member of the other sex if they wish to attain deliverance. In spite of all this and in spite of the distance between them and the Buddhist ideal of spiritual perfection, young women, because of the constraints imposed culturally on their sex, are paradoxically more thoroughly imbued with morality and are closer to monks and monasteries than young men. (It is unusual for a woman to drink alcohol or engage in physical violence.) In contrast, boys are the beneficiaries of an excessive indulgence, of too great a power over themselves and others. Attracting young men, especially the headstrong among them, toward religion by means of the martial arts and the promise of invulnerability is a way of transforming their erratic and dangerous strength into an energy from which society can benefit. Invulnerability is conceived of as a social discipline.

One more visit, and the *weikza* U Pandita enjoined his disciple to set about his mission at once: "Aung Thaung! Stop staying still. Act so that people can tell whether you are a crocodile or a piece of wood."

Just as what looked like a tree trunk on the surface of a river turns out to be the back of a crocodile, so Aung Thaung was to reveal himself. It was time that he made something of his "knowledge." However, nothing was divulged to him as to the significance of the innumerable cabalistic diagrams. The man would spend his entire life in ignorance of the meaning of what he sketched.

Much like the four *weikza*'s medium, Saturday's Son, and in keeping with a characteristic axiom, Aung Thaung "knows nothing." It is the *weikza* who know things. The disciple is in possession of a signal "knowledge" about which he understands nothing and over which he exercises no control. So the fact of his election is paired with the understanding that power has been delegated to him by the *weikza,* tempering impressions of his potency. Yet an ability to communicate the "knowledge" granted him by the *weikza* is said to go along with his function as a mediator, despite the fact that the substance and mastery of that knowledge escape him. Aung Thaung's vocation is to give something away, something eminent, that does not belong to him any more than it belongs to those who receive it. Beyond the enigma of the sense of the diagrams lies the mystery of the "knowledge" that makes them effective and that they transmit—the very mystery that we have tried to penetrate.

KNOWLEDGEABLE BUDDHISTS

While continuing to make his livelihood as a farmer, Aung Thaung started to spread the "knowledge" both in his native region and to those whom he met at the monastery of the four *weikza*. In line with his mission, he worked hard to form a group (*ahpwe*) based on the shared enjoyment of this "knowledge" and the powers that it confers. He produced one diagram for becoming a "member of the group" (*ahpwe-win*), then another for moving up to the rank of "master" (*hsaya*)—someone in a position to initiate new members, to "show the method [of invulnerability]" (*ni pya-*).

Recruitment expanded beyond the original target—morally deficient young men—from the very start. In effect, the "knowledge" Aung Thaung possesses is of two sorts. It includes, in addition to the power of invulnerability, the power to treat illnesses. Aung Thaung has never practiced martial arts or displayed his invulnerability. Instead he has built up a reputation on the basis of his skills as an exorcist, making afflictions attributed to evil spells (*payawga,* provoked by an external agent, either an invisible being or a sorcerer) disappear. So an aptitude for making someone invulnerable—that is, to immunize someone against external aggression—and an aptitude for fighting such aggression after the fact are combined here. They derive from a single strength, one both augmentative and purgative. This strength in fact both increases the capacity of an individual to whom it is transmitted to resist aggression and neutralizes an attack that has already been carried out. Someone who wishes to be protected by the holder of such strength or who has been cured by him often joins the ranks of his disciples. This explains the success of the Tactical Encirclement Group's recruitment.

There is more. Aung Thaung's "knowledge" has gone on to include within its purview the treatment of natural, organic maladies. It mixes together two types of specialization usually assigned to different individuals: treatment for evil spells and treatment for ordinary illnesses, thus both exorcism and indigenous or "English" medicine. Aung Thaung treats any sort of affliction. Many people suffering from natural diseases turn to him for assistance. Either they have tried everything—the hospital, several doctors, even treatment abroad—in vain, or they are too poor to be able to afford the services of "English medicine." Accompanied by a relative, they stay at his house one, two, three days, or sometimes longer, and they come back again if necessary. Aung Thaung observes their condition and decides which diagrams fit their illness. No compensation is required. Everyone makes some gift in accordance with his or her ability. A patient who has recovered decides, as a general rule, to join the group.

The "knowledge" propagated by its founder has gained legitimacy in tandem with the expansion of the group. Some disciples of the four *weikza,* men and women alike, have decided to avail themselves of membership without engaging in the practice of the martial arts. Belonging to the group simply makes up a part of their relationship with the four *weikza.*

How many members of the group are there today, thirty years after its founding? Five thousand, ten thousand, twenty thousand? No one knows. It has not been thought useful to put the slightest trace of an organization in place to manage its operation. The existence of the group depends on the person of Aung Thaung, who is its chief, its incarnation, and its living source. And the leader alone is in a position to confer the title of master on someone, by administering the requisite diagram in return for the sum of 100,000 *kyat.* (This amount has increased since the group's beginnings along with the cost of living.) Although this sum is by no means negligible, particularly in light of how modest the means of most prospective recipients of the honor are, the price of this very potent "knowledge," as its provider likes to remind people, is far less than the price of an ordinary cow (300,000 *kyat*). The spread of this "knowledge" has nonetheless assured Aung Thaung substantial revenues, which he is free to use as he pleases, including for his own personal needs if necessary. Despite this, the man persisted in working his fields. The four *weikza*'s medium, Saturday's Son, as long as he remained a layperson, did the same. In a rural milieu, agricultural chores set the rhythm of collective life. To stop devoting oneself to them is to set oneself apart. It appears that it is incumbent on those elected by the *weikza* to stay put, to keep their original social position and the values that it implies, at least up to a point. It is an integral part of their singular identity that they remain ordinary men.

At its start the group had no name. The four *weikza* got into the habit of calling it the "Group of Extraordinary Physical Strength" (Theikdi Bala Ahpwe). Once its demonstrations of invulnerability aroused a certain notoriety, it was subjected to an inquiry by the National Federation for the Martial Arts—in 1989, according to the most specific account—which led to its official recognition. This required fitting it out with a formal name. Some years earlier, in 1980, the government had undertaken a vast project of religious purification. Among its targets were certain groups of practitioners of the *weikza* path, pronounced dangerous to "true" or "pure" Buddhism. From the start, the authorities refused to let the term *"weikza"* or any other term that could be taken to refer to them (such as *theikdi,* "extraordinary powers") figure in the name they chose. A strange attitude, one might say, consisting of declaring war on a phenomenon on one front while indirectly encouraging its expansion on another. Here we come up against not a display of political power's duplicity but rather the ambivalent nature of the *weikza* phenomenon, which is taken at the same time to constitute a menace to the "true" Buddhism that Burmese Buddhism should be and to be an essential element of that same Buddhism. In other words, we come up against the nagging question intrinsic to Burmese identity and to the logic of differentiation at its heart: "Are we good Buddhists?"

The authorities suggested the name of "Setka Byuha Ahpwe." *Ahpwe,* a generic term, can be applied to any group, association, or committee. *Setka byuha* is a Pali compound. It is used so rarely in Burmese that its meaning is mysterious for many people, including many in the group. Aung Thaung defines it as follows: "a profound method, an extensive knowledge." One of his disciples with the rank of a master translates it as "an immediate skill," that is, a skill that makes someone invulnerable automatically; another translates it as "a method that gives you knowledge." The fact that each of these people can invest the phrase with a different meaning and that these meanings nevertheless all correspond to one another by referring to the idea of a special "knowledge" says much about the enterprise's fundamental coherence. In actual fact, *setka byuha,* an expression relating to military strategy, means "the tactic of encirclement."

If the possession and the diffusion of invulnerability are the distinctive signs of the group, the principle of its identity, they do not constitute its exclusive activity. The group's masters, like their leader, treat illnesses. Rescuing living beings (*thattawa ke-*) is, like the martial arts demonstrations, a means of supporting the religion. Displaying one's invulnerability and relieving suffering both aim to have the same effect: to arouse the desire to benefit by the protection and power that the group's members enjoy. This implies respecting Buddhist morality and practicing meditation (by reciting prayer beads, which intensifies a person's capacity for mental concentration). When they travel to villages for their demonstrations, the masters use some of Aung Thaung's diagrams, copied down in personal notebooks and eventually known to them by heart, to heal people who request such help. Many of them also receive patients at their homes. Curing (*hsay ku-*) has become so important to the group that a third rank has been introduced, an intermediate status between member and master, to which a specific initiatory diagram corresponds, one that can be administered by any master. This is the rank of "master [who cures] evil spells" (*payawga hsaya*)—that is, an exorcist—a wide-ranging title simply indicating that the master in question, who will as readily cure cancer as an eye problem, is qualified to combat an evil spell, which Burmese etiology takes as the cause of any persistent illness that resists ordinary treatment. There is no cabalistic pharmacopoeia strictly speaking. Masters use diagrams at their own discretion, according to what their "knowledge" and their experience suggest. From time to time, they turn to Aung Thaung to get a new design that will enable them to have done with some particularly obstinate affliction.

The key to a cure depends on "trampling" or "crushing" (*nin-*) the illness. In addition to giving someone diagrams to ingest, one technique a master uses consists of pressing a patient's body with his hands or even massaging a patient by treading on him or her with the heel of the foot. In the first case, a piece of paper with a diagram on it is put in the palms of the master's hands; in the second, the diagram is engraved on a stone plaque or sketched with ashes on a brick, the master stepping on it with his foot at regular intervals in order to infuse his heel with its power. By kneading a patient, who sometimes screams in pain when undergoing the diagram's action and must be restrained by several people, the master gathers the illness up in one spot and gets ready to expel it. This is effected by bleeding the patient: light pricks are made behind the knee, which is where the massage has made the illness descend. The blackish hue of the blood shows the treatment's effectiveness. The illness can also be expelled by means of defecating, thanks to a laxative swallowed after the massage. This treatment can be repeated, and if the situation demands it, it can go on for several months. Success is never certain. The diagrams used are only an aid (*aku*); the patient's karma and veneration of the Three Jewels, on the one hand, and the level of the master's spiritual accomplishment, on the other, also come into play. A truly potent master trying to expel an illness will only need give a patient a glass of water or pronounce a simple "Get out!" (*thwa-*) while fixing his mind on the four *weikza*.

It is a remarkable reversal: seeing those who were the most vulnerable, the most likely to introduce disorder into the collectivity, now capable of offering to its members relief from their ills. By so doing, they acquire a certain dignity, gaining for themselves a role and a validating activity. They also leave the village. The strength that has subdued them is not that of the local community, and it takes them far away for a time, granting them, in the very subjection that it imposes on them, a considerable liberty. Thus we find them released from the burden of familial and village constraints, unconcerned about their material survival (which is assured by the income their activities bring in), moving about some region of the country to display their extraordinary power and to heal people who are ill—putting up for a while at the monastery in Mebaygon or at Aung Thaung's, some of them even making it to a big city stadium for an official demonstration, puffed up all the while with a feeling of potency and of invulnerability. A journey of initiation? Many of them in any case come back calmer, readier to take up manhood, to take their place in the midst of the community. Indeed, do they not now know a bit more of the "knowledge" that the diagrams they ingest are said to confer on them?

INVULNERABILITY AND SOCIETY

From the time that his mission was revealed to him, Aung Thaung has never stopped sketching new designs for diagrams: squares with boxes filled in with unknown signs, letters, or numbers; figures composed of letters representing the Buddha, the saint Shin Upagok, a pagoda, an ogre (*bilu*), a dragon (*naga*); and so on. These diagrams, which only group members are authorized to see and to ingest (except for when they are used for curing), are endowed with energy of success, with strength. The leader recommends consuming them daily. "Don't you have to eat every day? It's just the same with diagrams," he tells his disciples. The designs are reproduced on Shan paper (made in Shan State), which is also called Maingkaing paper (after a town in that state). This modestly priced material is made out of blackberry pulp; its soft and supple texture makes it easy to ingest. Such a piece of paper is swallowed as it is or turned into ashes and mixed with a bit of water, or perhaps honey. It doesn't matter. Before ingesting it, a person will ideally have recited his or her prayer beads and made the declaration of truth in front of a Buddha altar. Nourishing themselves in this way, group members maintain and strengthen their invulnerability. Aung Thaung himself continues to ingest his diagrams because, as he puts it, he hasn't reached his destination yet. His goal is to become a *weikza,* more precisely an *in weikza,* a virtuoso of the cabalistic arts. Nevertheless, the diagrams cause him to feel such a great desire to be alone and to say his prayer beads that he avoids ingesting any when visitors, whether patients or disciples, are staying at his house, as is often the case.

Only masters have the privilege of reproducing the diagram designs put forth by Aung Thaung. Ordinary members must depend on those masters to get diagrams to ingest. The hierarchy within the group, with its three levels (leader, masters, members), corresponds to a one-way nutritional chain, one in which someone who gets fed is incapable of giving back what he has been given. Money that his disciples, both members and masters, give Aung Thaung as gifts, like the money given as gifts by disciples to the masters who have initiated them, can hardly be thought to equal in value the diagrams that have been bestowed on them. Such gifts are more a way of paying tribute, of acknowledging one's subjection. But let us not forget that Aung Thaung himself is a dependent. Doesn't his formidable power derive from the *weikza?* Doesn't this mean that the power he enjoys might be withdrawn at any moment? Members of the Tactical Encirclement Group like to tell incredible stories about their leader. But does constantly building up the man by attributing to him extraordinary abilities and actions amount only to affirming his potency and acknowledging his superiority, while also exalting the group of which he is the founder and implying that the people telling those stories are worthy of envy? Isn't it also a way to make subtly evident where it is that the leader's greatness comes from, to point out the origins of his stature—in brief, to remind people that he is and will remain what his subjects wish to make of him? Thus it is an inscrutable circle of servitude that makes the leader entirely subject to the good wishes of his subjects and that makes those subjects nevertheless entirely dependent on the leader whom they acknowledge as such, as if neither the former nor the latter had the upper hand and as if their relations bound them together, certainly, but beyond the control of either party.

Aung Thaung makes such variable comments about his diagram-producing activities that it is impossible to describe with any certainty the methods behind his impressive cabalistic compendium. Has he simply drawn for thirty years on the designs he has known, those that Bobo Aung and Bo Min Gaung taught him? Or has he made sketches by means of a kind of automatic writing, piloted at a distance by the four *weikza* and stimulating the constant creation of new cabalistic figures and signs? Whatever the explanation, there is no gainsaying that the *weikza* are the source of the diagrams' effectiveness. The diagrams are a means by which their power is represented and communicated. They constitute a manner of making material, visible, and incorporable an essence that concerns the transcendent. The diagrams' transcendent, which is to say unfathomable, origin explains why their meaning should be considered enigmatic. The question of what the symbolism of their constituent elements—letters, numbers, signs, figures— might be becomes almost incidental. (This does not prevent the specialists who produce them from endowing them with symbolism; that is, inscribing them within a system of correspondences, along the lines of the four letters *sa, da, ba,* and *wa,* which come up frequently in Burmese cabalistic practices and refer, among other things, to the four Buddhas who have appeared in this world cycle.) Aung Thaung understands nothing of what he sketches and hardly thinks about it. It's the same for all of his disciples. The four *weikza,* who could decipher the diagrams because they are their source, are present and could therefore be asked for clarification. But it would not come into anyone's head to interrogate them about the meaning of these diagrams that people keep ingesting and giving others to ingest. It is enough to know, or rather to accept, that the *weikza* inspire these representations and guarantee their effectiveness. By common accord, without anyone thinking about it, a set of signs is produced and reproduced, and these signs are potent even though largely arbitrary, because they are in the last instance dependent on the wishes of their authors, who determine both their types and their forms. Their power stems solely from believing, by those who consume them. The most important of the diagrams—that of initiation, which gives the "knowledge"—takes the form of an abstract representation, an assemblage of signs some of which are unrecognizable or indecipherable.[7]

With the knowledge that he possesses, Aung Thaung has the habit of saying, a dot made on a piece of paper is sufficient to create an active diagram. And said knowledge exempts someone in possession of it, if one wishes, from respecting the rules of production that condition the diagrams' efficacy (not speaking or not spitting, for example, while preparing a diagram). In short, the symbolic nature of the diagrams derives ultimately from the source from which they emanate,

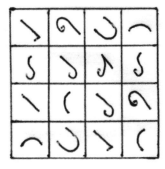

Figure 2   The initiatory diagram

and not from their graphic elements (the effect of figuration) or the means of their production (the effect of ritualization). They do not present images in order to signify; they signify what cannot be represented. It is in this that we can see their religious character. The diagrams are the result and the expression of an achievement—the realization of spiritual perfection or a state very close to it, in the status of *weikza*—which Buddhist ideology presents as inexpressible, ineffable. It is for this reason that everyone's aim is not to decipher them but rather to make them one's own, to incorporate them as a substance.

The literally blind faith of the Tactical Encirclement Group's members in the power of these incomprehensible sketches is very far from being peculiar to them. Burmese in general are inclined to put confidence, if not unconsciously, at least unthinkingly, in invulnerability procedures. This attitude has long been emphasized by disconcerted observers. As far back as foreign accounts of Burmese society of even minimal detail go—which is not all that far, actually, only to the end of the eighteenth century—we find mention of invulnerability practices in use among its people, women as well as men: tattoos of cabalistic diagrams; potent figures (the Buddha); plain dots; images paired with letters, words or formulas; amulets worn at the neck or on the wrist, consisting of a sheet of metal on which a cabalistic diagram has been sketched or an incantation recited; pieces of metal inserted under the skin bearing an inscription (letters, a formula); water or concoctions drunk after being filled with power by means of a recitation; and so on.[8] Some procedures lay claim to a total prophylaxis, providing protection against danger in any form. Others—a particular design for a tattoo, a particular type of amulet—offer more limited coverage, immunizing someone against a specific threat: a snake bite (a frequent occurrence when people are working in rice fields), aggression at the hand of a malevolent invisible being, sorcery, or bullets.

What invulnerability techniques have in common is their use of impression, incrustation, ingestion, or aggregation to add to someone's natural body a symbolic supplement—symbolic in the restricted sense given earlier; that is, relating to something whose source is extraordinary and unrepresentable. No one could possibly be, nor thinks or lays claim to being, invulnerable per se. Oddly, the thing that bears this force, which it contains and symbolizes, often turns out to be out of view. When it is not assimilated by being consumed, it is lodged beneath the skin, under someone's shirt, in the hair, inside someone's wallet or a little metal container. Tattoos are no exception to this tendency: unlike tattoos made of simple decorative motifs, a form of masculine adornment worn by almost all men, tattoos endowed with protective power are not only an impression made on the body but also an injection inside the body, one or more substances being added to the ink as a function of their intended effect. In any case, the first principle of invulnerability techniques is not to make something visible, in order to dissuade attack. The mark of invulnerability is rather a sign that someone does not reveal, a sign that a person masks or buries or incorporates, as if it were thereby appropriated and naturalized.

It is also a sign that its beneficiary does not understand. Invulnerability techniques take on an esoteric character. They include mysterious sketches; formulas or incantations, whose elements lend themselves to several interpretations (one letter for an entire sentence); and phrases in Pali, the language of Buddhist texts that few people know. Furthermore, their power depends on how they are combined, a combination whose logic is not clear, and not on the mere juxtaposition of their component parts. It is true that there are handbooks that focus, among other things, on the cabalistic arts. Circulating among a small minority of specialists who are not put off by their obscure and technical nature, they provide instruction on the rules for making diagrams. They establish correspondences among the thirty-three letters of the alphabet, the four constituent elements of matter (earth, water, fire, air), numbers, and some specific power (to gain protection from wild animals, to make oneself the object of others' love, etc.). They offer, above all, ready-to-use designs for diagrams indicating their function and the modalities of their ingestion. All the same, these works initiate readers into the cabalistic arts far more than they provide any infallible method for becoming a *weikza* or acquiring a specific power. For that matter, the potency attributed to a diagram is diminished as soon as the logic of its design is exposed and becomes accessible to one and all without distinction. Whether based on a cabalistic diagram or something else altogether, invulnerability techniques are fully effective only on the condition that their workings remain indecipherable.

These workings are not limited to an act of representation by figuration, pronouncement, or objectification. Simply reproducing the design of a diagram is not enough to take advantage of its power. Only certain people or beings are capable of charging the procedure with power, whether because, as people in this world, they are responsible for its realization or because, as invisible beings, they support it from afar. These people or beings are monks, ascetics, *weikza* and those aspiring to become *weikza,* or masters (*hsaya,* lay specialists of the techniques of invulnerability or healing gravitating toward the sphere of the *weikza* path). Their remarkable activating capacity stems from their status, which corresponds to a certain degree of spiritual achievement obtained through moral behavior and meditation, the latter allowing someone to attain a superior knowledge inaccessible to ordinary people. It may stem too, although to a lesser degree, from their originating from a region that is associated with a certain skill. For tattoos, "Shan masters" (*shan hsaya*), originating from the region in the northeast of the country that gives them their name, are renowned. Capable of providing invulnerability, these individuals are at the same time prohibited from using violence. Their condition forbids them from acting with ill will while, reciprocally, protecting them de facto from the ill will of others. In theory, any aggressive act perpetrated against them, whether a physical attack or an attack by means of sorcery or a spirit, is bound to fail because of their remarkable spiritual power. Thus invulnerability is useless to those individuals capable of producing it, because they are themselves located a priori off the field of play. The maker of invulnerability is never its beneficiary. The technique functions on the basis of the circulation of a socially founded and organized force. The system of invulnerability fits, on the level of values as well as on the level of process, with the primary structure of Burmese society: a hierarchical relationship of complementary opposition between the world-renouncer and the person in the world, between the monk and the layperson. The distinction between the producer and the consumer of invulnerability and the relationship that binds them together are part of this structure.

In sum, the force that supplies invulnerability, even though it is materialized and signified (if only as three small tattooed dots), is made invisible or close to it, as though it was integrated with its beneficiary. It is at the same time taken to be unintelligible: its hermetic nature is the guarantee of its effectiveness. And producing it requires the intervention of a special energy available only to certain individuals of recognized status. In addition, this force benefits everyone, but no one is in a position to take sole control of it or to gain complete mastery over it. It escapes an individual's grasp: some people can produce it without being able to use it; others can use it without being able to produce it. These different characteristics—invisibility, unfathomability, spirituality, and ungraspability—give the impression not of being logically independent but rather as being bound to one another. But by what thread? What is the axis on which invulnerability turns?

In August 1824, when the First Anglo-Burmese War, already in progress for several months, was not looking promising for the Burmese, the king dispatched a special regiment of fighters, much admired by the populace, called "the King's Invulnerables." That at least is what Major Snodgrass, a British participant in the events, informs us, without letting us know the Burmese term that he was translating.[9] These elite soldiers had animal designs tattooed on their bodies. They were above all famous because of the pieces of gold or silver, as well as precious stones, embedded in their flesh, a practice that gave rise to their reputation for invincibility. They positioned themselves at the frontlines, defying the enemy with a war dance while arousing the Burmese troops' fighting spirit. When these Invulnerables, armed with swords and muskets and shouting fierce curses at the enemy, launched an attack on the Shwedagon Pagoda in Yangon where the British had entrenched themselves, the "imaginary shield"[10] with which they had armed themselves, as Major Snodgrass, a skeptical and mocking witness of the event, put it, was useless against the British cannon fire, which caused a quick retreat after the collapse of the troops who were farthest forward. "A few devoted enthusiasts may have despised to fly," the Major writes ironically, "but as they all belonged to the same high-favoured caste, and had brought none of their less-favoured countrymen to witness their disgrace, the great body of them soon sought for safety in the jungle, where they, no doubt, invented a plausible account of their night's adventure, which, however effectual it may have proved in saving their credit, had also the good effect to us of preventing them in future from volunteering upon such desperate services."[11]

Yet despite obvious and bloody defeats, this type of "desperate" endeavor, an apparently senseless confrontation with an infinitely better armed adversary, was repeated in subsequent rebel movements that took place following the fall of the monarchy and the colonization of the entire country (1885–1900) and again in the course of the famous so-called Saya San Rebellion (1930–1932). Surely, the Burmese did not as a general rule hurl themselves into certain death: in these struggles they also conducted guerrilla warfare—striking an objective only then to disperse, leaving the enemy no time to react.[12] Nonetheless, resistance to the British occupation gave rise to striking incidents. Foreigners of that time who commented on the Saya San Rebellion, even the most sympathetic among them, were stupefied by the insurgents' recklessness. They attributed the widespread use of invulnerability techniques, along with the suicidal assaults that were its most spectacular manifestation, to "immemorial beliefs of the countryside" or to "superstitious belief in spells."[13] In these circumstances, invoking the notion of superstition enabled commentators to put a name to something that they could not or did not wish to understand. It was a way for them to place themselves in a relationship of radical alterity—at both a cultural and a temporal distance—vis-à-vis the Burmese, while supporting the colonial mentality, whether deliberately or not. Labeling invulnerability practices as the expression of a rustic and archaic psychology precluded commentators from recognizing their political and timely logic. Had the Burmese not believed themselves invulnerable, had they not shown themselves so confident, marching unprotected except for their swords and lances in the face of British cannon, the Burmese struggle would not have meant what it did. In techniques of invulnerability and the values and relations that they implied, the entire Burmese system of representations was brought into play. Had they stopped believing in invulnerability, it would have been useless to fight. Running into a massacre singing incantations supposed to paralyze the enemy amounted to proclaiming that Burmese society was invulnerable. Even if the colonizers had subjugated the country with their arms, they had in no way managed to crush the Burmese identity, an identity that every insurgent embodied inasmuch as his invulnerability techniques made him the bearer of the seal of the Burmese collectivity. Invulnerability techniques constituted the nation's delegation of power to its defenders. Their effectiveness lay not in their keeping the combatants safe from death: all the evidence indicated that they were powerless against bullets. Instead they were valuable in that they represented the continuity and the intensity of the sentiment of being Burmese.

The British showed in their own way how much they understood the link between invulnerability practices and resistance to colonial domination. After the Saya San Rebellion, the prosecutor who officiated at the first tribunal set up to judge the defendants asked the magistrates to consider all of the defendants with tattoos as rebels and guilty, even if no proof could be adduced as to their having participated in the revolt. The request was about to be approved by the head of the tribunal, an Englishman, when the Burmese judge who was seated beside him intervened. Lifting his robe to show the tattoos drawn on his arms and knees, he said to the presiding judge, "Judge, you may think that we are childish in our belief, but we all believe, especially the villagers, that these tattoo marks render us immune to snake bites."[14] While allowing for the predictable reaction of his British colleague, the judge was determined to affirm the legitimate and legal nature of invulnerability techniques, thought by all Burmese as an effective means of personal protection. Nonetheless, he qualified this generalization—"especially the villagers"—in such a way as to bring him, an educated, Anglophone, and urban person, closer to his foreign colleague. If we add to the layers of this subtle declaration that lifting the robe the judge was wearing, indicating which side he was on, suddenly revealed emblematic signs of the rebellion indelibly inscribed on his body, we can perceive the extraordinarily ambiguous position of Judge Ba U. In any case, by proving that it would be unjust to assume that invulnerability practices were coterminous with rebellion, this man saved the lives of a number of his compatriots. But the British prosecutor was not altogether wrong to suggest their equivalence. As long as invulnerability practices persisted—that is, as long as Burmese adhered to the values and principles that constituted in their eyes the substance and greatness of their nation—the colonial regime did indeed have a right to feel threatened.

By the same token, there is nothing improbable about the following assertion made by a member of the Tactical Encirclement Group: in case of war, Aung Thaung will give a cabalistic diagram to a thousand soldiers, each of whom will immediately and unconditionally find himself in possession of "extraordinary bodily power." In times of struggle, when the survival and fate of the group are at stake, those who find themselves granted invulnerability fulfill the function of representing the collectivity in its entirety. They personify and catalyze its will to resist or conquer. Their individuality and their strength are subsumed by the community.

That invulnerability should have played a significant role in political competition, a competition that generated divisiveness at the heart of Burmese society, in no way contradicts the principle of its articulation with collective identity. On the contrary. The small band that succeeded in entering the royal fort, on the night of October 4, 1782, with the aim of overthrowing the new monarch, Bodawhpaya, was headed by a specialist in invulnerability techniques (tattoos, diagrams, amulets). This leader, of Shan origin, known by the name of Nga Hpon, claimed to be the son of the last sovereign of the previous dynasty, who died in 1752.[15] In other words, the holder of royal authority, denounced as illegitimate, had to be routed with the help of a force imbued with a skill constitutive of the social order, an order in disarray that needed to be set right. The year after these events, Bodawhpaya himself buried cabalistic diagrams under the sentry boxes of the palace he was having built in Amarapura, with an eye to making it impregnable. The diagrams, rather than being displayed in the manner of signposts proclaiming the place's impregnability, were incorporated in the palace itself. The procedure, to which King Mindon (r. 1853–1878) had recourse in turn during the construction of his palace in Mandalay, emphasized the sovereign's full participation in the principles of the society that he dominated and embodied at the same time.[16] It contributed to the erection of the palace as a monumental expression of the royal function, a function of the collectivity's political personification. The palace, defended by cabalistic diagrams, was a replica and a microcosmic image of the society, both pervaded and protected by the techniques of invulnerability.

If on the basis of these various vignettes we were obliged to come up with a condensed statement, we would say, in Durkheimian fashion, that Burmese society hypostasizes its own strength in techniques of invulnerability. Out of the collectivity is born a power both different and superior to that of each of its members: the whole is much more, and much more potent, than the sum of its parts. One does not obtain invulnerability by simply adding up vulnerable individuals, no matter how many. In these enigmatic procedures and the extraordinary power that inheres in them, the society objectifies its power, it materializes it, it celebrates it, it spreads it about, and it imposes it on people. The artifact—whether in the form of a diagram, a tattoo, or an amulet—that gives rise to invulnerability constitutes something like a monogram that the society affixes to its members. If invulnerability's usages are drawn on at different levels, from royalty to a little group of male and female disciples gathered around a master, if these usages are many and sometimes contradictory, it is because the power of the collectivity acts at all orders of magnitude and because control over it is diffuse and disputed. That power cannot be reduced to a single and homogeneous current. It takes as many different forms as life in a society generates, life with its various orders of magnitude (from the individual to the family, the village, and so forth, to the nation), its diverse conceptions, its power relations, its tensions, its conflicts. The Tactical Encirclement Group constitutes one of the innumerable channels by means of which the power of the collectivity renews itself and spreads.

This insight enables us to understand better the different properties of invulnerability techniques. First of all is their invisibility, the way they are made intimately coextensive with an individual's person. As soon as invulnerability is seen to be the communication to the individual of the collectivity's power, it is clear that the means of that passage cannot remain external to that individual. It must become an integral part of his or her person, as though it had become a vital component thereof. An invulnerability technique is not a simple connection between the collectivity and the individual; it is a process of transformation of the latter by the former. Consequently, either the object bearing invulnerability is actually incorporated, a kind of literal representation of the movement of the collective power from the exterior to the interior of the person. Or this object occupies an ambiguous position, neither really external nor really internal, acting as a point of contact and transmission between the two (such as supports for invulnerability placed in someone's wallet or in a little container hung around one's neck; that is, hidden from the view of others without actually being incorporated). Tattoos, in this regard, become almost supercharged with meaning, combining the different mechanisms that ensure the efficacy of invulnerability techniques. They combine the two possibilities just mentioned, because a tattoo is both an inscription on the skin, at the point of juncture between the environment and a person's internal being, and the introduction of a substance into the body. In addition, the person making the tattoo, an itinerant figure circulating throughout society as if he were its traveling clerk, often accompanies his work with the recitation of more or less esoteric formulas. Invulnerability techniques are not accessories one might take on according to one's mood, as a function of how one wished to appear. They are a fragment of the self, an almost organic one, which is why people tend to naturalize them.

The second property is the esoteric nature of these techniques: because of their source and their extraordinary power, invulnerability techniques are projected beyond the level of normal individual comprehension and capacities, onto a level to which ordinary people have no access. Making them unintelligible to common mortals, and declaring them to be so, fits with their social, that is to say, supra-individual, origin. When a society sets its own energy in motion, it speaks a different language from that used for ordinary communication among its members.

Third, there is the role played by figures of distinguished spiritual achievement in the activation of these techniques. These individuals personify society's values and ideals; they are what society produces of the highest worth; they are individuals in whose fashioning it lays the greatest store and to whom it attributes the greatest authority. It is logical that such figures, endowed with an exceptional quantity of collective power, should be seen to influence the use and transmission of this power by charging a piece of paper, or a sheet of copper, or a bit of water with it. Concentrating in themselves all of what society finds best, they give back to others—less advantaged—a portion of what they have received. More precisely, to produce invulnerability, these figures act in the fashion of energy condensers. Collective power accumulates in their person, and they redistribute it in the form of a current of a special intensity. A monk does not just represent society's ideal; he is worked on by society and works for it, in an almost mechanical way. Yet unlike in the case of a machine, the return is variable; it depends on the degree to which the individual can rise to the collectivity's expectations.

Fourth, and finally, is the elusive character of invulnerability's power: what transcends individuals can hardly come back to specific individuals. Born out of the collectivity, invulnerability's power remains collective, inalienable. For it to be otherwise would risk having one person monopolize all social potency. While this power's producer, to whom it is of no use, is not in a position to use it for personal ends, to the detriment of others, its beneficiary is incapable of producing or controlling it. No one, as a result, appears who can take complete control of this power.

In short, invulnerability techniques' properties derive from the socially determined nature of the phenomenon. Invulnerability is society's reification of its own power, and invulnerability techniques are modes for the communication of this collective power—reification and also mystification, because neither party is aware of the true source of the power that gets distributed. To explain belief in invulnerability in terms of the demand, on the part of individuals, for magical protection against life's risks therefore puts things the wrong way around. Invulnerability practices can hardly derive from individuals' desires to save themselves from danger. They arise first of all from the collectivity's need to construct itself, to consolidate itself, to make itself manifest. Invulnerability is socially generated and determined before it is individually thinkable and possible.

The workings of invulnerability represent a constitutive part of the social contract. Having recourse to any invulnerability technique amounts to joining a social order, with its hierarchy and the relations that it presumes. This engagement is accomplished by the collectivity's investment in the body or the person of the individual, with the protection that follows from it. Just as through the institution of the state members of the collectivity renounce, theoretically, the use of violence in favor of a person or an entity that must in return guarantee them their personal safety, so through the institution of invulnerability people renounce, ideally, all inclination toward aggression or ill will in order to gain the benefit of personal protection. Invulnerability acts like a principle of civil law. Its frequent use by criminals is a significant perversion, inasmuch as it aims to confer legitimacy, the force of law, on an asocial act.[17] Relatedly, whoever diverges too far from the moral precepts of the collectivity loses the privilege of its protection and exposes himself to sanction: in the case of the Tactical Encirclement Group, a physical sanction (the sword that penetrates the flesh) and a social one (exclusion from the group). These sanctions indicate that the individual at fault no longer takes part in the group, that he has removed himself from it and set himself apart.

It becomes easier to appreciate in this light a comment made by Shway Yoe, alias James George Scott, one of the late nineteenth century's most knowledgeable experts on Burmese society and one of its most caustic observers: "the belief of every Burman in the efficacy of these tattooed charms is practically ineradicable."[18] The writer reported an incident in 1881 when a young man, having just gotten a tattoo, had himself thrown in the Yangon River with his feet and wrists bound in order to test immediately the effectiveness of the procedure. When the poor man disappeared in the waves, the British authorities accused the two tattooers of murder, to the great dismay of the Burmese. In their eyes, the failure of a procedure must be attributed not to the provider of invulnerability but rather to his beneficiary, because it is the latter whose inadequacy on the moral plane (failing to fulfill one of the rules ensuring the procedure's effectiveness) or whose bad karma (linked to some act in a previous life) has brought about that failure. To perpetuate itself, the collectivity, for whom the provider of invulnerability is something like its authorized representative, must remain infallible. Only its members can, in their individuality, and not insofar as they bear the imprint of the group's identity, be susceptible to getting disqualified.

There is more. From the moment that the workings of invulnerability operate like a transmitting apparatus for collective power and identity, it is as completely imbued with national ideology as with social ideology. The integrating current that invulnerability represents furthers the project of a sovereign, potent, and invincible nation. It is not irrelevant that Great-Master Aung Khaing, as a prelude to the Tactical Encirclement Group's members' demonstrations, recalls the Burmese military defeat at the hands of the British invaders and their subsequent subjection. If the Burmese had had the use of the technique taught by his group, he asserts, they would never have had to know "servitude" (*kyun bawa*). This fear of servitude haunts modern Burmese history, if we are to believe those Burmese authors who write that history today. A book about General-in-Chief Maha Bandoola, hero of the First Anglo-Burmese War, shows him haranguing his officers and commanders one day in November 1824. The general and his troops had rushed from Arakan to Danubyu, to the northwest of Yangon, in a forced march of several hundred kilometers in the midst of the rainy season. When the monsoon was over, they made their way to Yangon, occupied at that time by the British (who had repulsed the Invulnerables' assault the previous August). There they set up a siege. Just before the start of battle, Maha Bandoola exhorted the captains of his formidable army:

> "Commanders and officers! We have driven the English out of Danyawady [Arakan]. Since they could not come by land, they have made a detour and come by sea to invade our country. As a righteous people, we started the

war in the region of Danyawady in order to regain lands that are ours, unjustly taken from us. Rather than advancing out of covetousness, we have waited to see what the English-foreigners-whites were going to do. These insular English-foreigners-whites have a character different from ours. They want to crush us; they have come to challenge us. In these circumstances, if we take things lightly, our entire people will experience servitude. When it comes to historical glory, it is preferable to die fighting so that the virtue of the Burmese not fade rather than to become the slaves of a heretical [non-Buddhist] people. Today we must give our blood and our lives to win back our holy site [the Shwedagon pagoda]. This time, if we are victorious, we will only have to attack the English territory. So in the course of the battle, use your chest as a parapet and fight!"[19]

Alas! The Burmese were defeated and forced to retreat. Every one of the innumerable soldiers whose cadavers were strewn about the battlefield, the British later found, bore an invulnerability charm of one sort or another, although, commented Major Snodgrass ironically, "on this occasion they [the charms] seemed to have completely lost their virtue."[20] Maha Bandoola died a few months later, in early April, killed by a British bomb that hit his fort in Danubyu. As soon as the news became known, his army disbanded.[21]

It seems as though it is the drama of August 1824, and of all the other struggles that followed it along much the same lines with respect to both their circumstances and their outcomes, that the members of the Tactical Encirclement Group were reenacting in the course of their demonstrations, which amount to an anamnesis, in the etymological sense of the term; that is, the act of recalling something to memory. But the outcome is reversed: in their performances, the Burmese are victors, triumphing over their invisible but persistent adversary. The group's demonstrations, replicas of the war dances of the Invulnerables of 1824, proceed from a double necessity, one that requires exorcising the colonial defeat while still retaining its memory and bitterness, foundational sentiments in the Burmese national identity.

Indeed—although Victorious and I never heard this mentioned by our interlocutors—the district of Minbu, where the cult of the four *weikza* that was at the origin of the Tactical Encirclement Group was born and developed, was the site from 1886 to 1888 of one of the most formidable resistance movements against the British occupation in Upper Burma. The principal rebel chief, Bo Swe, who was to perish in October 1887 after having ruled for a time over the southern part of the district, was assisted by a monk who guaranteed invulnerability to Bo

Swe's men. The monk gave the insurgents water or ashes (of cabalistic diagrams, probably) to drink; these substances had had an incantation recited over them thirty-seven times. He inscribed cabalistic signs or letters on the face or chest of each of the combatants.[22] The Tactical Encirclement Group's recruits know nothing of the details of these lost battles, preferring to read martial arts novels over history books. They are nonetheless bearers, with their very bodies, of a certain collective memory, making themselves at the same time both reminders of the colonial wound and performers of an alternative possibility. With them, history comes alive in two ways, because it is placed in their bodies (as the "knowledge" that they have internalized) and because it is reinterpreted.

Speaking of the past at these invulnerability shows, a past marked by a combination of impotence and infamy, Great-Master Aung Khaing addresses the present. Because, he says in effect, we now have possession of this extraordinary "knowledge" that makes us invulnerable, it is up to us to use it to make sure the Burmese never again undergo servitude, that they never so much as even worry about falling back into servitude—to use it also "to make Myanmar known to the world." Members of the Tactical Encirclement Group have represented the country at traditional Asian martial arts competitions in Malaysia, China, and the Philippines, with some success. "Myanmar first in the world!" (*kanba hma myanma hay*), as the conventional formula has it, has become the motto of the group's masters, who intone it in the course of the demonstrations. Yet this desire for potency and this wish to be great, don't they involve to some degree the generation of a state of servitude? Don't they contain the seed of a totalizing power? The specter of servitude haunts the battered conscience of the Burmese, shutting them up in the trap of tyranny.

THE LAND OF THE BUDDHA'S KIN

In the Buddha's time, recount the four *weikza,* there lived a king who aspired to becoming a *thakiwin min-myo,* a "member of the royal Sākya group" (the Buddha's group of origin, ruling over the small kingdom of Kapilavatthu).[23] To this end, the king asked the Sākya to give him a wife. But the Buddha's kin, wishing to maintain the purity of their group, customarily married among themselves. They picked out one of their slaves and offered her in marriage to the king, passing her off as a princess.

The couple had a son named Witatuba. After succeeding his father on the throne, Witatuba went to the country of the Sākya to pay homage to his supposed parents. At the palace, when people learned of his imminent arrival, they made sure that all those younger than him, who would have had to prostrate themselves in his presence, would not encounter him. Only his elders received him as a guest. Witatuba paid them homage and then left. On his way, he noticed that he had forgotten his sword and turned back.

At the palace, he saw the servants using milk to purify the spot where he had been seated. Witatuba left the scene, filled with shame and anger. On his return to his own country, he asked his mother for an explanation. She revealed to him that she was only a slave. The young man was all the more enraged. He resolved to kill all of the Sākya. But when he was marching with his troops toward their capital, he met up with the Buddha, who saved his kin by dissuading him from carrying out his plan.

But Witatuba's vindictive rage soon returned. He organized a second expedition. Once again, the Buddha convinced him to give it up. The third time, the Master did not intervene. It was inevitable that his kin would suffer the consequences of the immoral act that they had committed in a previous life in killing members of Witatuba's family, who at that time were in the form of fish. When Witatuba attacked the palace, some of the Sākya managed to flee. The rest were massacred.

On his return trip, the mass murderer and his troops were carried away as they were trying to cross a river. They drowned.[24]

There the story ends. The story continues, nonetheless, some 2,500 years later, in contemporary Burma. This massacre of the Sākya is actually more than an edifying tale in which social aspiration, marriage rules, scheming, the thirst for vengeance, and the inexorability of fate are each called on in turn to serve as plot devices in an exemplary drama, one leading to carnage followed by slaughter. The incident constitutes the starting point for the singular project conceived of by the four *weikza:* to gather together the kin of the Buddha who were unable to reach nirvana during the Master's life because of the massacre perpetrated by Witatuba and to set them on the path to deliverance during their current lives. According to Great-Master Aung Khaing, the *weikza* are counting on the Tactical Encirclement Group's activities to realize this great plan. To the founder and leader of the group, Aung Thaung, they have entrusted the mission of searching for and reuniting in his organization the *thakiwin min-myo,* the members of the royal Sākya group. Both this mission and the story in which it is rooted touch on the mythic origins of the Burmese nation and on the double principle that informs its modern configuration, which is both a religious principle and a racial one.

The story of the massacre of the Sākya that the *weikza* tell derives from an account to be found in the Theravadin Buddhist corpus of classical texts. The

original version of the tragedy appears, with a few variations, in both the preamble to the story of a previous life of the Buddha and in a commentary on the canonical book of the *Dhammapada*.[25] It appears to be the second of these texts,
the commentary, that inspired the redactor of the *New Bagan Chronicle,* which
dates from 1785. Up until that time, the chronicles retracing the genealogy of the
Burmese kingdoms and dynasties from their origins, the oldest known example
of which goes back to the fifteenth century, made no mention of the massacre of
the Sākya, and perforce no mention of the role of that event in the genesis of the
Burmese monarchy. The incorporation of the story into the royal historiography
instituted "Burma" as the place of asylum for one of the Sākya, who was then
deemed the founder of the kingdom of Tagaung, legendary predecessor of the
historical Burmese kingdoms. The express assertion of this filiation backed up a
centuries-long movement aiming to confer on Burmese dynasties the prestigious
stamp of the Sākya. Poems composed between the fourteenth and seventeenth
centuries in honor of kings or princes already contained a reference to this relationship between Burmese monarchs and the Buddha's natal group.[26]

The compilation of the *Glass Palace Chronicle* on the orders of King Bagyidaw (r. 1819–1837) completed the process. The experts charged with this undertaking attributed not only one but two foundings of the kingdom of Tagaung to
the Sākya. These Sākya, in both instances, would have fled as far as what is today
Burmese territory as a consequence of a debacle. The first kingdom of Tagaung is
said to have been created by a king of Kapilavatthu who was to have reached
Burma with his army after a military defeat. It was to have collapsed after a long
history, broken by an external attack. The massacre perpetrated by Witatuba
would then be the starting point for the restoration of this earlier kingdom. Having described the causes and the course of the massacre, the chronicle reports
that one of the princes who survived, obliged to remain abroad, lived in various
parts of what is contemporary Burma. He founded several royal cities and married a descendant of the Sākya who had arrived in Burma long before, at the time
of their first migration. After making this advantageous alliance, a means both
for respecting the Sākya norm of endogamy and integrating himself into the history of the country, the refugee prince retied the strings, temporarily loosened, of
the "Burmese" monarchy by taking up residence in Tagaung and reestablishing
the earlier kingdom. Everyone who has ruled in Burma since, proclaims the
chronicle (which remains the principal historical source for the Burmese), de-
scends in a direct line from this Sākya stock established in Tagaung. This means
that the eminent royal group of the Sākya, the natal group, has been perpetuated
in all its purity through the successive Burmese dynasties.[27]

The abolition of the monarchy in 1886, although removing from the political stage the living incarnation of the Sākya line, did not put an end to the idea of a potent connection between the Burmese and the Buddha's kin group. In the context of a fight against the colonial regime, the disappearance of royalty encouraged the extension of the Sākya label to apply to the entire population. Members of one of the most important anticolonial groups, the "We Burmese" movement (Do Bama), founded in 1930, composed a song that enjoyed immediate success and was soon declared the national anthem. The song begins by invoking the name of the Sākya founder of the first kingdom of Tagaung. It then recalls the military greatness of the Burmese nation, which had in its time conquered both Thailand and India. The subject of the phrase in this case is "We Burmese who are of the Sākya group" (*Do bama thaki myo ha mo*).[28]

Of the "Sākya group": this particular translation has been chosen for its semantic neutrality. There is in fact a remarkable indeterminacy as to the status of the entity consisting of the Sākya, that very entity that the four *weikza* seek after a fashion to revive. In the Western literature on Buddhism, the Sākya are described variously as a "tribe," a "clan," a "race," and more rarely as a "lineage" or a "people." This diversity of labels is all the more disconcerting because writers do not judge it necessary to justify their preference for one over another nor to explain what they mean by each term.[29] If specialists seem to have trouble determining what the Sākya were, it is probably because the texts themselves are vague on this point and even contradictory. They simply refer to the "Sākya" as a group name. No further specification is provided, other than at times adding the word *vamsa,* which is what is intended by *"win"* in the Burmese compound *thakiwin.* The meaning of this qualifier, however, is ambiguous, because it can refer as easily to a family, a lineage, or a race.[30] Thus simply analyzing the constituent parts of the expression *thakiwin min-myo* does not capture its precise meaning.

In these circumstances, we must turn to both vernacular commentary and usage and see what interpretation emerges. There is an aura of purity, of racial purity, attached to the glorious Sākya name. The Sākya's wish to maintain the purity of their blood, evident in their strict adherence to the rule of endogamy, is almost proverbial: it is emphasized by the texts and is well known to the Burmese. This principle of identity turns out to be contained within their name. Theravadin sources relate that the Sākya's ancestor, King Okkāka, to ensure that his favorite son would succeed him on the throne, exiled all his other children. The latter founded Kapilavatthu. Anxious above all not to "break the group apart" (*amyo hpyet-*), in the words of the monk who recounted the story to Victorious and me, they forbade marriage to anyone outside the group. There were nine of them. The eldest sister was given the status of mother, and the others married each other. Getting wind of this, Okkāka said admiringly: "My children are really smart!" The Pali term "sākya" that he used to describe the family's talents, and which in Burmese is rendered as *swan,* meaning "to be strong, potent, effective," came to label his posterity in its entirety.[31] So it is a remarkable and significant fact that the distinctive continuity of the Sākya stems not from the—fundamentally ethical—chain of cause and effect on which Buddhist reasoning is usually based, but rather on that continuity's perpetuation through biological reproduction. Physical principles, in this instance, overtake the karmic principle in the generation of beings' lives. Beyond the particular shading relating to the desire for purity, the designation "Sākya" is tinged with a suggestion of superiority. The Sākya are said to descend in a direct line from the first king of this world, Mahāsammata, elected to reestablish moral order after the decadence of the original golden age.[32]

In light of this combination of themes of origins, consanguinity, reproduction, purity, and preeminence over other groups, it is indeed a racial connotation that is contained within the notion of *thakiwin min-myo.* To convey the full semantic breadth of the expression, it would be appropriate to speak of a "member of the supreme royal race of the Sākya." Yet this powerfully charged expression takes on a different sense in the case of the mission in which the Tactical Encirclement Group is so invested. Following the four *weikza,* Great-Master Aung Khaing maintains that whoever joins the cult must be taken to be the reincarnation of one of the Buddha's relatives and, for this reason, a *thakiwin min-myo.* In this perspective, being a member of the royal group of the Sākya means being a Buddhist; that is, venerating the Three Jewels and conforming to the ethic of the Five Precepts. Being a (good) Buddhist means adhering to the cult of the four *weikza.* The title of *thakiwin min-myo* has been specially conferred by U Pandita on his elite disciples who participated in his life-prolonging ceremony in 1975 and made its success possible.

Such a loose understanding of the notion of *thakiwin min-myo* obliterates, without quite eliminating, the principle of racial purity that was attached to it originally. It bases belonging to the royal group of the Sākya on a religious principle. Stories that disciples of the four *weikza* relate are telling with respect to the consequences of this change in meaning. At the Energy Center in Mebaygon, rumor has it that in Kayah State, where guerillas are waging a war against the government, those men who had given up their arms miraculously escaped the reprisals of their former comrades when they became members of the Tactical Encirclement Group: bullets intended for them did not come out of the gun or missed their target. Defecting from the rebels and becoming integrated into the national community are thought to go along with the entry into the group and accession to the status of *thakiwin min-myo*—in other words, with an individual's affirming his Buddhist identity and what follows from that identity, which surpasses his ethnic origin (in this case, Kayah). Ingesting the diagram of initiation, which means receiving the "knowledge," amounts to incorporating the nation. The diagram is a national substance, and what takes place through its ingestion might be called "natiophagy": the consumption of collective symbols to assimilate the identity and power of the national community.

Thus the redefinition of the category of *thakiwin min-myo* enters into a redefinition of the nation, articulated on the basis of a religious, rather more than a racial, reference, thereby making the category a more inclusive one. Although the label of "member of the royal group of the Sākya" was the marker of the Burman group in the colonial era, it now includes within its purview the ensemble of non-Burman groups (Shan, Kayin, Kayah, etc.), representing about a third of the national population. The label functions as a unifying term, as a way to transcend the divisions among ethnic groups within the national community.

There are nevertheless citizens of the nation who are not Buddhists. Muslims, Christians, Hindus, and practitioners of spirit cults are estimated to represent about 10 percent of the Burmese population. The vast majority of them belong to ethnic minorities. In light of the notion that only Buddhists are citizens of the nation in the fullest sense of the word, this makes them appear to be individuals in need of conversion, an alterity in need of being reduced. In Loikaw, the capital of Kayah State, the Tactical Encirclement Group's expansion coincides with an insidious war carried out by representatives of the national authorities against the Christian churches that have become established in the area. The Burmese authorities are striving to remove all signs of the Christian presence from the landscape. At the other end of the country, in the west, members of the group circulate in Chin villages bordering on Central Burma, villages that have always had relations with that region. These villages are either Buddhist, in which case the aim is to counter the supposed Christian encroachment, or Christian, in which case the aim is to bring about conversions.[33]

What about the many Buddhists (Thai, Lao, Western, etc.) who are not of Burmese nationality? Do they have a right to the title of *thakiwin min-myo*? Although Great-Master Aung Khaing states that any Buddhist, no matter what his or her origins—social, ethnic, or national—can be regarded as a member of the royal group of the Sākya if that person observes the religion's fundamental prescriptions, it is not possible for a foreigner to become a member of the Tactical

Encirclement Group. This impossibility stems from the requirement for official permission to enroll foreign recruits, something not yet granted. Has anyone thought about putting the request to the authorities concerned? It is as though the broadening of the field of attribution of the *thakiwin min-myo* label stopped by the nature of things at the nation's borders. It is easier, declared a Tactical Encirclement Group master, for a person of Burmese nationality, a Chin for example, to become Buddhist than for a foreigner. In other words, the inhabitants of Burma are predisposed to be Buddhist.

The project of rallying together the members of the royal group of the Sākya and the spreading of invulnerability, which are as a result of the Tactical Encirclement Group's activities one and the same thing, follow from a double movement, if not from a double wish, of national configuration and national incorporation. On the one hand, the nation as a whole gets drawn onto the area enclosed by the contemporary borders of the country. The arbitrary way in which territory got carved up in the process of defining Burma's borders becomes the basis of a common essence: being Burmese predisposes someone to be Buddhist. On the other hand, every boundary within the whole should be effaced by working to realize the putative nature—being Buddhist—of every member of the national body. This implies eliminating religious identities deemed either foreign or backward—with the exception of Muslims, who are perceived as unassimilable, fundamentally different. In a way the Tactical Encirclement Group's leaders seek to reestablish in the present, in both religious and national terms, the legendary kingdom of Tagaung.

What is striking about this process of national construction, in which their effort participates, is its incompleteness. Not only do the non-Buddhists remain non-Buddhist, resisting actions intended to bring about their conversion but, in addition, the consciousness of the Buddhists remains deeply marked by the territorial and ethnic divisions that contradict the ideal of national fusion. What does a Shan from Kengtung, a city located in the east of the country, say when he goes to Mandalay or Yangon? "I'm going to Burma" (*myanma pyi thwa-*), as though his region of residence constituted a different country. Ask people of the Burman group what is their ethnic origin (*ba lu-myo le,* literally, "What sort of person are you?"), and often, instead of simply saying "Burman" (*bama*), they will respond "pure Burman" (*bama sit sit*), a hint of superiority showing through in the phrase.

Great-Master Aung Khaing knows from his own experience the ineradicable diversity of the Burmese nation. Of Arakanese origin, he married a Padaung woman, the iconic symbol of ethnicity in Burma because of the spectacular feature that emphasizes their alterity: Padaung women, known abroad by the un-flattering label of "giraffe women," wear around their necks a number of golden necklaces accumulated over time, which deform and lengthen that part of their body. The Great-Master's wife, an irony of fate, is not Buddhist. She is Catholic, and her brothers are priests. She receives Saturday's Son with reverence when he comes to Loikaw, but she has nevertheless not converted. She has a habit of stat-ing, not without a touch of malice, that she will consent to becoming Buddhist if the *weikza* make her family rich. The Great-Master's four children are Bud-dhists when they are at Mebaygon, but Catholic when they are with their mother's family.

Against the propensity of groups to set themselves apart, a force that dis-members the national body and whose power he experiences in his very own home, Great-Master pits a rhetoric of common origins. All the country's populations—the Bama [Burmans], the Chin, the Kayah, and so on—he declares, descend from a single stock, which he locates, without further specificity, in the region of the oldest Arakanese kingdoms. The groups derived from this stock, who peopled Arakan, would have spread through contemporary Burma, and out of this dispersion would have resulted the formation of the contemporary groups. In other words, in the face of difficulty, the discourse gets inverted: the racial logic becomes primary once again, the basis of unity. No doubt this represents an idiosyncratic theory of the nation's origins. Still, it resonates with history as told by the chronicles, and it is in keeping with history as it has been written at the instigation of the military regime in place since the coup d'état in 1988. This gov-ernment has sought, often by Ubuesque means, to solve a double dilemma that troubles the political consciousness of the Burmese: the intimately linked ques-tions of the nation's origins and of its unity.[34]

Should we then simply take the Great-Master's discourse as an extension of the military regime's propaganda? Such discourse—that of Great-Master, that of the authorities, and that of many others still—displays the vagaries, the ambi-guities, and the contradictions in the process of constructing the Burmese na-tional identity. They are attempts to generate this identity by radical means. They appeal to a constellation of notions, conflating several theories of the nation's origins. All or a segment of the inhabitants of Burma would be both *thakiwin min-myo* and *myanma lu-myo,* both sustainers of the royal group of the Sākya and descendants of a people of ethnically and culturally indivisible origins, whether autochthonous or immigrant. These theories bring into play a principle, an inclu-sive one, of adherence to the Buddhist religion, particularly to its claims to a uni-versal ethic, and another principle, an exclusive one, of racial purity. Invulnerability practices, by way of the Tactical Encirclement Group's work, turn out to be one of the sites for these theories' expression, one of the sites where, as a result, the diverse foundations of the nation get bound together: the moral and the natural, the cultural and the biological.

AND FINALLY, A TERRIFYING QUESTION

The account sketched here in successive strokes, based on a description of the Tactical Encirclement Group's activities and an analysis of the ins and outs of the invulnerability-providing "knowledge" the group diffuses, has cast a sidelong glance at the political situation in contemporary Burma, that of a country suffering the iron-fisted rule of a ferocious and authoritarian military regime. Such an account relies on a hypothesis—namely, that it would be impossible to truly grasp the nature of the drama that has played out in Burma over the past several decades if—attributing the condition of tyranny solely to the thirst for power of a certain number of generals and to their hateful ways—we refused to consider servitude a collective construct, a community's own self-"encirclement," one that, as a community wishing itself to be singular and great, it cannot completely escape. Thus it is the enigma of "voluntary servitude" that we must reconsider.[35] But is that possible? Is it even acceptable to do so?

When the discourse of the state aspires to hegemony, inscribing its mark on the landscape, institutions, newspapers, even down to each and every book published, whose first page, no matter what the nature of the book's content, must be given over to the principal official slogans; when furthermore, this discourse is generated by a regime whose governing ways are that of tyranny and one that is, one can confidently state, hated by the population, it is neither obvious nor even admissible for an anthropologist to stick to the principle of neutrality, which consists of giving up value judgments in favor of an impartial interpretation or explanation. However, it is this principle, by requiring us to give up setting a threshold of any kind as to what is acceptable—that is, by widening to the maximum degree the boundaries of culture even to the point of eliminating the idea of savagery—that has made it possible to treat headhunting or cannibalism as objects of scientific attention, in the fullest sense, wherein the will to describe and understand takes precedence over naive fascination, repulsion, or anathema. There is, like it or not, a strain of inhumanity in the practice of anthropology that is the condition of its possibility. Let us note in passing that this makes the idea of a society dominated by the anthropological perspective—a society in which every act, no matter how "barbarous," would find its justification—frightening.

To think about difference, as anthropology aims to do, does not mean championing it. This applies as much to tyranny as to headhunting or cannibalism.

Granted, tyranny does not appear a priori to be a cultural institution. It is not articulated on the basis of a symbolic system and does not fulfill a social function. It produces neither meaning, nor equilibrium, nor order, other perhaps than the order of the most powerful. In its pure form it is, to give it an approximate definition, the monopolizing of power over a society by an individual or a group of individuals, a total monopoly and an illegitimate one, because it is sustained by brute force on one side and fear on the other. Tyranny is a source of suffering for the immense majority of the population, which desires its end. Usurping power, often the way in which a tyrannical government gets established, sets the style of governance from the start: an economy of the arbitrary. However, the very fact that it is prevalent in so many regions of the world means that the tyrannical situation certainly merits the attention of "the science of man." Nothing, assuredly, prevents anthropologists from putting their experience and knowledge of the material to work in service of a cause, to become engaged, fighting along with others against a system that they have taken as their goal to parse. But when a scientific undertaking and an ideological one then get combined in anthropologists' actions, when a value judgment underlies their interpretive project, when understanding does not confine itself to disentangling the way things are but goes on to implicate decisions as to what should—or shouldn't—be, anthropologists' perception of the reality they have observed and the rendering of it they propose are not, as is the case for any representation, only reductive. They are truncated, and indeed, whether knowingly or not, altered. It needs to be kept clear: anthropology serves no purpose and is at the service of no one. It is free—and consequently insolent. This is what makes it so necessary and so useful. No matter how distant this ideal of independence of mind may have been and may remain, nothing prevents us from aspiring to it.

The mechanism that confers on the anthropologist's vision of the world a determining role in the production of knowledge does not apply solely to the study of conditions of tyranny. It is inherent to the anthropological endeavor. But it takes on a singular clarity in such situations. In contrast to headhunting and cannibalism, exotic practices that remain the almost exclusive privilege of distant societies, tyranny touches a nerve in the Western political consciousness, because the great historical narrative of that part of the world centers on the centuries-long—and conflict-filled—fight for individual rights and liberties: for "democracy." Faced with tyranny, anthropologists are no longer just in the land of the Other. They are taken back to their own history and their own condition.

To consider tyranny "there" as not an abnormality but rather as a normal institution would be to justify its establishment or reestablishment "here" among us. The suffering of others becomes the mirror of the suffering, whether past or virtual, of the anthropologists' own society. One cannot therefore apply two different standards: down with relativism! From this vantage point, tyranny constitutes an unacceptable universal. There is no logic to this system, other than the thirst for power, violence, and terror, leavened with just a touch of ideology. In short, tyranny is to a certain degree both unthinkable and inscrutable.

Tyranny makes it, furthermore, all the more difficult for Western observers to escape themselves and the constraints of their own understanding of the situation, because in tyrannical contexts access to the field is always complicated. In the Burmese case, in a country that has been governed by the army since the coup d'état of 1962, foreigners are forbidden to live in a village, or even in town, or to be hosted by a Burmese family without special authorization. Research activities are subject to surveillance that, far from foolproof, nonetheless puts real constraints on carrying out one's quest. It is currently impossible to engage in fieldwork concerning local political activity. By depriving everyone of direct access to the field, at least for everything touching on politics, the only substantive material the authorities leave available is official discourse as propagated by state entities or the discourse of the opposition disseminated outside the country. The study of politics risks as a result becoming reduced to its formal ideological dimensions, supplemented with bits and pieces of information and conversation gathered by chance from face-to-face encounter or events witnessed firsthand. The distance imposed between observers and the reality of the tyrannical situation is likely to induce them to use their imagination to convey this reality, an imagination nourished by the most compelling Western ruminations on the workings of tyranny. Indeed, much like headhunting or cannibalism, tyranny fascinates, even as it repulses, the Western imagination; this fascination is both made evident and fed by works, such as those by George Orwell and Michel Foucault, on total power and its machinery.

Out of this double impossibility—the impossibility of thinking of tyranny as a normal situation and the impossibility of doing an ethnography of the tyrannical condition—there arises a marked tendency to reify the constituent parts of tyranny as two opposed entities: the tyrants and the tyrannized. On one side, violence, arbitrariness, propaganda, and nonsense; on the other, resistance, impotence, truth, and subtlety. On one side, Evil; on the other, Good. And if we see individuals participating in the system that subjugates them, it can only be due to either opportunism or the inescapable imperative of survival.[36] The tendency to draw an absolute dichotomy between masters and subjects becomes all the stronger because it corresponds to a certain degree to the discourse of the tyrannized themselves. In this way, the problem of responsibility gets resolved as soon as it is posed, and in the same gesture, the terrifying question of voluntary servitude gets excluded as well.

Writes Étienne de La Boétie:

> I would simply like to understand how it is that so many men, so many cities, so many nations, sometimes support a single Tyrant's every act, when he has no authority other than what they give him, has no power to harm them except to the degree that they wish to endure it, and could do them no harm if they did not prefer to suffer his every act rather than to contradict him. It is truly surprising (and yet so common that one should bewail rather than be surprised by it!), to see millions and millions of people, miserably subjugated, their heads bowed down under an appalling yoke, not because they have been constrained by *force majeure* but because they have been fascinated, one might even say, bewitched, by the mere name of a single man whom they should neither dread, since he is alone, nor cherish, since he is in his treatment of them all both inhuman and cruel.[37]

Once the secondary causes of constraint, habit, dumbing down, and illusion have been exposed, La Boétie discerns the ultimate source of this incredible and unspeakable will to serve, of this consent on the part of all to the reign of one alone: people's susceptibility to corruption on the basis of their self-interest or fear.

Although La Boétie's reflections on a tyrannical regime's systematic corruption of individual morality illuminate much about the contemporary situation in Burma, an anthropologist will pause longer on a different engine of tyranny, one that La Boétie mentions in passing, but not without a certain disdain: belief—for example, in the notion that kings are endowed with magical powers.[38] La Boétie touches on the question of collective representations, both their making and their consequences. If his pamphlet has enjoyed such long-lasting fame, it is, among other reasons, due to the ambiguity that lies in his definition of his object, leaving the door open to diverse interpretations concerning the type of political regime he has in mind. The tyrannical principle that La Boétie analyzes relates as much to a monarchical regime whose existence enjoys cultural acceptance (including the divine right of kings) as it does to a dictatorial regime based on the will of one or several all-powerful individuals. For this author, there is clearly no difference between these two types of regime. More precisely, every tyrannical system relies, in varying proportions, on one or another of these foundations. No tyrannical government can be either entirely legitimate or entirely illegitimate.

The Marxist anthropologist Maurice Godelier has formulated this perspective in broad sociological terms, although without reference to La Boétie's work. The relations of domination at work at the heart of any society, Godelier suggests, consist of a mix of violence and consent. Godelier tends to place greater weight on the side of consent, taking it to be the decisive factor. This gives a particular direction to anthropological research: "to understand how social groups and individuals can cooperate to a certain degree in the production and reproduction of their own subordination, and even exploitation." For there to be castes, classes, or states, it is necessary for these institutions, no matter what conflicts of interest they generate, to be thought by all to be necessary and useful, and so legitimate. Godelier is careful not to include cases of forced consent, measures imposed by force alone, in the realm of the legitimate, thereby banishing them from analysis in a single stroke.[39] Yet do such cases exist? What is interesting and difficult in La Boétie's essay stems from the fact that the author does not dissociate tyranny from collective bonds, or political servitude from cultural servitude. The servile process, a form of denaturing that, in La Boétie's terms, makes of man a beast,[40] depends in part on the movement that makes of beast a man, that is to say, establishes society. It is impossible therefore to make liberty the opposite of servitude. To live in a cultural system—that is, to have access to the means of being in the world—implies being subordinated to a set of representations whose arbitrariness goes largely or entirely unnoticed, just as to live in a tyrannical system means being moved by a power many of whose devices go undetected. It is for this reason, furthermore, that defining servitude in absolute terms turns out to be impossible: where does liberty end and servitude begin? Do all the members of a society share a single conception of these two states and so the same attitude toward their own condition?

It is one thing, however, to claim that certain cultural representations foster tyranny's reign and another thing to seek to discern what about a culture, enacted day after day, might have the unintended consequence of sustaining domination by the few. The former view would mean claiming that the theory of karma helps explain the current political condition of the Burmese. Karmic theory would incite submission and passivity: Burmese would conceive of military dictatorship as the result of an irremediably bad collective karma. Those concerned do, indeed, sometimes account for their situation in these terms. But that would mean ignoring the fact that the same theory, as has been frequently observed, can serve Burmese just as well to explain a sudden political reversal and a change of regime. The latter view would mean looking at what happens and what plays out in minuscule social contexts. It is this procedure that we have followed in focusing on a tiny cog in the tyrannical system, understood as a set of social, cultural, and historical elements that participate in the tyrannical system and its perpetuation within a community: a group of disciples of the four *weikza* who specialize in martial arts. The point was to draw attention to the paradox that makes of the quest for invulnerability a source of servitude.[41]

Not all Burmese have recourse to invulnerability techniques. Some, in fact, do not believe in them or say that they do not do so, displaying a (relative) skepticism that is no doubt just as longstanding as the invulnerability practices themselves. It is also far from true that all the four *weikza*'s disciples are unanimous in applauding the Tactical Encirclement Group's activities. Some find it inappropriate to promote the practice of martial arts in the context of an undertaking of a spiritual nature. Others evince a mocking skepticism: an odd sort of superman, this Aung Thaung, to whom members of his group attribute the status of a *weikza* yet who must rely on medical injections to keep himself in good health. The Tactical Encirclement Group's leader has always been treated coolly by a segment of the cult's urban and wealthy disciples. He was and remains in their eyes a peasant, a provincial. Along with other disciples of rural origins, he was long entrusted with the most unpleasant and wearisome tasks (clearing, cleaning, carrying), while their betters kept the nobler duties, involving direct contact with the *weikza* and their medium, for themselves. To this very day, even though he has become a central figure in the cult—it is a sight to be seen when, each year at the time of the Festival of Success, members of the Tactical Encirclement Group come from all over the country and hurry to pay him homage and give him a gift in the building where he awaits them at the Energy Monastery—he remains at a remove from the circle of the privileged. As for Great-Master Aung Khaing, chief commander of the Tactical Encirclement Group for Kayah State, who sometimes imagines himself governing all of Burma, he arouses mixed feelings, even among his own subordinates, however respectful they may appear in his presence. For beneath his show of being a fervent defender of Buddhist morality, he is sometimes an arrogant man who rules over his tiny universe with an immense pettiness.

It remains the case that in several parts of the country, young people, members of the Tactical Encirclement Group, have bricks broken on their heads to prove their invulnerability. These broken bricks are so many stones to add to the building of the nation and so, in part, to that of tyranny. The group's demonstrations are charged with forces whose full import its recruits, only too happy to have at their disposal a space where they can show off their skills and blossom, fail to perceive. The bitter taste of colonial humiliation, the will to power, the dream of a golden age restored, and the radical desire of unity, all of which pervade these demonstrations, nourish a vision of the national community founded on a leveling of individuals, on a refusal of difference. When the nation is thought of on the basis of an exclusive racial and religious communion, doesn't the danger lie in everyone's submission to a uniform and totalitarian conception of society? Nationalism and servitude, even if the former was supposed to bring liberation from the latter, seem on the contrary to show elective affinities, each with the other.

The activity that saves our young Burmese from the fate of being bad boys, opening a path—for some so tortuous—to the age of manhood, this very activity that bruits their invulnerability turns out to be weighted down by a past and an ideology that keep them in chains. It is in the relationship with history, at the heart of the cult of the four *weikza* and the activities and discourse that this cult generates, that one of servitude's spontaneous mechanisms can be spotted. For the four *weikza* and their disciples, all the most telling moments of the national past make up a single and consistent tale that gets crystallized in the present. The cult focuses on a certain number of classical points of reference, particularly the golden age of the life of the Buddha and the Burmese royal kingdom of Bagan between the eleventh and the thirteenth centuries. Discontinuities are ignored or, as in the case of the colonial period, their anomalous character is emphasized. In this perspective, the present is atemporal; it reflects a permanent condition, a continuity. This is not a fiction produced by the anthropologist but rather an illusion with which the indigenous fool themselves. The four *weikza,* who claim to do everything like the Buddha and whose lives, thanks to their longevity, cover the essential part of Burmese history (U Kawwida, the oldest, was born in 968, at the dawn of the Bagan period), constitute the focal point of this immobile history. From the Buddha up until them, they assert in effect, Buddhism has remained true to its essence. Therein lies a conception of history in which the present is constantly projected back onto the past and the past constantly cast back onto the present. There is no mythical time strictly speaking, because the present contains within itself both the past in its entirety and all the promises of the past. This atemporal temporality is capable of supporting a representation and a construction of the nation in which the heterogeneous ensemble that makes up that nation is fantasized as gathered into a unitary whole.[42] This whole implies a dual postulate—that there is a natural affinity between the Burmese and Buddhism and that all the ethnic groups of Burma share a common origin—

which lays down an enchanting but alienating conception of what it means to belong to the community.

In the end, political servitude cannot be said to stem from its being desired or assented to. It stems instead from its being the consequence, following a circuitous path that the anthropologist tries hard to trace, of a certain way of organizing collective life. The fact that it depends first and foremost on violence and terror does not rule out looking for its social and cultural elements, conceived not in determinist terms (no culture contains within itself the institution of tyranny) but rather in terms of uncontrollable devices in the collective machinery. To tell the truth, no such demonstration has been made here. My ethnography does not allow me to make incontrovertible claims that there is a clear link between the Tactical Encirclement Group's activities and the reproduction of political servitude. A link remains missing, one that would reveal their connection transparently. But the inadequacy of the demonstration was inevitable, because what I have tried to do is to illuminate an aspect of servitude's invisible architecture rather than its tangible parts. I wanted to reveal a relationship of suitability or affinity, rather than a causal one, between elements of collective ideology and a tyrannical situation. Above all, I wanted to grasp in real life how servitude gets fashioned not only at the level of representations but also in the pursuit of a useful and necessary social activity.

There remains in all this a certain worry as to whether social and cultural processes may get out of control, a kind of dark Durkheimianism. This pessimism is both diminished and intensified by the share of responsibility attributable to everyone in conditions of voluntary servitude. The cards are not played out in advance: all parties are in a position to curb or to exacerbate the deleterious effects of collective mechanisms. The contrast appears almost archetypically in the figures of Major Zaw Win and Great-Master Aung Khaing. The two men personify the idea of individual conscience and that of unconsciousness, respectively, in the face of the collectivity and its institutions' potential to grind people down. But these are figures whom the anthropologist has fashioned, on the basis of his data, for the purposes of argument.[43] In truth, the contrasting tendencies incarnated in the anthropologist's rendering by the Major and the Great-Master are to varying degrees constituent elements of any Burmese, including these two: love of freedom and the communitarian imperative are bound together and at war with each other in each of them.

5 Trial by Fire

THE MANUFACTURING OF AN EVENT

Thursday, February 19, 2004. It is about 1:00 a.m. when two officers of the law, coming from Minbu, arrive at the four *weikza*'s monastery. The forces of order often carry out their operations in the middle of the night, especially when they concern state security. Surprise makes escape more difficult. In addition, a nighttime operation, because it takes place unobserved by the neighbors, safeguards against any attempted collective resistance. It is never really clear whether it is police officers or agents of the military intelligence services who come to the monastery. The impersonal pronoun that Burmese use—"them"—labels both the government and all those who act in its name.

The Festival of Success finished more than a week ago; life at the monastery has reverted to its habitual rhythm, punctuated by the arrival of groups of disciples, appearances by the *weikza,* and Saturday's Son's trips. Victorious and I left three days after the end of the festival. Victorious returned to Yangon, where he had things to do; I headed for Pindaya, in Shan State, to inquire about the death and funeral of a highly venerated monk. We are to meet up again on March 9 at 6:00 a.m. at the bus station in the city of Pyay and then pay a visit to Aung Thaung, the leader of the Tactical Encirclement Group. After that visit I will leave Burma and will not get wind of the forces of order's operation at the monastery until I reach Singapore, in April. Victorious, notified by a relative, will write me with the news.

At that hour, in the village as at the monastery, everyone or close to everyone is asleep. The representatives of the authorities proceed to the building where Saturday's Son lives. They are expected. Some time before, the *weikza*'s medium informed one of the monastery's nuns that a serious problem was going to arise. He urged the disciples to speak very carefully. This evening, the *weikza* appeared. "Success" is coming, they said repeatedly; in other words, Bodaw Bo Htun Aung's life-prolonging ceremony was about to be performed. But "obstacles" (*ahnaung ashet*) were going to occur. They told the disciples not to leave the monastery after nightfall during this critical period. Furthermore, they instructed them to keep bookies, who in normal times take bets on illegal lotteries, away from the site.[1] After the *weikza* appeared, Saturday's Son was massaged by two lay assistants in order to relieve his rheumatism. The monk wondered aloud, "Wouldn't it be a good idea for me to leave on a trip?" At another point he asked, "Aren't those men here yet?" Noticing that he seemed to be putting off going to bed, one of the assistants asked him, "Venerable, have you still not gone to bed?" "No, and for a reason," Saturday's Son replied.

In the presence of the medium and of Great-Master Aung Khaing, who has been sent for, the officers proceed to search the Monastery of Noble Success where the four *weikza* customarily appear. In the lowered ceiling, they find a coconut; in the room located in the front right corner, they find some copies of a booklet about the cult that a foreign disciple has had printed and distributed without the censorship office's permission. All this is material to use for later convictions. They force Great-Master to sign a document listing the results of the search. Saturday's Son is interrogated. An officer asks him to recite the four fundamental rules of monastic discipline, those concerning infractions that result in exclusion from the monastic community. "I don't know," the monk answers. He is arrested and taken to the Minbu police station, then transferred to Magway. There he is disrobed—a monk cannot be put in prison. They put him in a cell dressed in laymen's clothes.

It is not the first time that Saturday's Son has been arrested and imprisoned. In the 1960s, at the urging of Colonel Mya Maung, some opium smokers from Kachin State came to the Energy Center in hopes of getting detoxified. One group, as a sign of their success and gratitude, gave a poppy ball to the *weikza*'s medium, who placed it on the altar to the Buddha. Then a malevolent villager took advantage of the situation to turn in Saturday's Son. The medium was arrested by the Minbu police, and the offending material was seized and sent to Yangon. The experts in the capital, nevertheless, found only tamarind paste, a brown-colored cooking ingredient, in the supposed ball of opium. Saturday's Son, imprisoned for three months, was then released.

A second arrest took place in 1992. Agents suddenly appeared at the monastery and without making an investigation of any kind ordered the monk to follow them. Saturday's Son was taken to Yangon for questioning before being sent back to Minbu and put in temporary detention at the police station. Some people say that monks in the area or the village head, with whom his relations were tense, had accused him of subversive tendencies. Cults that grow up around figures possessed of supernatural powers are susceptible of turning into movements of political contestation or of provoking disorder by disturbing some institutional hierarchy. The Energy Center's activities have always been under surveillance. Some people say that Saturday's Son was accused of taking on several roles at once (Bodaw Bo Htun Aung, U Pandita)—that is, of being the mastermind of an immense deception. But while the medium was in prison, the four *weikza* appeared in the flesh at the Monastery of Noble Success. Saturday's Son's misadventure, they said, was a test set for the disciples in light of U Kawwida's soon-to-be observed life-prolonging ceremony. It was appropriate to sort out the true disciples from the others, those who, in light of the circumstances, would desert the monastery. Indeed, some of the disciples, fearing that the authorities would turn to them next, distanced themselves from the cult. (All of this took place barely four years after the bloody suppression of popular demonstrations in 1988 and the coup d'état that then followed.) The most committed, however, rallied to its side. Several of them busied themselves seeking help from the top echelons: they had to go all the way to a national leader, one of the four generals who controlled the regime. Even though he was under arrest, and so dressed as a layman, Saturday's Son was permitted to move about freely from 6:00 a.m. until 6:00 p.m. and simply had to spend the night at the police station. His guards, whom he offered to feed, allowed a free-standing hut to be constructed for him, rather than making him stay in a cell. When his former wife, being treated for a heart problem in the capital, passed away, he was allowed to go there to attend her funeral. He enjoyed the Minbu police's hospitality for almost a year before being released, without having been put on trial.

The arrest of Saturday's Son in 2004, the third in fifty years, is explained variously. The reasons brought forward enable the disciples, who are unaware of where the attack on the cult comes from, to trot out some of their favorite themes. By means of this recapitulation, the incident is inscribed in the cult's weft: it becomes meaningful, and at the same time it structures that weft in turn. Some envious monks in the area would have once again incriminated the medium, hoping to bring about his definitive disgrace and thereby getting control of his large and wealthy monastery. An article of law would forbid monks from being possessed: the arrest would have been based on this article. Saturday's Son would be on the verge of "exiting;" the *weikza* would have brought the situation about in order to "call" him more easily to Dragoness Mountain. It would be a matter of instilling in the man the desire to leave behind a world filled with suffering. One of Saturday's Son's drivers was said to have reported to a military officer that the monk had in his possession a living ball of mercury. The officer would have told this to his superiors, who, wishing to gain the benefit of the alchemy ball's powers for themselves, would have demanded it from Saturday's Son in vain. The medium would then be experiencing the consequences of that refusal. Every life-prolonging ceremony has taken place under a different head of state. Yet since 1992 the same person has ruled the country. Disciples speak of the need for a change in the head of state before Bodaw Bo Htun Aung's ceremony, the last one still in need of being accomplished, can take place. But the "higher-ups" don't like people to speak of their fall—whence the military intelligence services' attack on the cult. And so forth.

No matter what the nature of the explanation put forth, everyone interprets Saturday's Son's arrest as a typical sign of what is to come. Bodaw Bo Htun Aung's life-prolonging ceremony is imminent, and the incident constitutes a typical case of "disturbances," difficulties that arise as the great event draws near. People cite as evidence for this the problems that punctuated preparations for U Kawwida's ceremony. The building intended to shelter the *weikza* had been built in 1992, after a new head of state had taken charge. But it had been necessary to wait another two years before performing the ceremony (in December 1994). In the meantime, Saturday's Son was arrested. And a nun who had come and taken up residence at the monastery had caused great worry by fighting with other residents and entering into ambiguous relations with some laypeople. (She was expelled.) Various "disturbances" have to take place in the same way before Bodaw Bo Htun Aung can undergo the trial by fire. The *weikza* know this; they talk about it, as do their disciples. It seems as though the remarkable success about to be realized must be compensated beforehand by a series of prior calamities; that is, to purify fate's path of its inevitable negative portion. Allowing these disturbances to take place, but on the margins, means keeping the negative portion away from what really matters: performing the ceremony. Misfortune, the *weikza* intimate to their disciples, is a part of success.

For several years now the cult's disciples have been awaiting Bodaw Bo Htun Aung's ceremony. How many times were Victorious and I, returning from Mebaygon, met with the burning question, "What's going on with the Bodaw matter?" The ceremony is not named explicitly so as to avoid drawing baleful forces down on the event. People speak of the "Bodaw matter" (Bodaw *keiksa*), of the "Bodaw undertaking" (Bodaw *lokngan*), of the "Bodaw project" (Bodaw *alok*). Victorious and I, despite our having stayed at the monastery, knew no more about it than other people. The event would take place very quickly and with the greatest possible discretion. A list of participants to be called together to perform the ceremony—at night, at the Site of Success—would be drawn up at the last moment. It's like getting ready to attack an enemy army, the *weikza* like to say. The operation is planned in secret, and the troops aren't told about it until the moment they must throw themselves into battle. Otherwise their adversary might get wind of the plan and take preventive action.

The building for Bodaw Bo Htun Aung, his Cave of Success, has not been built yet. Nor has any change in the country's leadership taken place in the interim. Still there are constant rumors about the current head of state's retirement. And no one would be willing to place bets on what the *weikza* will decide. If they decided that the moment was propitious, with respect especially to the alignment of the stars, things could get started impromptu, despite the absence of any changes at the top. In 1999, an ordination hall was built at the Site of Success for Bodaw Bo Htun Aung's use. He will become a monk before undergoing the trial by fire: he will achieve in this way some measure of equality with the three other *weikza*. The disciples are on the alert, ready to rush to the Energy Center at a sign from Saturday's Son. All of them hope to be numbered among the several dozen or hundreds of the elect. Several false alarms have already occurred, with the most impatient people making a dash for Mebaygon on the basis of mere rumors. In anticipation of the event, people resolve to take up specific practices, such as eating vegetarian for a certain length of time or reciting their prayer beads every day. They share the merit that results with Bodaw Bo Htun Aung so that he will meet with success when he undergoes his future trial. When you go to war, you ready your munitions.

The four *weikza* keep stoking the fires of this feverish anticipation. Their sermons are shot through with references to the ceremony. Two weeks ago, on the eve of the Festival of Success (which celebrates the *weikza*'s successful completion of previous life-prolonging ceremonies), Bodaw Bo Htun Aung concluded the recitation of his life before a large and passionate audience with the following promise-filled proclamation: "U Pandita succeeded! U Oktamagyaw succeeded! U Kawwida succeeded! If I succeed, I'm telling you I will not forget you! Do you hear?" Then he questioned the wildly excited crowd. "Isn't there anyone who wishes to ask for something from the *weikza?*" A group of women native to Arakan asked that the prodigy of the appearance of the Buddha relics be performed. The *weikza* had at their disposal four bottles of perfume for the process, alluding to the four figures—an old man, a sick man, a dead man, and an ascetic—the sight of whom induced Prince Siddhattha, the future Buddha, to renounce the world. The *weikza* gave them to Great-Master Aung Khaing to distribute among those in the audience. The Arakanese women got two bottles, and a group from Bago the other two. An unfortunate choice! By relying on the literal meaning of some persons' and place's names, the *weikza* had actually set things up as a portent (*ateik*) capable of producing energy of success. Had the disciple Pyizon, whose name means "accomplished, fulfilled, granted, complete," been given a bottle at the hands of Aung Khaing ("success" and "steady") who lives in Loikaw (a word that, changed slightly, means "we will succeed easily"), Bodaw Bo Htun Aung's ceremony, for which everything at the Site of Success was ready, would have been successfully performed that very night. It was a Wednesday, a day that pairs well with Saturday, the *weikza*'s day of birth. Bodaw Bo Htun Aung immediately lamented the unintended error on the part of Great-Master Aung Khaing. Later, U Pandita revealed both the plan for the ceremony and the reason for its postponement. Throughout the evening, every time they appeared, the *weikza* bewailed the undoing of the portent and the chance everyone had missed to participate in such an important event. The ceremony would take place neither that night nor even that year, they said, pushing the possibility of its enactment back to the month of Kahson (either April or May, after the turn of the Burmese new year). When the séance was over, Saturday's Son, who never attends the *weikza*'s appearances, came in to speak to the crowd for a few minutes. He turned the knife one more time. Several people had been sent to the Site of Success in preparation for the ceremony and were waiting for the *weikza*'s instructions; but the plan was canceled, the portent generating success not having been taken up. Pyizon will suffer the ill effects of this failure. It behooved him, when the bottles were being distributed, to make insistent demands for one of them. Yet he had failed to react. And in contrast to Great-Master, he neglected to ask the four *weikza*'s forgiveness for this oversight. He will fall sick. After eleven days in the hospital, the doctor will say his case is desperate and order that he be released so that he can die at home. Bodaw Bo Htun Aung will show up in his hospital room at this point and assure the disciple of his support. After long months of terrible suffering, the man will regain his health.

On February 11, 2004, several days after the unfortunate failure of this portent's realization and the day after the conclusion of the Festival of Success, Bodaw Bo Htun Aung repeated that preparations for his "undertaking" had been called off. There were too many "disturbances," he said. Hardly had he said this but a group of people cried out in surprise at a coconut's sudden fall. The *weikza* joked: "If when I enter the fire (*hpo win-,* a name for the life-prolonging ceremony) you are frightened like that and run away, I'll die. It is because you are supposed to take part in it that I'm not carrying out my project!"

The ceremony's time span thus spreads over years, during which time the coming event grows larger with the accretion of both individual and collective experiences, as well as the exciting wait. Well before its enactment, the ceremony is a tangible, living, waxing reality. It outstrips its performance, engraved in people's memories and evoked in their speech. To think about it outside this chronology, reducing it to its mere enactment, would be to diminish its import and its meaningfulness. It would be to suggest that simply by determining its structure we could gauge the charge and efficacy of a rite that transforms an individual's condition and engages to varying degrees something vital for all its participants. This is a necessary but not a sufficient step. If the ceremony is effective, if it prolongs the *weikza*'s life, it can do this in part because of the role it plays in the cult's disciples' imaginary, both before and after its actual enactment. The ceremony, in other words, is not simply carried out: it is also thought, represented, and spoken about. It exists, it is experienced, and it is put to use in people's minds as much as in fact. It has its contexts, the many elements that are not inherent to its execution but are related to it. We are obliged to take into account all of these dimensions; otherwise we risk placing the event outside history and outside time. It is in a sense a longitudinal event: even if it constitutes a delimited moment of rupture with ordinary time, it is experienced lastingly.

MYTH, RITUAL, AND HISTORY

Monday, December 1, 1975, the fourteenth day of the waning moon of Tazaungmon, 1337. Thirty-six lay disciples, chosen on the basis of their moral rectitude, their ability for mental concentration, and their fidelity, are gathered at the Mebaygon monastery at the invitation of Saturday's Son. Present, among others, are Maung Maung, Doctor Sein Yi, Major Zaw Win, Kyaw Khaing, Mingyi Sein Hlaing, Lieutenant-Colonel Thein Han, Ba Yi, and Mya Than, along with the sole woman to be invited, Kyin Myaing. Missing from the ranks is Colonel Mya Maung who, named a minister at the start of the 1970s, died suddenly in a train that was taking him to Katha in Kachin State. But Hpay Myint is also there, and he will be able to add the story of these memorable several days to the next edition of his book on the cult. The four *weikza* have emphasized without letup the importance of the undertaking, which they consider a historic event worthy of inclusion in the history books. A second disciple, Ohn, has also decided to document the event. His manuscript of 148 pages, *A work, drawn from personal experience, on the stage of entering the state of fruition [leading to nirvana],* will remain unpublished, although two hundred copies will be printed furtively for distribution among the cult's disciples. The censors would no doubt have refused permission to publish it. Hpay Myint's work, however, will be reedited, with the addition of ninety pages devoted to the ceremony. The anthropologist, when coming upon these minutely detailed descriptions many years later, is ecstatic.

Such retellings constitute firsthand accounts that provide information not only about the course of the ceremony as it is performed down to its tiniest details but also about the way the cult's disciples perceive and live the event; that is, about the tonality of the native experience. They illuminate the ceremony in its temporal, psychological, and dramatic complexity. Relying on these writings, but as they are enriched and clarified by information drawn from research conducted thirty years later, it becomes possible to follow step by step the event's construction and to recount it in Burmese terms.[2] Reproducing indigenous discourse should not, certainly, take the place of analysis. Yet it contributes nonetheless to our understanding, in that it reveals a certain way of perceiving the ceremony. Furthermore, the way in which Burmese describe and speak about the ceremony turns out to play a part in that very ceremony, in the process of its construction and in its implementation. Today, the ceremonies that have already taken place live on through the texts that recount them, especially the work of Hpay Myint. His work, supplemented by Major Zaw Win's account of U Oktamagyaw's 1989 ceremony and reprinted and available in return for a donation to the four *weikza* at the Energy Center, remains the cult's bible. The *weikza* mention it in their sermons, inviting the disciples to refer to it.

No reason was given for making U Pandita, at the age of 719 years, the first candidate for the trial by fire, rather than U Kawwida, who had recently passed the 1,000-year mark—being the maximum length of a *weikza*'s life, according to a theory specific to the cult.[3] Opinions differ about the ceremony's effect: will it prolong the *weikza*'s life by a thousand years; will it multiply his life's normal length by a factor of five, raising it to five thousand years; or will it add another thousand years for each day spent in the fire? In any case, the risk run is great. It is enough to consider, along with the disciples who know this story because they have heard it related so often in sermons, what happened to the *weikza* Wimala, a monk during the reign of Anawratha (r. 1044–1077). Wimala was on a quest to find an assistant whom he could trust to help him accomplish his own life-prolonging ceremony. He chose his disciple Tha Det, telling him, "I am going to enter the fire. One day [spent in the fire], a thousand years of life. If I succeed, I will watch over you throughout your life. And if you want to become a *weikza*, I'll call you."

"Trust me, Venerable! I, your disciple, will remain at my post for more than three hours."

The two men wandered about from Mount Sinkyan to Mount Popa, looking for a propitious place to hold the ceremony. They found the ideal location in the area of Dragoness Mountain: a flat space about a hundred feet long, with a hole of three feet in diameter at its center. They piled up logs of *limonia acidissima* (*thanatkha*), red sandalwood (*padauk*), and sandalwood (*nantha*), a thousand logs altogether, in reference to the number of years being sought. They doused the pyre with a flammable substance. When everything was ready, Wimala took his place in the hole at the center of the pyre, with Tha Det in a circle drawn nearby.

"Tha Det, my life is in your hands. For the next three hours, don't leave your place!"

"Trust me, Venerable!"

The disciple tossed the first ball of fire (*mi lon*). The woodpile caught fire. Evil creatures (*meikhsa*)—ghosts, demons—immediately appeared. (The ceremony, a heroic effort undertaken in the name of Buddhism's supreme goal, access to nirvana, arouses a violent reaction from envious and hostile beings.) They tried to frighten the disciple into leaving the ceremonial circle, to no effect. The *weikza* for his part waved his fan and meditated in the middle of the flames. After one hour, the first ball having succeeded, Tha Det tossed the second. He saw his mother, his father, his wife, and his children all begging him to come help them immediately. He looked at his family, and then at Wimala, and thought to himself, "The great monk's matter is primary. Let my wife and my children die if need be!" The second ball had succeeded. He tossed the third and last ball. A young woman appeared, dazzling in her grace and beauty, with a gorgeous complexion, dressed in light green and golden clothing. She said, "Tha Det, there is a sumptuous residence ready for us where we can live together. The person in the fire will only bring about your destruction. It's lucky I have come in time. Look, I am here beside you." Overcome by this enchanting apparition, the disciple conceived a non-*weikza* desire (*a-weikza tahna*). He left his circle to approach the young woman. The latter's appearance changed into something horrific. Tha Det, gone mad, died at once. As for the great *weikza* Wimala, he perished in the fire.

It is significant that the *weikza* place Wimala's life in the reign of Anawratha; that is, in the second half of the eleventh century. For Burmese historiography, this period represents the era during which the country took on its contemporary territorial dimensions. It is a time of great religious reform, with royal sponsorship helping orthodox Theravada Buddhism spread throughout the population. The *weikza* path and the life-prolonging ceremony, in particular, seem on the basis of this historical embedding to take part in the movement of Burma's Buddhicization and unification. At least the story describing the first trial by fire, the oldest and only instance the *weikza* bring up, attests to the Burmese Buddhist authenticity of the practice.

At first glance, it appears to provide a mythical charter for the contemporary performance of life-prolonging ceremonies. Examined more closely, however, the prototype appears both primitive and negative. The script for the ceremony planned by the great *weikza* Wimala seems rudimentary. Only a single lay disciple contributes his labor; the test takes place without any supporting action to enhance the chances of its success; and no words are even pronounced in the course of its execution. This ritual poverty contrasts with the sophistication of the ceremonies organized by the four *weikza*. For that matter, far from recalling an archetype whose model should be reproduced in order to copy its success, the story of the great *weikza* Wimala ends in disaster. Of course, this dramatic outcome is intended to emphasize the disciples' vital role in the ceremony; the slightest wavering on their part would cause their death and that of the *weikza*. Other aspects of the ceremony require no particular elaboration, and it is understandable that they could be treated only briefly in the story. Still, apart from the message addressed to the disciples in this story, there remains the matter of the place of the four *weikza* in history. At the same time that the reference to Anawratha is obligatory, conferring on the trial by fire a historical and Buddhist pedigree, the mythic coefficient linked to the great sovereign's reign is diminished. The real myth, in the sense of an event or era taken up to serve as a reference or model, is not to be found in the past, a site of failure. It is conjugated in the present, which the four *weikza* and their disciples are in the process of constructing. It is impossible to understand the central place that organizing life-prolonging ceremonies enjoys in the life of the cult, the emotions that they arouse, and the imaginativeness the *weikza* display as they plan them out without taking into account this deeply held conviction that all involved are collaborating in the production of a myth, a charter for future generations. Everything fits together to support the impression that this is the first time, an unprecedented realization of the time of success. In fact, the myth and the rite stand in neither isomorphic nor inverted relation to each other but rather in one of repair: the rite successfully achieves what the myth presents as possible but failed. The rite makes the myth and the myth makes history.

And how is history thought about in Burma? By breaking time up into a series of reigns. An event is characterized by being placed "under the reign of." The rule, stated by the cult's members although never commented on by the four *weikza,* according to which each life-prolonging ceremony necessarily takes place under the government of a different head of state—and so implying that, in a phrase often repeated among the disciples, a "change of ruler" (*min pyaung min hlwe*) is necessary to hold the ceremony—is nothing other than an expression of the *weikza*'s stated desire to "remain in history" (*thamaing kyan-*). To the reign of a head of state is thus linked the most striking religious event, of which the *weikza* are the authors. Each ceremony has its own stamp. Thus future generations will learn history as they repeat the formula that the *weikza* never fail to pronounce in the course of their sermons: "The great monk U Pandita succeeded under the reign of General Ne Win [1962–1988]; the great monk U Oktamagyaw succeeded under the reign of General Saw Maung [1988–1992]; the great monk U Kawwida succeeded under the reign of General Than Shwe [1992–2010]." The formula will be completed once Bodaw Bo Htun Aung has succeeded. The *weikza* know well that, in order to create history, you have to produce myth. Let us listen to U Pandita conclude today, after three ceremonies already performed, his telling of the story of the great *weikza* Wimala:

> "We, in contrast, we enjoy success! We do not fail like them [Wimala and his disciple]. We do not enter the fire with only a single disciple. For U Pandita, there were seventy-eight people altogether [actually, thirty-nine]; for U Oktamagyaw, one hundred and ten people; for U Kawwida, more than three hundred people. There were lots of people! As for how we will proceed for Bodaw Bo Htun Aung, we have been thinking about this for fifty-three years. We are crazed because we want Burma, in light of our success, to become known throughout the world. Yes, we are crazed! But we are not crazed with desire. We are crazed with meditation (*bawana*)."

The wish to convert the present time into mythic time, into a golden age, explains the denigration of Wimala's past attempt. This wish shows more broadly the cult's millenarian tendencies. So U Kawwida speaks during his appearances in the flesh:

> "Our aspiration, our horizon, our goalpost is a great era when those who have entered the stream, those who will not return, those who will only return once, and the saints [that is, the four categories of individuals sure to reach nirvana] are so numerous that a chicken won't be able to roost [in the crowd]; [an era] when there will be no need to look for gold or silver; the era of those who have entered the stream, of those who will not return,

of those who will only return once, and of the saints, of rich female donors like Withaka and of rich male donors like Anahtapein [two figures said to have lived at the time of the Buddha]. This time is near, do you hear?"

The disciples of the cult take such a promise seriously. Nevertheless, despite the proud boasts of the *weikza,* this promise does not seem to be thought likely to come true soon. Yet no one appears disappointed that the anticipated reality does not materialize. What counts is less the actual realization of the millennium than the collective maintenance of expectation: waiting is a constitutive principle, among others, of the cult's dynamic.

PREPARING FOR THE CEREMONY

The four *weikza* have been referring to U Pandita's ceremony since the mid-1960s. Ten years have passed; only now do they believe that the time has come. In the meantime, the Energy Monastery has been for the most part completed. The first building and a pagoda twenty-seven cubits in height (about a dozen meters) were built in 1972–1973; they were named the Monastery and the Pagoda of Noble Success, respectively. Saturday's Son took up residence there after he was ordained as a monk. The following year the Monastery and the Pagoda of the Noble Country's Peace were built. The two sets of buildings complement each other: one pair diffuses success energy, the other calming energy; one fosters prosperity, the other harmony.

In late 1974 U Pandita stopped appearing in the flesh. After that time he participates solely by possessing Saturday's Son. This development was intended to turn "false" disciples away from the cult, people who frequented the monastery for purely worldly ends and who would be put off by the *weikza's* absence. Once they were cleared out, it would be possible to proceed with the ceremony without disturbance, at least by them.

The ceremony will take place a few hundred meters from the Energy Monastery, at the Site of Success, on the spot where in 1298 U Pandita, at the age of forty-one, having succeeded his ball of mercury, "exited." Two Bo trees whose trunks have joined together to form an arch grow there. They were planted by Bodaw Bo Htun Aung in the 1860s, prior to his "exit." The four *weikza,* after their reappearance in the world in 1952, indicated the importance of this spot and named it the place most conducive to the success of their life-prolonging ceremonies. Saturday's Son's father-in-law, Pan Aung, was the owner of these grounds; he made a gift of them to the cult. They had previously been referred to as the "Site of the Pauk Trees" (Pauk Chaung), because trees of this species, called "false teak," made up a small forest. The *weikza* kept the name. *Pauk-* is also a verb that means "to succeed, to win": the Site of the Pauk Trees is the Site of Success.

The place was feared, because thieves had used its woods as a hiding place. Pan Aung, helped by several villagers, worked five days straight to clear it. The task complete, he went blind—an act of revenge taken by the spirits of the felled trees, the *weikza* said. In 1974, a monastery and, more important, the Cave of Success—Aung Gu (the word *gu,* "cave, cavern," also denotes a hollow and solid building, such as a tomb)—were built a few meters from the entwined Bo trees. U Pandita will undergo the trial by fire there. The building, made of durable materials, measures 4.5 by 3.7 meters; it is 2.4 meters high. The roof is flat; its four corners are decorated with statues of the four guardian deities of the universe, the center by a pagoda nine arm-lengths (four meters) in height. The door, located on the side of the entwined Bo trees, is made out of iron; it is closed from the outside by means of a sliding bar secured with a padlock. An opening eleven inches (twenty-seven centimeters) in diameter has been made in the west wall, two meters above the ground. It is through this hole that the four balls required for the performance of the ceremony will be thrown.

Inside the building, a Buddha altar with a statue has been placed on the east wall. In the middle of the room, in line with the pagoda that stands on top of the building, is a circular space, about an inch lower than the level of the floor and twenty-seven inches (about a meter) in diameter. U Pandita will place himself in this circle for the duration of the trial by fire. When exactly will that be? The *weikza* will not announce it until the last minute, in an effort to stave off, as much as possible, any potential disturbances. The disciples present on this day, December 1, 1975, have responded to Saturday's Son's call without knowing anything about the event to take place. It would be surprising for it to take place the next day, Tuesday, which is an inappropriate day because of the dark moon. The ceremony is more likely to be held on Thursday, the day of U Pandita's birth.

In the course of the afternoon, two of the three invited monks—all of whom enjoy considerable seniority, having been men of the cloth for sixty-two, fifty-four, and forty-nine years, respectively—deliver the Nine Precepts to the lay disciples gathered on the first floor of the Monastery of Noble Success.[4] The *weikza* have asked that the monks guarantee the moral purity of the participants several times a day. The disciples also recite their prayer beads and practice the Buddhist virtue of loving-kindness. Their spiritual force must be raised to the maximum degree. The accumulation of energy will help ensure a triumph over unwonted disturbances.

The *weikza* possess Saturday's Son or appear in the flesh. They give initial instructions concerning the ceremony, while reminding the disciples of what is at stake and what difficulties lie in store. They say not a word about when exactly it will happen. In this mix of waiting and mobilization, the atmosphere becomes more intense. It is like an army waiting on high alert for their leaders to give the signal to rush into battle.

The next day, December 2, 1975, the disciples go to the Site of Success at an early hour. U Oktamagyaw, the most erudite of the four *weikza*, is supervising the preparations, and he has ordered that the statue of the Buddha that stands on the altar of the Cave of Success be moved. It would otherwise risk being damaged in the course of the ceremony. After they have paid homage to the cave and cleaned up around it, the disciples make a human chain starting from that building. They pass the Buddha from hand to hand. Each person forming a link in the chain, having passed the statue along, goes to take his place at the head of the chain to receive the statue and pass it along again, until it reaches the Energy Monastery. For the rest of the day, U Oktamagyaw continues to excite the disciples through the good offices of Saturday's Son. No one yet knows when the ceremony will take place.

5:00 P.M.

Doctor Sein Yi, Ohn, and a third disciple, Kyi Shwe, are sent to the Site of Success to arrange acacia wood in a pyre. They place one thousand small pieces of wood in the circle located in the middle of the cave, the number making reference to the normal life-span of *weikza* or to the number of years obtained by means of the ceremony—opinions vary on this point. They then set logs three feet in length and about two inches in diameter in an east-west direction, ten of them altogether representing the *weikza*'s ten extraordinary powers (*theikdi*). Finally, they pile seven logs, referring to the seven qualities of the virtuous man, at each of the four cardinal points of the pyre.[5] Four stone statues of the Buddha, brought from the Energy Monastery, are placed on the altar. They correspond to the four Buddhas who have appeared in turn during this world cycle. When everything is ready, the door is locked with a key. Ohn and Kyi Shwe stay behind to guard the cave. They recite prophylactic texts (*payeik*) or say their beads. Doctor Sein Yi returns to the monastery to report to Saturday's Son.

6:00 P.M.

Saturday's Son, under U Oktamagyaw's telepathic guidance,[6] presents himself at the Site of Success. He inspects the cave, pronounces himself satisfied, and leaves.

8:00 P.M.

The disciples gather on the first floor of the Monastery of Noble Success. A sonorous recording of one of the *weikza*'s sermons is played. It concerns the words addressed by the gods of Tusita heaven to one of their own, the future Buddha. They inform him that it is time for him to give up his divine state in order to be reborn in the belly of Queen Maya and to enter into his last life, in the course of which he will attain Awakening.

Saturday's Son makes his entrance at the conclusion of the cassette. He is possessed by U Oktamagyaw. Following the *weikza*'s instructions, two groups of lay disciples are drawn up, sixteen people in each: the "country group," led by Maung Maung of Minbu, and the "Yangon group," led by Aung Khaing. The Yangon group includes a seventeenth member in the person of Kyin Myaing, fifty-four years old, who, as Hpay Myint in his chronicle suggests, contributes the feminine energy (*ma dat*) indispensable to the ceremony's success. A third and final group, the "Mandalay group," is made up of the three remaining lay disciples native to that city: Chit Kyaw, Mya Than, and Ba Yi. Thus the entire nation—that is, both the countryside and the two capitals—will be represented in the ceremony.

U Oktamagyaw asks Doctor Sein Yi to count up the numbered badges the disciples will wear. Each badge consists of a photograph of U Pandita encircled by the following inscription: "The Noble Venerable Great Monk U Pandita, Mebaygon Success Center, Minbu." The doctor counts forty-seven instead of fifty. Others check this in turn, with the same result. The numbers two, three, and four are missing. Might the *weikza* have come up with some portent productive of success $(2+3+4=9)$? U Oktamagyaw possesses Saturday's Son to order Major Zaw Win to renumber the badges by hand so as to get a complete series. The badges are then handed over to the groups' leaders, who distribute them, numbers one to sixteen going to the country disciples. Nevertheless, the participants are not granted permission to put them on. The excitement wanes. It looks as though it's all just a matter of getting things ready so that the event will take place without incident on Thursday.

9:00 P.M.

A piece of cloth is laid on the floor of the monastery's main hall. The disciples lay personal possessions on it—an energy ball, a set of prayer beads, a cabalistic diagram, and so on. Doctor Sein Yi adds a curing stick that the *weikza* have given him. Aung Khaing, the Doctor, and the Major take the set of objects and the stick to the Site of Success. They put them on the Buddha altar inside the cave.

10:00 P.M.

Possessing Saturday's Son, U Oktamagyaw asks for the "three precious medicinal balls" (*yadana hsay-lon*) needed for the performance of the ceremony. They had been passed along from one disciple's house to another's for several months so that people could pay them homage. They were then entrusted to three individuals to whom the privilege will be given to throw them onto the pyre: Mingyi Sein Hlaing (Yangon), Shwe Pyi (Ledaing village, in Pwint-pyu township), and Kyaw Khaing (Minbu). Bodaw Bo Htun Aung made the three balls according to the instructions of the three *weikza* monks. They are a mix of *weikza* ingredients (*weikza hsay*) and ingredients that Bodaw Bo Htun Aung is said to have gone searching for on the slopes of the Himalayas. Called balls, they actually look like cones whose tops have been removed; they resemble miniature pagodas. An inch and a half in height, they are an inch and a quarter in diameter at the base, which is slightly oval, and an inch at the top. They are gilded. There is a fourth ball, the "medicinal ball of success" (*aung hsay-lon*), which only Saturday's Son is capable of handling. He will throw this ball onto the pyre first in order to light it.

The Mandalay group is put in charge of safeguarding the three balls. These balls are placed on the altar of the Monastery of Noble Success, where they will be removed at the last minute.

10:30 P.M.

U Oktamagyaw orders that the other disciples be transported by car to the Site of Success. The three monks, then Saturday's Son and the Yangon group, and finally the country group are dispatched. Contrary to all expectations, the ceremony will take place this very night.

10:45 P.M.

At the Site of Success, U Oktamagyaw possesses Saturday's Son. He gathers the disciples together in the hall of the monastery built near the cave.

Some grains of popped rice (*pauk pauk*, literally, "successful, successful") are laid in the middle of the hall. (Such grains of rice are often thrown up in the air at the conclusion of religious ceremonies to signal their successful accomplishment.) Monks and laypeople recite prophylactic texts, and then each receives a handful of grains of rice. They are yellow, Buddhism's color, for the monks; white, signifying moral purity, fidelity, and loving-kindness, for the country group; and red, signifying bravery and righteousness, for the Yangon group.

U Oktamagyaw, through the intermediary of Saturday's Son, explains how the ceremony will proceed. He insists that the disciples follow its timing scrupulously. Watches are synchronized in order to avoid any confusion.

11:10 P.M.
U Oktamagyaw asks the disciples to tread on the ground of success that surrounds the cave. The only person remaining in the monastery is an oil-fields worker who has been called to take charge of the electricity and lighting. He will not take part in the ceremony.

The laypeople form four rows of eight persons facing the cave's outside eastern wall (the side with the Buddha altar). The country disciples form the first two rows, those from Yangon the next two, and Kyin Myaing is alone at the rear. Each of the three monks takes a position at one of the outside corners of the cave, with Saturday's Son occupying the fourth one, the southwest corner (corresponding to his day of birth). At this moment, U Kawwida suddenly appears in the flesh.

> "Disciples, we have planned U Pandita's ceremony in minute detail. Disciples, do not hope to get gold or silver! Gold and silver are worldly things. They do you no good. Hope only to get supramundane goods. No one is ever certain of getting the worldly things they wish, such as gold or silver. Now the most important moment for your master, U Pandita, has arrived. Be vigilant. Do not let down your guard. Pay constant attention. No matter what unwonted disturbances arise, do not abandon your mission. No matter how frightening things get, do not be afraid. Stay in the circle, holding fast to the weapon of morality, fidelity, patience, and loving-kindness. You can place yourself at any of three sides of the building [the side of the Buddha altar is excluded]. Fear nothing. . . ."

After preaching to the participants for a while, U Kawwida recites the Nine Precepts to them. Then, taking a few steps back, he disappears into thin air. In the meantime, U Pandita has appeared. He speaks in a marvelous voice no one has ever heard him use before: "Because we *weikza* trust and believe in the word and the loving-kindness of our disciples, I, U Pandita, am putting my life in your hands. I am going to enter the fire. Disciples, act with loyalty and loving-kindness. Be vigilant so that you can fulfill your mission."

U Pandita walks around the cave, passing along the south side and then entering the building from the north side where the door has been opened. His head covered with his robe, he sits in the posture of meditation in the middle of the pyre, facing the Buddha altar. The four monks leave their places and walk in order of seniority to the entrance of the cave, where they throw grains of popped rice onto the *weikza* while shouting, "The great monk U Pandita has succeeded!" The lay disciples do the same, from the country group's leader, Maung Maung, to Kyin Myaing. The door to the cave is closed back up. Of the two copies of the key to the padlock, one is in the care of Major Zaw Win, the other in the care of a second disciple. Saturday's Son, under the *weikza*'s telepathic guidance, is directing operations. He allows the participants, who returned to their places, to break out of their rows. Two disciples are sent to the Monastery of Noble Success to let the Mandalay group know that it is time to bring the three precious medicinal balls.

11:45 P.M.
Aung Khaing, the leader of the Yangon group, has been charged with marking off the ceremonial space. He uses grains of popped rice to trace a circle with a radius of five cubits around the cave. The circle widens supernaturally on one side to include the entwined Bo trees. The term used to describe this action, "to lay down a line" (*si khya-*), is also applied to the procedure of reciting phrases to prevent malevolent beings (*nanabawa*) from entering the designated space. The disciples will engage in this recitation while the ceremony proceeds.

No participant can leave the circle at this point. To do so would risk causing the entire endeavor to fail, as happened to the great *weikza* Wimala. Leaving the circle would amount to punching a hole in the invisible wall that protects the space around the cave. Evil entities would then pour in. The monks get up on a bamboo platform propped up against the western wall of the cave. The lay disciples divide themselves into two groups standing on the ground on the two other sides, the country group in the south, the Yangon group in the north. The leaders of the two groups are seated close to Saturday's Son, ready to take his orders. Everyone recites their prayer beads.

Popped rice is thrown a second time, this time through the hole put in the western wall, which the platform makes accessible. A light bulb casts a weak light on the inside of the cave. The monks and lay disciples move past the opening while throwing rice and reciting the formula, "The great monk U Pandita has succeeded!"

Finally, U Pandita stands up and reaches the packet of objects and the curing stick placed earlier on the Buddha altar through the hole, while stating, "Success!" The objects are suffused with power.

12:10 A.M.

The Mandalay group and the two disciples who went to summon them appear. It was not otiose to have five men bring the balls: terrifying creatures or even rival *weikza* often try to grab balls in an effort to make the ceremony fail. Having arrived without major difficulty, they wait outside the circle, in the Saturday corner. The oil-fields worker comes and throws a few grains of popped rice and then leaves the circle. The five men enter it. From this point on no one is permitted to enter the ceremonial space. Chit Kyaw hands the balls to Saturday's Son. Along with the four other disciples, he then throws popped rice into the cave before rejoining the rest of the participants.

Saturday's Son calls Mingyi Sein Hlaing, Shwe Pyi, and Kyaw Khaing up onto the platform. He sprinkles their hands with perfume and then gives each of them one precious medicinal ball. He keeps the ball of success for himself, getting ready to throw it through the hole in order to light the pyre U Pandita is sitting on. Absolute silence reigns. All that can be heard is the clicking of the prayer beads the disciples are fingering.

A LUXURIANT SYMBOLISM

At the moment at which Saturday's Son is getting ready to throw the ball of success onto the pyre, two years have passed since The-in Gu Hsayadaw, one of the most highly venerated meditation teachers in the country, died.[7] The great monk, weakened by disease, succumbed in the Yangon General Hospital on July 8, 1973. He was sixty years old. His terrible suffering, he said shortly before his death, was the consequence of evil deeds he had committed in previous lives. He was obliged to pay off his karmic debts (*wut kyway hsat-*) before reaching nirvana. Now, two years after his death, his funeral has still not been performed. Two factions formed at the time of his death, and they continue to fight with one another. One group insists that his body be preserved; the other insists that it be cremated. Each camp has tried to mobilize eminent monks and potent political figures on its side.

No monastic institution exists that can settle the matter and impose an incontestable decision. Only lay authorities can assert a solution. Indeed, it is their responsibility to do so. It is up to them to make sure that the quarrel not lead to a formal division within the monastic community. Such an eventuality would lead to the creation of two distinct groups (*gaing*), each one defending a different conception of funerals, and that cleavage would divide laypeople along similar lines, becoming a source of disorder. So the Yangon Division Council, in association with representatives of the army and of the Department of Religious Affairs, will intervene in February 1976 to put an end to the lengthy dispute. The Council will order that the great monk's body be cremated. Was this not the case for the Buddha, and shouldn't it therefore be forever the same for monks in Burmese society? Partisans of the body's preservation will nevertheless refuse to give in. They will try to get a hold of the body, in vain. They will be arrested and put in prison. When the funeral takes place, in April 1976, policemen will be posted along the route of the cortege to safeguard the body's safety.

At the same time that the medium and the four *weikza*'s disciples are risking their lives in order to allow U Pandita to prolong his, others, elsewhere, are confronting one another in unremitting struggle around a dead man's body. But what drives some of them to fight against The-in Gu Hsayadaw's cremation when this is the consecrated way to treat a monk's remains? Their demand to preserve his body seems all the more aberrant in light of the fact that cremation is the means par excellence for confirming a figure's sainthood. Following a cremation, people set about looking for relics (*datdaw*) among the ashes. Such relics take the form of smooth little stones, the results of a bodily transformation brought about by fire's impact and due to the deceased's spiritual perfection. The appearance of relics is deemed the tangible and irrefutable proof of sainthood, its sole mode of valid certification, although it can be further corroborated by other signs postmortem, such as the body's resistance to physical putrefaction for as long as it is on display and the fact that the dead man's hair continues to grow. Yet at the same time, cremation has the effect of terminating a cycle of sainthood. Relics arouse far less fervor than does a saint during his lifetime, and a cult of relics is susceptible to no real growth. Such is the paradox of cremation: it provides definitive assurance of sainthood, but the saint now has no, or very little, social life. This explains the vehemence of the quarrel surrounding The-in Gu Hsayadaw's corpse. To cremate the monk's body would allow his sainthood to be given incontestable expression; to preserve it would be to fight, against all comers, for his continued presence in the world.

The trial that U Pandita is about to undergo makes it possible to escape this terrible dilemma. Does it not consist in cremating the *weikza*, but with the aim of prolonging his life and his presence? In the funeral of an ordinary monk—one not considered a saint—the fire's action, by causing the body's disappearance, both causes and signifies the dissociation of the deceased from the world; it illustrates the principle of impermanence for a figure who is thought of as the emblem of the Buddhist religion and its teachings. Yet the remarkable fact is that a *weikza*, given that he neither dies nor is reincarnated, is fireproof. Flames cannot consume a *weikza*'s body. This is the mark of his spiritual accomplishment, just as the appearance of relics is for a saint. A *weikza,* for that matter, does not receive a funeral properly speaking. He "exits" in one of two ways: "alive" (*ashin htwet*) or "dead" (*athay htwet*). In the first case, the *weikza* vanishes into thin air—body and soul, we might say, leaving no trace (except sometimes, when it is a monk, his robe). In the second case, he abandons his physical body (*yok*) at the moment of his apparent death in order to continue his existence by means of a spiritual body (*nan*). The body of a *weikza* of this second type is, as a general rule, placed in a tomb and not burned. It would not burn in any case. Thus the permanent nature of the *weikza*'s physical body is a sign of his unique continuity. In the course of a life-prolonging ceremony intended to ensure this continuity, the *weikza* is submitted to fire's action, which has in the first instance no effect: his body remains unscathed.

The trial by fire confirms, then, the impossibility of the *weikza*'s funeral in order to better suggest his victory over death. The rite makes sense as the reverse of the scenario of a monk's funeral. This probably explains why the only layperson among the four *weikza,* Bodaw Bo Htun Aung, will be obliged to be ordained as a monk before undergoing the ritual. The symbolism of impermanence and separation that surrounds a funerary cremation is less pronounced in the case of a layperson than that of a monk, such symbolism alluding to Buddhist principles of which a monk is the embodiment.

The *weikza*'s body is not only fireproof but it is also regenerated by fire. The life-prolonging ceremony is labeled in two ways, which are sometimes paired: *hpo win-,* "to enter the hearth or the kiln"—that is, to enter the fire[8]—and *mi htun ku-,* "to be transformed, to pass from one state to another by means of fire." Some words from these phrases are in use in the field of alchemy. *Hpo* is the name for the hearth in which the crucible containing an energy ball is placed; the verb *htun-,* made into a substantive, supplies the name for an alloy that, by bringing about a change of properties or state, causes mercury to solidify. Although none of the *weikza* ever said anything along these lines, one of the smartest of the disciples, a monk and a respected sermon-giver, believes that the life-prolonging ceremony is modeled after alchemy. The trial by fire, he suggests, encapsulates the process whereby an energy ball is transformed into a living ball. Just as an alchemist uses ingredients (*hsay,* in the sense of drug, medicine, or potion) to transform the material of his ball, making it die and then come back to life, so the first of the medicinal balls, the one that Saturday's Son throws onto the pyre, serves to make the *weikza*'s physical material die, and the three that follow, thrown by the disciples, make it come back to life, thereby granting him an extraordinary longevity. The monk supports this interpretation by reference to a photograph taken at the time of U Oktamagyaw's ceremony in 1989. Saturday's Son had tossed the ball of success, and the pyre had caught fire. The photograph shows, in the middle of the flames, the *weikza*'s body reduced to a tiny size, that of a newborn baby, an eloquent image of his rejuvenation. The three other balls brought U Oktamagyaw back to normal size, while at the same time increasing his vital strength. Furthermore, just as in alchemy changes in the color of the flames in the hearth indicate the course of the transformative process going on inside the crucible containing the liquefied ball, so in the course of the ceremony changes in the color of the flames of the pyre after each ball is thrown onto it indicate the course of the process of the *weikza*'s regeneration. The *weikza,* for their part, describe the life-prolonging ceremony as an exercise in purification (*thanshinyay*). But isn't the alchemical process a purification, precisely, of an energy ball?

Drawing an analogy between the life-prolonging ceremony and alchemical operations makes it possible to liken a *weikza* to an energy ball whose success depends on the action of his disciples; the latter are placed in the same position as the alchemist. As noted earlier,[9] an energy ball "represents a living double of the person, one in which it is possible to project and look upon oneself in the present or future, and on the basis of which, above all, it is possible to work long and hard on the self." This double, however, is not a faithful copy of its owner; it is not a simple extension of his person, because it can take precedence over the original. It seems as though in the life-prolonging ceremony, in which the *weikza* is treated like an alchemical energy ball, people are representing the real, not the conventional, relationship between the *weikza* figure and the human community: if in normal times he is taken to be the master of his disciples, at the time of the ceremony he is shown instead to be created by them. Whereas alchemical operations require the *weikza*'s assistance to reach their goal, the trial by fire requires the disciples' assistance to succeed. If in the former case the disciples depend on the *weikza,* in the latter case it is the reverse. At the time of the ceremony, the community presents its own work of collective sublimation—strictly speaking, it makes the *weikza*—a project that it usually accomplishes unknowingly, assigning a *weikza* the status of an independent—superior and active—reality. Still, we can hardly speak of demystification. The ceremony does not bring about any real movement toward revelation and disalienation. It is the *weikza,* not the disciples, who produce the balls essential to the ceremony's successful conclusion; the *weikza* still keep things in their hands. The reversal, although obvious, is not total.

In truth, a life-prolonging ceremony sometimes takes place according to methods in which fire is absent. The operation can also be accomplished by the action of earth (*myay htun ku-*) or of water (*yay htun ku-*). In the first case, the *weikza* is buried for several days, guarded by the disciples; in the second, he is thrown, heavily weighted down, into a river, where he dedicates himself for a time to submarine meditation. If he comes out of the trial alive, he has succeeded. The energy of the earth or water will have been transmitted to him, as is that of fire in the case of incineration. Aside from this explanation in the idiom of energy, aside from the meaning of the ceremony as it is conceived of by the four *weikza,* what links these different types of trials appears to be the ability to survive whatever causes death, to surpass death.[10]

Surpassing death and regenerating life: the analogy between the ceremony and the alchemical process is not the only one with which to account for the ceremony's revitalizing effect. Others present themselves. Shortly before U Pandita's ceremony, Bodaw Bo Htun Aung, while possessing Saturday's Son, remarked that carrying out the ceremony was like a snake shedding its skin. At the trial's end, U Pandita would not move out of the cave for months, like a snake that, after shedding his skin, stays sheltered because of its fragile condition. It is relevant, furthermore, that what was played through the loudspeakers on the evening of the event was a sermon about the future Buddha's entry into his final life. He was called to give up his celestial condition in order to be reborn in human form in the belly of Queen Maya. It is worth asking—no hypothesis should be left unexamined—if the "cave" in which the *weikza* undergoes the trial by fire has something to do with a mother's womb, the disciples throwing balls through the hole suggesting an insemination. In fact, does the *weikza*'s prolonged stay inside, after the ceremony, recall the period of intrauterine gestation? Behind the metaphor of regeneration would then stand, although less emphasized, that of rebirth. The two metaphors are not mutually exclusive, issuing from a symbolic thought that conceives of the ceremony on the basis of several models (funerals, alchemy, rebirth) with overlapping imagery. In any case, the choice of the sermon reiterates, once again, the fundamental identification of the *weikza* with the Buddha.

Even though it is richly meaningful, a life-prolonging ceremony is not actually essential. There are famous *weikza* whose careers include no such ceremony. Bo Min Gaung and Bobo Aung are among them. About the latter figure, patron of the cabalistic arts, it is said that as a young man he inherited a book of copper plates showing cabalistic designs from a layperson who became a *weikza* after he triumphed in the trial by fire. Bobo Aung studied these designs and attained "knowledge" without further difficulty and without needing to extend the power of longevity he acquired thereby.[11] Still, even if it is not indispensable, the life-prolonging ceremony as it is imagined and implemented at the Energy Center of Mebaygon represents an apotheosis of the extraordinary—and the extraordinary is indeed essential to *weikza* cults.

ORDEAL AND TRUTH

12:20 A.M.
Boom! At the time determined by the *weikza* to be auspicious, Saturday's Son has thrown the ball of success through the cave's hole while pronouncing the word, "Success!" The explosion, like a stick of dynamite's, is so strong that it can be felt in the surrounding area over a five-kilometer radius. Fire invades the whole of the structure's interior. The force of the explosion is such that it throws Saturday's Son backward on the platform, while the iron door of the cave is thrown off its hinges, falling on two disciples sitting in the first row. The flames shooting out through the opening burn their legs while they lie unconscious, pinned under the heavy door. The flames almost reach Major Zaw Win, who is standing on the northwest side. It takes great resolve on his part not to step back beyond the confines of the ceremonial circle. The surprise is so great that for several seconds everyone is too stunned to react.

Saturday's Son, regaining his senses, jumps off the platform, screaming, "What happened? What happened?" He is afraid that U Pandita, unable to withstand the explosion, has left the structure. But the *weikza* is there, seated in the middle of the pyre. Reassured, the medium orders the door once again to be closed. Eight disciples, braving the blaze, pick the door up and put it back in place. They use the bamboo platform to prop it up.

Doctor Sein Yi and a disciple, a medical officer by profession, attend to the two wounded disciples, who have been carried over to the northwest side. One of them has regained consciousness. The other remains unconscious. The Doctor, who has left his first-aid kit at the Energy Monastery, waves the curing stick he got from the *weikza* over the unconscious disciple's body. It has no effect. Consternation and fear: the man is believed dead. A few minutes later he opens his eyes. Two other disciples have suffered light burns.

Suddenly, Ohn, standing in the northwest corner, cries out, "Oh, monk, don't enter the circle, don't enter the circle!" The disciple, who is unaware that the monk living at the Site of Success has been sent to the Energy Monastery for the ceremony, sees him approaching, apparently intending to help out. In response to the disciple's scream, the figure turns back, grows huge, and suddenly disappears. Ohn and about four or five others who have seen the apparition understand that it was a malevolent being. At the same moment, on the southeast side, Mya Than and Ba Yi notice frightening shapes walking toward them. They point their flashlights at them, and the shapes disappear. Elsewhere, several disciples observe the oil-fields worker approaching the circle. In actual fact, the man remains motionless under a lamp in the monastery. He is watching the events helplessly.

12:26 A.M.
The time comes to throw the first of the three precious balls. On Saturday's Son's instruction, Mingyi Sein Hlaing, determined to sacrifice his life in the service of the *weikza,* places himself close to the hole. At 12:27 a.m., he pronounces the formula, "The great monk U Pandita has succeeded!" and tosses the ball. He lowers his head to protect himself from the expected explosion. Nothing happens. The flames inside the cave change color momentarily, going from yellow to light green to purple, before returning to their original color. The first ball's success reassures the disciples.

12:35 A.M.
"The great monk U Pandita has succeeded!" On Saturday's Son's instruction, Shwe Pyi throws the second ball. Once again, the color of the flames changes briefly.

12.45 A.M.
"The great monk U Pandita has succeeded!" Kyaw Khaing throws the third and last ball. One more time, the color of the flames changes.

"Success! Success! Success! The great monk U Pandita has succeeded!" proclaims Saturday's Son. "Success! Success! Success! The great monk U Pandita has succeeded!" repeat the disciples in unison, their cry of victory piercing the night.

12:55 A.M.
Saturday's Son grants the disciples permission to leave the ceremonial circle. But people stay on to enjoy themselves and congratulate one another for another ten minutes or so, before moving to the adjoining structure to spend the night. Like soldiers returned from battle, the disciples, unable to sleep, run back over the course of events and celebrate their success. The Doctor tends to the injured, four people altogether, who are suffering from burns and broken bones. One of them will need to be hospitalized.

1:30 A.M.

Saturday's Son has sent for two bricklayers from the town of Sagu who are staying in one of the buildings of the Energy Monastery. They have been called on for help with the ceremony. When they get to the Site of Success, they pour cold water on the still red-hot door. They take out the platform and replace it with a bamboo pole to prop up the door while they seal it and the entrance to the cave with bricks and cement. The hole in the west wall through which the balls were thrown is also walled up with bricks and cement. The bricklayers work until dawn under the watchful gaze of about ten disciples who have come back to the area near the cave.

In the morning, the three missing badges turn up. Wasn't their absence an effort to throw things off, exclaims Ohn in his recounting of the event, pointing out that the Buddha encountered numerous difficulties because of the Evil One (Man Nat)?

In the evening, U Kawwida appears in the flesh. He speaks to the disciples:

> "Thanks to you, disciples, your master, U Pandita, has succeeded in the trial by fire ceremony. Doesn't that make you happy? Your master, U Pandita, succeeded in the task of entering the fire in the course of three hours. But now he is like a snake who has just shed its skin. His skin is very tender and fragile, and he can't go outside. Are you happy? Say, disciples, don't be downcast [because you can't pay homage to U Pandita yet]. Fasten your attention on the Three Jewels and meditate!"

Three days after the ceremony, Doctor Sein Yi, Major Zaw Win, and one other disciple, put in charge of completing repairs to the cave, call a painter from Minbu. The artisan sketches a circle on the wall covering the door in the form of the Wheel of the Doctrine, divided into twenty-four sections, corresponding to the twenty-four sections of the canonical text of the *Pahtan*. Around the circle are written the words, "The great monk U Pandita has succeeded!" At the base there is another formula, "Long life [to U Pandita]!" (*siyan teikhtatu*), which is a formula commonly used with reference to Buddhism, such as in the phrase "Long life to the religion of the Buddha!" (*bokda thathana siyan teikhtatu*). Just above the walled-in door, he paints a flag in the religion's colors along with the inscription, "The Buddha has succeeded!"

Yes, without a doubt, the Buddha—which is to say, the *weikza*—has succeeded. Yet catastrophe was only barely averted. Four people were injured, one of them requiring hospitalization. What would have happened had the Major or one of the others, in the midst of the confusion caused by the explosion and the shooting flames, stepped outside the limits of the ceremonial space? The *weikza* and their disciples are not exaggerating when they emphasize the dangers of the life-prolonging ceremony and the heroism of its participants. Yet it is precisely these grave risks that give the event all its power and value. Success is uncertain: unlike an initiation ceremony or a wedding, in which the outcome is in a sense predetermined, a life-prolonging ceremony is an adventure, a hazardous and perilous one—and it is these very qualities that grant it its mythic stature. Weakness on anyone's part would mean death to the entire group of participants. Uncertainty and danger: these two elements of the risks run are pushed to the limit, because the participants' lives are at stake. And even if we deem some threats fanciful, such as the apparition of frightening shapes, real incontestable dangers remain. In the second ceremony, conducted on behalf of U Oktamagyaw in February 1989, another violent explosion will occur after Saturday's Son throws the ball of success. The explosion will blast the cave's walls outward, displace the roof, and leave the medium in a half-conscious state for more than an hour. Had the walls collapsed, comments Major Zaw Win in his description of the event, there would have been many victims. The event will take place, furthermore, only a few months after the repression of widespread demonstrations and the military coup d'état of September 18, 1988, during a period when martial law was imposed. Gathering a hundred or so people together at night and setting off a loud explosion was at the very least risky and could have landed the disciples in prison.

Yet far from being avoided, the risk seemed to be sought out. It is tangible, lived, staged, and glorified because it is inherent to the effectiveness of the ceremony. Shouldn't it be a mortal danger that is confronted if what is sought is the power of life? If the category existed, we would have to classify the life-prolonging ceremony among "rites of the extreme." Because it implies life-threatening risks, it takes on the character of an ordeal, a trial to which a person is subjected (throwing him into water or fire, for example) to determine his innocence or guilt. Doesn't the success of the ceremony demonstrate that the *weikza* and their disciples both possess and personify the Truth?

INCORPORATING SUCCESS

Monday, April 26, 1976. Disciples and the merely curious have been flocking to the monastery since yesterday. It is believed that the ceremony to open the Cave of Success will take place on this Wednesday, the first day of the waxing moon of Kahson. Bodaw Bo Htun Aung had indeed announced that the cave would be opened either in the month of Dabaung (*paung-* meaning "to gather, to be together") or in the month of Kahson (*hson-* meaning "to meet").[12] Dabaung went by without anything happening.

Five months have passed since the trial by fire. During the weeks following the event, people came from all over to pay homage, indirectly, to the *weikza* shut up within the cave. Some of the disciples took turns guarding the Site of Success day and night. They were especially afraid that villagers or people from the oil fields, patently skeptical, would try to smash open the cave at night.

At the Energy Monastery, the small pagoda squeezed between the two recently built pagodas has been restored and heightened to make it equal in size to its sisters. It is the Wish-Fulfillment Pagoda (Hsutaung-pyay Hpaya). A huge building, the Wish-Fulfillment Preaching Hall, is under construction a few meters away, financed by a married couple among the disciples.

8:00 P.M.

Saturday's Son, guided telepathically by the *weikza,* tells the disciples to gather on the upper floor of the Monastery of Noble Success and to recite their prayer beads. Shortly thereafter, one of the monks who participated in the life-prolonging ceremony takes his place on the preaching chair. He recites a long hagiographic poem about U Pandita. Saturday's Son, possessed by U Oktamagyaw, goes next. He celebrates once again the success of the trial by fire and announces that the cave will be opened this evening. However, the door remains walled up; the propitious moment has not yet arrived. The disciples will have to content themselves with opening the hole on the western facade, through which the balls were thrown. Doctor Sein Yi, Lieutenant-Colonel Thein Han, Kyaw Khaing, and one more disciple must go to the Site of Success and use an iron stick to mark with a cross the spot where the hole is. While Saturday's Son is giving these instructions, U Pandita appears in the flesh. He enters via the room located at the front right corner of the hall. The audience pays him homage with great emotion, the same emotion, Ohn notes in his account, as that of the Buddha's disciples when the Master came back to earth after a three-month stay in one of the heavens where he had preached the Buddhist doctrine to his mother (reincarnated as a divine being). U Pandita's appearance has changed. He has grown younger, like a snake after it has shed its skin. He addresses the crowd: he has come from the cave to express his gratitude to the disciples who have enabled him to undergo the trial successfully.

9:00 P.M.

U Pandita leaves the hall. The four disciples named by U Oktamagyaw leave for the Site of Success.

U Kawwida and Bodaw Bo Htun Aung appear in turn. They preach briefly. Bodaw Bo Htun Aung entertains the audience with a show of his supernatural powers.

11:00 P.M.

Once the *weikza* have left, the disciples recite their prayer beads while awaiting further instructions.

ABOUT 1:00 A.M.

Hpay Myint has fallen asleep while reciting his beads. Maung Maung wakes him up. Saturday's Son wants to see him right now. The medium, possessed by U Oktamagyaw, tells the writer that the monks—the three who participated in the trial by fire, plus a fourth who had not made it in time—would open the hole at 1:45. Hpay Myint will go with them. Saturday's Son hands him a piece of paper with a poem about the ceremony of entering the fire. The disciple must read it while the monks do their work.

Hpay Myint leaves along with the four monks and Colonel Ba Htay (who missed the trial by fire because he had been held up by his official responsibilities). Just when the vehicle is about to set off, a fifth monk living at the Energy Monastery joins the group on Saturday's Son's instruction.

1:45 A.M.

At the time determined by the *weikza* to be auspicious, one of the monks strikes the first blow with a pickaxe at the spot where a cross has been sketched on the western wall of the cave. The other monks then take turns doing the same while Hpay Myint reads the poem by flashlight. The hole is opened up before he has finished reading the poem. A breath of hot air comes out of the structure. It is so hot that it is impossible to keep an arm in the hole for very long. An ordinary man would die in a matter of minutes inside the cave.

Each person looks through the hole in turn. Six large candles are burning in front of the four statues of the Buddha. Cups of water and five vases holding fresh flowers are placed on the altar as well. The room smells like perfume. Hpay Myint is reminded of a famous episode in Buddhist history: Emperor Asoka's discovery of the Buddha's relics, which King Azatatat and the monk Maha Katthapa had had encased two hundred years earlier, after the Master's death, in a building that was made impenetrable. When Asoka managed to make his way into the reliquary, the four oil lamps that the king and the monk had placed there were still burning, and the flowers had not faded, despite the passage of two centuries.

U Pandita is no longer in the cave. The disciples notice, in the center of the room, a large pile of ashes, the remains of the pyre in the middle of which the *weikza* stayed during the ceremony.

News that the cave has been opened reaches the Energy Monastery. In spite of the lateness of the hour, the disciples rush to the Site of Success. They look through the hole to see inside the cave. U Kawwida appears in the flesh on the east side and speaks to the disciples. U Pandita pops up under the entwined Bo trees. The activity lasts the whole night.

THE NEXT DAY, 8:00 P.M.
Once one of the monks, as happens every evening, has recited the poem relating U Pandita's life, Saturday's Son arrives and, possessed by U Oktamagyaw, orders the disciples to proceed to the Site of Success. They must all throw popped rice inside the cave while stating their names, viz., "Disciple Sein Yi, Venerable!," "Disciple Zaw Win, Venerable!," and so on, and then shout, "The great monk U Pandita has succeeded!" The point is to generate a portent productive of success energy. Celebrating U Pandita's triumph, which took place on a Tuesday, will help make all things whose name begins with a letter linked to this day (according to the Burmese system of correspondences)—in particular, rice, oil, and salt—become abundant in the country and also help bring prosperity more generally. Then U Kawwida appears and delivers the Nine Precepts, next Bodaw Bo Htun Aung, and finally U Pandita, who reminds the disciples of their mission and sends them off in small groups. "All right, I'm leaving. The disciples will be getting to the Cave of Success," he says. When the first disciples throw popped rice through the cave's hole, they see the *weikza* inside. He strolls or sits while reciting his prayer beads.

SUNDAY, MAY 2
Early in the morning, Saturday's Son, possessed by U Oktamagyaw, states that it is time for the disciples to ask U Pandita for the ashes from the ceremony's pyre so that they can share them among themselves. Colonel Ba Htay and his family are given the job. Doctor Sein Yi, Kyin Myaing, and others will follow in Saturday's Son's vehicle.

The Colonel must first go find a monk, and his group reaches the cave after the other group. The other disciples are already filing past the hole. They are throwing popped rice while stating their names and making the identical request of the *weikza:* "Give us the success energy ashes (*aung dat pya*), Venerable!" When it gets to be the last disciple's turn, the position of the stars being propitious, U Pandita hands him a bag filled with ashes through the hole. The disciple tucks them securely under his shirt, and the two groups return to the Energy Monastery, where everyone is waiting.

Saturday's Son, possessed by U Oktamagyaw, lays claim to the bag. He hands it to a monk. Assisted by Major Zaw Win among others, the monk spends the rest of the day preparing tiny paper packets, each one containing a little more than one gram of ashes.

In the evening, U Pandita, with Saturday's Son as his intermediary, arranges the distribution of the ashes. He recommends swallowing them with honey. People who participated in the trial by fire and some other people who did virtuous deeds in previous lives receive the packets, one per person, plus ashes from alchemical work and a handkerchief with cabalistic designs sketched on it. The rest of the disciples who are present get only alchemy ashes or amulets. The disciples are now free to go; they will leave the monastery the next day. Some extend their stay at the request of the *weikza.*

Thus consuming the success energy ashes will not be done collectively. The ashes will be swallowed by the disciples on their own, at whatever time and in whatever circumstances they wish. That the long ceremonial cycle (December 1, 1975, to May 2, 1976), of which the collection of the ashes marks the endpoint and which points to its complete success, should conclude with a simple distribution of the ashes and not with a rite of communion in the form of an energy feast, is emblematic of the kind of individualism that obtains throughout the cult and in Burmese society more broadly. The ashes, whose consumption enables a person to incorporate the *weikza*'s energy in order to prolong their life and eventually attain the same status as a *weikza,* are not uniform in their effect. Their power varies according to the spiritual energy of the person who swallows them; that is, according to someone's degree of morality and mental concentration, as well as his store of virtue capital. They are the fruit of a collective effort, but it isn't as though everyone who has the extraordinary opportunity of eating them will benefit equally from their power. Even though they could not on principle be produced without the existence of a community—one of the motivations that made the *weikza* decide to reappear in the world in 1952 was to form this community of disciples capable of supporting them in the trial by fire—in the end the ashes throw every individual back on himself and on his own fate. The meticulous care with which both of the ceremony's chroniclers, Hpay Myint and Ohn, identified each of the event's forty participants, including Saturday's Son, and indicated their respective roles, whether planned or not, over the course of the proceedings, certainly shows a shared sense that they are writing a page for the history books, one in which the actors deserve individual recognition. But doing so also reflects a logic whereby each person's acts are always being tallied, as part of the continuous process by which each person fashions his or her own fate. It is not at all the same thing to have thrown one of the precious balls or to have recited one's prayer beads in the midst of the other disciples, to have been in possession of one of the copies of the key to the cave or to have come to the aid of the injured after the explosion. From each according to his abilities, to each according to his merit.

Individually assimilating the *weikza*'s strength by consuming the remains of the pyre in which he placed himself and that was the site of his regeneration can be linked to anthropophagy—an anthropophagy attenuated by means of a substitution, the ashes being suffused with the *weikza*'s being rather than being the *weikza*'s ashes. This anthropophagical inclination is hardly surprising in light of the theory of energy that supports the *weikza* path and the Burmese conception of life. If you can swallow cabalistic diagrams in order to increase your personal vitality, why would you not eat some *weikza*? No doubt it is one thing to eat symbols and quite another to eat the human flesh of a *weikza*. But let us listen, once again, to those most knowledgeable: the four *weikza* themselves. Their telling of the story of the great *weikza* Wimala, in the time of Bagan, does not end with the tragic failure of the ceremony. While the ill-fated pyre was still smoking, they say, the Great Monk of Bame (Bame Hsayadaw) and his lay assistant came upon it while they were wandering about the forest in search of medicinal plants. Bame Hsayadaw suspected that the body was that of a *weikza* who had attempted the trial by fire. He ordered his assistant to gather up the remains of flesh. On returning to his monastery, he tasted it: it was indeed some *weikza* flesh. Anxious to please the king and the kingdom's power holders, he wished to make his discovery known to them and to invite them to share with him this desirable food. Before leaving, to make sure that the two Indian brothers living in his monastery would not go near it, he told them that it was deadly poisonous. Nonetheless, the two brothers ate it all up. They were Byatwi and Byatta, the *weikza* say in conclusion, without needing to go on, because these figures from the Bagan period, whose disobedience earned them extraordinary powers, are well known to Burmese.[13]

It should be noted in passing that historical chronology has been mixed up a bit here, because Bame Hsayadaw, a famous representative of the *weikza* path, is usually said to have lived not in the eleventh but rather at the turn of the seventeenth century.[14] The *weikza* have taken their inspiration from a famous story that the royal chronicles situated during the reign of Anawratha. They adapt it, just as they adapt stories from the canonical texts. Nonetheless, the cult's disciples, by swallowing ashes from the pyre, repeat quite closely Byatwi's and Byatta's deed, yet with the critical difference that this time the ceremony was successful. They swallow what they have produced. They give themselves life in taking in what they have given life to. The *weikza*, fashioned by the collectivity, is consumed by each of its members. Their anthropophagy is an individual incorporation of the collectivity's strength. Consuming the ashes closes the ceremonial cycle by reestablishing conventional truth, after having, for one danger-filled night, partially overturned it. The disciples are once again dependent on the *weikza*.

THE ANTHROPOLOGIST'S HANDIWORK

Sunday, August 15, 2004. Victorious arrives alone at the Energy Monastery. I am in Singapore. Saturday's Son has been released on July 20, after five months in detention. The cult's disciples have turned to the older brother of one of the most powerful people in the government, a man who used to be a regular visitor at the monastery in Mebaygon, asking him to intervene to bring the matter to a close. It is said that before his release, Saturday's Son was forced to sign a document saying that he would no longer be subject to possession and that he would accept no gifts. The police in Magway were sorry to see him go. The medium gave his jailers food and, thanks to the *weikza*, provided them with precious information about numbers that would be drawn in the lottery. In addition, disciples who came to visit him paid their way in.

The monastery suffered the consequences of Saturday's Son's arrest during these five months. The *weikza* no longer appeared. The influx of visitors diminished, as did their gifts, and money to feed the residents, whether religious or lay, became sparse. In these difficult circumstances, Great-Master Aung Khaing struggled to keep the place running. At the beginning of June, short of supplies, he was obliged to buy from sellers at the market on credit. This made him anxious, and he appealed to the *weikza*, begging them to provide him some solution to the money problem. One night a girl surrounded by three cows appeared to him in a dream. Great-Master, an avid follower of the Thai lottery—in which people place bets, via bookmakers' illegal networks, on the last three digits of the bimonthly drawings—interpreted the scene as a sign sent to him by the *weikza*. All that remained to do was to decipher the sign. The cows (*nwa*) referred to the letter *na,* so Saturday, and thus the number seven. There were three of them, with just one girl: 731. Still, the girl was in the middle of the cows: 713. Aung Khaing's bet brought him a considerable sum—no one knows exactly how much. The monastery, for a while at least, was free from want.

When Victorious enters, the residents, with whom he has gotten along well on previous visits, greet him with a mix of surprise and reserve. They don't appear hostile but rather polite and cool. Contrary to usual practice, he is not invited to spend the night there. Victorious has decided it would be better to stay at a small guesthouse in Minbu anyway. Several people avoid him, as though fearful of being questioned.

The young woman who runs the modest tea shop at the foot of the Monastery of Noble Success, where Victorious and I used to take our evening meal, tells him straight out:

> "Victorious, be careful not to go asking questions all over the place, okay? Don't go asking everybody about stuff like you did before. People get nervous when they see you coming. Because they thought it was because of you and Ko Yin Maung [my Burmese name] that Saturday's Son got arrested. The way you ask for details about everything, people get the impression you must belong to the military intelligence services. And then Saturday's Son got arrested not long after the end of the Festival of Success, just after you guys left. So it looks like your handiwork. But people get it now that he has been freed [and they know that the questions that he got asked during his incarceration had nothing to do with what you guys asked about]."

Misfortunes never come singly. The Irrawaddy River rose exceptionally high that year. In July, the floodwaters reached the edge of the village, more than a kilometer from the riverbed. For twenty days, the water was a meter and a half deep. All the supplies—cement and sand—that had been bought and stored at the Site of Success in preparation for the construction of a cave for Bodaw Bo Htun Aung's life-prolonging ceremony were swept away. That, Saturday's Son tells Victorious, is another disturbance, a sign that the ceremony is drawing near. The medium has come from Mandalay where he is spending the season of retreat. He seems in excellent form; he even gained a bit of weight during his time in jail.

The next morning, Saturday's Son gives twelve monks breakfast, seven from the monastery and five guests, to mark the twelfth anniversary of the death of his wife. He has them served vermicelli soup (*kyazan*), a portent productive of success energy that will help him live (*san-*) a long time (*kyakya*).[15] He is seventy-seven years old. Long live the four *weikza!*

Notes

A Word to the Reader

1. The phrase "mode of representation" is borrowed from George Marcus and Michael Fischer's work *Anthropology as Cultural Critique: An Experimental Moment in the Human Sciences* (1986).

2. Gérard de Nerval's words are quoted by Edward Said (1979 [1978]: 101).

Chapter 1: From Belief to Believing

1. This man, who appears only in Chapter 1, is not to be confused with Major Zaw Win, who appears throughout.

2. The narrative recounted in this section is mostly drawn from Hpay Myint (1990 [1972], 1–16). Part of this book has been translated into English recently (see Kunsal Kassapa 2005). I did not, however, use or consult this translation.

3. Information about Gyan, *alias* Weikza Gyan, has been enriched with data provided by an interview with Gyan herself and by a book on the *weikza* U Nareinda (Yadanabonpyan Meditation Center's Support Association for Religion 1959, 23–40).

4. On the famous *weikza* Bobo Aung, including his multiplying the letter *wa* on the king's palace walls, see Htin Aung (1962, 57–60), Ferguson and Mendelson (1981, 67–68, 72), Foxeus (2011, 51–57, 112–114), and Rozenberg (2011, 102–104).

5. See Spiro (1967, 2–8; 1970, 5–6, 26–28).

6. See Spiro (1970, xi).

7. See Spiro (1967, 8–10; 1970, 15–16).

8. Spiro's comments on the *weikza* phenomenon are to be found in chapter 7, titled "Esoteric Buddhism: A Religion of Chiliastic Expectations," in his *Buddhism and Society* (1970, 170–187).

9. Ibid., 183–184.

10. *Yok-wada* means literally "materialism," in reference to Western philosophical materialism. Yet, in this context, it cannot be translated as such. The monk used a neologism, *seik-wada,* to contrast with *yok-wada.*

11. The question was inspired by a paper titled "Theravāda Philosophy 101: Teaching the Abhidhamma in Thailand," presented by Justin T. McDaniel at the conference *Exploring*

Theravāda Studies: Intellectual Trends and the Future of a Field of Study (Asia Research Institute, National University of Singapore, 12–14 August, 2004). See McDaniel (2008).

12. On Thailand's related economic and religious booms, see Jackson (1999).

13. Spiro (1970, 180n22).

14. See Sangermano (1995 [1833], 215–216).

15. Spiro (1970, 180; the square brackets are Spiro's). The correct spelling of the second name quoted is not U Kya Nyein, but U Kyaw Nyein.

16. Malinowski's tireless Socratic question is mentioned in André Devyver's introduction to the French translation of *Argonauts of the Western Pacific* (Devyver 1993 [1963], 11).

17. The material in this section pertains to a long-established concern for the problem of "belief" in anthropology. Critical works in this regard are by Evans-Pritchard (1937), Mannoni (1969), Needham (1972), Southwold (1979), Sperber (1982), Lenclud (1990), Bazin (1991), Pouillon (1993, 17–36), and Favret-Saada (1995 [1977]). If my distinction between belief and believing and my wish to study the passage from the former to the latter are primarily based on Burmese activities, representations, and discourses, they nonetheless converge with issues raised in the above works. But I would argue that establishing a clear terminological distinction between belief and believing allows the anthropologist to avoid some of the stalemates in which the authors of these works leave us marooned. Or at least it allows us to move beyond their analyses. This terminology, I should emphasize, has been devised independently of the ways others may have defined and used the term "believing." For instance, the well-known French sociologist of religion, Danièle Hervieu-Léger, drawing inspiration from the writings of Michel de Certeau, confers on the term a maximum semantic extension: "believing," for Hervieu-Léger (1993, 105–106), encompasses what I find it necessary to distinguish in terms of "belief," on the one hand, and "believing," on the other hand.

18. The Burmese communist stance toward Buddhism and Buddhist principles I discuss here reflects what an ex-member of rebel communist communities explained to me. (He, like the man in the story recounted here, ultimately became a staunch disciple of the Mebaygon *weikza* and was living at their monastery as a layman during my stays there.) Niklas Foxeus (2011, 372–375) presents another instance of the radical opposition between Buddhism and communism in his description of a *weikza* cult whose leaders have been engaged in a battle against "enemies" of Buddhism, including communism. Yet some Burmese ideologists, on the contrary, undertook from the 1930s onward to reconcile Marxism with Buddhism (see Sarkisyanz 1965, 166–179).

19. The formulaic phrase, "To be Burmese is to be Buddhist," may actually have been coined at the beginning of the twentieth century by the Burmese founders of the Young Men's Buddhist Association (Schober 2011, 66). Yet one never hears this phrase in Burma today; it does not seem to have become a Burmese saying strictly speaking.

20. If one follows Gustaaf Houtman (1990a) and Alexey Kirichenko (2009), the question commonly asked by Burmese today, "What is your religion?" (*ba batha kokwe tha*

le), would be, in its phrasing and spirit, an offshoot of the Christian missionizing and the British colonization of Burma in the nineteenth century. Under this foreign influence, the word *batha* (originally, "language") would have become the Burmese equivalent of the Western idea of "religion," hitherto absent from the Burmese context. In precolonial Burma, in this view, only the more general term "*thathana*," meaning the teaching given by a Buddha and its different expressions—doctrine, ethics, monastic community, institutions, relics, edifices, and so on—would have been in use. The historian Patrick Pranke (personal communication) notes, however, that "the word *batha* appears already (once) in the [religious chronicle] *Vamsadipani* (*circa* 1790), conveying a meaning akin to religion." If one adds that F. K. Lehman (personal communication), both an anthropologist and a linguist, remarks for his part that *batha* would actually be better translated as "doctrine" than as "religion," one gains a sense of how vexing this matter of Burmese usage is.

21. See Spiro (1967, 80–89).

22. The following description of Dragoness Mountain is taken from Hpay Myint (1990, 107–109). His source, he writes, is the *weikza* Bodaw Bo Htun Aung. Brown Mountain (Taung Nyo), where the *weikza* U Nareinda lives, is described in similar terms (Yadana-bonpyan Meditation Center's Support Association for Religion 1959, 14–19) as is, less elaborately, the Mountain of Splendid Trees (Thiri Yokkha Taung), where the *weikza* Maha Theikdi (master of the famous *weikza* Bame Hsayadaw) resides (Maha Myaing Hsayadaw 1962, vol. 1, 5–6).

23. The idea that something is strange or extraordinary is commonly expressed in Burmese using the verbs "*htuzan-*" or "*htukhya-*."

24. "Je sais bien, mais quand même . . ." ("I very well know, but still . . .") is the title of an article by Octave Mannoni (1969).

25. Ibid., 16; emphasis in original.

26. I dealt in quite a different manner with these feats and the way they contribute to believing's workings in an earlier article (Rozenberg 2009b).

27. U Kawwida's question to Aung Khaing regarding the trip to Magway with Victorious and me refers to what is described in Chapter 4, in the section "A demonstration of invulnerability."

28. On the definition of the *weikza* figure, including the distinction between mundane and supramundane *weikza,* see Rozenberg (2010b, 42–68), which includes relevant scholarly references.

29. See Vernant (1996, 339–351).

30. See Rozenberg (2010b, 30–39), which includes references to the work of other scholars.

31. *Hpaya-nge* is normally the Burmese word for *pacceka buddha,* an individual who attains enlightenment outside the time of a Buddhist dispensation; that is, by himself, without benefiting from the teachings of a Buddha (Ministry of Education 1993, 323). Such a

meaning, however, is not adequate here. I therefore opted for the literal translation "little Buddha."

32. Donald K. Swearer (2004, 109–115) presents the solutions given by some well-known Western students of Buddhism to the question as to the presence/absence of the Buddha. Swearer's entire book is concerned with the issue of how the presence of the Buddha is instantiated through the consecration ritual of the Master's image.

33. The fact that, from the point of view of Burmese Buddhists, the question is badly stated was also noted by Spiro (1970, 147–153), whose inquiries among Burmese Buddhists concerning the issue of whether the Buddha is dead or alive elicited diverse and contradictory answers.

34. For the Buddha's words about the uselessness of appointing a leader of the monastic community to succeed him, see Walshe (1995 [1987], 245) and Rhys Davids and Rhys Davids (1951 [1910], 107–109).

35. Rudolf Otto's ideas about the realm of the numinous are expressed in his famous book about "the idea of the holy" (Otto 1952).

36. My emphasis on the collective elaboration of reality, drawing on a concrete representation provided by the *weikza,* was stimulated by Edward Schieffelin's essay (1985), especially its illuminating conclusion.

37. Comments Niklas Foxeus (2011, 130–138) made on the subject of supernatural powers in Buddhism, both Burmese and Pali, alerted me to my regrettable ignorance, at the time when I wrote the discussion that appears here, of some relevant work. Particularly germane is an article by Phyllis Granoff about how Buddhist texts approach "the ambiguity of miracles." Granoff (1996, 79–88) shows that the writers of ancient Buddhist texts shared today's Burmese Buddhists' concern with the source of miracles and supernatural powers when trying to interpret their significance. Also of note is a special section of the *Journal of the International Association of Buddhist Studies* dedicated to "miracles and superhuman powers in South and Southeast Asian Buddhist traditions" (Fiordalis 2010 [2011]).

38. See Shwe Zan Aung (1912).

39. See Frazer (1922, 48–60).

40. I have been helped here by John Holt's inspiring work in which he emphasizes the centrality of soteriology for the definition of what is religious and what is not in the Theravādin Sinhalese context (Holt 1991).

41. In the index to *Buddhism and Society,* the entry "magician" refers the reader to "*weikza*" (1970, 502). In this book, Spiro qualifies the *weikza* phenomenon as "anti-Buddhist" (ibid., 164).

42. Michael M. Ames, in his essay "Buddha and the Dancing Goblins: A Theory of Magic and Religion" (1964), based on his research on Sri Lankan Buddhism, formulated an approach that is more sophisticated than the dualistic opposition between the mundane

and the supramundane. He suggested that magic or "magical rituals" (in this case, healing rituals taking the form of spirit propitiation ceremonies) should be taken as "transitional devices that mediate between the profane world and sacred Buddhist concerns" (ibid., 80). His, however, is a structural approach built on a distinction between the functions of two complementary ritual systems, Buddhism and the spirits cults, so much so that the potential existence of phenomena that would arouse contrasting interpretations (are they magical or religious?) by Sri Lankan Buddhists is passed over in complete silence, and the mundane (or in this author's terminology, magical) component of the Buddhist monks' activities is ignored.

43. Works mentioned here (some of which are referred to elsewhere in Chapter 1) almost all relate to the issue of religion, magic, and science or to the issue of belief and believing. These are Malinowski (1935, 1948), Evans-Pritchard (1937), Weber (1958), Lévi-Strauss (1963, 1966), Lévy-Bruhl (1966 [1910]), Spiro (1967, 1970), Mauss and Hubert (1972 [1902–1903]), Needham (1972), Tambiah (1990), Hume (1992), and Horton (1993).

44. The very common practice of *yadaya* consists, as a general principle, of an action intended to influence the course of fate—either prophylactically, in order to avoid strokes of bad luck, or *a posteriori,* in order to alleviate some misfortune. *Yadaya* is often defined as a way to fight against "bad karma" (*kan hso-*) and a way to attenuate "suffering" (*dokkha*) in the Buddhist sense of the term; that is, all sources of dissatisfaction or sorrow. People don't say in Burmese "to make a *yadaya,*" but rather "to crush something with a *yadaya*" (*yadaya khyay-*), in the sense of getting rid of a real or virtual problem by means of a specific procedure (see Tosa 2005, Leehey 2010 [especially 124–136], and Rozenberg 2011).

45. According to Burmese astrology, a week has eight days, Wednesday being divided into two. Each day corresponds to a planet and a direction. When people go to a pagoda, they will usually choose to be seated at the place whose direction corresponds to their day of birth.

46. The Five Precepts are those that every Buddhist layperson should theoretically respect: to abstain from killing any living being, from stealing, from adultery, from telling lies, and from taking any intoxicant.

47. A "declaration of truth" consists of stating, in front of a Buddha altar or a pagoda, one's virtuous deeds (performed or yet to be performed, in accordance with a vow / resolution) and the wish to obtain specific benefits as a consequence of those deeds.

48. The five Buddhas are the five Buddhas of this world cycle: Kaukkathangon/Kakusandha, Gawnagon/Konāgāmana, Katthapa/Kassapa, Gawtama/Gotama, and (still to appear) Areinmaydayya/Arimetteya.

49. These are the five common kinds of *weikza,* defined according to the technique mastered by the individual.

50. Twenty-seven is an auspicious number, because two plus seven equals nine, the most auspicious number for Burmese Buddhists.

51. *Arahan* is the shortened Pali characterization of the first of the Nine Supreme Qualities of the Buddha. It is common to use such shortened characterizations of these qualities to recite one's prayer beads.

52. One hundred and eight is an auspicious number, referring both to the 108 signs inscribed on the Buddha's footprints and to the figure nine (1+8=9). The Burmese word for bamboo (ဝါး) is made of the consonant *wa* (ဝ), which is associated with a person born on Wednesday morning. In addition, fresh leaves (*nyunt*) symbolize the newly born and undamaged, the best in other words, in contrast to the state of a sick person.

53. According to a monk knowledgeable in Pali, the form "*bokdaw*" corresponds to the nominative declension of the noun *bokda*. For the accusative, it would be *bokdan*. And so on. The remainder of the sentence (*aung byi*) is not in Pali, but in Burmese.

54. See Lévi-Strauss (1963). The three short following quotations are from pp. 198–199.

55. I should note that I make this comparison without raising the question of the validity of Claude Lévi-Strauss's characterization, which has been disputed. Among others, Michael Taussig (1987, 460–461), calling into question Lévi-Strauss's interpretation, pointed out that the Cuna shaman's special language is probably not understood by the patient.

56. See Malinowski (1935, 55).

57. This idea stands in contrast with David N. Gellner's approach, whereby he distinguishes three kinds of religion: soteriological (or salvation), instrumental, and social (or communal). He classifies curative rites, as well as those concerning success on an exam or in business, in the category of instrumental religion, without taking into account that what he calls instrumental religion may in certain circumstances actually be used to express a soteriological reality. He indeed insists on what he considers to be the much neater boundary between soteriology and worldly religion in Theravada Buddhism than in Mahayana Buddhism (Gellner 2001, 14, 70–71, 93–95). Gellner's approach is quite similar to that of Spiro (1970, 29–187). Spiro distinguished, famously, between four kinds of Buddhism—Nibbanic Buddhism, Kammatic Buddhism, Apotropaic (Magical) Buddhism, and Esoteric Buddhism—thereby ignoring some elements that make of Buddhism a single whole (for a criticism of his work in this respect, see Lehman 1972, 377). The distinction made by these authors between magical (or instrumental) Buddhism and soteriological/ Nibbanic Buddhism originates in part in the Weberian paradigm (see the discussion on this paradigm later in the present chapter). In a work in progress, I show how this misleading distinction has been pervasive in the approach to various cults from Theravadin Southeast Asia that are analogous to *weikza* cults.

The idea that the *weikza*'s action, in the end, although it has a curative aim and is therefore instrumental (mundane), is endowed with a mystical signification and is therefore soteriological (supramundane), may also be compared with John Clifford Holt's discussion of the categories *laukika* (mundane) and *lōkōttara* (supramundane) in the context of Sinhalese religion (Holt 1991, 19–26). Holt posits that these categories or orientations "are not … mutually exclusive or essentially contrastive in nature" but, "rather, complementary" (ibid., 25). "For example," he writes, "the curing of physical illness is a *laukika* concern but also an existential requirement for one to be in a condition to make spiritual progress. Illness is also a form of *dukkha* (suffering). *Laukika* acts, therefore, may also be regarded as 'religious acts' insofar as they inhibit the experience of *dukkha* and ultimately serve a *lōkōttara* purpose, even indirectly" (ibid., 24). What this conceptualization misses, however, is precisely the potential mystical/soteriological signification of curative acts themselves, beyond the immediate contribution they make to the well-being of Buddhists.

58. Here I use the account given to me by Doctor Sein Yi of his first encounter with the Mebaygon *weikza*. It differs in some particulars, although not in spirit, from the account he provided thirty years earlier to Hpay Myint (1990 [1972], 158–187).

59. See Aristote (2008, 115).

60. Rhys Davids and Stede (1972 [1921–1925], 710).

61. See Horner (1940, 176–177).

62. For instances of the mention of the eighteen *sippa* in the *Jātaka,* see Cowell (1895, 126, 203, 285).

63. Rhys Davids (1925 [1890], 6).

64. Quotations from the *Brahma-gāla Sutta* are formulas repeatedly stated in the text (see Rhys Davids 1923 [1899], 26–55).

65. Ibid., 69.

66. Ibid., 76–95.

67. U Kawwida's words are quoted by Hpay Myint (1990 [1972], 277–278).

68. Any student of Buddhism will recognize here a contradistinctive reference to the title of Walpola Rahula's classical work *What the Buddha Taught* (1959).

69. To summarize the episode of Pukkusa's conversion, I have relied on the translations of the *Mahā Parinibbāna Sutta* by Maurice Walshe (1995 [1987], 258–260) and T. W. and C. A. F. Rhys Davids (1951 [1910], 141–145). The words pronounced by Pukkusa are from Walshe's translation (1995 [1987], 259).

70. Rhys Davids and Rhys Davids (1951 [1910], 144n1).

71. This and the following paragraphs offer a brief and incomplete presentation of some orientations in the early Western study of Buddhism. For more complete critical approaches to the early Western study of Buddhism, see Reynolds (1976, 37–40), Almond (1988), Hallisey (1995), and Schopen (1997 [1991]).

72. Weber (1958, 225).

73. For the successive quotations from Oldenberg's work, see Oldenberg (1928 [1882], 184–187).

74. Ibid., 81.

75. For Senart's methodological statements, see Senart (1882, xi–xii).

76. Mus (1990 [1935], *50).

77. For the interpretation of the seven first steps of the Buddha, see ibid., *66–*71.

78. Mus speaks of the "mystical imagination" of ancient India (ibid., *64).

79. For this and the previous quotation, see ibid., *127; see also *197–*198.

80. See Rozenberg (2005a) for a discussion on the relation between the anthropology of Buddhism and Buddhology.

81. See Strong (2001, 107–112, 120).

82. See Ray (1999 [1994], 44–78). The biography is the *Buddhacarita,* written by Aśvaghoṣa by the first century of our era.

83. Ibid., 51.

84. Ibid.

85. Ibid., 61.

86. Ibid., 62.

87. In his entry, "Magic (Buddhist)," written for the *Encyclopaedia of Religion and Ethics* (1915), Louis de La Vallée Poussin took as an example of "magic powers" the ten extraordinary powers (*iddhi*) of the Buddhist saint.

88. Swearer (2004, 28–29).

89. Ibid., 3–4.

90. Ibid., 14.

91. I would also refer the reader to my study of Buddhist sainthood in Burma (Rozenberg 2010b), entitled *Renunciation and Power,* which shows how in the case of contemporary saints what might look like a "paradox" turns out, on closer examination, to be perfectly coherent.

Chapter 2: Being a Disciple, Fashioning a Cult

1. According to a Burmese Buddhist manual written in English, the Nine Supreme Qualities (or Virtues) of the Buddha are as follows: (1) "he is worthy of special veneration by all men, devas and brahmas"; (2) "he has fully realized all that should be known by himself"; (3) "he is proficient in supreme knowledge and in the practice of morality"; (4) "he speaks only what is true and beneficial"; (5) "he knows all the three Lokas, namely *satta-loka*–the world of living beings, *saṅkhāra-loka*–the world of conditioned things, and *okāsa-loka*–the planes of existences"; (6) "he is the incomparable charioteer who is adept in taming who deserve to be tamed"; (7) "he is the guiding teacher of all devas and men"; (8)

"he himself is the Enlightened One, and he can enlighten others"; and (9) "he is the most exalted and most glorious One" (Ministry of Religious Affairs 1997, 175–177).

2.   For the Burmese system of correspondences between days, planets, and letters, see Shway Yoe (1963 [1909], 4–8).

3.   On the uses of *payeik* (*paritta* in Pali) in the Burmese context, see Spiro (1970, 140–161, 248–250, 263–271).

4.   On Shin Thiwali (Sīvalī Thera in Pali), see Duroiselle (1922–1923).

5.   The list of the ten *theikdi* characteristic of the *weikza* may vary somewhat according to interlocutors. A Burmese text translated by Patrick Pranke provides the following list: "overcoming old age; freedom from disease; the ability to extend one's life span beyond one hundred to more than a thousand or even ten thousand years; the ability to transform nonprecious metals into gold and silver; the ability to make oneself dear to all living beings; immunity from weapons, fire and poison, whereby the body cannot be stabbed, cut by blades, nor injured by blows; the ability to pass through the earth and mountains, and to travel above the surface of the ground; the ability to fly through the sky; the ability to travel over water as if it were solid earth; the ability to disappear, and to create duplicate bodies of oneself at will" (Pranke 1995, 350).

6.   Most of this section appeared as a separate article (Rozenberg 2010a).

7.   To date we have only summary descriptions of the Burmese practice of alchemy. These are, in the chronological order of their original dates of publication: Shway Yoe (1963 [1909], 401–405), Htin Aung (1962, 41–54), Nash (1973 [1965], 190–192), Spiro (1970, 164–171), and Tosa (2005, 160).

The origins of Burmese alchemy are obscure. Htin Aung (1962, 41) declares, without citing any source, that Burmese alchemy derives from Indian alchemy. Melford E. Spiro (1970, 165) argues that it derives "probably from Chinese and Indian alchemy." These two statements are no doubt based on certain similarities among elements of these different types of alchemy. It remains a question—impossible to resolve—what among these similarities follows from cultural diffusion and what follows from comparable but independent developments in each context.

8.   The idea that the word *aggiyat* means "art of fire" is a folk (and nonetheless significant) etymology based on the homonymy between အဂ္ဂိရတ် (correct spelling) and အဂ္ဂိရပ် ("wrong" spelling), *yat* (ရပ်) referring to any art. The true etymology of *aggiyat* remains unknown, as we do not know what *yat* (ရပ်) refers to.

9.   For a list of the nine "bodies" (*yok-dat*) and nine (or twelve) "minds" (*nan-dat*), see Htin Aung (1962, 47–48).

10.   On U Paramawunnatheikdi, see Schober (1989, 285–293).

11.   On Burmese astrology, see Bernot (1967, vol. 1, 154–197), Schober (1980), Tosa (2005), and Coderey (2011, 67–73, *passim*).

12. Doctor Sein Yi's misadventure echoes a famous story in the popular historiography of the medieval period of Bagan (see Htin Aung 1962, 51–54, and Spiro 1970, 167).

13. See Eliade (1977, 137).

14. The Major explained to me that he had been told Panaikkhaya's story by the *weikza* U Pandita. The story, he added, could also be found in royal chronicles (see Pe Maung Tin and Luce 1960 [1923], 105–106).

15. The idea of a "dynamic" conception of language was borrowed (unconsciously) from Bronislaw Malinowski (1935, 52).

16. The designation "superstitious function" was coined with a hint of mischievousness. Lévi-Straussian structural anthropology called "symbolic function" the unconscious ability of the human mind to impose formal meaning onto reality (see Izard and Bonte 1979, 12). The idea that there exists an underlying structure to any cultural elaboration has made it possible to make sense of narratives or practices that anthropologists and especially folklorists had sometimes assimilated to various manifestations of primitive or popular superstition. To use the expression "superstitious function" amounts to combining two phrases, "symbolic function" and "superstition," which, in the history of anthropology, pertain to two antithetical approaches.

17. On Setkya Min, the Prince of the Universe, and Burmese expectations of his return, see Mendelson (1961a, 1961b), Sarkisyanz (1965, 149–165), Spiro (1970, 171–180), Ferguson and Mendelson (1981, 67–68, 72), Prager (2003), Candier (2005), and Foxeus (2011).

18. Regarding the *dat yaik dat hsin* procedure and the way in which the notion of *dat* informs it, see also Tosa (2005).

19. Gustaaf Houtman (1990b) and Ingrid Jordt (2007) deal at length with the spread of meditation practice among the laity in twentieth-century Burma.

20. For Major Zaw Win's account of U Oktamagyaw's life-prolonging ceremony, see Hpay Myint (1990, 397–487). The biography of U Oktamagyaw is found on pp. 470–485.

21. The remarkable action attributed to Kyin Myaing by her children is not mentioned in either account of U Pandita's life-prolonging ceremony (Hpay Myint 1990, 304–394; Ohn n.d.).

22. For references on Bobo Aung, see note 4 of Chapter 1; on Bo Ming Gaung, see Mendelson (1963, 798–803). Concerning Bo Paukhsein, see the section "Fashioning a cult" of Chapter 2.

23. Here I simply reproduce the contents of conversations with a few Burmese Buddhist nuns. Ingrid Jordt (1988), Hiroko Kawanami (1990, 1997), and Laure Carbonnel (2009) provide a much more systematic account of nuns in the Burmese Buddhist context.

24. Bodaw Bo Htun Aung sometimes relates his own biography on the occasion of his appearances in the flesh. It can also be found in Hpay Myint's book (1990 [1972], 88–111).

25. The course attended by Major Zaw Win was most likely held at the Central School of Political Science established in Mingaladon in 1963 to train members of the Burma Socialist Programme Party (Fistié 1985, 186).

26. On the Security and Administrative Committees, see Bunge (1983, 59).

27. The demonstrations of December 1974 are briefly described by Pierre Fistié (1985, 275–276).

28. The booklet, written by Thaw Zin (1965) on the occasion of the "exit" of Bo Paukhsein, has recently been incorporated into a larger book about Bo Paukhsein (Win Tin U 2002), wherein it constitutes the first two chapters.

29. On Shin Eizagona, see Htin Aung (1962, 51–54).

30. For developments on Muslims in Burma and Buddhist attitudes toward them, see also Foxeus (2011, 371–372, 375–383), who provides all the relevant references (ibid., 376n1345). A study of Burmese Hindus and Hinduism remains to be done.

31. "Peace and Development Councils" was the name given to governing bodies from the state level to the local level between 1997 and 2011.

32. On the notion of *dat,* see also Tosa (2005).

33. On the Burmese physiological conception of disease and its relation to *dat,* see Coderey's synthesis (2011, 53–58).

34. The notion of *pahtan hset* is often taken by Burmese to be synonymous with *yay set,* literally "drop of water;" that is, the belief that two individuals or more, who are joined to one another in relations of kinship, friendship, or love in their current lives, performed a meritorious deed together in a past existence, a deed marked by the pouring of water on earth. Both notions express the principle of a predestination of current relationships or encounters between people. On *yay set,* see Kumada (2001, 91–126).

35. For more comprehensive information regarding Burmese conceptions of karma (*kan*), see the entry for "karma" in Melford E. Spiro's book index (1970) and that for "kan" in Manning Nash's book index (1973 [1965]).

36. The Burmese conception of fate stands in contrast here with the Western notion of fate as illustrated by Yvonne Verdier's anthropological reflections on the idea of fate both in a French village (Verdier 1979, 77–82) and in Thomas Hardy's literary work (Verdier 1995, 29–168; see also the introduction by Claudine Fabre-Vassas and Daniel Fabre to this posthumous book of Verdier).

Chapter 3: The Possessed

1. The following narrative of Htun Yin's encounter with the *weikza* is taken from Hpay Myint (1990 [1972], 112–121).

2. The first paragraph of the section is an implicit contrast between possession by a *weikza* (*dat si-*) and possession by a spirit from the pantheon of the Thirty-Seven Lords (*nat pu-*). Such a contrast is often made by disciples of *weikza* cults with the intention of promoting the former and disparaging the latter. For instance, the book on U Nareinda, the *weikza* who possessed the young woman Gyan in the 1950s, puts forward a systematic physical and phenomenological comparison and distinction between the two modes of possession. (Significantly, it also equates possession by a spirit with possession by a witch [*sun pu-*].) The comparison is said to have been formulated and elaborated on by the *weikza* U Nareinda while he preached through Gyan so that people would not confuse the two modes of possession: possession by a *weikza* and possession by a spirit or a witch (Yadanabonpyan Meditation Center's Support Association for Religion 1959, 69–74). Major Zaw Win expounded similar ideas to me. Bénédicte Brac de la Perrière, who has written extensively on possession in the Thirty-Seven Lords' spirit cult (see especially Brac de la Perrière 1989), recently started to study the *weikza* phenomenon and to compare modes of possession by *weikza* and spirits (Brac de la Perrière 2012). She argues that the features of possession by *weikza,* which would actually be closer, technically, to "inspiration" than to possession (on this distinction, see Rouget 1980, 54–58), would have taken shape through a process of differentiation from the standard occurrence of possession in the Burmese context, possession by a spirit.

3. The committee that tested U Nareinda and the intervention of exorcist monks are mentioned in the book on this *weikza* and his teachings (Yadanabonpyan Meditation Center's Support Association for Religion 1959, 25–26). Gyan also told Victorious and me about the investigating committee.

4. The exorcism of Saturday's Son is narrated by Hpay Myint (1990 [1972], 129–132). For a case of possession by a *okzazaung* and its exorcism, see Spiro (1967, 174–203).

5. The religious reform of 1980 led to the expulsion from the monastic community of more than three hundred monks and novices judged guilty of grave disciplinary violations, in most cases for having engaged in sexual relations. It also involved an inquiry into *weikza* cults and their leaders, who were deemed to profess heterodox views. On this reform, see Tin Maung Maung Than (1988; 1993) and Lubeigt (1990).

6. Under the powerful impulse of the government and especially that of Prime Minister U Nu (see Smith 1965, 140–229), the 1950s were a time of great expansion in every religious domain, including the practice of lay meditation and the *weikza* cults.

7. The "eleven fires" (*mi hsetit ba*) are greed, hatred, delusion, birth, old age, death, anxiety, grief, suffering, helplessness, and distress (Awbatha 1955, 411). An identical list was given to me by a disciple of the Mebaygon *weikza*.

8. The book on U Nareinda was published by the Yadanabonpyan Meditation Center's Support Association for Religion (1959).

Chapter 4: In Quest of Invulnerability

1.   On cabalistic diagrams (*in, sama*), see also Patton (2012).

2.   The "101 populations" (*lu-myo 101 ba*) is a standard expression to designate the entirety of the world's population, that is, the seven Burmese populations, the four Mon populations, the thirty Shan populations, and the sixty foreign populations (Awbatha 1955, 479).

3.   The number "84,000," sometimes abridged to "80,000," is the commonly cited number of persons who shall become *weikza*. The number derives from the "84,000 sections" of the Pali canon.

4.   Another version of the future Buddha's trial can be found in the biography of the Buddha translated from the Burmese by Bishop Bigandet in the nineteenth century. In this version, the young prince offers evidence of his competence in the eighteen sciences not on the occasion of his marriage but after it, when some members of his family voice some doubts regarding his personal abilities and therefore his capacity to succeed his father, the king (Bigandet 1878 [1866], 55–56).

5.   Awbatha (1955, 13–16) provides three different lists of the eighteen sciences, drawn from three different sources. On the eighteen sciences in canonical texts and in Burmese texts from the fifteenth century onward, see Lammerts (2010, 401–414).

6.   Aung Thaung, who is given to few words in any case, has little to say about his past and about the history of the Tactical Encirclement Group. A biography of the man has, however, been written and published privately for the edification of members of the group, to whom it is sold. It was a very pleasant surprise for Victorious and me to come upon its author when we went to visit Aung Thaung a month and a half after our trip to Magway University with Great-Master Aung Khaing. We had heard about the work at the Mebaygon Monastery, but had been denied access to it in the absence of the author's express permission. The writer, an official retired from the Department of Commerce, had never been a member of the Setka Byuha Ahpwe. But as a writer specializing in Buddhism, in the late 1980s he had heard about Aung Thaung's extraordinary healing powers, and, obviously in search of new topics, had decided to come to meet him. In 1995, he published his work on Aung Thaung and his younger brother, Khin Maung Yin, who has helped him lead the group since its creation, as well as on the Tactical Encirclement Group's practices. I had actually made a special trip to Kyaukme (a town in Shan State, on the road between Pyin Oo Lwin [Maymyo] and Lashio) to meet the author, to discuss his research, and get a copy of his book. To no avail: all I had was the pseudonym the author had used when he published the work, and despite the help of local men of letters, it had turned out to be impossible to figure out his real name and his address. After I had pretty much given up all hope, Victorious and I came upon him when we got to Aung Thaung's. You can imagine the delight this caused me, a treasure seeker in my own way. Better still: the man was waiting for me! He had heard from a member of the Tactical Encirclement Group that I had talked about going to see Aung Thaung while we were in Mebaygon, and he had come on a visit under his own steam in order to meet me. Nevertheless, he had waited patiently for close to

two weeks not to place a copy of his work ceremoniously in my hands, but rather to talk business. I had explained in Mebaygon that I had carried out earlier research in Burma, and some people, understanding that much money and effort had been expended to undertake this new project on the four *weikza,* imagined that I must have made a fortune on the earlier project. If I was so anxious to get a copy of the man's work, it was obviously in order to translate it and make money off it. That at least was what a member of the Tactical Encirclement Group had managed to talk the man into thinking. So the writer approached Victorious to let him know his terms. He had first intended to set the price for his work at $10,000 but would, he said, settle if need be for $2,000. Victorious made no headway trying to explain to him what my research consisted of. The man wouldn't budge. He was sure that I traveled with thousands of dollars in my wallet to pay for my ethnographic purchases. I never got a copy of the work.

7.   I should mention that I did not obtain the secret initiation diagram by stealth. It was willingly given to me by Aung Thaung himself.

8.   Sangermano (1995 [1833], 148–149), who stayed in Burma from 1783 to 1808, writes of some invulnerability procedures. For more detailed descriptions, see Scott and Hardiman (1900–1901, part 1, vol. 2, 77–82), Shway Yoe (1963 [1909], 39–47), Hildburgh (1909), Hla Baw (1940), Nash (1973 [1965], 181–182), and Spiro (1967, 35–37).

9.   See Snodgrass (1997 [1827], 64–71).

10.   Ibid., 70.

11.   Ibid., 70–71. The end of the last sentence has been cut.

12.   A history of movements of resistance to colonial occupation has been written by Parimal Ghosh (2000), who provides references to existing sources in English. However, except for Saya San Rebellion (ibid., 145–179) and, marginally, two other earlier occurrences in 1857 (ibid., 59–60) and in the 1920s (ibid., 136), this author makes no mention of the uses of invulnerability techniques. In relation to Saya San Rebellion, he refers to several examples of desperate attacks by rebels equipped with invulnerability charms (ibid., 154, 157, 167). But most rebel groups, from 1885 onward, instead used the "hit and run tactic" (ibid., 82).

13.   The phrase "immemorial beliefs of the countryside" is from Maurice Collis (1996 [1938], 211) and "superstitious belief in spells" (*la superstition des sortilèges*) is from C. V. Warren (1938, 54). Maurice Collis was a magistrate in Yangon at the beginning of Saya San Rebellion, and C. V. Warren worked for a forestry company in Burma in the early 1930s. I was made aware of these sources by Maitrii Aung-Thwin's PhD dissertation, now published as a book (Aung-Thwin 2011). In it, Aung-Thwin offers a critical deconstruction of the colonial and scholarly readings of the "Saya San Rebellion" (a late designation dating back only to 1958, as he shows), including interpretations of the use of invulnerability techniques in the course of the rebellion.

14.   See Ba U (1959 [1958], 109). Again, I am indebted to Maitrii Aung-Thwin for this reference. In his work, the author disentangles the equation made by the British authorities

between tattooing as an invulnerability technique and rebellion (2011, 96–97, 122–125). Still, in a way, the British were not so wrong in taking them to be equivalent.

15. On Nga Hpon's attempt to overthrow the king, see Koenig (1990, 209) and Toe Hla (2002 [1993], 212).

16. For the burying of diagrams by Bodawhpaya and then Mindon during the construction of their royal palace, see Toe Hla (2002 [1993], 212).

17. On the use made by criminals of invulnerability techniques, see Hla Baw (1940).

18. Shway Yoe (1963 [1909], 47).

19. Thein Maung (1991, 77–78).

20. Snodgrass (1997 [1827], 114).

21. The death of Maha Bandoola is described by Snodgrass (1997 [1827], 173–177).

22. The resistance movements in the Minbu District are described by Scott and Hardiman (1900–1901, part 1, vol. 1, 134–137, 167–169), who also write about the techniques of the monk assisting Bo Swe (ibid., part 1, vol. 2, 81–82).

23. Most of this section has been published in the French language as part of an article about the idea of "race" in contemporary Buddhist Burma (Rozenberg 2008).

24. Witatuba's story was apparently a standard element in preaching in the 1950s—at the time of the advent of the Mebaygon cult—because it is referred to, without any further details (as if the story was well known by the reader), in the book on the *weikza* U Nareinda (Yadanabonpyan Meditation Center's Support Association for Religion 1959, 59).

25. See Cowell (1901, 91–96) for a translation of the *Bhadda-Sāla-Jātaka* (no. 465) in the preamble to which the massacre of the Sākya is recounted, and Malalasekera (1960 [1937], vol. 2, 876–877, 971–972) for a summary of the passage in question in the commentary of the *Dhammapada*. See also the comparative analysis by André Bareau (1981) of the sources expounding the massacre of the Sākya.

26. My information on the incorporation of this story into Burmese poetry and chronicles comes from Pe Maung Tin in his introduction to the partial translation of the *Glass Palace Chronicle* he made with G. H. Luce (Pe Maung Tin and Luce 1960 [1923], xiii–xx; see also Koenig 1990, 87). Pe Maung Tin reviews various chronicles, making general summaries of their contents. In reading his presentation of the *New Pagan Chronicle* (a source I have not been able to look at), it is not very clear whether this chronicle contains, as is more probable, the full story of the massacre of the Sākya or only mentions the migration of the Sākya to Burma after the massacre (Pe Maung Tin and Luce 1960 [1923], xv–xvi). The *Arakanese (Rakhaing) Chronicle,* written before 1775, seems to include the story of Witatuba, if I read Pe Maung Tin's introduction (ibid., xviii) correctly.

27. For the account of the story in the *Glass Palace Chronicle,* see Pe Maung Tin and Luce (1960 [1923], 1–4). The claim that all Burmese kings descend from the Sākya is on p. 6.

28. On the song of the Do Bama movement, see Khin Yi (1988, 6–10). The Burmese version of the song is included in a supplement to the book, which I was not able to consult. I looked at the song in the entry relating to the Do Bama movement in the *Myanmar Encyclopaedia* (1961, 44).

29. A survey of a few scholarly works on Buddhism over the course of more than a century reveals the degree of uncertainty surrounding the exact nature of the Sākya group. Within the space of only two pages, Hermann Oldenberg (1928 [1882], 98–99) labels the Sākya, successively, as a "family," a "line," an "aristocratic community," a "race," and, finally, a "stock." G. P. Malalasekera (1960 [1937], volume II, 969) characterizes the Sākya as a "tribe" that "probably" included several clans (in Pali, *gottā*); nevertheless, the same author also mentions the Sākya's concern for "the purity of their race" (ibid., 970). Alfred Foucher (1993 [1949], 34) uses the phrase "oligarchic clan" about the Sākya and, when he wants to render more faithfully the Buddhist view, speaks of the "noblest of the race." André Bareau (1985, 16) takes on the label of "tribe," of which the Gotama formed one of the clans; elsewhere, in a collection of his articles, "race" and "tribe" appear alternatively (Bareau 1995, passim). Richard F. Gombrich (1995 [1988], 49, 236) uses the terms "community" or "people" and declares his distrust of the usual term, "tribe," which, he mentions, has no Sanskrit or Pali equivalent. Môhan Wijayaratna (1998, 13), who obviously sees the difficulty, confines himself to a cautious "country of the Sākya" and characterizes the Sākya as a group of "aristocratic warriors." Finally, the hesitation is tangible in John S. Strong's book about the Buddha's biography (2001, 35): on the same page, one finds, linked to the term Sākya, the terms "clan," "tribe," or "lineage," the last word referring to the Buddha's prestigious forebears.

30. For the etymology of *thakiwin,* see Ministry of Education (1993, 492), and for the translations of *vaṁsa,* see Rhys Davids and Stede (1972 [1921–1925], 590).

31. For a scholarly summary of the origins of the Sākya label and for the related Buddhist textual references, see Malalasekera (1960 [1937], vol. 2, 970).

Here I translate the expression *amyo hpyet-* literally, but this expression also has the metaphorical meaning of "bringing dishonour to one's family, ancestry, race or nation" (Ministry of Education 1993, 580).

32. On the link between the Sākya and Mahāsammata, see Mingun Hsayadaw (1990–1998, vol. 2, first part [1994], 7) and Malalasekera (1960 [1937], vol. 2, 565–566).

33. The Buddhicization process does not only involve the elimination of alternative religious identities. It also implies a nationwide homogenization of Buddhist practices; that is, the erasing of regional Buddhist particularities (for some examples, see Robinne 2000, and Mersan 2005, 131–132).

34. On the government's policy and discourse since 1988 in relation to the combined issue of national origins and national unity, see Houtman (1999, especially pp. 142–147).

35. This concluding section in particular, and the entire Chapter 4 in general, takes up the thread of some personal reflections on the Burmese political situation (see Rozenberg

2005b, 2009b). The general thrust of these reflections is a reformulation of the idea of "voluntary servitude" initially put forward by Étienne de La Boétie (2002 [1976]; 1983). My understanding of La Boétie's work has been helped by several commentarial texts: the texts by various authors included with an edition of the work (La Boétie 2002 [1976]) and Simone Goyard-Fabre's introduction to another edition (La Boétie 1983). A passage from one of these commentarial texts, a text by Miguel Abensour and Marcel Gauchet, was used as an epigraph to Chapter 4 in an earlier version of *The Immortals:* "Thus it is impossible to understand *servitude* as *passivity.* A people's servitude is not definable by reference to people's not thinking of insurrection, to the fact that people do not always revolt. People do revolt and in a sense never stop revolting. But the question of servitude stands apart from the potential for uprisings. It is important to understand that servitude inhabits even the very moment of revolt, that it accompanies it the length of its journey. Servitude remains inside the movement that wishes to produce freedom. The real measures that would give rise to freedom have not yet been taken, and therein lies the enigma" (translated from Abensour and Gauchet 2002 [1976], 30).

36. Instances of such a tendency toward dichotomizing the tyrants and the tyrannized in the treatment of the contemporary Burmese political situation can be found in two works, one by Gustaaf Houtman (1999) and another by Monique Skidmore (2004), however different they may otherwise be. Ingrid Jordt (2007) and Ardeth Maung Thawnghmung (2004) offer a different, more grassroots, and less politically correct approach, closer to the one that I believe necessary to pursue.

37. La Boétie (2002 [1976], 194–195).

38. On belief, which La Boétie names "credulity," see ibid., 227.

39. For relevant passages, see Godelier (1992 [1984], 23–25, 205–206). The quotation is from p. 24. The author does not cite La Boétie, and I do not know whether or in what way La Boétie figured in his thinking.

40. The exact expression of La Boétie concerns liberation and goes as follows: "from a beast once again becoming a man" (La Boétie 2002 [1976], 199).

41. The paradox lies in the association of the terms (and situations) "invulnerability" and "servitude," of course, but I also implicitly refer here to a scholarly approach to invulnerability techniques emphasizing their importance in "peasant rebellions throughout Southeast Asia" (Turton 1991, 156), rather than their disciplinary social and political effects.

42. The phrase "unitary whole" ("l'Un" in French) refers to La Boétie's work and a comment on it made by Pierre Clastres (2002 [1976]).

43. Elsewhere, I have set out briefly my conception of "anthropological characters" (Rozenberg 2010a, 191–194). On the parable-like or allegorical dimension of anthropological discourse, see Clifford (1986).

Chapter 5: Trial by Fire

1. On illegal lotteries in Burma, see Rozenberg (2005b).

2. The detailed account of U Pandita's life-prolonging ceremony in this and the following sections relies mainly on the descriptions by Hpay Myint (1990, 304–394) and Ohn (n.d.). The 1990 edition of Hpay Myint's book also includes an account of U Oktamagyaw's 1989 life-prolonging ceremony written by Major Zaw Win (Hpay Myint 1990, 397–487). Another disciple of the cult chronicled U Kawwida's 1994 life-prolonging ceremony (Mandala Than Hla 1997).

3. The idea that the maximum length of a *weikza*'s life is one thousand years is not very common today, but it was also present in U Nareinda's cult (Yadanabonpyan Meditation Center's Support Association for Religion 1959, 45). The Mebaygon cult of the four *weikza*—that is, the undertaking of their medium Saturday's Son—seems to owe much to this earlier, nearby cult.

4. The Nine Precepts are to abstain from killing any living being, from stealing, from performing a sexual act, from telling lies, from taking an intoxicant, from taking food after midday, from attending entertainment shows (dance, singing, etc.) and from using perfume or other cosmetics, from staying on a luxury seat or bed, and to meditate on loving-kindness.

5. According to Awbatha (1955, 570), the seven qualities of the virtuous man (*thudawgaung okza yadana khunit ba*) are equivalent to the seven qualities of the noble man (*ariya okza khunit ba*), which are faith in the Three Gems and in karmic law, morality, shame before bad things, fear of bad things, the supranormal ability to see and hear things, generosity, and understanding, in the sense of spiritual accomplishment (ibid., 47).

6. The phrase "telepathic guidance" (of Saturday's Son by a *weikza*) is a translation of the Burmese phrase *dat hsaung-*, which, Hpay Myint explains (1990, 365), is one of the three ways the four *weikza* manifest themselves: the first mode is appearing in the flesh; the second is possessing Saturday's Son (*dat si-*); and the third is by intimating that, although they do not appear in the flesh, they are present thanks to a connection established with Saturday's Son (*dat hsaung-*).

7. Most of the following four paragraphs is taken from Rozenberg (2011).

8. The name for the trial by fire (*hpo win-*) actually has two possible spellings in Burmese, with exactly the same pronunciation. The first spelling (ဖို ဝင်-) means "to enter the hearth/fire" and refers to the event's actual procedures. The second spelling (ဖိုလ် ဝင်-) means "to enter the state of fruition." This would normally mean attaining one of the four states leading to nirvana, but such an understanding would refer to the supramundane (*lawkoktara*) understanding of *hpo* (ဖိုလ်). The latter word has also a mundane (*lawki*) sense, referring to the fact of extending one's *weikza* life for another one thousand years so as to continue supporting religion and practicing meditation while awaiting the Buddha's final appearance (Ohn n.d., 54–56). I suspect that the second spelling is a reworking with the intent of equating the life-prolonging ceremony with a successful quest for nirvana. Interestingly,

the spelling of the phrase oscillates, without notice, between the two possibilities in the 1990 edition of Hpay Myint's book or, to be more precise, in Major Zaw Win's account of U Oktamagyaw's life-prolonging ceremony (1989) appended to this book. On p. 408, instead of ဓို ဝင် - as in the preceding pages (pp. 397–407), it suddenly becomes ဓိုလ် ဝင် - in the running head at the top of the page; it then reverts to the former from p. 414 onward. The same oscillation occurs again and again thereafter (from pp. 424–428, 440–444, 456–460, and 472–476). Maung Ohn (n.d.), in his account of U Pandita's life-prolonging ceremony, uses only the second spelling (ဓိုလ် ဝင် -).

9. See, in Chapter 2, the section titled "The art of self-fashioning," dealing with the practice of alchemy.

10. An example of a trial by fire is provided by Htin Aung (1962, 57–59), who also offers a brief description of a trial by earth (ibid., 43–44; see also Spiro 1970, 170). In these works, by contrast with the case of the Mebaygon cult, such trials are said to be the condition to become a fully accomplished *weikza* and to "exit" (and not to prolong the existence of someone who has already become a *weikza*). The book on the *weikza* U Nareinda puts forward a still different view. It restricts the necessity of a trial to one kind of *weikza,* the *weikza* of medicine (*hsay weikza*), who, it is declared, is unable, in contrast to the other kinds of *weikza,* to "exit alive" (*ashin htwet*) and must undergo such a trial to "exit dead" (*athay htwet*). It mentions the three kinds of trials (by fire, by earth, or by water) and describes the trial by fire (Yadanabonpyan Meditation Center's Support Association for Religion 1959, 51–55).

11. On Bobo Aung's obtaining the book of brass plates, see Htin Aung (1962, 57–59). Interestingly, the book was obtained from a *weikza* who had successfully undergone the trial by fire. Another instance of obtaining knowledge of the *weikza* arts through the gift of a manuscript by a full-fledged *weikza* can be found in the biography of the *weikza* Bame Hsayadaw (U Nandathara), who was born in 933 of the Burmese era or 1572 C.E. (see Maha Myaing Hsayadaw 1962, vol. 1, 5–8).

12. *Hson* is spelled differently in "Kahson" and in "to meet" (*hson-*), but the pronunciation is identical.

13. For the story of Byatwi and Byatta, see Htin Aung (1962, 67–73).

14. For a biography of Bame Hsayadaw, see Maha Myaing Hsayadaw (1962, vol. 1, 5–10).

15. "*Kyazan*" is normally written ကြာဆံ. But the common pronunciation is similar to ကြာစံ; hence, the portent with the verb *san-* (စံ -).

Bibliography

REFERENCES IN BURMESE

Awbatha (Ashin Awbatha Biwantha). 1955 (1317 Burmese era). *Dictionary of research.* Yangon: Pyinna Nanda Press (579 pages).

[အသျှင်ဩ ဘာသာဘိဝံသ ။ ၁၃၁၇ (၁၉၅၅) ။ သုတေသနသရုပ်ပြ အဘိဓါန် ။ ရန်ကုန်၊ ပညာနန္ဒ ပုံနှိပ်တိုက်]

Hpay Myint. 1990 (2nd ed.; 1st ed. 1972). *Biography of the great monk* weikza *venerable Pandita and biography of Bodaw Bo Htun Aung.* South Okkalapa (Yangon): Gaba Alin Yaung Press (487 pages).

[ဖေမြင့် ။ ၁၉၉၀ ။ ဝိဇ္ဇာရေ မဟာထေရ ဘဒ္ဒန္တပဏ္ဍိတ ထေရုပ္ပတ္တိ နှင့် ဘိုးတော် ဘိုးထွန်းအောင် ၏ အတ္ထုပ္ပတ္တိ ။ တောင် ဥက္ကလာပ၊ ကမ္ဘာ့အလင်းရောင်စာပေ]

Maha Myaing Hsayadaw (U Wannadaza). 1962 (1324 Burmese era, month of Thitingyut; third edition). *Treatise of the great monk Bame, alias Bame Weikza, on the great extraordinary powers.* Mandalay: Pitakatdaw Pyanpwayay Press (2 vols.: 138 and 139 pages).

[မဟာမြိုင်ဆရာတော် (ဦးဝဏ္ဏဇေ) ။ ၁၃၂၄ (၁၉၆၂)၊ သီတင်းကျွတ်လ ။ ဗားမဲ့ဆရာတော်ဘုရားကြီး ၏ ဗားမဲ့ဝိဇ္ဇာ အမည်ရှိသောမဟာသိဒ္ဓိကျမ်းရင်းကြီး ။ မန္တလေး၊ ပိဋကတ်တော်ပြန့်ပွားရေး ပုံနှိပ်တိုက်]

Mandala Than Hla. 1997. *Biography of the venerable Kawwida, genuine account of the* weikza *trial by fire, and biography of the great monk Saturday's Son.* Yangon: Tet Lan Press (251 pages).

[မဏ္ဍလာသန်းလှ ။ ၁၉၉၇ ။ ဘဒ္ဒန္တကောဝိဒ ထေရုပ္ပတ္တိ ၊ဝိဇ္ဇာမီးတုံကူးဖြစ်ရပ်မှန် နှင့် စနေသားဆရာတော် အတ္ထုပ္ပတ္တိ ။ ရန်ကုန်၊ တက်လမ်းစာပေ]

Myanmar Encyclopaedia. Vol. 5. 1961. Yangon: Sapay Beikman (500 pages).

[၁၉၆၁ ။ မြန်မာ့စွယ်စုံကျမ်း၊ အတွဲ ၅ ။ ရန်ကုန်၊ စာပေဗိမာန်]

Ohn (Maung). N.d. *Work, drawn from personal experience, on the stage of entering the state of fruition.* Published at the author's expense (148 pages).

[အုန်း (မောင်) ။ ကိုယ်တွေ့မှတ်တမ်း ဖိုလ်ဝင်စခန်း စာစောင်]

Thaw Zin. 1965 (1326 Burmese era). *A short history of the work for religion of the great monk U Paukhsein (U Weikzadara) from Yangon.* Yangon: Sape Press (20 pages).

[သော်ဇင် ။ ၁၃၂၆ (၁၉၆၅)၊ တပို့တွဲလ ။ ဘုန်းဘုရားကြီး ဦးပေါက်ဆိန် (ဦးဝိဇ္ဇာရေ) မဟာရန်ကုန် ၏ သာသနာ ပြု သမိုင်း အကျဉ်းချုပ် ။ ရန်ကုန်၊ စပယ်ပုံနှိပ်တိုက်]

Thein Maung. 1991. *The Burmese hero General Maha Bandoola.* Yangon: Sapay Beikman (108 pages).

[သိမ်းမောင် ။ ၁၉၉၁ ။ မြန်မာ့သူရဲကောင်း စစ်သူကြီး မဟာဗန္ဓုလ ။ ရန်ကုန်၊ စာပေဗိမာန်]

Toe Hla (Doctor). 2002 [1993]. *Konbaung, the golden country of Alaungmintayagyi.* Yangon: Sapay Lawka.

[တိုးလှ (ဒေါက်တာ) ။ ၂၀၀၂ (၁၉၉၃) ။ အလောင်းမင်းတရားကြီး ၏ ကုန်းဘောင်ရွှေပြည် ။ ရန်ကု၊ စာပေလောက]

Win Tin U. 2002. *The journey for religious work of the venerable monk U Weikzadara Bo Paukhsein and their opinions.* Yangon: Sitthidaw Press (143 pages).

[ဝင်းတင့်ဦး ။ ၂၀၀၂ ။ ဘုန်းဘုရား ဘိုးပေါက်ဆိန် ဦးဝိဇ္ဇာရေ ၏ သာသနာပြုခရီး နှင့် သူတို့အမြင် ။ ရန်ကုန် ၊ စစ်သည်တော်စာပေ]
Yadanabonpyan Meditation Center's Support Association for Religion. 1959 (1320 Burmese era). *Treatise on practice from the essence of religion.* Paygon (Minbu District): published at the authors' expense (315 pages).

[ရတနာဘုံပျံ ပဋိပတ္တိဋ္ဌာန သာသနာ့နုဂ္ဂဟအဖွဲ့ ။ ၁၃၂၀ (၁၉၅၉) ၊ တန်ခူးလ ။ သာသနာ့အဆီ ကျင့်ဝသီ ကျမ်း ။ ပေကုန်း (မင်းဘူးခရိုင်)]

OTHER REFERENCES

Abensour, M., and M. Gauchet. 2002 [1976]. Présentation: Les leçons de la servitude et leur destin. In *Le discours de la servitude volontaire,* by É. de La Boétie, 7–44. Paris: Éditions Payot & Rivages.

Almond, P. C. 1988. *The British discovery of Buddhism.* Cambridge: Cambridge University Press.

Ames, M. M. 1964. Buddha and the dancing goblins: A theory of magic and religion. *American Anthropologist* 66, no. 1: 75–82.

Aristote. 2008. *La poétique: Introduction, traduction, notes, étude de Gérard Lambin.* Paris: Éditions L'Harmattan.

Aung-Thwin, M. 2011. *The return of the Galon King: History, law, and rebellion in colonial Burma.* Ohio University Research in International Studies, Southeast Asia Series no. 119. Athens: Ohio University Press.

Bareau, A. 1981. Le massacre des Śākya: Essai d'interprétation. *Bulletin de l'École française d'Extrême-Orient* 69: 45–73.

———. 1985. *En suivant Bouddha.* Paris: Philippe Lebaud Éditeur.

———. 1995. *Recherches sur* la biographie *du Buddha dans les Sūtrapitaka et les Vinayapitaka anciens.* Vol. 3: *Articles complémentaires.* Paris: Presses de l'École française d'Extrême-Orient.

Ba U. 1959 [1958]. *My Burma: The autobiography of a president.* New York: Taplinger.

Bazin, J. 1991. Les fantômes de Mme Du Deffand: Exercices sur la croyance. *Critique. Revue générale des publications françaises et étrangères* 47, no. 529–530: 492–511.

Bernot, L. 1967. *Les paysans arakanais du Pakistan oriental: L'histoire, le monde végétal et l'organisation sociale des réfugiés Marma (Mog).* 2 vols. Paris: Mouton & Co.

Bigandet, P. A. (translated from the English by V. Gauvain). 1878 [1866]. *Vie ou légende de Gaudama, le Bouddha des Birmans, et Notices sur les Phongyies ou moines birmans.* Paris: Ernest Leroux Éditeur.

Brac de la Perrière, B. 1989. *Les rituels de possession en Birmanie: Du culte d'État aux cérémonies privées.* Paris: Éditions Recherche sur les Civilisations.

———. 2012. Spirits versus *weikza:* Two competing ways of mediation. *Journal of Burma Studies* 16, no. 2: 149–179.

Bunge, F. M. 1983. *Burma, a country study.* Washington, DC: American University (Area Handbook Series).

Candier, A. 2005. Imagination and knowledge: Some comments on rumours in the mid-nineteenth century Konbaung court. In *Traditions of knowledge in Southeast Asia,* part 1, 165–191. Yangon: Myanmar Historical Commission.

Carbonnel, L. 2009. On the ambivalence of female monasticism in Theravāda Buddhism. *Asian Ethnology* 68, no. 2: 265–282.

Clastres, P. 2002 [1976]. Liberté, malencontre, innommable. In *Le discours de la servitude volontaire,* by É. de La Boétie, 247–267. Paris: Éditions Payot & Rivages.

Clifford, J. 1986. On ethnographic allegory. In *Writing culture: The poetics and politics of ethnography,* edited by J. Clifford and G. E. Marcus, 98–121. Berkeley: University of California Press.

Coderey, C. 2011. Les maîtres du "reste": La quête de l'équilibre dans les conceptions et les pratiques thérapeutiques en Arakan (Birmanie). PhD diss., Aix-Marseille University.

Collis, M. 1996 [1938]. *Trials in Burma.* Bangkok: Ava Publishing House.

Cowell, E. B., ed. 1895. *The Jātaka or stories of the Buddha's former births.* Vol. 1. Cambridge: Cambridge University Press.

———, ed. 1901. *The Jātaka or stories of the Buddha's former births.* Vol. 4. Cambridge: Cambridge University Press.

Devyver, A. 1993 [1963]. Présentation. In *Les Argonautes du Pacifique occidental,* by B. Malinowski, 7–44. Paris: Gallimard.

Duroiselle, C. 1922–1923. *Report of the superintendent, archaeological survey, Burma.* Rangoon: Office of the Superintendent–Government Press.

Eliade, M. 1977. *Forgerons et alchimistes.* Paris: Flammarion.

Evans-Pritchard, E. E. 1937. *Witchcraft, oracles and magic among the Azande.* London: Oxford University Press.

Favret-Saada, J. 1995 [1977]. *Les mots, la mort, les sorts.* Paris: Éditions Gallimard.

Ferguson, J. P., and E. M. Mendelson. 1981. Masters of the Buddhist occult: The Burmese weikzas. In *Essays on Burma,* edited by J. P. Ferguson, 62–80. Contributions to Asian Studies, vol. 16. Leiden: E. J. Brill.

Fiordalis, D. V., ed. 2010 (2011). Miracles and superhuman powers in South and Southeast Asian Buddhist traditions (contributions to a panel at the Fifteenth Congress of the International Association of Buddhist Studies, Atlanta, June 23–28, 2008). *Journal of the International Association of Buddhist Studies* 33, no. 1–2: 381–554.

Fistié, P. 1985. *La Birmanie ou la quête de l'unité: Le problème de la cohésion nationale dans la Birmanie contemporaine et sa perspective historique.* Paris: École française d'Extrême-Orient.

Foucher, A. 1993 [1949]. *La vie du Bouddha, d'après les textes et les monuments de l'Inde.* Paris: Librairie d'Amérique et d'Orient.

Foxeus, N. 2011. The Buddhist world emperor's mission: Millenarian Buddhism in postcolonial Burma. PhD diss., Stockholm University.

Frazer, J. G. 1922. *The golden bough: A study in magic and religion.* London: MacMillan and Co.

Gellner, D. N. 2001. *The anthropology of Buddhism and Hinduism: Weberian themes.* New Delhi: Oxford University Press.

Ghosh, P. 2000. *Brave men of the hills: Resistance and rebellion in Burma, 1825–1932.* New Delhi: Manohar Publishers.

Godelier, M. 1992 [1984]. *L'idéel et le matériel.* Paris: Fayard.

Gombrich, R. F. 1995 [1988]. *Theravāda Buddhism: A social history from ancient Benares to modern Colombo.* London: Routledge.

Granoff, P. 1996. The ambiguity of miracles: Buddhist understandings of supernatural power. *East and West* 46, no. 1–2: 79–96.

Hallisey, C. 1995. Roads taken and not taken in the study of Theravāda Buddhism. In *Curators of the Buddha: The study of Buddhism under colonialism,* edited by D. S. Lopez Jr., 31–61. Chicago: University of Chicago Press.

Hervieu-Léger, D. 1993. *La religion pour mémoire.* Paris: Les Éditions du Cerf.

Hildburgh, W. L. 1909. Notes on some Burmese amulets and magical objects. *Journal of the Royal Anthropological Institute of Great Britain and Ireland* 39: 397–407.

Hla Baw. 1940. Superstitions of Burmese criminals. *Journal of the Burma Research Society* 30, part 2: 376–383.

Holt, J. C. 1991. *Buddha in the crown: Avalokiteśvara in the Buddhist traditions of Sri Lanka.* New York: Oxford University Press.

Horner, I. B. 1940. *The book of the discipline.* Vol. 2: *Suttavibhanga.* London: Oxford University Press.

Horton, R. 1993. *Patterns of thought in Africa and the West: Essays on magic, religion and science.* Cambridge: Cambridge University Press.

Houtman, G. 1990a. How a foreigner invented "Buddhendom" in Burmese: From tha-tha-na to bok-da' batha. *Journal of the Anthropological Society at Oxford* 21, no. 2: 113–128.

———. 1990b. Traditions of Buddhist practice in Burma. PhD diss., University of London, School of Oriental and African Studies.

———. 1999. *Mental culture in Burmese crisis politics: Aung San Suu Kyi and the National League for Democracy.* Tokyo: Tokyo University Institute for the Study of Languages and Cultures of Asia and Africa (monograph no. 33).

Htin Aung. 1962. *Folk elements in Burmese Buddhism.* London: Oxford University Press.

Hume, D. 1992. *Writings on religion.* Edited by A. Flew. La Salle, IL: Open Court.

Izard, M., and P. Bonte. 1979. Avant-propos. In *La fonction symbolique,* edited by M. Izard and P. Bonte, 9–15. Paris: Éditions Gallimard.

Jackson, P.A. 1999. The enchanting spirit of Thai capitalism: The cult of Luang Phor Khoon and the post-modernization of Thai Buddhism. *South East Asia Research* 7, no. 1: 5–60.

Jordt, I. 1988. Bhikkhuni, thilashin, mae-chii: Women who renounce the world in Burma, Thailand and the classical Pali Buddhist texts. *Crossroads: An Interdisciplinary Journal of Southeast Asian Studies* 4, no. 1: 31–39.

———. 2007. *Burma's mass lay meditation movement: Buddhism and the cultural construction of power.* Ohio University Research in International Studies, Southeast Asia Series no. 115. Athens: Ohio University Press.

Kawanami, H. 1990. The religious standing of Burmese Buddhist nuns (thilà-shin): The ten precepts and religious respect words. *Journal of the International Association of Buddhist Studies* 13: 17–40.

———. 1997. Buddhist nuns in transition: The case of Burmese thilà-shin. In *Indian insights: Buddhism, Brahmanism and Bhakti,* edited by P. Connolly and S. Hamilton, 209–224. London: Luzac Oriental.

Khin Yi. 1988. *The Dobama movement in Burma (1930–1938)*. Ithaca, NY: Cornell University Southeast Asia Program.

Kirichenko, A. 2009. From thathanadaw to Theravāda Buddhism: Constructions of religion and religious identity in nineteenth- and early twentieth-century Myanmar. In *Casting faiths: Imperialism and the transformation of religion in East and Southeast Asia*, edited by T. D. DuBois, 23–45. New York: Palgrave MacMillan.

Koenig, W. J. 1990. *The Burmese polity, 1752–1819: Politics, administration, and social organization in the early Kon-baung period*. Ann Arbor: University of Michigan Center for South and Southeast Asian Studies.

Kumada, N. 2001. In the world of rebirths: Politics, economy and society of Burmese Buddhists. PhD diss., Wolfson College, Cambridge.

Kunsal Kassapa (Ashin), trans. 2005. *Wonders of Mebegon village: Historical record of an event never revealed before*. Chonburi, Thailand: Nagamasa Centre.

La Boétie, Étienne (de). 1983. *Discours de la servitude volontaire*. Paris: Éditions Flammarion.

———. 2002 [1976]. *Le discours de la servitude volontaire*. Paris: Éditions Payot & Rivages.

Lammerts, D. C. 2010. Buddhism and written law: Dhammasattha manuscripts and texts in premodern Burma. PhD diss., Cornell University.

La Vallée Poussin, Louis de. 1915. Magic (Buddhist). In *Encyclopaedia of religion and ethics*, vol. 8, edited by J. Hasting, 255–257. Edinburgh: T. & T. Clark.

Leehey, J. 2010. Open secrets, hidden meanings: Censorship, esoteric power, and contested authority in urban Burma in the 1990s. PhD diss., University of Washington.

Lehman, F. K. 1972. Doctrine, practice, and belief in Theravāda Buddhism. *Journal of Asian Studies* 31, no. 2: 373–380.

Lenclud, G. 1990. Vues de l'esprit, art de l'autre: L'ethnologie et les croyances en pays de savoir. *Terrain* 14: 5–19.

Lévi-Strauss, C. (translated from the French by C. Jacobson and B. Grundfest Schoepf). 1963. The effectiveness of symbols. In *Structural anthropology*, by C. Lévi-Strauss, 186–205. New York: Basic Books.

———. 1966 [1962]. *The savage mind*. London: Weidenfeld and Nicolson.

Lévy-Bruhl, L. (translated from the French by L. A. Clare). 1966 [1910]. *How natives think*. New York: Washington Square Press.

Lubeigt, G. 1990. L'organisation du Sangha birman. In *Bouddhismes et sociétés asiatiques: clergés, sociétés et pouvoirs*, edited by A. Forest, E. Kato, and L. Vandermeersch, 125–154. Paris: L'Harmattan–Sophia University.

Malalasekera, G. P. 1960 [1937]. *Dictionary of Pāli proper names*. 2 vols. London: Luzac & Company.

Malinowski, B. 1935. *Coral gardens and their magic: A study of the methods of tilling the soil and of agricultural rites in the Trobriand islands*. Vol. 2: *The language of magic and gardening*. New York: American Book Company.

———. 1948. *Magic, science and religion and other essays*. Glencoe, IL: Free Press.

Mannoni, O. 1969. Je sais bien, mais quand même... In *Clefs pour l'Imaginaire ou l'Autre Scène*, by O. Mannoni, 9–33. Paris: Éditions du Seuil.

Marcus, G. E., and M. J. Fischer. 1986. *Anthropology as cultural critique: An experimental moment in the human sciences.* Chicago: University of Chicago Press.

Mauss, M., and H. Hubert. 1972. Esquisse d'une théorie générale de la magie [1902–1903]. In *Sociologie et anthropologie,* by M. Mauss, 1–141. Paris: Presses Universitaires de France.

McDaniel, J. T. 2008. *Gathering leaves & lifting words: Histories of Buddhist monastic education in Laos and Thailand.* Seattle: University of Washington Press.

Mendelson, E. M. 1961a. The king of the Weaving Mountain. *Journal of the Central Asian Society* 48, parts 3 and 4: 229–237.

———. 1961b. A messianic Buddhist association in Upper Burma. *Bulletin of the School of African and Oriental Studies* 24, part 3: 560–580.

———. 1963. Observations on a tour in the region of Mount Popa, Central Burma. *France-Asie* 19, no. 179: 780–807.

Mersan, A. (de). 2005. L'expression du particularisme arakanais dans la Birmanie contemporaine. *Moussons* 8: 117–141.

Mingun Hsayadaw (translated from the Burmese by Ko Lay, Tin Lwin, and Tin Oo). 1990–1998. *The Great Chronicle of Buddhas.* 6 vols. Yangon: Ti Ni Publishing Centre.

Ministry of Education. 1993. *Myanmar–English dictionary.* Yangon: Department of the Myanmar Language Commission.

Ministry of Religious Affairs. 1997. *The teachings of the Buddha (basic level).* Yangon: Ministry of Religious Affairs.

Mus, P. 1990 [1935]. *Barabudur: Esquisse d'une histoire du bouddhisme fondée sur la critique archéologique des textes.* Paris: Éditions Arma Artis.

Nash, M. 1973 [1965]. *The golden road to modernity: Village life in contemporary Burma.* Chicago: University of Chicago Press.

Needham, R. 1972. *Belief, language, and experience.* Oxford: Basil Blackwell.

Okell, J. 1972. *A guide to the Romanization of Burmese.* London: Royal Asiatic Society.

Oldenberg, H. (translated from the German by W. Hoey). 1928 [1882]. *Buddha: His life, his doctrine, his order.* London: Luzac & Co.

Otto, R. (translated from the German by J. W. Harvey). 1952. *The idea of the holy: An inquiry into the non-rational factor in the idea of the divine and its relation to the rational.* London: Oxford University Press.

Patton, T. N. 2012. In pursuit of the sorcerer's power: Sacred diagrams as technologies of potency. *Contemporary Buddhism* 13, no. 2: 1–19.

Pe Maung Tin, and G. H. Luce, trans. 1960 [1923]. *The Glass Palace chronicle of the kings of Burma.* Rangoon: Rangoon University Press.

Pouillon, J. 1993. Le cru et le su. In *Le cru et le su,* by J. Pouillon, 17–36. Paris: Éditions du Seuil.

Prager, S. 2003. The coming of the "future king": Burmese minlaung expectations before and during the Second World War. *Journal of Burma Studies* 8: 1–32.

Pranke, P. 1995. On becoming a Buddhist wizard. In *Buddhism in practice,* edited by D. S. Lopez Jr., 343–358. Princeton, N.J.: Princeton University Press.

Rahula, W. 1959. *What the Buddha taught.* Oxford: Oneworld Publications.

Ray, R. A. 1999 [1994]. *Buddhist saints in India: A study in Buddhist values and orientations*. New York: Oxford University Press.

Reynolds, F. 1976. The many lives of the Buddha: A study of sacred biography and Theravāda tradition. In *The biographical process: Studies in the history and psychology of religion*, edited by F. E. Reynolds and D. Capps, 37–61. Paris: Mouton.

Rhys Davids, T. W., trans. 1923 [1899]. *Dialogues of the Buddha, Part 1: Sacred books of the Buddhists*. Vol. 2. London: Humphrey Milford and Oxford University Press.

———, trans. 1925 [1890]. *The questions of King Milinda* (part I). London: Oxford University Press.

Rhys Davids, T. W., and C. A. F. Rhys Davids, trans. 1951 [1910]. *Dialogues of the Buddha*. Part 2: *Sacred books of the Buddhists*. Vol. 3. London: Luzac & Company.

Rhys Davids, T. W., and W. Stede. 1972 [1921–1925]. *The Pali Text Society's Pali-English dictionary*. London: Routledge & Kegan Paul.

Robinne, F. 2000. *Fils et maîtres du lac: Relations interethniques dans l'État Shan de Birmanie*. Paris: CNRS Éditions and Éditions de la Maison des Sciences de l'Homme.

Rouget, G. 1980. *La musique et la transe: Esquisse d'une théorie générale des relations de la musique et de la possession*. Paris: Éditions Gallimard.

Rozenberg, G. 2005a. Anthropology and the Buddhological imagination: Reconstructing the invisible life of texts. *Aséanie: Sciences humaines en Asie du Sud-Est* 16: 41–60.

———. 2005b. The cheaters: Journey to the land of the lottery. In *Burma at the turn of the 21st century*, edited by M. Skidmore, 19–40. Honolulu: University of Hawai'i Press.

———. 2008. Être birman, c'est être bouddhiste . . . In *Birmanie contemporaine*, edited by G. Defert, 29–52. Bangkok: Irasec/Les Indes savantes.

———. 2009a. How "the generals" think: Gustaaf Houtman and the enigma of the Burmese military regime. *Aséanie: Sciences humaines en Asie du Sud-Est* 24: 11–31.

———. 2009b. L'invraisemblance du surnaturel: Fiction et réalité dans un culte bouddhique birman. *Archives de sciences sociales des religions* 145: 129–146.

——— (translated from the French by W. Keeler). 2010a. The alchemist and his ball. *Journal of Burma Studies* 14: 187–228.

——— (translated from the French by J. Hackett). 2010b. *Renunciation and power: The quest for sainthood in contemporary Burma*. New Haven: Yale Southeast Asia Studies.

——— (translated from the French by W. Keeler). 2011. The saint who did not want to die: The multiple deaths of an immortal Burmese holy man. *Journal of Burma Studies* 15, no. 1: 69–119.

Said, E. W. 1979 [1978]. *Orientalism*. New York: Vintage Books.

Sangermano. 1995 [1833]. *The Burmese Empire a hundred years ago*. Bangkok: White Orchid Press.

Sarkisyanz, M. 1965. *Buddhist backgrounds of the Burmese revolution*. The Hague: Martinus Nijhoff.

Schieffelin, E. L. 1985. Performance and the cultural construction of reality. *American Ethnologist* 12, no. 4: 707–724.

Schober, J. S. 1980. On Burmese horoscopes. *South East Asian Review* 5, no. 1: 43–56.

———. 1989. Paths to enlightenment: Theravada Buddhism in Upper Burma. PhD diss., University of Illinois.

———. 2011. *Modern Buddhist conjunctures in Myanmar: Cultural narratives, colonial legacies, and civil society.* Honolulu: University of Hawai'i Press.

Schopen, G. 1997. Archaeology and Protestant presuppositions in the study of Indian Buddhism [1991]. In *Bones, stones, and Buddhist monks: Collected papers on the archaeology, epigraphy, and texts of monastic Buddhism in India,* edited by G. Schopen, 1–22. Honolulu: University of Hawai'i Press.

Scott, J. G., and J. P. Hardiman, eds. 1900–1901. *Gazetteer of Upper Burma and the Shan States.* 5 vols. Rangoon: Government Printing.

Senart, E. 1882. *Essai sur la légende du Buddha, son caractère et ses origines.* Paris: Ernest Leroux Éditeur.

Shway Yoe (James George Scott). 1963 [1909]. *The Burman: His life and notions.* New York: Norton Library.

Shwe Zan Aung. 1912. Hypnotism in Burma. *Journal of the Burma Research Society* 2: 44–56.

Skidmore, M. 2004. *Karaoke fascism: Burma and the politics of fear.* Philadelphia: University of Pennsylvania Press.

Smith, D. E. 1965. *Religion and politics in Burma.* Princeton, N.J.: Princeton University Press.

Snodgrass, J. J. 1997 [1827]. *The Burmese war (1824–1826).* Bangkok: Ava Publishing House.

Southwold, M. 1979. Religious belief. *Man* (new series) 14, no. 4: 628–644.

Sperber, D. 1982. Les croyances apparemment irrationnelles. In *Le savoir des anthropologues: Trois essais,* by D. Sperber, 49–85. Paris: Hermann.

Spiro, M. E. 1967. *Burmese supernaturalism: A study in the explanation and reduction of suffering.* Englewood Cliffs, NJ: Prentice-Hall.

———. 1970. *Buddhism and society: A great tradition and its Burmese vicissitudes.* London: George Allen & Unwin.

Strong, J. S. 2001. *The Buddha: A short biography.* Oxford: Oneworld Publications.

Swearer, D. K. 2004. *Becoming the Buddha: The ritual of image consecration in Thailand.* Princeton, N.J.: Princeton University Press.

Tambiah, S. J. 1990. *Magic, science, religion, and the scope of rationality.* Cambridge: Cambridge University Press.

Taussig, M. 1987. *Shamanism, colonialism, and the wild man: A study in terror and healing.* Chicago: University of Chicago Press.

Thawnghmung, A. M. 2004. *Behind the teak curtain: Authoritarianism, agricultural policies and political legitimacy in rural Burma/Myanmar.* London: Kegan Paul.

Tin Maung Maung Than. 1988. The Sangha and Sasana in socialist Burma. *Sojourn: Social Issues in Southeast Asia* 3, no. 1: 26–61.

———. 1993. Sangha reforms and renewal of Sasana in Myanmar: Historical trends and contemporary practice. In *Buddhist trends in Southeast Asia,* edited by T. Ling, 6–63. Singapore: Institute of Southeast Asian Studies.

Tosa, K. 2005. The chicken and the scorpion: Rumor, counternarratives, and the political uses of Buddhism. In *Burma at the turn of the 21st century,* edited by M. Skidmore, 154–173. Honolulu: University of Hawai'i Press.

Turton, A. 1991. Invulnerability and local knowledge. In *Thai constructions of knowledge,* edited by M. Chitakasem and A. Turton, 155–182. London: School of Oriental and African Studies.

Verdier, Y. 1979. *Façons de dire, façons de faire: La laveuse, la couturière, la cuisinière.* Paris: Éditions Gallimard.

———. 1995. *Coutume et destin: Thomas Hardy et autres essais.* Paris: Éditions Gallimard.

Vernant, J. P. 1996. *Mythe et pensée chez les Grecs: Études de psychologie historique.* Paris: La Découverte/Poche.

Walshe, M., trans. 1995 [1987]. *The Long Discourses of the Buddha: A translation of the Dīgha Nikāya.* Boston: Wisdom Publications.

Warren, C. V. 1938. *Dans la jungle de Birmanie.* Paris: Payot.

Weber, M. (translated and edited by H. H. Gerth and D. Martindale). 1958. *The religion of India: The sociology of Hinduism and Buddhism.* Glencoe, IL: Free Press.

Wijayaratna, M. 1998. *Le dernier voyage du Bouddha: Avec la traduction intégrale du Mahā-Parinibbāna-sutta.* Paris: Éditions Lis.

Index

Abensour, Miguel, 293n35
actions, inherent potency of, 107
Ālāra Kālāma, 68–69
alchemy, 86–105; ascetic's fire method
 (*yathay hpo*) of energy ball creation,
 100–101, astrology and, 96–97;
 conclusions on, 102–105; fire's
 importance to, 89–90, 92–93; origins of,
 285n7; overview, 86–87; prevalence of
 practice of, 11, 13; Sein Yi's practice of,
 59, 60, 98; Spiro on, 13; U Thakkara's
 practice of, 87–89, 94–95, 99–101;
 transformation of energy balls and,
 90–94; trials by fire, comparison with,
 262–264; uncertainty of, 63, 95–97;
 weikza's intervention in, 101–102; Zaw
 Win's interest in, 83. *See also* balls of
 energy
Ames, Michael M., 280–281n42
anthropologists, Clifford's trope of, xii
anthropology: analysis, methods of,
 xxiii; inhumanity in, 234–235;
 problem of belief in, 278n17; of religion,
 classical issues of, xxi; representation
 in, xxi
anthropophagy, 273–274
Aristotle, on stories, 64
asit tit-khu, atu tit-htaung, ayaung tit-thein
 ("One real, a thousand fakes, and a
 hundred thousand imposters"), 23
astrology, 96–97, 114
ateik (past, omen, future), 107–108
ateik lok- ("doing an *ateik*"), 108–109, 113,
 246–247
atemporal temporality, of Burma,
 240–241
Aung, Bobo, 264
Aung Khaing, Great-Master: ambitions of,
 198; Burmese ethnic diversity, experience

of, 232–233; career of, 185–187;
 financial difficulties faced by, 274–275;
 importance of, 200; law officers' visit
 and, 243; life-prolonging ceremony of
 Bodaw Bo Htun Aung and, 246–247;
 perceptions of, 239; on servitude, 226;
 at Tactical Encirclement Group
 demonstration, 190–195; on *thakiwin
 min- myo,* 230, 231–232; on *weikza*'s
 Sākya project, 227
Aung Khaing (of Yangon), 256, 259
Aung Thaung, 190–192, 201–210, 220, 227,
 239
Aung-Thwin, Maitrii, 290n13, 290–291n14
ayuahsa (belief, customary understanding),
 15–16

Ba Htay, 270, 271
balls of energy (*datlon, dat* balls):
 alchemists, relationship to, 102–104;
 methods of production of, 105–106;
 preparation for, 88–91; as receptacles
 of vital energy, 157; transformation of,
 and path to becoming a *weikza,* 91–101;
 weikza, comparison with, 263; Zaw
 Win's, 81–82, 83
Bame Hsayadaw (Great Monk of Bame),
 273–274
Bareau, André, 292n29
Ba U, Judge, 219–220
Ba Yi, 122–124, 144–145, 153, 154, 256,
 266
being called (by the *weikza*), 118, 120–122,
 124, 125, 206
belief, 14–19, 278n17
believing: belief vs., 14, 278n17; Burmese
 words for, 15–19; drama of, 18–19;
 effectiveness of, 53; importance of, 55;
 influence of disciples' importance on, 59;

About the Author

Holding a PhD in social anthropology from Ecole des Hautes Etudes en Sciences Sociales (Paris, 2001), Guillaume Rozenberg has been a researcher at the French National Center of Scientific Research, posted to the Center for Social Anthropology in Toulouse, France, since 2004. His research focuses on the anthropology of religion, specifically, Buddhist virtuoso figures and the cults they give rise to in contemporary Burma. He is the author of *Renunciation and Power: The Quest for Sainthood in Contemporary Burma* (Yale University Southeast Asia Studies, monograph 59, 2010) and coeditor of *Champions of Buddhism: Weikza Cults in Contemporary Burma* (NUS Press, 2014).

Production Notes for Rozenberg / *The Immortals*

Cover design by Mardee Melton

Composition by Westchester Publishing Services
with display type in Palatino Linotype and text in
Garamond Premier Pro.

Printing and binding by Sheridan Books, Inc.

Printed on 60 lb. House White Opaque, 466 ppi.